Bring History Alive!

A Sourcebook for Teaching World History

EDITED BY:

Ross E. Dunn
David Vigilante

National Center for History in the Schools
University of California, Los Angeles

Ordering Information

Bring History Alive: A Sourcebook for Teaching World History
ISBN 0-9633218-6-2

Contact:

UCLA Book Zone
The UCLA Store
308 Westwood Plaza
Ackerman Union
Los Angeles, CA 90024-8311
Phone: (310) 206-0788
Fax: (310) 825-0382

Cover illustration: Two centers of higher learning dating to the Middle Ages.
Left: Corpus Christi College (founded 1352 CE), Cambridge University,
England. Right: al-Azhar University (founded 970 CE), Cairo.

INTRODUCTION

This book is a resource manual created by teachers and for teachers. It is not a curricular plan, not a textbook, and not a prescribed set of classroom exercises. It is presented for the consideration of those who wish to engage in an inquiry-based approach to historical knowledge and historical understanding. We hope that if your house catches on fire, this is the one book you'll reach for on your way out the door.

Bring History Alive! has a history of its own. A large majority of the classroom activities presented here were first published as illustrative examples of how students could master the *National Standards for World History*. The controversy over the National Standards is a story in itself, one that would take an entire chapter—perhaps even a book—to rehearse and analyze. It need only be said here that these examples of student achievement, not to be confused with the standards themselves, were omitted from the revised version of the World History Standards, published in April 1996. Hundreds of teachers have strongly urged that these teaching activities be republished, with appropriate revisions and improvement.

How were the classroom activities written in the first instance? They are the work of a task force of teachers from various parts of the country, and evenly divided among elementary, middle, and high school teachers, who worked from 1992 to 1994 at UCLA as part of the National History Standards Project. The National Center for History in the Schools selected these teachers after soliciting nominations from nine principal organizations that participated in the project: the American Historical Association, the Association for Supervision and Curriculum Development, the Council of Chief State School Officers, the Council for State Social Studies Specialists, the National Council for History Education, the National Council for the Social Studies, the Organization of American Historians, the Organization of History Teachers, and the World History Association. Most of the examples written by these teachers have been tried out in their own classrooms.

In preparing this book for publication, its editors have combed the original examples of student achievement to ensure that each activity raises questions about important topics without dictating or inferring answers. The activities and questions are meant to be open-ended. They are invitations to explore historical issues, problems, patterns, ideas, values, interests, motives, and personalities. Many thoughtful critiques of the hundreds of classroom activities are gratefully acknowledged, and the editors have carefully considered every criticism and suggestion. Many of the original examples have been discarded; others have been newly created; many have been rewritten.

Though numbering in the hundreds, the activities are explicitly not meant to add up to a curriculum. Nor are they intended to cover every important topic—or every personage—in world history. Such a comprehensive book would be overwhelming. It is true that the examples have been created by a diverse group of accomplished teachers who have tried to spotlight what inexperienced or overburdened colleagues will find most helpful, and this means giving pride of place to the less familiar rather than to activities that have been conventionally addressed for years.

Every reader of this book should understand that the teaching examples are simply examples—ones chosen to enliven classrooms with material that is not customarily found in curricular materials. It goes without saying that teachers will chose as they like from these examples, redesign them to meet their students' needs, and, we hope, find in them particles of inspiration that will lead teachers to create many others of their own.

The teaching examples, organized by grade level and by era, are supplemented by essays of two kinds. In Part I, we have brought together a number of essays that explore ways to approach, organize, and conceptualize the teaching of world history, a discipline that, unlike the Western civilization course, lacks a hallowed tradition of classroom practice and that in fact is still being invented. These essays also present classroom strategies that colleagues have been putting to use over the past several years, strategies that can help make the human past lively and intelligible and that inspire students to become active, inquisitive, skillful learners.

In Part II, essays have been selected to introduce each of the nine eras of world history. None of these essays describes the era, defines the era, or addresses all the major events and issues of the era. Rather, each essay addresses a particular topic or theme relevant to the era. Regard each essay as a pep pill, not a nostrum; simply a lively essay to help get students thinking.

While this volume is a stand-alone resource book, it has several links to the *National Standards for World History*. First, the nine eras are borrowed from the National Standards, though as these standards point out, the periodization of history is always arbitrary and open to negotiation. Second, Part I, Historical Thinking Skills, is reprinted from the National History Standards because these skills are the *sine qua non* of historical literacy. Third, Part III draws upon the resources provided in the National History Standards, although the resources recommended here have been substantially enlarged.

The editors of this volume wish to thank five exceptional teachers from different parts of the country who reviewed all the classroom activities in the first edition of the *National Standards for World History* and made numerous suggestions and creative new contributions: Avi Black, Anne Chapman, Robert Rittner, Donna Rogers-Beard, and Donald Woodruff.

We also gratefully acknowledge the members of the Advisory Board of the National Center for History in the Schools who reviewed the format, design, and philosophy of the book: Joyce Appleby, Robert Bain, Jerry H. Bentley, Daniel Berman, Linda Black, Douglas Greenberg, Melinda Hennessey, Linda Heywood, David Hollinger, Evelyn Hu-DeHart, Donna Rogers-Beard, Gloria Sesso, Donald Woodruff, and Judith P. Zinsser.

Ross E. Dunn
David Vigilante

Los Angeles, California
October 1996

TABLE OF CONTENTS

Approaching World History: Foundations of Good Teaching

Rationale: Why Study History*

The Case for History in Our Schools

Americans have long said that universal education is essential to securing the people's rights to life, liberty, and the pursuit of happiness. But those who run our schools have rarely agreed on what is most worth teaching to every learner in a modern democratic society. So difficult has this question appeared that we have repeatedly turned away from it, to busy ourselves instead with methods and logistics, as though these were more important and could be applied without regard to the subject matter we choose to teach, or our purposes in choosing it. The consequences are evident. All subjects and disciplines have suffered, at all levels of schooling from kindergarten through the graduate years.

By its nature, history has suffered more than most subjects from permissive or simply ill-founded curriculum making. History's enormous scope and detail require more choices than many people, educators and historians included, are able or willing to make. It is, and ought to be, complex and often controversial. In its style and methods, it is both an art and a science. As a school subject, it embraces both the humanities and the social studies, neither of which can prosper without history's context and perspectives. It is the most synthesizing of all the disciplines, not just another bundle of subject-matter, but a way of ordering and apprehending reality. To be well taught it calls for more than ordinary knowledge and pedagogical skill on the part of those who teach it. As historians and teachers of history, we must admit its difficulties

---

*Reprinted from *Lessons From History, Essential Understandings and Historical Perspectives Students Should Acquire*, edited by Charlotte Crabtree, Gary B. Nash, Paul Gagnon, Scott Waugh (Los Angeles, CA: The National Center for History in the Schools, 1992), pp. 1-10.

and labor to overcome them, for if the proper place of history in our schools is not accepted by the public and those who shape the schools, the larger campaign to improve the quality, and equality, of American education will surely fail.

Why Study History?

The purposes of historical study must reflect the three ultimate purposes of education in a free society: to prepare the individual for a career of work, to sustain life; for active citizenship, to safeguard liberty and justice; and for the private pursuit of happiness. The last of these purposes—personal fulfillment, whether it be defined in secular or spiritual terms—is of first importance, providing the reason we struggle to maintain life and liberty, its necessary conditions. Each of the three aims of education, of course, calls for traits of minds and character that are useful to the other two. Historical study contributes to all three, but in preparing the individual for citizenship and for personal fulfillment its offerings are unique, and together with those of literature and philosophy, are indispensable.

The argument for more history in the schools and for its centrality to the social studies has usually stressed its role in preparing informed, sophisticated citizens. Thomas Jefferson long ago prescribed history for all who would take part in self-government because it would "enable every man to judge for himself what will secure or endanger his freedom." History's main use, he believed, was to prepare people for things yet to come. By reflecting on the past, on other times, other people, other nations, they would be able "to judge of the future" and to make up their own minds on the "actions and designs of men."

In 1892, the Committee of Ten's subcommittee on History, Civil Government, and Political Economy (which included Woodrow Wilson) urged that four years of history be required for all secondary school students, whether or not they were destined for college, because history, more than any other subject, readied the student to exercise "a salutary influence upon the affairs of his country." It was, they said, vital to "the invaluable mental power which we call judgment." A succession of committees, from the American Historical Association's "Seven" in 1899 through its study panels in the 1930s, pressed similar arguments for history as the basis for civic education.

Nearing the end of the 20th century, in a populous and ethnically and racially diverse society caught up in an interdependent global society, we reaffirm the central importance of history in preparing students to exercise their rights and responsibilities in the democratic political process. AS historians of human behavior, we know better than to claim too much. "Neither history nor any social studies course intended to teach citizenship can *make* good citizens," said the Council for Basic Education's Commission on the Teaching of History in 1982; but without knowing the past, citizens cannot know the choices before them. And historian William McNeill, in a report for the American Historical Association in 1985, similarly argued that "democratic citizenship and effective participation in the determination of public policy require citizens to share a collective memory, organized into historical knowledge and belief."

Lacking a collective memory of important things, people lapse into political amnesia, unable to see what newspapers are saying, to hear what is in (or left out of) a speech, or to talk to each other about public questions. A historical education should prepare us for times of trouble, when we are tempted to put aside inefficient democracy and to lash out, to exclude, or to oppress others. Why have past societies fallen or survived, turned ugly or retained their humanity? Citizens need to know and to be able to tell each other, before it grows too late, what struggles and sacrifices have had to be accepted, what comforts given up, to keep freedom and justice alive. Historical knowledge and historical perspective ward off panic, cynicism, self-pity, and resignation.

Students of history come to see as James Howard and Thomas Mendenhall said in *Making History Come Alive*, that not every difficulty is a problem and not every problem is a crisis. To take but one example, democracy must cherish both liberty and equality. The two impulses repeatedly clash, yet each is necessary to the other. This "concept" may serve as a starting point, but only history can each us why it is so, by presenting the tough human experience that has convinced us of it. Students then grasp why conflict is to be expected—even welcomed—and is not some failure of a system that should run itself and leave them alone. They also understand how hard it has been to improve human life but how often it has nonetheless been done in the past. Historical study has a way (annoying to some) of rejecting both optimism and pessimism, of refusing us the comforts of either. In sum, it offers citizens the sense of reality and proportion that is the first mark of political wisdom.

It is hard to see how better to prepare students for life in the 21st century, about which there is so much talk these days in the social studies field. Unhappily, enthusiasts for "futures studies" are quick to reject history and the humanities in general as "past-oriented" and thereby useless in preparing citizens for what is to come. Apart from flying in the face of centuries of human experience, such notions ignore—as they would have our young people do—everything that can be learned from the lives of countless men and women whose historical and humanistic education prepared them for great work in the "futures" of their own eras. If they knew how to meet the unexpected, it was not out of formulas and "skills" but out of first knowing themselves and the human condition. History, philosophy, biography, literature, and the arts had liberated their imaginations, informed their judgments, and imbued them with a sense of human dignity. The social sciences standing alone help to describe today's and tomorrow's problems, but they alone cannot explain them; nor should they be expected to nourish those values and qualities of mind required to deal with them wisely. For these purposes the long-term explanatory perspectives that history provides and the habits of thought it uniquely develops are essential.

Along with educating citizens for public affairs—a role it shares with the social sciences—history has a deeper, even more fundamental responsibility: the cultivation of the individual private person, in whom self-knowledge and self-respect support a life of dignity and fulfillment. The public and private purposes of educational and historical study are, of course, inescapably interrelated. Only the self-respecting, fully-rounded person is likely to make a good citizen for a self-governing society, as ready to serve as to resist, depending upon the circumstances of the hour. Only a free society can provide a setting for personal dignity and fulfillment, what Jefferson called the pursuit of happiness.

The liberal education of the private person is preeminently the role of history and the humanities. The study of history reveals the long, hard path of human striving for dignity. It can be, as Jerry Martin puts it, "a source of *pietas*, the reverent acknowledgment of the sources of one's being." Historical memory is the key to self-identity, to seeing one's place in the stream of time, in the story of humankind. We are part of an ancient chain and the hand of the past is upon us—for good and ill—as our hands will rest on our descendants in the future. Such perspective is essential to one's morale, perhaps even to sanity, in a complex, troubled present. "It is true that history cannot satisfy our appetite when we are hungry, nor keep us warm when the cold wind blows," says the New York Chinatown History Project. "But it is also true that if younger generations do not understand the hardships and triumphs of their elders, then we will be a people without a past. As such, we will be like water without a source, a tree without roots."

The human mind seems to require a usable past. Unfurnished with historical knowledge that approximates reality, we are like to conjure up a past that is false or nostalgic, misleading in one form or other. Or we may subscribe to versions of the past peddled by partisan or special interests. Either way we are deluded, lose our way, perhaps even become dangerous to ourselves and our contemporaries, not to speak of posterity. We remain prisoners of our milieu, ignorant, in bliss or despair, of the possibility for personal liberation that history opens to us by revealing the immense range of approaches people have taken to political, economic, and social life, to personal integrity and salvation, to cultural creativity.

The dignity of free choice can proceed only out of knowing the alternatives possible in private and public life, the knowledge that only history, and the humanities taught in conjunction with history, can provide. Is such education "past-oriented" and obsolete? Exactly the contrary. The study of history opens to students the great case book of centuries of human experience. The quicker the pace of change, the higher the flood of "information," the more troubled and confused we become, the more relevant and essential history becomes in preparing people for private life and public auction.

As to the third purpose of education—preparation for work—historical studies are central for such careers as journalism, law, diplomacy, international business, government service, politics, the military, teaching, and management of many public and private enterprises. Knowledge of history informs many other academic disciplines and creative professions. Insofar as personal morale, integrity, and dignity are conducive to all kinds of good work, history's contributions are obvious, as is its development of analytical skills and modes of critical judgment. As more and more employers assert the importance of a liberal education to their workers' inventiveness, their aptitude for continued learning and changes of career, the uses of historical studies should be more commonly appreciated.

Given the importance of history for all three purposes of education, and its centrality to citizenship and personal life, it is clear that both the amount and the quality of history taught in American schools must be sufficient to the task. That they are clearly not sufficient has alarmed many observers in recent years. In 1975, a report by the executive secretary of the Organization of American Historians, Richard S. Kirkendall, found history enrollments shrinking and history being displaced by other social studies subjects. In 1982 the Council for Basic Education's Commission on the Teaching of History deplored both the quantity and the quality of history being taught in the schools. History, said the Commission's report, was "overshadowed and undervalued in the curriculum, often neglected by professional historians, and found boring by many students."

Data reported by the National Center for Education Statistics indicated that in 1981-82 only 60 percent of the nation's high schools were offering a comprehensive course in United States history, though courses in state history, special eras, or special topics were being offered in some of the schools not providing the basic United States history course. By 1989-90 this picture had improved, probably as a result of the curriculum reforms launched in 1983. A national survey conducted in 1989-90 by the National Center for History in the Schools found that 89.9 percent of the high schools were offering one or more General Enrollment classes in United States history, and an additional 5 percent not offering the General Enrollment course were offering one or more special enrollment classes such as Advanced Placement or Remedial.

Fully 5 percent of the high schools, however, were offering no United States history courses, and of the courses that were offered, only 81 percent provided a full year of instruction; the rest were offered for one semester or less. Only 70.2 percent of the high schools were offering a General Enrollment course in world history, with only 66 percent of these schools requiring the course for graduation. Only 3.7 percent were offering a course in Western Civilization, a significant decline from a decade earlier when 14 percent were offering such a course. Serious problems were observed in the middle school/junior high school offerings. Close to 40 percent were offering no courses in United States history and 87 percent reported offering no courses in world history. For a significant number of students, then, the only history they currently study is what is offered in a year or less of high school instruction.

The gap between what a modern democratic school system needs and what the curriculum in this country now provides is very great. Putting aside for a moment the paucity of history in the elementary and middle school curriculum of most schools, there is simply no way that the one and one-half years, or less, of history now taken by the average American high school student can possibly fulfill the purposes we have set forth above, or develop the essential knowledge and understandings we shall presently discuss. This view is shared by every major reform proposal of recent years. Theodore Sizer, in *Horace's Compromise* (1984), makes the joint study of history and ideas one of his four required areas of learning throughout the secondary years. *The Paideia Program* (1984) places narrative history and geography at the core of the social studies from the upper elementary years through high school. In the Carnegie report, *High School* (1983), Ernest Boyer recommended a year of United States History, a year of Western Civilization, and at least a term's study of a non-Western society. The Council for Basic Education's report of 1984 set an "irreducible minimum" of two years of American history, one of European and the historical study of at least one non-European society in depth. In 1987, the American Federation of teachers published *Education for Democracy: A Statement of Principles*, signed by 150 national leaders across the political spectrum, and calling for the reordering of the entire social studies curriculum around a continuing core of history and geography. Also in 1987 the National Endowment for the Humanities issued *American Memory*, Lynne V. Cheney's report on humanities in the schools, which urged that "both history and enduring works of literature" be a part of every school year for every student. Most recently, the Bradley Commission recommended that the social studies curriculum from kindergarten through grade six be history-centered and that no fewer than four years of history be required of all students sometime during the six-year span from 7th through 12th grade.

All of these reports set reasonable goals, and they also agree that a reformed social studies curriculum should be required of all students in common, regardless of their "track" or further vocational and educational plans. Only such a common core is democratic, because wherever the curriculum in history and ideas is truncated or optional, the students' right to know is violated and democracy is wanting. Something is wrong when the learning often considered necessary and appropriate for university-bound students is treated as unnecessary or irrelevant for the others. This first principle of democratic education, enunciated by the Committee of Ten a century ago, is an idea whose time has come again. In order that it not again be abandoned, diverse and imaginative teaching methods must be applied in developing the common core of what is most worth learning with all of our diverse learners. A common core and varied methods are the twin imperatives for democratic schooling. A curriculum that is trivial, optional, or differentiated according to track produces a class system of education, no matter how innovative the methods or how many students receive a diploma. But the most wondrous subject matter just as surely produces a class system of education if inflexible teaching methods and school structures impede its being conveyed to the great majority of young people.

Methods: Historical Thinking Skills*

The study of history, as noted earlier, rests on knowledge of facts, dates, names, places, events, and ideas. In addition, true historical understanding requires students to engage in historical thinking: to raise questions and to marshal solid evidence in support of their answers; to go beyond the facts presented in their textbooks and examine the historical record for themselves; to consult documents, journals, diaries, artifacts, historic sites, works of art, quantitative data, and other evidence from the past, and to do so imaginatively—taking into account the historical context in which these records were created and comparing the multiple points of view of those on the scene at the time.

Real historical understanding requires that students have opportunity to create historical narratives and arguments of their own. Such narratives and arguments may take many forms—essays, debates, and editorials, for instance. They can be initiated in a variety of ways. None, however, more powerfully initiates historical thinking than those issues, past and present, that challenge students to enter knowledgeably into the historical record and to bring sound historical perspectives to bear in the analysis of a problem.

Historical understanding also requires that students thoughtfully read the historical narratives created by others. Well-written historical narratives are interpretative, revealing and explaining connections, change, and consequences. They are also analytical, combining lively storytelling and biography with conceptual analysis drawn from all relevant disciplines. Such narratives promote essential skills in historical thinking.

Reading such narratives requires that students analyze the assumptions—stated and unstated—from which the narrative was constructed and assess the strength of the evidence presented. It requires that students consider the significance of what the author included as well as chose to omit—the absence, for example, of the voices and experiences of other men and women who were also an important part of the history of their time. Also, it requires that students examine the interpretative nature of history, comparing, for example, alternative historical narratives written by historians who have given different weight to the political, economic, social, and/or technological causes of events and who have developed competing interpretations of the significance of those events.

Students engaged in activities of the kinds just considered will draw upon skills in the following five interconnected dimensions of historical thinking:

1. Chronological Thinking
2. Historical Comprehension
3. Historical Analysis and Interpretation
4. Historical Research Capabilities
5. Historical Issues-Analysis and Decision-Making

These skills, while presented in five separate categories, are nonetheless **interactive and mutually supportive.** In conducting historical research or creating a historical argument of their

---

*Reprinted from National Standards for History, Basic Edition, National Center for History in the Schools, UCLA (Los Angeles, CA: The National Center for History in the Schools, 1996), pp. 59-70.

own, for example, students must be able to draw upon skills in all five categories. Beyond the skills of conducting their research, students must, for example, be able to comprehend historical documents and records, analyze their relevance, develop interpretations of the document(s) they select, and demonstrate a sound grasp of the historical chronology and context in which the issue, problem, or events they are addressing developed.

In short, these five sets of skills, developed in the following pages as the five Standards in Historical Thinking, are statements of the **outcomes** we desire students to achieve. They are not mutually exclusive when put into practice, nor do they prescribe a particular teaching sequence to be followed. Teachers will draw upon all these Thinking Standards, as appropriate, to develop their teaching plans and to guide students through challenging programs of study in history.

Finally, it is important to point out that these five sets of Standards in Historical Thinking are defined in the following pages largely independent of historical content in order to specify the quality of thinking desired for each. It is essential to understand, however, that these skills do not develop, nor can they be practiced, in a vacuum. Every one of these skills requires specific historical content in order to function.

STANDARD 1

Chronological Thinking

Chronological thinking is at the heart of historical reasoning. Without a strong sense of chronology—of when events occurred and in what temporal order—it is impossible for students to examine relationships among those events or to explain historical causality. Chronology provides the mental scaffolding for organizing historical thought.

In developing students' chronological thinking, instructional time should be given to the use of well-constructed **historical narratives**: literary narratives including biographies and historical literature, and well-written narrative histories that have the quality of "stories well told." Well-crafted narratives such as these have the power to grip and hold students' attention. Thus engaged, the reader is able to focus on what the narrator discloses: the temporal structure of events unfolding over time, the actions and intentions of those who were there, the temporal connections between antecedents and their consequences.

In the middle and high school years, students should be able to use their mathematical skills to measure time by years, decades, centuries, and millennia; to calculate time from the fixed points of the calendar system (BC or BCE and AD or CE); and to interpret the data presented in time lines.

Students should be able to analyze *patterns of historical duration*, demonstrated, for example, by the more than two hundred years the United States Constitution and the government it created has endured.

Students should also be able to analyze *patterns of historical succession* illustrated, for example, in the development, over time, of ever larger systems of interaction, beginning with trade among settlements of the Neolithic world; continuing through the growth of the great land empires of Rome, Han China, the Islamic world, and the Mongols; expanding in the early modern era when Europeans crossed the Atlantic and Pacific, and established the first world-wide networks of trade and communication; and culminating with the global systems of trade and communication of the modern world.

Standard 1: The student thinks chronologically:

Therefore, the student is able to:

A. **Distinguish between past, present, and future time.**

B. **Identify the temporal structure of a historical narrative or story:** its beginning, middle, and end (the latter defined as the outcome of a particular beginning).

C. **Establish temporal order in constructing historical narratives of their own:** working forward from some beginning through its development, to some end or outcome; working *backward* from some issue, problem, or event to explain its origins and its development over time.

D. **Measure and calculate calendar time** by days, weeks, months, years, decades, centuries, and millennia, from fixed points of the calendar system: BC (before Christ) and AD (*Anno Domini,* "in the year of our Lord") in the Gregorian calendar and the contemporary secular designation for these same dates, BCE (before the Common Era) and CE (in the Common Era); and compare with the fixed points of other calendar systems such as the Roman (753 BC, the founding of the city of Rome) and the Muslim (622 AD, the hegira).

E. **Interpret data presented in timelines and create timelines** by designating appropriate equidistant intervals of time and recording events according to the temporal order in which they occurred.

F. **Reconstruct patterns of historical succession and duration** in which historical developments have unfolded, and apply them to **explain historical continuity and change.**

G. **Compare alternative models for periodization** by identifying the organizing principles on which each is based.

STANDARD 2

Historical Comprehension

One of the defining features of historical narratives is their believable recounting of human events. Beyond that, historical narratives also have the power to disclose the intentions of the people involved, the difficulties they encountered, and the complex world in which such historical figures actually lived. To read historical stories, biographies, autobiographies, and narratives with comprehension, students must develop the ability to read imaginatively, to take into account what the narrative reveals of the humanity of the individuals involved—their motives and intentions, their values and ideas, their hopes, doubts, fears, strengths, and weaknesses. Comprehending historical narratives requires, also, that students develop historical perspectives, the ability to describe the past on its own terms, through the eyes and experiences of those who were there. By studying the literature, diaries, letters, debates, arts, and artifacts of past peoples, students should learn to avoid "present-mindedness" by not judging the past solely in terms of the norms and values of today but taking into account the historical context in which the events unfolded.

Acquiring these skills begins in the early years of childhood, through the use of superbly written biographies that capture children's imagination and provide them an important foundation for continuing historical study. As students move into middle grades and high school years, historical literature should continue to occupy an important place in the curriculum, capturing historical events with dramatic immediacy, engaging students' interests, and fostering deeper understanding of the times and cultural milieu in which events occurred.

Beyond these important outcomes, students should also develop the skills needed to comprehend—historical narratives that *explain* as well as recount the course of events and that *analyze* relationships among the various forces which were present at the time and influenced the ways events unfolded. These skills include: 1) identifying the central question the historical narrative seeks to answer; 2) defining the purpose, perspective, or point of view from which the narrative has been constructed; 3) reading the historical explanation or analysis with meaning; 4) recognizing the rhetorical cues that signal how the author has organized the text.

Comprehending historical narratives will also be facilitated if students are able to draw upon the data presented in historical maps; visual, mathematical, and quantitative data presented in a variety of graphic organizers; and a variety of visual sources such as historical photographs, political cartoons, paintings, and architecture in order to clarify, illustrate, or elaborate upon the information presented in the text.

Standard 2: The student comprehends a variety of historical sources:

Therefore, the student is able to:

A. **Identify the author or source of the historical document or narrative and assess its credibility.**

B. **Reconstruct the literal meaning of a historical passage** by identifying who was involved, what happened, where it happened, what events led to these developments, and what consequences or outcomes followed.

C. **Identify the central question(s)** the historical narrative addresses and the purpose, perspective, or point of view from which it has been constructed.

D. **Differentiate between historical facts and historical interpretations** but acknowledge that the two are related; that the facts the historian reports are selected and reflect therefore the historian's judgement of what is most significant about the past.

E. **Read historical narratives imaginatively,** taking into account what the narrative reveals of the humanity of the individuals involved—their probable values, outlook, motives, hopes, fears, strengths, and weaknesses.

F. **Appreciate historical perspectives**—the ability (a) to describe the past on its own terms, through the eyes and experiences of those who were there, as revealed through their literature, diaries, letters, debates, arts, artifacts, and the like; (b) the historical context in which the event unfolded—the values, outlook, options, and contingencies of that time and place; and (c) to avoid "present-mindededness," judging the past solely in terms of present-day norms and values.

G. **Draw upon data in historical maps** in order to obtain or clarify information on the geographic setting in which the historical event occurred, its relative and absolute location, the distances and directions involved, the natural and man-made features of the place, and critical relationships in the spatial distributions of those features and historical event occurring there.

H. **Utilize visual, mathematical, and quantitative data** presented in charts, tables, pie and bar graphs, flow charts, Venn diagrams, and other graphic organizers to clarify, illustrate, or elaborate upon information presented in the historical narrative.

I. **Draw upon visual, literary, and musical sources** including: a) photographs, paintings, cartoons, and architectural drawings; b) novels, poetry, and plays; and, c) folk, popular and classical music, to clarify, illustrate, or elaborate upon information presented in the historical narrative.

STANDARD 3

Historical Analysis and Interpretation

One of the most common problems in helping students to become thoughtful readers of historical narrative is the compulsion students feel to find the one right answer, the one essential fact, the one authoritative interpretation. "Am I on the right track?" "Is this what you want?" they ask. Or, worse yet, they rush to closure, reporting back as self-evident truths the facts or conclusions presented in the document or text.

These problems are deeply rooted in the conventional ways in which textbooks have presented history: a succession of facts marching straight to a settled outcome. To overcome these problems requires the use of more than a single source: of history books other than textbooks and of a rich variety of historical documents and artifacts that present alternative voices, accounts, and interpretations or perspectives on the past.

Students need to realize that historians may differ on the facts they incorporate in the development of their narratives, and disagree as well on how those facts are to be interpreted. Thus, "history" is usually taken to mean what happened in the past; but *written* history is a dialogue among historians not only about what happened but about why and how it happened, how it affected other happenings, and how much importance it ought to be assigned. The study of history is not only remembering answers. It requires following and evaluating arguments and arriving at usable, even if tentative, conclusions based on the available evidence.

To engage in these activities requires that students draw upon their skills of *historical comprehension* as well as go beyond those skills to conduct *thoughtful analyses* of the line of reasoning or argument in which the historian has engaged in creating the narrative. There is no sharp line separating the skills involved in comprehension and in analysis. For example, unless students are first able to comprehend what a document, historical narrative, or artifact divulges concerning the ideas, perspectives, or beliefs of a particular person, culture, or era, it is impossible for students to engage in the analytic skills of comparing the ideas, perspectives, or beliefs held by different individuals, cultures, or societies at a particular time, or of comparing instances of continuity and change in ideas, perspectives, and beliefs over time. Similarly, unless students comprehend the credibility of the historical documents, artifacts, or other records on which the historian bases his or her interpretation of the past, students will be unable to analyze whether a narrative is grounded on sound historical evidence and merits, therefore, their thoughtful attention. In this sense certain of the skills involved in comprehension not only overlap the skills involved in analysis, but are essential to conducting these more demanding analytic activities. Analysis, however, builds beyond the skills of comprehension, and carries the student more deeply into assessing the authority of historical records themselves, assessing the adequacy of the historical evidence on which the historian has drawn, and determining the soundness of the interpretations historians have created from the evidence. It goes without saying that, in acquiring these skills, students also develop the capability to differentiate between expressions of opinion, no matter how passionately delivered, and informed hypotheses soundly grounded in historical evidence.

Well-written historical narrative has the power to promote students' analysis of historical causality—of how change occurs in society, of how human intentions matter, and how ends are influenced by the means of carrying them out, in what has been called the tangle of process and outcomes. Few challenges can be more fascinating to students than unraveling the often dramatic complications of cause. And nothing is more dangerous than a simple, monocausal explanation of past experiences and present problems.

Finally, well-written historical narratives can also alert students to the traps of *lineality and inevitability*. Students must understand the relevance of the past to their own times, but they need also to avoid the trap of lineality, of drawing straight lines between past and present, as though earlier movements were being propelled teleologically toward some rendezvous with destiny in the late 20th century.

A related trap is that of thinking that events have unfolded inevitably—that the way things are is the way they had to be, and thus that humankind lacks free will and the capacity for making choice. Unless students can conceive that history could have turned out differently, they may unconsciously accept the notion that the future is also inevitable or predetermined, and that human agency and individual action count for nothing. No attitude is more likely to feed civic apathy, cynicism, and resignation—precisely what we hope the study of history will fend off. Whether in dealing with the main narrative or with a topic in depth, we must always try, in one historian's words, to "restore to the past the options it once had."

Standard 3: The student engages in historical analysis and interpretation:

Therefore, the student is able to:

A. **Compare and contrast differing sets of ideas**, values, personalities, behaviors, and institutions by identifying likenesses and differences.

B. **Consider multiple perspectives** of various peoples in the past by demonstrating their differing motives, beliefs, interests, hopes, and fears.

C. **Analyze cause-and-effect relationships** bearing in mind **multiple causation** including (a) **the importance of the individual** in history; (b) **the influence of ideas**, human interests, and beliefs; and (c) **the role of chance**, the accidental and the irrational.

D. **Draw comparisons across eras and regions in order to define enduring issues** that transcend regional and temporal boundaries.

E. **Distinguish between unsupported expressions of opinion and informed hypotheses grounded in historical evidence.**

F. **Compare competing historical narratives.**

G. **Challenge arguments of historical inevitability** by formulating examples of historical contingency, of how different choices could have led to different consequences.

H. **Hold interpretations of history as tentative**, subject to changes as new information is uncovered, new voices heard, and new interpretations broached.

I. **Evaluate major debates among historians** concerning alternative interpretations of the past.

J. **Hypothesize the influence of the past**, including both the limitations and the opportunities made possible by past decisions.

STANDARD 4

Historical Research Capabilities

Perhaps no aspect of historical thinking is as exciting to students or as productive of their growth in historical thinking as "doing history." Such inquiries can arise at critical turning points in the historical narrative presented in the text. They might be generated by encounters with historical documents, eyewitness accounts, letters, diaries, artifacts, photos, a visit to a historic site, a record of oral history, or other evidence of the past. Worthy inquiries are especially likely to develop if the documents students encounter are rich with the voices of people caught up in the event and sufficiently diverse to bring alive to students the interests, beliefs, and concerns of people with differing backgrounds and opposing viewpoints on the event.

In this process students' contextual knowledge of the historical period in which the document or artifact was created becomes critically important. Only a few records of the event will be available to students. Filling in the gaps, evaluating the records they have available, and imaginatively constructing a sound historical argument or narrative requires a larger context of meaning.

Historical inquiry proceeds with the formulation of a problem or set of questions worth pursuing. In the most direct approach, students might be encouraged to analyze a document, record, or site itself. Who produced it, when, how, and why? What is the evidence of its authenticity, authority, and credibility? What does it tell them of the point of view, background, and interests of its author or creator? What else must they discover in order to construct a useful story, explanation, or narrative of the event of which this document or artifact is a part? What interpretation can they derive from their data, and what argument can they support in the historical narrative they create from the data?

In this process students' contextual knowledge of the historical period in which the document or artifact was created becomes critically important. Only a few records of the event will be available to students. Filling in the gaps, evaluating the records they have available, and imaginatively constructing a sound historical argument or narrative requires a larger context of meaning.

For these purposes, students' ongoing narrative study of history provides important support, revealing the larger context. But just as the ongoing narrative study, supported by but not limited to the textbook, provides a meaningful context in which students' inquiries can develop, it is these inquiries themselves that imbue the era with deeper meaning. Hence the importance of providing students documents or other records beyond materials included in the textbook, that will allow students to challenge textbook interpretations, to raise new questions about the event, to investigate the perspectives of those whose voices do not appear in the textbook accounts, or to plumb an issue that the textbook largely or in part bypassed.

Under these conditions, students will view their inquiries as creative contributions. They will better understand that written history is a human construction, that certain judgments about the past are tentative and arguable, and that historians regard their work as critical inquiry, pursued as ongoing explorations and debates with other historians. By their active engagement in historical inquiry, students will learn for themselves why historians are continuously reinterpreting the past, and why new interpretations emerge not only from uncovering new evidence but from rethinking old evidence in the light of new ideas springing up in our own times. Students then can also see why the good historian, like the good teacher, is interested not in manipulation or indoctrination but in acting as the honest messenger from the past—not interested in possessing students' minds but in presenting them with the power to possess their own.

Standard 4: The student conducts historical research:

Therefore, the student is able to:

A. **Formulate historical questions** from encounters with historical documents, eyewitness accounts, letters, diaries, artifacts, photos, historical sites, art, architecture, and other records from the past.

B. **Obtain historical data from a variety of sources,** including: library and museum collections, historic sites, historical photos, journals, diaries, eyewitness accounts, newspapers, and the like; documentary films, oral testimony from living witnesses, censuses, tax records, city directories, statistical compilations, and economic indicators

C. **Interrogate historical data** by uncovering the social, political, and economic context in which it was created; testing the data source for its credibility, authority, authenticity, internal consistency and completeness; and detecting and evaluating bias, distortion, and propaganda by omission, suppression, or invention of facts.

D. **Identify the gaps in the available records and marshal contextual knowledge and perspectives of the time and place** in order to elaborate imaginatively upon the evidence, fill in the gaps deductively, and construct a sound historical interpretation.

E. **Employ quantitative analysis** in order to explore such topics as changes in family size and composition, migration patterns, wealth distribution, and changes in the economy.

F. **Support interpretations with historical evidence** in order to construct closely reasoned arguments rather than facile opinions.

STANDARD 5

Historical Issues-Analysis and Decision-Making

Issue-centered analysis and decision-making activities place students squarely at the center of historical dilemmas and problems faced at critical moments in the past and the near-present. Entering into such moments, confronting the issues or problems of the time, analyzing the alternatives available to those on the scene, evaluating the consequences that might have followed those options for action that were not chosen, and comparing with the consequences of those that were adopted, are activities that foster students' deep, personal involvement in these events.

If well chosen, these activities also promote capacities vital to a democratic citizenry: the capacity to identify and define public policy issues and ethical dilemmas; analyze the range of interests and values held by the many persons caught up in the situation and affected by its outcome; locate and organize the data required to assess the consequences of alternative approaches to resolving the dilemma; assess the ethical implications as well as the comparative costs and benefits of each approach; and evaluate a particular course of action in light of all of the above and, in the case of historical issues-analysis, in light also of its long-term consequences revealed in the historical record.

Because important historical issues are frequently value-laden, they also open opportunities to consider the moral convictions contributing to social actions taken. For example, what moral and political dilemmas did Lincoln face when, in his Emancipation Proclamation, he decided to free only those slaves behind the Confederate lines? The point to be made is that teachers should not use critical events to hammer home a particular "moral lesson" or ethical teaching. Not only will many students reject that approach; it fails also to take into account the processes through which students acquire the complex skills of principled thinking and moral reasoning.

When students are invited to judge morally the conduct of historical actors, they should be encouraged to analyze the values that inform the judgment. In some instances, this will be an easy task. Students judging the Holocaust or slavery as evils will probably be able to articulate the foundation for their judgment. In other cases, a student's effort to reach a moral judgment may produce a healthy student exercise in analyzing values, and may, in some instances, lead him or her to recognize the historically conditioned nature of a particular moral value he or she may be invoking.

Particularly challenging are the many social issues throughout United States history on which multiple interests and different values have come to bear. Issues of civil rights or equal education opportunity, of the right to choice vs. the right to life, and of criminal justice have all brought such conflicts to the fore. When these conflicts have not been resolved within the social and political institutions of the nation, they have regularly found their way into the judicial system, often going to the Supreme Court for resolution.

As the history course approaches the present era, such inquiries assume special relevance, confronting students with issues that resonate in today's headlines and invite their participation in lively debates, simulations, and socratic seminars—settings in which they can confront alternative policy recommendations, judge their ethical implications, challenge one another's assessments, and acquire further skills in the public presentation and defense of positions. In these analyses, teachers have the special responsibility of helping students differentiate between (1) relevant historical antecedents and (2) those that are clearly inappropriate and irrelevant. Students need to learn how to use their knowledge of history (or the past) to bring sound historical analysis to the service of informed decision making.

Standard 5: The student engages in historical issues-analysis and decision-making:

Therefore, the student is able to:

A. **Identify issues and problems in the past** and analyze the interests, values, perspectives, and points of view of those involved in the situation.

B. **Marshal evidence of antecedent circumstances** and current factors contributing to contemporary problems and alternative courses of action.

C. **Identify relevant historical antecedents** and differentiate from those that are inappropriate and irrelevant to contemporary issues.

D. **Evaluate alternative courses of action,** keeping in mind the information available at the time, in terms of ethical considerations, the interests of those affected by the decision, and the long- and short-term consequences of each.

E. **Formulate a position or course of action on an issue** by identifying the nature of the problem, analyzing the underlying factors contributing to the problem, and choosing a plausible solution from a choice of carefully evaluated options.

F. **Evaluate the implementation of a decision** by analyzing the interests it served; estimating the position, power, and priority of each player involved; assessing the ethical dimensions of the decision; and evaluating its costs and benefits from a variety of perspectives.

*Students at West Milford
High School, West Milford, NJ.
Photo by John Jordan*

Explorations

Adding Inquiry To The "Inquiry" Method*
by Clair W. Keller

Clair Keller outlines approaches to teaching based on open-ended questions which engage students in the study of history. The teacher's role is to encourage curiosity; to motivate students using a creative process of describing, explaining, and evaluating data. Based on observations as classroom teacher and supervisor of student teachers, Keller argues that what usually passes for class discussions are one-to-one exchanges rather than a mutual commitment of teacher and student to investigate and utilize data. In the following article Keller offers several practical approaches to the development of creative inquiry in the classroom.

The author holds a joint appointment in History and Education at Iowa State University. He teaches colonial history and social studies methods classes as well as supervising student teachers. He taught for ten years in high schools near Seattle.

The newest method promising instant success in teaching social studies, "packaged inquiry," does not seem to provide students with the open-end experiences the term "inquiry" implies. In fact, "Inquiry," as it is now being commercially packaged, actually prevents the student from practicing at least two essential and creative skills he must learn in order to be inquisitive and skeptical, a true inquirer. First, by providing questions similar to those at the "end of the chapter," the materials stifle the opportunity to ask questions; second, the materials limit the scope of investigation by selecting the data from which a student is to draw conclusions. There is increasing danger that, in the hands of many teachers, these new materials will become new textbooks rather than new methods of teaching.

It is possible for students and teachers through the use of open-end questions to become truly engaged in creative inquiry, by which we mean the process of explaining various relationships between social science phenomena by developing inquiry models to ask the questions needed to solve, clarify or explain a subject.

The method we advocate is based upon the following suppositions.

1. That the most important learning which takes place in a classroom is not what is taught but the way it is taught (a Marshall McLuhan derivative).
2. That the primary objective of social studies teaching should be to provide students with the skills needed to explore and explain relationships between various kinds of social science data.
3. That the above objectives can best be accomplished when students and teachers are mutually engaged in the process.

The ability to ask the right questions is at the center of inquiry and good teaching. Yet teachers either are not being taught to ask good questions or they are not using this training successfully, judging from the observations of this writer as both classroom teacher and supervisor of student teachers. Class discussions are usually a one-to-one exchange between teacher and student: one question asked, one question answered. More honest and less time consuming would be giving the questions to the students in written form—either with or without answers—rather than continuing the pointless charade of "guess what I'm thinking." Included in this charade are those questions requiring several parts for a full answer, for while they are

---

*Reprinted from *The History Teacher*, Vol. IV, No. 1 (Nov. 1970), pp. 47-53.

more complex, they differ only in length. When teachers quit talking and begin listening to their students, they usually hear a recapitulation of the lecture or textbook. The argument so often offered to justify such a catechism is that students must know the "facts" before they can think. Even granting this dubious assumption, few teachers ever get beyond the first level. Most social studies teaching stops at the point where it should be beginning.

In contrast to the "guess what I'm thinking" approach to class discussions, teachers need to ask questions for which there are no pat answers. These questions generally fall into two categories: those which focus upon the subject matter of the discipline and those which focus upon the methodology of the discipline. Both are essential, but the latter are the most crucial and the most neglected. As far as the social sciences are concerned, a student's education will never become self-starting until he can skillfully propose questions leading to investigation and utilization of the data of the social sciences.

To teach students to ask such questions, the teacher's role must change so that he too is engaged in a creative process of describing, explaining and evaluating the various relationships between data in the social sciences. Such an approach calls for a new honesty in the classroom as class discussions shift from "question-and-answer" to a mutual commitment of finding out. Think of the excitement and revelation when students discover that the teacher also wants to learn, It could be contagious.

Most inquiry models follow the steps outlined by Massialas and Cox in *Inquiry in the Social Studies*, consisting of Orientation, Hypothesis Formation, Exploration, Evidencing and Generalizing. These steps are usable, but the Exploration and Evidencing parts should be expanded. Students need to speculate, not only in forming the original hypothesis, but in "Evidencing" as well, by answering the question: How can we know that my hypothesis is valid? Students speculate in model building, first, by determining what questions need to be answered to prove the hypothesis, and second, by deciding what evidence would be needed to substantiate these answers. It is here that the student and teacher become engaged in creative inquiry.

Inquiry itself presupposes curiosity. The first step—and the major role of the teacher—is to present an episode in the class which enables students to hypothesize about the subject under investigation. It is this class session which should make each student's reaction and line of inquiry unique, momentum coming from the dialogue of students and teacher. This can be done in numerous ways; a great deal depends upon the imagination and resources of the teacher in making students curious and motivating them—although the motivation can grow with the process itself. Visual presentations are often effective. Some current films are designed to raise questions or get students to hypothesize. Another approach is providing students with conflicting interpretations. An imaginative teacher can utilize the textbook as well, as has been illustrated by Massialas and Cox, encouraging students to speculate about the subject. For the purposes of demonstrating this approach to inquiry, the causes of the American Revolution will serve as the "medium" through which the "message" will be explained. These speculations might include some of the following statements about the causes of revolutions in general and about the American Revolution in particular:

Revolutions occur when people are poor or getting poorer.
Revolutions occur when people's rights are taken away by a despotic government.
People revolt because they want greater voice in their own affairs.
Revolutions occur because the masses are led by a few agitators.

The American Colonists declared independence in order to escape the mercantile system.

The American Colonists revolted because they wanted to have a greater control over their own lives.

The American Colonists wanted to main the control of their own affairs to which they had become accustomed prior to 1763.

For purposes of illustration, the class will test the last statement.

The teacher should turn to developing a model substantiating the claim that the "American Colonists" sought independence in order to maintain the control over their own affairs to which they had grown accustomed prior to 1763." The process involves several interacting episodes consisting of determining what kinds of data are needed for verification, if they exist, where they can be found, and whether they are reliable. Model building and data accumulation should go on simultaneously as questions are raised and data collected to answer them or supportive statements made in class.

Model building should begin with speculation about the requirements necessary for verification. Such speculation could consist of the following:

Colonists must have had control over their own affairs prior to 1763.

Colonists must have believed that this freedom existed.

This idea must have been sufficiently widespread to have a mass following.

The colonists must have believed that this freedom was disappearing.

Those who were responsible for independence must have believed that

Great Britain was substantially reducing local control.

Each statement is then evidenced. First the class must determine what kind of evidence would substantiate the statement and then proceed to gather that which exists. If the data cannot be acquired, or if they do not exist, then students need to recognize the weakness of the supporting statement. For example, class discussion and investigation of the statement, "Colonists must have had control over their own affairs prior to 1763," might revolve around the following:

What affairs would be important for the colonists to control?
  Control over their livelihood.
  Control over the way they were governed.
How would you determine that colonists had control over their own livelihood?
  Must identify what colonists did to make a living and that they were unhampered in these pursuits.
  Show that the colonists were not prohibited from pursuing some economic endeavors that were important to their economic welfare.
How would you establish that the colonists had control over their own political affairs?
  Must identify what political institutions were important to the Colonists.
  Must show that these political institutions were controlled by the Colonists.
How would you determine what political institutions were important to the colonists?
  Those institutions which had the greatest effect upon their lives.
  Those institutions which, if not controlled, could significantly alter their lives.

What data would you accept to identify those political institutions which were important to the colonists.

Answers might include:

Statements by colonists to that effect.
Polls which asked the question, which of these institutions are you most concerned with?
Analysis of decisions made by institutions and the impact these decisions had on the lives of people.
Analysis which shows what institutions received greatest participation by colonists.
Which political institutions produced the greatest struggle for control among the colonists and between the colonists and Great Britain.

When specific data has been identified, students must locate and gather the data. Again the work could be divided among groups in the class and research begun as students search for the data. It is obvious that a reasonably good library or resource center would be required. If sufficient resources are not available, topics should be pursued which lend themselves to the materials readily obtainable.

Model building is complex and varies greatly in sophistication. The example illustrated above would certainly pose difficulty for the average high school class in American history. It is possible, however, to relate the questions mentioned above to more contemporary and perhaps more understandable issues without sacrificing the open-endedness of this approach. Such an investigation could begin by asking and pursuing the following:

What political institutions are most important today?
How could we find out?
Who would you ask?
Who should decide which institutions are most important?
What kind of data would you accept as verification that certain political institutions were most important?

A discussion of a possible analogy to the colonial period could then be developed.

How valid is an analogy between the present and the colonial evaluation?
How would you decide is such an analogy were valid?
What assumptions would have to be made if the analogy were valid?

Once a model has been constructed it provides a useful tool for analysis of various interpretations by comparing the arguments and data historians used with that developed in the class model. The emphasis which each interpretation places on parts of the model not only identifies the interpretation more clearly but helps to account for the differences.

This approach can easily be adapted to different forms of instruction. It lends itself to individual instruction for it enables a student to do two things: first, choose his own topic; second, develop his own model at his own level of sophistication. Group work may be more feasible, however, because a large amount of interaction between student and teacher and among students is desirable. Group work best provides for such interaction, as well as affording the opportunity for variety. Because data from all the social sciences are useful for evidencing, this method make possible a true inter-disciplinary approach.

The development of a new technique in the teaching of social studies does not mean that it should be employed exclusively. Social studies teaching should be eclectic. The procedure suggested in this article is flexible enough to allow teachers to use as little or as much as students can digest. It can be implemented as rapidly or as slowly as teachers desire. It can be the focal point for an entire course, a unit, ore merely a day's work. The procedure can be adopted by an entire school system which provides workshops and training for the teachers or by an individual teacher who, after reading this article, understands the technique. No new materials need be purchased, although a good selection of primary and secondary sources are necessary. Even here, it is possible to collect materials for a particular unit and follow this process without a large investment. What makes this proposal acceptable is that it focuses upon the art of teaching and not, as so many proposals of today, upon expensive gimmickry.

Students examining primary sources at the Copeley Library, La Jolla, CA. Photo by Richard Del Rio

The Case for "Big History"*
by David Christian

David Christian presents a case for teaching world history on a larger timescale. He writes, "We cannot fully understand the past few millennia without understanding the far longer period of time in which all members of our own species lived as gatherers and hunters...." In opening the study of history to the larger picture it will become necessary to breach the walls of convention and transgress "the traditional boundaries between the discipline of history and other disciplines, such as prehistory, biology, geology, and cosmology." Christian discusses some of the objections to and merits of "big history." He describes a course that illustrates some of the practicalities of his approach.

David Christian is a professor of history at Macquarie University in Sydney, Australia. He has been a leader in advancing world history teaching on that continent.

What is the scale on which history should be studied? The establishment of the *Journal of World History* already implies a radical answer to that question in geographical terms, the appropriate scale may be the whole of the world. In this paper, I will defend an equally radical answer to the temporal aspect of the same question: what is the time scale on which history should be studied? I will argue that the appropriate time scale for the study of history may be the whole of time. In other words, historians should be prepared to explore the past on many different time scales up to that of the universe itself—a scale of between 10 and 20 billion years. This is what I mean by "big history." Readers of this journal will already be familiar with the case for world history. I will argue that a similar case can be made for teaching and writing about the past on these even larger time scales.

As I understand it, the case for world history turns to a large extent on the belief of many historians that the discipline of history has failed to find an adequate balance between the opposing demands of detail and generality. In the century since Ranke, historians have devoted themselves with great energy and great success to the task of documenting the past. And they have accumulated a vast amount of information about the history of a number of modern societies, in particular those with European or Mediterranean roots. But in history, as in any other academic discipline, you must look beyond the details if you are to understand their meaning, to see how they fit together. We need large-scale maps if we are to see each part of our subject in its context. Unfortunately, historians have become so absorbed in detailed research that they have tended to neglect the job of building these larger-scale maps of the past. Indeed, many historians deliberately neglect the task of generalization in the belief that the facts will eventually speak for themselves when enough of them have been accumulated, forgetting that it is we alone who can give the "facts" a voice. The result of this one-sided approach to historical research is a discipline that has plenty of information but a fragmented and parochial vision of its field of inquiry. Not surprisingly, it has become harder and harder to explain to those we teach and those we write for why they should bother to study history at all.

World history is, among other things, an attempt to redress this balance. The point is expressed well by David Sweet in a recent discussion of efforts to organize graduate study in world history:

---

*Reprinted from *Journal of World History*, Vol. 2, No. 2 (Fall 1991), pp. 223-238.

Perhaps the best argument for a program in world history is that it represents a long-overdue recognition by members of *our* profession that in the end history is all of one piece—that it is the whole story of humanity, seen in the context of humanity's changing relationship to nature. This includes an acknowledgment that all parts of that story are of importance to the whole, and that they have full meaning only when seen somehow in relation to the whole.

Arguments of this kind will be familiar to readers of the *Journal of World History*. But the arguments that apply to world history are also true at larger scales. We cannot fully understand the past few millennia without understanding the far longer period of time in which all members of our own species lived as gatherers and hunters, and without understanding the changes that led to the emergence of the earliest agrarian communities and the first urban civilizations. Paleolithic society, in its turn, cannot be fully understood without some idea of the evolution of our own species over several million years. That however requires some grasp of the history of life on earth, and so on. Such arguments may seem to lead us to an endless regress, but it is now clear that they do not. According to modern Big Bang cosmology, the universe itself has a history, with a clear and identifiable beginning somewhere between 10 and 20 billion years ago. We can say nothing of what happened before this time; indeed time itself was created in the Big Bang. So this time scale is different from others. If there is an absolute framework for the study of the past, this is it. If the past can be studied whole, this is the scale within which to do it.

By "big history," then, I mean the exploration of the past on all these different scales, up to the scale of the universe itself. In what follows I will first discuss some possible objections to big history; then I will describe in general terms, and with some specific examples, some of its merits; and finally I will describe a university course in big history as an illustration of some of the practicalities of teaching history on this largest of all possible scales.

Some Objections to Big History

If the idea of big history seems strange at first sight, that is largely because it breaches in an even more spectacular way than world history a number of well-established conventions about the ways in which history is best taught and written. To explore the past on a very large scale means going beyond conventional ideas about the time scales on which history is best studied, and it means transgressing the traditional boundaries between the discipline of history and other disciplines, such as prehistory, biology, geology, and cosmology. Can these conventions about time scale and discipline boundaries be breached with impunity? For my own part, I am sure that they can; I believe that they are indeed little more than conventions and that breaching them can only be healthy.

To take first the issue of time scales. Although there are a number of outstanding exceptions (several of whom have played an active role in the establishment of the World History Association), the vast majority of professional historians continue to explore the past on the time scale of a human lifetime. Most courses tend to be taught, and most books tend to be written, on time scales from a decade or two to a century or so. Two similar, but opposite, objections are often raised against those who attempt to survey the past on larger scales. One is that large-scale history means sacrificing detail and retreating into empty generalities; the opposite objection is that at the large scale there is simply too much information for the historian to handle.

The same reply can be made to both objections: the very notion of detail is relative. What is central at one scale may be detail at another and may vanish entirely at the very largest scales. Some questions require the telephoto lens; others require the wide-angle lens. And as one shifts from smaller to larger scales, the loss of detail is, in any case, balanced by the fact that larger objects come into view, objects so large that they cannot be seen whole from close up. So there is no single appropriate level of "graininess" for the historian; nor is there any reason to regard the conventional time scales as sacrosanct. The amount of detail required depends purely on the nature of the question being asked.

This principle applies to all time scales. If the questions being asked concern the origins of human society or the human impact on the environment, then clearly we must be prepared to view the past on a scale of many millions of years. If our questions concern the significance of intelligence or of life in the universe, they require an even larger scale. All that is required to pursue such questions is a willingness to shift lenses in a way that is familiar in principle to all historians, even if its application on so heroic a scale may induce a degree of vertigo the first time around. No difficulty of principle is involved, although the shaking of such well-established conventions does require a considerable effort both of the imagination and the intellect.

This leads to a second criticism of large-scale history, one that concerns expertise. In tackling questions on these huge scales, the historian is bound to breach conventional discipline boundaries as well as conventional time scales. Can historians legitimately stray like this beyond their patch? Clearly, no single scholar can acquire an expert's knowledge in all the different disciplines that have a bearing on history at the very large scale. But this does not mean that the historian should abandon such questions. If a question requires some knowledge of biology or geology, then so be it. All that is required is a willingness to exploit the division of intellectual labor that exists in all our universities. Far from being unusual, this is normal procedure in any science; indeed it is normal procedure within and among the many subdisciplines that make up history. Besides, such borrowing is more feasible today than it would have been even a decade ago; there exist now numerous fine works of popularization by specialists in many different academic disciplines, works that offer scholarly, up-to-date, and lucid summaries of the contemporary state of knowledge in different fields. So there is no fundamental objection to the crossing of discipline boundaries; the difficulties are purely practical.

The obvious objections to big history, then, reflect little more than the inertia of existing conventions about the way history should be taught and written. In principle, there is nothing to prevent the historian from considering the past at very large scales and using essentially the same skills of research, judgment, and analysis that would apply at more conventional scales. What are the positive arguments for big history? They follow from the negative arguments I have just discussed.

First, big history permits the asking of very large questions and therefore encourages the search for larger meanings in the past. If world history allows us to see the history of specific societies in a global context, history on even larger time scales allows us to consider the history of humanity as a whole in *its* context. It therefore invites us to ask questions about the relationship between the history of our own species and that of other living things. And it invites us to go back even further and try to place the history of life itself in a larger context. In this way, big history encourages us to ask questions about our place in the universe. It leads us back to the sort of questions that have been answered in many societies by creation myths. This suggests that history could play as significant a role in modern industrial society as traditional creation myths have played in nonindustrial societies; but it will do so only if it asks questions as large and profound as those posed in traditional creation myths.

In the second place, big history allows us to tackle these large questions with new approaches and new models because it encourages the drawing of new links between different academic disciplines. It can be seen, therefore, as an appropriate response to the intellectual apartheid between "the two cultures" of science and the humanities that C. P. Snow discussed in a famous lecture delivered in 1959.

So far, the discussion has been at a very general level. In what follows, I would like to give some specific illustrations of each of these arguments. First I will discuss a specific historical issue that can be approached at several different scales, the issue of economic growth in human history. What is the scale on which such a question can best be discussed, and how do different time scales affect the way we view the question and its implications? I will argue that this is a question better debated at scales even larger than those conventional within the field of world history.

On the scale adopted in most histories of human society, growth of some kind, involving changed technology and increases in productivity, is palpably there. So it is easy to think of change, or even "progress," as a basic characteristic of human history, perhaps even a defining characteristic of our species. E. L. Jones has made these assumptions explicit in a series of recent studies that have done much to put large-scale historical questions on the agenda for professional historians. "Let us assume," he writes in a recent essay, "that a propensity for growth has been widely present in human society. This does not commit us to a neoclassical maximising position. Not everyone need be engaged in maximising on every margin at once. All that is needed is to accept that a desire to reduce material poverty is commonplace in our species, as well it might be considering that poverty exacts such a penalty in terms of dead babies, or at any rate of children without shoes." On the scale of 5,000 years, this is all very plausible. And Jones himself has assembled the evidence for a long-term trend toward both extensive and intensive growth over this period.

But is 5,000 years really the appropriate scale if our concern is with human beings and the societies they have created? If we are asking questions about the "propensities" or "desires" of the human species, surely the appropriate time scale is that of the species as a whole. How big is that? The earliest fossil evidence for Australopithecines, the first members of the hominid family, dates back about 4 million years. The first evidence for *Homo habilis,* the earliest species that modern physical anthropologists are willing to classify within the genus *Homo,* dates back almost 3 million years. The larger-brained species, *Homo erectus,* first appears in the record about 1.9 million years ago. The relationship between *Homo erectus* and our own species, *Homo sapiens,* is a subject of great controversy, but an age of between 50,000 and 400,000 years for *Homo sapiens* would cover most positions within this controversy, and a figure of 250,000 years is a reasonable compromise. So, on this evidence, when did human history begin? For my purposes, a precise answer is not important. One could argue that "humans" have existed for 5 million years. But even on the more modest scale of 250,000 years, a question posed on a scale of a mere 5,000 years is likely to produce aberrant answers.

What does the problem of growth look like on the larger scale? If we take world population as a measure of the capacity of human societies to support growth, then the story of human history over several hundreds of thousands of years is one of small populations and local fluctuations that have left little trace in the historical record, and then a sudden and spectacular burst of growth in recent times. Early hominid populations were probably of the same order of magnitude as those of other great apes in recent times: perhaps 1 million, all living in Africa. We must presume that the migrations that led *Homo erectus* out of Africa and into the colder climates of Eurasia about 1 million years ago (migrations that might have been accompanied by the mastery of fire), led to a considerable increase in the world population of hominids, which suggests that 2 to 4 million may be a reasonable guess for the world population 250,000 years ago. By 10,000 years ago, when forms of agriculture and permanent settlements began to appear in several distinct parts of the world, the population of the world could hardly have been more than 10 million. On these very rough estimates, human populations increased from perhaps 2 million to 10 million over a period of some 250,000 years, and most evidence for intensification comes from the last 40,000 years of that huge range. This is a rate of growth so imperceptible that no modern economist would want to apply the word "growth" to it, and any "propensity for growth" one may claim to observe on this scale begins to look a pretty spectral thing.

In contrast, during the last 10,000 years, human populations have risen from 10 million to about 200 million (2,000 years ago), and then, in an even more spectacular acceleration, to nearly 5 billion today. On this reckoning, human history consists of about 250,000 years of relative stasis followed by a mere 10,000 years of growth, most of which has been concentrated into the last few hundred years. In other words, even on a rather restricted definition of our species, growth has occupied a mere 4% of its history; the really spectacular growth has occurred in the last 0.2% of that history.

The accompanying figure graphs no more than the last two and a half millennia of human population growth. To get a sense of human population growth over 250,000 years, one would have to add a further ninety-nine graphs to the left, and on most of those graphs, the line representing human population would merge into the graph's base line. Only in the last three or four graphs would it begin to rise above that line.

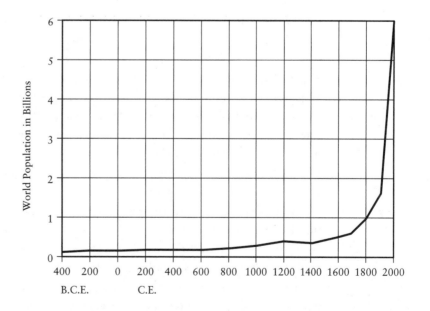

Figure 1. World Population, 400 B.C.E. to 2000 C.E.

To the extent that population growth can serve as a surrogate for growth in average levels of productivity, we must conclude that growth, far from being the normal condition of humanity, is an aberration. The growth that E. L. Jones has documented over the past 5,000 years is evidence not for the normality of growth, but rather for a sudden breakdown in an ancient equilibrium between a large mammal species and the environment it inhabits. Carlo Cipolla comments: "A biologist, looking at the diagram showing the recent growth of world population in a long-range perspective, said that he had the impression of being in the presence of the growth curve of a microbe population in a body suddenly struck by some infectious disease. The 'bacillus' man is taking over the world." Why did this particular large species of mammal suddenly begin to display the demographic behavior of a plague species? On the scale of human history as a whole, this is the really interesting question.

A slightly different way of saying the same thing is to point out (what everyone knows, although few expend much intellectual effort on the fact) that the history of human beings has been above all a history of hunter-gatherer societies.' In an important sense, hunting and gathering are the "natural" activities of human beings, and what has occurred in the last 5,000 years is profoundly "unnatural." There is nothing "natural" about the state, or civilization, or economic growth. The entire history of agrarian and now industrial civilizations is from this point of view a curious and rather surprising coda tacked onto the end of human history.

The large perspective affects our approach to the problem of growth in other ways, too, for it raises a host of further issues, some of which are ethical, and some of which need to be discussed on a very large scale indeed. Should we admire the explosive growth of the past few millennia? Is it, perhaps, what distinguishes us from other living species? Or can we identify similar turning points in the history of other living species? Is human history governed, ultimately, by the rhythms of natural history as a whole? What is the likely impact of our own history on the history of the planet as a whole? Is the rapid growth of human society proof of a fertility in invention so astonishing (and so untypical of animal species as a whole) that it will continually outstrip the dangers it creates? Casual judgments about such questions lie behind much historical writing, so it is important that the questions be posed seriously and clearly. They should also be debated rigorously if history is to take itself seriously as a discussion of what it means to be human, a discussion that inevitably has ethical dimensions.

A discussion of "growth" highlights another advantage of thinking about the past on a very large scale. Thinking about the very long term means thinking about very large trends. This makes it possible to discuss the future in ways that are not possible if historians concentrate on the short term. Is accelerating economic growth a trend that can be projected forward indefinitely into the future? Presumably not, simply because the mathematics of such a trend will soon lead us toward some embarrassing infinities: infinite population growth, infinite increase in consumption, and so on. So we can be certain, after exploring these very long trends, that they can not be projected indefinitely into the future. What, precisely, does that mean? What mechanisms will alter the accelerating trends we now observe? Will they be Malthusian in nature? Or climatic or ecological? Or will they involve rational human intervention? And when will the trend change? These questions, of vast significance for our view of the next few hundred years and for our understanding of political and economic decisions that have to be made today, can be tackled seriously by historians only if we look more seriously at very long trends. What drives the long-term trends? What drives the machinery of growth in the very long term?" How fast can that machine go, and at what point is it likely to stall? By raising questions of this sort, big history may make it possible to end the ancient historians' taboo on discussion of the future as well as the past. That taboo made sense, but only as long as historians refused to discuss trends large enough to yield significant hints about the future. These examples should indicate some of the ways in which large-scale history can make it easier to pose fundamental questions that cannot be tackled at smaller scales.

I also suggested earlier that one of the virtues of big history may be that it will encourage historians to become more familiar with the models, techniques, habits of thinking, and types of evidence used in other disciplines. This in turn may help historians view their own discipline in new ways. I would like to give a brief illustration of what I mean. It concerns the problem of agriculture and its origins, and it draws on the work of David Rindos. Rindos seeks the answer to a historical question (the reasons for the emergence of agriculture) using a Darwinian paradigm. He argues that the emergence of agriculture is a familiar process in natural history, where it can be described as a form of coevolution, the evolution of a symbiotic relationship between two very different species. Agriculture is not unique to humans, for many other species of animals, including several types of ants, can also be said to have developed forms of agriculture, or "domestication," in which the animal aids in the reproductive success of an edible plant. Within the Darwinian paradigm, coevolution, whether of ants and trees or of humans and grains, is a mutual process, one to which both partners contribute something. It is also an essentially blind process, one that involves no element of conscious intention. Here is Rindos's definition of "domestication":

> Domestication is a coevolutionary process in which any given taxon diverges from an original gene pool and establishes a symbiotic protection and dispersal relationship with the animal feeding upon it. This symbiosis is facilitated by adaptations (changes in the morphology, physiology, or autoecology) within the plant population and by changes in behavior by the animal.

In the case of human agriculture, coevolution was presumably encouraged by the fact that hunter-gatherers were likely to scatter the seeds of plants they favored around frequently used camp sites. Plants that offered the most attractive taste were the ones most likely to be selected in this way, so these plants were most likely to flourish near camp sites. This is what Rindos calls the "dump-heap model for agricultural origins."

Is Rindos merely using a Darwinian analogy here, or is he claiming that the Darwinian arguments can be applied directly to human history? As I understand it, he claims (after preparing his ground with an elaborate exorcism of the ghost of Herbert Spencer) that the argument is more than analogy; however, the Darwinian argument needs to be modified in some important respects before it can be used as a tool for the interpretation of human history. As his definition of "domestication" suggests, in the natural world coevolution, although it requires behavioral changes, also involves genetic change in both partners to the relationship. In the case of the human domestication of grains, this is not necessarily true. It is certainly true that agriculture encouraged rapid genetic change on one side of the evolving relationship, that of the plants; but Rindos's argument does not require that this be true of both sides. Human groups evolved culturally. Their behaviors and cultures changed in ways that maximized the benefits they procured from domesticated plants, and simultaneously improved the reproductive chances of the plants. So in this case, coevolution involved change on one side and behavioral change on the other. This line of argument leads Rindos to the notion of "cultural evolution": "Behavior, like any other phenotypic trait of an organism, is amenable to selection. Thus behaviors may influence the differential reproductive success of a lineage over time. If the presence of a new behavior increases the probability that a lineage will prosper (in numerical terms), the change in behavior has increased the fitness of that lineage."

At issue here is not whether Rindos's account of agricultural origins is right or wrong. The crucial point is that historians can only gain by considering seriously the ways in which other disciplines solve problems. Drawing closer links between the traditional content and methodology of history and that of other disciplines can only enrich the theoretical and methodological toolbox available to historians.

A History of 15 Billion Years

But is big history manageable in practice? In particular, can history be taught at this scale? The best proof is in the doing. At Macquarie University in Sydney, we have been teaching since 1989 a first-year history course that does just what I have proposed. It discusses history on many different time scales, beginning with that of the universe itself.' Naturally, this course is only one of many possible ways of approaching big history, and the specific ways we approach it may or may not be palatable to other historians. But our experience suggests that there is nothing particularly difficult about teaching such a course once one has shifted mental gears. So I will end with a brief description of our approach to big history.

The Macquarie course is taught over thirteen weeks; it offers two lectures a week and one tutorial. Lecturers come from many different disciplines: astronomy, geology, biology, palaeontology, anthropology, prehistory, classical history, and modern history.

The course begins with lectures on time and creation myths. The lecture on time offers an introductory discussion of the medium within which historians operate (for the most part without questioning it); the lecture attempts to demonstrate the differences in conceptions of the nature of time in different societies and to help students begin to grasp large and unfamiliar time scales. The second lecture discusses creation myths from many different societies. Its aim is to suggest that history itself may best be regarded as a form of modern "creation myth," in the sense that it reflects the best attempts of our society to answer questions about origins, just as the Genesis account or the creation myths of Australian Aboriginal society reflect the attempts of very different societies to answer fundamental questions about the origins of the heavens, the planet, living things, human beings, and human society. The drawing of this parallel is also a way of suggesting that history, like traditional creation myths, can pose questions of the most fundamental kind. And this, it seems to me, is the first payoff for the teacher of a course on this scale; no special effort is required to explain why the subject matter being taught is important. Its importance is self-evident.

After these introductory lectures, the course starts at the beginning, offering a narrative that is unconventional only because of the scale on which it tells its story. Two lectures given by a professional astronomer discuss current theories on the origins of the universe itself and the clusters of galaxies and stars that are the largest structures the universe contains. Two lectures are given on the history of the solar system and the history of the earth and its atmosphere. These are followed by lectures summarizing current theories and evidence on the origins of life on earth, the main laws of biological evolution, and the main stages of the evolution of life. A lecture on the evolution of human beings from apelike ancestors follows. Our own species appears in the course only in the fifth week of the thirteen-week course.

Given the influence of conventional discipline boundaries, this appearance inevitably marks a crucial turning point in the course. This is the point at which disciplines conventionally classified as "sciences" are left behind in favor of disciplines conventionally classified as "social sciences" or "humanities." The transition requires some discussion of what is meant by the conventional distinction between scientific and nonscientific disciplines, which in turn requires some discussion of the nature of the "truths" offered by both scientists and historians. So at this point there is an introductory lecture on theories of science, which poses the question: is history less scientific than science? (The answer is a cautious but qualified "No.") This lecture is designed to highlight the way in which big history can pose issues not just of content, but also of methodology. Is history a science? In what sense can it claim to offer truths more certain than those of traditional creation myths? Should history aspire to its own "paradigms" (in the sense made familiar in the work of Thomas Kuhn)?'s Is there any fundamental difference between the types of evidence offered by scientists and those offered by historians? (Is a written document fundamentally different from the redshifted spectrum of a distant galaxy?) How useful are models? Problems of historical methodology do not vanish when history is viewed on a large scale; on the contrary, they can be posed more clearly when the methodologies and types of argument used by historians are contrasted with those of researchers in many other disciplines. To ensure that this is true, lecturers and tutors in the course concentrate at every point on the *evidence* for the theories they are discussing.

From this point, the content of the Macquarie course should be more familiar.' Lectures follow on the nature of paleolithic societies and the significance of hunter-gatherer technologies and life-styles in the past and present. Then come lectures on the emergence of agriculture, the earliest political and class structures, and the very earliest civilizations. Only at this point, in the ninth week of the course, do we begin to discuss problems that come within the domain of conventional history writing. Later lectures discuss early civilizations and the classical civilizations of Europe, Asia, and the Americas. Discussion of pre-Columbian America is particularly fruitful as it poses fascinating questions about the parallel development of agrarian civilizations in parts of the globe that seem to have had no cultural contact for many thousands of years. Then there is a series of lectures on the emergence of a distinctively modern world and the nature of the world we inhabit at the end of the second millennium of the Christian calendar.

The final lecture, given jointly by myself (a historian) and a colleague who is a biologist, attempts an overview of the course as a whole. It asks a question that can only be asked in this kind of course: is there a discernible pattern to the past? It poses the question on three different scales—that of humanity, the planet, and the universe. Our answer? Yes, there are large patterns. In some sense history, at all three levels is a fugue whose two major themes are entropy (which leads to imbalance, the decline of complex entities, and a sort of "running down" of the universe) and, as a sort of counterpoint, the creative forces that manage to form and sustain complex but temporary equilibria despite the pressure of entropy. These fragile equilibrium systems include galaxies, stars, the earth, the biosphere (what James Lovelock has referred to as "Gaia"), social structures of various kinds, living things, and human beings. These are all entities that achieve a temporary but always precarious balance, undergo periodic crises, reestablish new equilibria, but eventually succumb to the larger forces of imbalance represented by the principle of "entropy." They all share the rhythm of "punctuated equilibrium" that Stephen Jay Gould and Niles Eldredge have detected in the history of life on earth. These are entities that live, develop, and then die. Such patterns can be found at all time scales, so in this sense history is, as the mathematicians of chaos would say, "self similar." Seen in this perspective, human history is the story of one such equilibrium system, which exists on the scale of a million or so years. And the history of the last few thousand years deals with the experience of that system as a long period of equilibrium was punctuated by a period of turbulence and instability. In this perspective, the most profound question that can be asked by a member of the species *Homo sapiens* living in the modern era is this: will human society manage to establish a new equilibrium of some kind? Or will it succumb to the forces of entropy?

Coda

This paper has been concerned with presenting the case for big history. It may seem, therefore, that it constitutes an attack on "small history." So I will conclude by emphasizing that this is not so. My real complaint is not that historians have concentrated on the details; it is that the profession has tended in the century since Ranke to define its task almost exclusively in terms of detailed research. As a result, historians have neglected the larger questions of meaning, significance, and wholeness that can alone give some point to the details. If history is to reestablish its centrality as a discussion about what it means to be human, it must renew the interest in the large scale that was taken for granted by historians in the days before history became a "science."

Photo by Bert Seal,
San Diego County Office of
Education

Central Themes for World History*
by Ross E. Dunn

Why teach world history? Countering arguments that world history courses are by nature superficial, Dunn confronts problems of coverage and offers practical suggestions for instituting a viable course organized around patterns of change that involved peoples of different cultures in shared experience. He recommends a course syllabus that focuses on the 'big picture' of world change in whatever age is being studied. The essay is a call for establishing global history in the school curriculum.

Ross Dunn is Professor of History at San Diego State University and Director of World History Projects for the National Center for History in the Schools at UCLA. He served as first president of the World History Association and is the author of *The Adventure of Ibn Battuta, A Muslim Traveler of the 14th Century*.

One day not very long ago, I went into a fruit and vegetable market in my neighborhood. While looking over the avocados, I noticed that the clerks were speaking foreign language among themselves. I thought it might be Arabic but I was not sure. So I asked one of the clerks if the owners of the market had come from an Arabic-speaking country. The woman bristled slightly, then replied, "No, we are not Arabs. We are Kooor-dish!" Ever since then, my wife and I have called this store the "Kooor-dish market." In fact, the Kurds later sold it to people of Iranian descent. The Persians in turn sold it to the present owners, who are Arabs of Palestinian origin. Then there is the neighborhood meat and fish market that we frequent. Its proprietors are Arabic-speaking Chaldean Christians who emigrated from Iraq. Indeed, my Southern California city has become so cosmopolitan in the past decade that if I am to appreciate the cultural background and family origins of my immigrant neighbors, I can no longer think of classifying them crudely as "Middle Easterners" or "Orientals." I am obliged, rather, to know whether my neighbor is Kurd or Turk, Persian or Afghani, Palestinian or Syrian, Chaldean or Maronite.

The presence in America of newcomers from such diverse parts of the world is largely a manifestation of particular migratory movements that have developed only in recent years. As I drive down an avenue of my city and see commercial signs in Persian, Chinese, Vietnamese, and several other scripts that are totally foreign to me, I wonder whether in their school classes my children will learn something about the places from which these settlers came and why they abandoned their natal homes for California. I wonder how their resettlement relates to the grand, world-scale patterns of migration in the late twentieth century as well as to the three centuries of earlier migration that contributed to the making of the American people.

History and World History

If the young people of my city are to make any sense at all of such issues as world migration, issues that impinge directly on their lives, their school curriculum ought to include world history, and as much of it as possible. Students must be offered the knowledge and conceptual skill with which they can at least begin to address intelligently the great global questions of our time. History must be the foundation of their world studies because only by examining the past will they locate themselves in humanity's drama and come to be aware that the world they experience is the way it is because of social processes that were activated decades, centuries, or millennia before they were born. To limit their global education to reviews of current events or to a purely contemporary study of other societies is to sow on much too shallow ground.

---

*Reprinted from *Historical Literacy: The Case for History in American Schools*, Ed. Paul Gagnon and the Bradley Commission on History in American Schools. Boston: Houghton-Mifflin, 1989.

The idea that history education and international competence should be closely tied to one another in the school curriculum has been one of the themes in the national education debate of the past five years. Many teachers and scholars have been demanding that history as a discipline replace conceptually fragmented and excessively present-minded programs in social studies as the core of both the humanities and social science curricula. Many who share that view also specify a program of historical studies that replaces, or supplements, the traditional Western civilization course with one that embraces humanity as a whole.

Many educators, however, express uncertainty, if not alarm, about the practical problems of teaching world history. When teachers whose classroom experience has been limited to American history, Western civilization, or world geography agree (or are ordered) to plunge into world history, they may face multiple challenges of learning large new bodies of knowledge, abandoning topics that have been part of their canon for decades, radically reordering their periodization schemes, finding innovative classroom strategies, and even thinking about history in general as they never have before. Compared to Western civilization or the conventional geography course, world-scale history is still a comparatively unproven teaching field. Every teacher must be something of a pioneer in the search for an effective conceptual approach.

The most common blueprint for organizing a world history course has been simply to divide humankind into cultural or civilizational units, then to address each in turn, usually covering its history over a span of several centuries. Most textbooks take this approach, and indeed most educators and publishers seem to have assumed that world history must be primarily the serial study of a variety of foreign cultures plus the West. For example, Matthew Downey and Douglas Alder, both champions of world history, argue that "instead of discovering only their own Western heritage, students should learn to appreciate other cultures as well.... They need to know about cultures other than those of the West if the United States is to compete economically with...non-Western nations." In *What Do Our 17-Year-Olds Know?*, Diane Ravitch and Chester Finn recommend that students "study the history of Western Europe for a full year, and the history of other major nations and cultures for another full year."

Global History as the Study of Processes

The internationalist sentiment behind these recommendations should be taken seriously in all our schools. Defining world history, however, as fundamentally a study tour of civilizations in different parts of the earth has, I think, impeded the working out of a more integrated and dynamic conception of the global past. By assuming that civilizations are disparate chunks of humanity, bounded off from one another in space and time, and that therefore they must be the primal units of historical study, global educators have put themselves up a pedagogical tree where there may be nothing more to do except prune and shape the facts and concepts that are to be taught about each "culture."

The fact is that from the early Stone Age to the present, human beings have interacted in all sorts of aggregations that are not caged within one cultural tradition or another. Indeed, many of the most important events in history, even in ancient times, have been played out on a map bigger than any single country or civilization. If the aim of world history is, as it should be, to make sense of the larger, more extensive patterns of the past, then the patterns themselves, not separate cultures, ought to be the leading categories for sorting out and organizing the raw material that students will be asked to learn.

One of the recurrent complaints against the social studies in recent years has been that they are too abstractly analytical, too lacking in good narrative storytelling. Yet the very concept of "culture," and particularly "traditional culture," is often misleadingly presented to students as something static and immutable, having more to do with archaic institutions, immemorial customs, and ritual behavior than with dynamic and rationally explainable change. History as a series of separate, parallel culture stories is often not very exciting because in the end the narratives go nowhere. One week the students "do" African history, the next week India, and so on. None of the events occurring inside these "cultures" is related to a broader framework of world-historical meaning. So students miss out on some of the choicest dramas of world history, epic accounts played out across continents and oceans. These stories go unrecognized and unstudied because teachers and textbooks have found no way to bring them into the space-time limits of one conventionally defined culture or another.

Let us see how some of the recurrent questions about teaching world history might be answered if we imagine a course that takes the human community as a whole, rather than bounded cultures, as the primary field of study and that stresses in each era of the past the larger-scale patterns of change that have brought the world to its present state of complexity and interdependence. I will use the term "global history" as the most precise way to describe this kind of course, recognizing that the phrase has also and more generally been applied to any history studies that embrace the non-West as well as Europe

Such a global history would be chronologically organized—that is, it would have a narrative structure, though a looser one than U.S. and European surveys often have. Students would follow a world time line that stirs awareness of the interrelations of societies from one century to the next and that invites continuous comparison of events occurring in different parts of the world. Each primary unit of the course would be organized around an important chain of events (and I use the term "event" broadly to include relatively long-term developments) whose impact was wide enough to involve peoples of differing cultures in a shared experience. These "big" events would provide the common reference point for investigating and comparing other events and trends that relate more narrowly to particular civilizations and cultural groups.

Moreover, such overarching events would also determine the periodization of the course—that is, the major divisions of time to be studied one after another. Making clear to students causal links between one "era" and another on the world historical level is a challenge because we are so used to thinking about divisions of the past, excepting for the last century or two, only as they relate to particular countries or civilizations. World history cannot, as U.S. and Western surveys have done, trace a single narrative line of history, neatly sliced up, against the background of a relatively unified, coherent cultural development. Creative solutions to the problem of periodization in global history will in every case depend on teachers' willingness to stand back and scan the world scene for significant patterns of cause and effect from greater distances than they have usually done, and at the same time to break through civilizational categories that would predetermine the ordering of historical time.

How might a major unit of study look in a course whose aim is to get students to think "globally"? Imagine an early unit whose primary focus is the invention and spread of iron technology, a historical event of great importance for large areas of Eurasia and Africa between about 1200 and 800 B.C. This development had a transforming effect on societies all across Eurasia and northern Africa. Moreover, set against the very long term of history, it affected much of the Eastern Hemisphere (though not the Western) in a relatively short span of time. The how, why, and where of the spread of iron would give rough geosocial and chronological shape to the unit of study and provide the leading comparative idea from which to launch discussion of other events in China, India, the Middle East, and the Mediterranean region during about a four-hundred-year period.

The objective here would not be to give the unit a narrowly technological focus but rather to provide students with a conceptual trunk line from which to undertake explorations of similarities, differences, and interconnections between one part of the world and another during *a particular period of time*. Students would be invited to think about an important, far-reaching change, such as the social effects of iron tool-making, as an integrated historical process, letting the process itself determine which cultural milieus are to be included in the study rather than fragmenting and obscuring the process by demoting it to merely a subsidiary aspect of the history of this civilization or that. Students could thereby observe events occurring in different parts of the world at the same time and consider how these events might be interrelated or at least compared.

In this course, then, students would at the broadest level of generalization be investigating historical processes rather than "cultures" on the map. By "process" I mean simply an identifiable pattern of change. Historical processes are like stories: They have beginnings, middles, and ends. As in a Western civilization course, students would study processes in different arenas of human action. Some would transcend the frontiers of a particular country or civilization (e.g., the Atlantic slave trade), others would not (e.g., the sixteenth-century Reformation). The aim of this approach is not to deny the importance of cultural forces in history. The ups and downs of particular civilizations are themselves important processes that need to be studied. The point is that the stories of civilizations should not be permitted to limit or confuse the teacher's efforts to help students see the "big picture" of world change in whatever age is being studied. History is distorted and ethnocentrism is only encouraged when we lead students to conclude that civilizations are self-contained and self-perpetuating and that their relationship to neighboring or distant societies is of no real importance. A major drawback of the traditional Western civilization course is its common presumption that the rise of Europe (and of the U.S.) to world economic and military dominance in the twentieth century can be adequately explained simply by looking back over the history of the West, neglecting the world context into which each age of Western history was born.

Content of a Global History Course

Because the human community has moved over the long run of time from a sparse population and the isolated autonomy of small groups to global crowding and intricate interdependence, it is naturally easier to identify complex, large-scale patterns of change in the world in recent centuries than, say, in paleolithic times (except for fundamental but very long-term changes such as the progress of early tool-making or agriculture). Even so, the weeks of a course devoted to ancient history can still center on world-historical events that transcend the conventional civilizational modules. One of these would be the spread of iron already mentioned. Another might be the Indo-European expansion out of Central Asia between about 1700 and 1200 B.C., a phenomenon that deeply affected subsequent history all across Eurasia. A third might be the flowering of Greek commerce and culture from 800 to 200 B.C., a process that could be presented to students not merely as an early episode in the narrative of the "Western tradition," but more accurately and more dramatically as the rise of an Eastern Mediterranean-Black Sea civilization whose language, ideas, and aesthetics proved irresistible to peoples all around the rim of that dual sea and as far east as China.

In the millennium between A.D, 500 and 1500, patterns of human interaction involving very large numbers of people become increasingly evident. The remarkable growth of trans-hemispheric trade and travel, the long-distance migrations and predations of steppe peoples, and the rise of gigantic new empires that spanned two or more major civilizations all indicated the end of a world of divided regions. Indeed, it was during this period that all-Eurasia, together with the northern and eastern rims of Africa, began to take on a kind of history of its own, a history that is almost completely obscured in the culture-based course. Some of the big events that might provide the main headings of study include:

- The rise of Islam as a movement not just of the Middle East but of the whole region of arid lands stretching from Iberia to India.
- The near industrial revolution in China under the Song Dynasty and its effects on trade and economic development all across Eurasia.
- The military, economic, and cultural expansion of Latin Europe, a development that embraced an area stretching from Scotland to Palestine.
- The explosion of the Mongols and the hemispheric consequences of the conquests.
- The Black Death, not only as a chapter in the history of Western Europe but as a trans-Eurasian event that had long lasting effects on Central Asia, China, and the Middle East as well as on Europe.

In working up a syllabus for the modern age, that is, the centuries after 1500, international and truly global patterns are easily thrown into relief. Some of them are commonly taught in the traditional Western civilization course, but more as extensions of European history than as world processes. Some well-used topics recast in the global mold might include:

- Popular revolts and democratic revolutions between 1750 and 1850, not simply as aspects of European or American history, but as movements sweeping the "Atlantic basin"—that is, including Latin America and even West Africa.
- The early industrialization of Europe, not as a phenomenon entirely conceived and brought forth in England, but as a process involving economic interrelations worldwide.
- The New Imperialism, less as a study of intra-European conflicts abroad than as an encounter between Europeans and African or Asian peoples.

Some less obvious topics for the modern age might include:

- The demographic and cultural effects of the worldwide exchange of plants and animals that occurred in the century after Columbus.
- The surge of Islamic expansion in Eurasia and in Africa in the sixteenth century.
- The process in the twentieth century of environmental intervention and planetary pollution and their effects on world population and economy.

Insofar as students begin to think about world history, both the remote and the recent past, in terms of such supranational topics as these, they should gain a more holistic view of their global heritage, as well as freedom from the perverse and narcissistic notion that "our" historical experience (America's and Europe's) has for all but the most recent decades been almost completely alien from "theirs" (Africa's, China's, and so on). Our profession has no greater responsibility than to offer students a broad base of world-historical knowledge and conceptual skill with which they may recognize and begin to confront the numerous problems of our planet, problems that no single nation or cultural group can hope to solve by itself.

The Social Sciences or the Humanities: Where Does Global History Fit?

Implementing a more process-oriented world history will, of course, take more than merely adopting a new textbook and a revised set of outlines. Other commitments and choices must also be made that may or may not be compatible with the individual teacher's education, habits, and convictions. One question has to do with locating global history's disciplinary "home." Should it be in the care of humanists or social scientists, or of both?

The kind of world-scale history advocated here will inevitably engage the political, social, and economic behavior of people acting in groups (tribes, empires, trading corporations, religious communities, and so on). It will also emphasize many subsurface currents of change, like the effects on society of new technology, of which people were for the most part unconscious at the time the changes were happening. Therefore, teachers well grounded in the social sciences and the sorts of questions those disciplines ask might on the whole be more willing to innovate in global history than teachers inclined to humanistic subjects.

Since the humanities are eminently concerned with the values, achievements, and enduring styles of particular civilizations, some teachers might well be hesitant to offer a course that would constrain them from giving analytical primacy to the cultural and social continuities within each of the great traditions. But a clear choice must be made. A world history course can center on the serial study of several civilizations, stressing chronological strings of causation within each, as is commonly done in Western civilization courses. Or it can focus on the study of world-historical processes, emphasizing for each defined period of history those forces that embraced different peoples in shared experience. It may to some degree do both at the same time, but only at the risk of conceptual ambiguity and organizational confusion if one or the other approach is not clearly, explicitly dominant. Each approach is valid and teachable. But the global alternative, it should be made plain, does give precedence to the interrelations of peoples in each historic age over the cultural factors that divide them.

Since global history does carry something of a social scientific bias, teachers and textbook writers should be warned that the humane and dramatic dimensions of the past are no less important in this kind of course than in any other. If global historians fall so in love with economic systems-building, technological diffusion, or comparative demography that they forget to animate the past with personalities, deeds, and works of the mind and spirit, then their students will remain as indifferent to the discipline as they now generally appear to be. Global history may require new vocabularies and a certain amount of abstract formulation, but its classroom lessons must also be salted with vivid stories, artistic images, and the portrayal of great events and ideas.

Global History and the Problem of Coverage

When teachers consider world history for the first time, one hears a common refrain: "I could never get past World War Two in my Western civ class. How can I take on global history without running out of time at the Battle of Lepanto?" The simplest solution to the problem of coverage is, of course, to make the program of study longer. At present the world's past is surveyed in one year in most of the schools and universities where it is taught. A two-year sequence of global history is probably to be preferred. California addressed the issue in 1987 by designing a three-year program of courses: ancient history in the sixth grade, A.D. 500 to the late eighteenth century in the seventh, and modern history in the tenth.

Yet even if world history is given generous scope in the curriculum, teachers must still carefully select what is to go into their syllabus and what is not. Skeptics about world history have often contended that such a course is impractical because no one can teach "everything" in a year's time. The charge itself is suspect since any ordering of the past involves a great deal of choosing between one potentially relevant fact and another. Indeed, the typical European history survey excludes mountains of historical information that is significant in some context. I know of no Western civ course that probes seriously into Charlemagne's conquest of Saxony, the commercial dynamics of medieval Amalfi, or the domestic politics of interwar Denmark. Western civ, rather, puts into relief the integrative, transnational patterns of European history (e.g., the Renaissance, the rise of fascism), anchoring them to empirical ground with concrete illustrations, examples, primary source readings, biography, and so on. A successful global history course will follow a similar scheme, except that the historical processes to be studied will often involve a larger scene of human interaction than one civilization or another.

The task of deciding which peoples to introduce to students and which to ignore is easier to accomplish if those choices are related to the world-historical processes to be studied. Australian aborigines might enter the scene only as they figure in a unit on the nineteenth-century overseas migrations of European settlers and their ensuing encounters with indigenous groups. Peoples of the Amazon basin or the Arctic Circle might reasonably be excluded from the course altogether. A textbook aiming to "democratize" world history by awarding a section or paragraph to every ethnic group in every corner of the planet would be chaotic and pointless. On the other hand, a course might go equally wrong if it focuses too narrowly on patterns of change among literate elites and urbanized societies. A genuinely global course could hardly neglect, for example, the tent-dwelling pastoralists of Central Asia, people who seem marginal indeed in modern times but who in earlier ages activated chains of events that reverberated all across Eurasia.

Is Global History Inevitably Superficial?

Even if a global history course is assiduously selective, can time be found for more than superficial study of most topics? The California *History-Social Science Framework* rightly commends the study of "major historical events and periods in depth as opposed to superficial skimming of enormous amounts of material," and it denounces syllabi and textbooks that make students "feel that they are on a forced march across many centuries and continents." American history and Western civ surveys have long been notorious for skating over the surface of the past. When a world history course requires students to jog breathlessly across the chronologies of seven or eight different civilizations, they might indeed end up with less historical comprehension than they had at the start. We must reject any syllabus that substitutes memorization of countless free-floating facts for unhurried reflection on the meaning of the past.

Like an effective Western civilization course, a good global history avoids frantic exertions to "mention" as many facts and topics as possible. The difference lies in the questions asked. And the kinds of questions global historians should be formulating are far from superficial. Students can study momentous historical processes "in depth" as readily as they can study particular cultures. When they are allowed to rove over the whole world scene, they are likely to perceive important patterns of change that might not be identified at all in their Western civ class.

For example, what would a world-historical approach make of the fifteenth- to sixteenth-century Age of Exploration, a period usually treated in both Western civ and culture-oriented classes largely as a stage in the evolution of the Western tradition? Here are a few of the questions that might be asked: What relationship did European commercial enterprise in Africa and Asia have to the earlier expansion of a transhemispheric trading system run largely by Muslims? Why did Western Europeans succeed in discovering America and circumnavigating the globe when, as of the early fifteenth century, the Chinese were in several respects more likely candidates to undertake those adventures? How did the migration of old-world disease microorganisms across the Atlantic affect the success of Iberian conquest and settlement in America? What conditions all around the rim of the Atlantic led to the forced migration of millions of Africans to America?

Such questions are essential to explaining how the world's peoples and cultures got to be as thoroughly entangled as they are today. To grapple with these issues, students must learn how to think comparatively about the past and to recognize large-scale patterns. Answers to the queries posed in a global history class might be simple and straightforward or confoundingly intricate, but they will require more than superficial thinking and skimming. World history textbooks will probably continue to "mention" more facts than they should, simply because of the diverse requirements and tastes of the teaching market that uses them. But they can become more useful as they strive to integrate world history, to incorporate more discussion of the often hidden streams of change, and to accent comparative analyses.

Geography in Global History

Geography is a vital partner in making world history intelligible. A global approach must inevitably emphasize the pervasive impact of climate, vegetation, and natural resources on the larger-scale events of history. It should also exhibit to students vivid mental pictures of the scenic travels of soldiers, sailors, merchants, and monks, as well as of the migration of religious truths, scientific ideas, and new technologies, spreading here and there over the surface of the earth.

Global history should require students to think about spatial geography, names and places, the locations of major mountains, rivers, islands, and straits, as well as empires, nations, and cities. But they should be discouraged from concluding that political and cultural boundaries are all they need to grasp geographical reality. Rather, they should develop an astronaut's view of the earth, a holistic grasp of the patterns that mountains, plateaus, ocean basins, and winds make in relation to one another. They should, for example, think of the whole Eurasian landmass as a single stage where important historical events have occurred. They should learn why so much history was carried on the oscillating monsoons of the Southern Seas. They should learn about the crucial role of pastoral peoples in world history by seeing that great band of arid land that runs all the way across the Eastern Hemisphere from the Sahara to the Gobi. To learn global history, in short, is to cultivate an integral vision of the world's geographical personality.

Contemporary Problems and Universal Themes in Global History

Whatever innovations teachers make to enliven global history, they would do well, I have argued, to lay the subject out along a chronological line. When it comes to organizing time, they should teach the old-fashioned way, starting somewhere back in the reaches of time and connecting the links of cause and effect as they move forward.

Some educators, however, hold a contrasting view: The study of the past should be wrapped up in a series of essentially sociological, humanistic, or contemporary topics—that is, on the persistent and ever-recurring problems of the race: war and peace, slavery and freedom, human rights, the condition of women, and so on. Such headings, they say, should determine the order of study, and students should be free to slide back and forth in time as they search for the "origins" of each "problem." This approach reflects the ideas of the "new social studies" movement of the past three decades in its advocacy of the study of contemporary issues "in historical perspective."

Many teachers have been skeptical of such a topical approach, and rightly so. In its more rigid forms, topic-centered social studies isolates selected aspects of history from the wider social context in which they are situated, and it treats historical facts as so many bits of "background information" to help explain conditions of the present. Students are denied the opportunity to learn the chronological relationship of events to one another or to contemplate the full range of possible causes and effects of processes being studied. History as data presumed useful to today's citizens erases history as story and drama.

On the other hand, meditations on the universal riddles of humankind should not be consigned brusquely to English and civics teachers. Indeed, a good global history course will not fail to wrestle with at least a few of the immemorial issues that inform our hopes, fears, and moral values. These questions can be embodied in selected themes that weave through the entire course in counterpoint to the narrative story being told. A teacher might select, for example, the impact of nationalism as a leading world-historical theme. When students mentally connect one era with another ("The demands of these African nationalists sound like the same things the leaders of the French Revolution were saying!"), the teacher knows they are following the thematic thread. One caution: play only a few topical songs. Attempting to work the students through too many of the ageless questions, however thought-provoking, can blur the conceptual structure of the course and detract from its central purpose, which is to reconstruct and interpret *history*.

Several prominent educators have argued vigorously in the past few years that since the political and cultural heritage of American society lies largely in the West, the history of the West should dominate the curriculum. Advocates of global education have answered that, yes, our children should learn about Western civilization, but they also must study other cultures in order to function intelligently in a shrinking world and to appreciate the diverse heritages of many new Americans. The argument of such internationalists is valid but inadequate on its own. It assumes that a variety of "world cultures" can reasonably be investigated *ad seriatim* and largely in isolation from one another, and that then the result can rightly be called world history. But their approach obscures the fact that the social context of all history is ultimately the globe itself. And it fails to refute the argument that since the crowded curriculum allows no time for detailed study of several cultures, schools should devote their time to "our own."

The remarkable role of the West in world history must obviously figure large in a global history course. The fact remains, however, that even if the Western tradition shaped most of us, the rise of that tradition occurred within a world context that shaped much of *it*. However valuable it is to work the study of Western civilization and several other selected heritages into the school day, the fundamental question is whether we can afford to permit young Americans to graduate without having at least tried to erect in their minds a framework for thinking about the long run of change in the world in something grander than narrow cultural or nationalistic terms. Are the supracultural processes that, in all their complexity, shaped our own world worth understanding? If so, then the search for a teachable world history becomes more imperative every day.

Patterns and Comparisons in the Human Drama*
by Jean Elliott Johnson

Jean Johnson presents a model for constructing a world history course that helps students "move chronologically through time and space so they see history as a seamless web involving both the universal and the particular, both cultural and materialist factors." Suggesting that we look at history as a drama, the author provides a conceptual framework in nine acts, each exploring central themes and ideas in world history.

Jean Elliott Johnson taught history at Friends Seminary in New York City. She created curriculum materials for American schools while serving as a resident consultant in New Delhi, India, and she is the co-author of *Through Indian Eyes* and *Gods in Hinduism*.

In the 1990s in the United States, we are struggling with two apparently contradictory forces. One is the ostensible homogenization of the world through trade, travel and instant communication and the other is the intense, and often virulent concern for what Geertz identifies as "primordial attachments" to race, religion, language, and ethnicity. These two seemingly contradictory forces are not only the focus of much popular debate, they are also exerting profound influences on how we reconstruct world history, specifically in debates between materialist vs. culturalist historians and universalist vs. particularist historian.

Historians who believe in an ever-homogenizing world focus primarily on material factors such as technology and economic arrangements. They include, among others, Wallerstein and his world system, Abu-Lughod and her cross-cultural trade patterns, and much of William McNeill's historical writing. Their materialist model stresses trade, consumerism, warfare, disease, demography and technology. The competing paradigm, reflected by scholars such as Hodgson, Geertz, and Huntington, focuses more on cultural factors such as religion and worldview and suggests that humans cannot exist except as cultural beings who make symbolic meanings of their lives and even of "material" objects such as plows, potter's wheels, corn, or jet planes. This group stresses values, worldviews, religion and long-lasting "moods and motivations" for human action.

In addition to the materialist/culturalist debate, there is a second related dichotomy between particularist and universalist historians. The former insist we must analyze places like Song China and Benin Africa in their local contexts; and the latter, for a better understanding of the past, would place them into world movements like climatic changes, industrialism and modernization. The universalizers may also include some of the "culturalists" like Fukuyama who see ideologies like liberalism engulfing local cultures (recalling Christian nations of sixteenth and seventeenth century Europe that espoused a universal faith for all peoples). Many current "universalizers" cling to the nineteenth century evolutionary model and, fascinated by the consumerism that has come to dominate American culture since World War II (itself a universalizing symbol), postulate a facile concept of "modernization" that they imagine sweeping away all vestiges of "traditionalism." Many who see a new material global culture developing believe that all peoples are striving for modernity defined by "wealth and power" and cite as evidence consumers of Blue Jeans and rap tapes, worldwide. Universal modernizers often suggest cultural diversity is what "modern man" will trade in for a "better" standards of living. The uproar that accompanied Huntington's article in *Foreign Affairs* on the clash of cultures, and the assault on multiculturalism, suggests that many Americans support both materialism and universalism as the major criteria for social and historical analysis.

*Reprinted from *The History Teacher*, Vol. 27, No. 4 (1994), pp. 434-447.

The dualistic way scholars formulate these issues grows out of a deeply seated Western cultural construct. Instead of getting caught in this either/or debate, suspend faith in Aristotle and other champions of dualism, for a moment, and imagine the importance of both material and cultural dimensions of the human past. Acknowledge, also, the importance of both particular and universal tendencies without dichotomizing either of these pairs of opposites. The distinct historic development of cultural or civilizational perspectives or worldviews must be an integral part of how we conceptualize World history, but so should the common experiences and universal tendencies. World history must include the historical development of non-materialist or culturally diverse dimensions of human experience without sacrificing coverage of inventions, modes of production, trade and diseases? How can all four dimensions inform our conceptualization and teaching of a genuine World history? How can we help our students move chronologically through time and space so they see history as a seamless web involving both the universal and the particular, both cultural and materialist factors?

At the outset, we must take multiple worldviews seriously. By "worldviews," I mean such things as beliefs and values, cultural ethos, way of life, civilizational orientation, or basic religious and philosophical assumptions underlying particular societies. Understanding diverse worldviews is difficult since we tend to believe our own worldview is normative. To transcend the medium of our own thought requires learning what we have become without knowing it. Immersed in a particular worldview, we assume it is universal, and we tend to forget that, as Mumford reminds us, "No two cultures live perceptually in the same kind of space and time."

Acknowledging diverse worldviews is especially difficult for those of us who cling to Western exceptionalism. When we take multiple worldviews seriously, the Western experience must stand alongside other perspectives, and we should realize that our own worldview is a deviation from someone else's norm. Giving up Western exceptionalism, culminating in the belief that the West is the only "modern" civilization or the ultimate cultural achievement of all human evolution, is perhaps the most important principle, and source of major contention, behind some of the current efforts to reconceptualize World history.

Not only are worldviews important in World history, they change over time. The aversion to taking religion seriously in the classroom and in textbooks since the 1950s, as well as time constraints when teachers must cover so much material, leads to a tendency to fossilize faiths and ignore how worldviews change. Teachers, textbooks, and curriculum guides often present a particular worldview, such as Confucian values or the Hindu way of life, only once, early in the course or text, usually at the formative basis of the civilization. The result is that certain views get labelled traditional and remain so in the minds of students. This is one of the major reasons students come away believing in Western exceptionalism, since teachers almost always present the Western cultural experience historically and the rest of the world as timeless "cultural areas." At the height of the Cold War, John Foster Dulles is reported to have asked Prime Minister Nehru, "Are you with us or against us?" Nehru answered, "Yes." Nehru's response was not any more traditional than Dulles's. Each reflected his own cultural perspective, one Hindu and the other Presbyterian, and each has been and continues to change over time. We must eschew identifying the West during the last three hundred years as modern and classifying other cultures as traditional. We cannot offer frozen time frames of any civilization, but must trace the permutations and adjustments of worldviews through time and space. You and I take it for granted that technology changes over time; worldviews do as well.

One possible way to conceptualizing World history so that both the material and the cultural, both the universal and the particular, are included is to identify certain reoccurring patterns and then examine how they are manifest over time and in different places. Once we understand the patterns as both local manifestations and as ideal types, we can apply them in various areas of the world and return to them at different periods of time. Patterning is one way to cover a great deal of information efficiently and it makes sense pedagogically as well.

What I am calling patterns are really concepts or ideal types that reoccur. In my own course, I vary the ones I use from year to year, but some useful patterns include what it means to be human, contrasts between settled and nomadic lifestyles, characteristics of urban life, reasons for nomadic invasions and possible result of the interaction of nomadic invaders and urban centers, the concept of empire, trade and cultural diffusion, characteristics of universal religions and their institutionalizations, and long-lasting moods and motivations—the flavor and style—of specific civilizations.

Using reoccurring patterns is pedagogically sound. In the first place, establishing reoccurring patterns provides a way to make a great deal of information intelligible. Think of the vast amount of possible information in World history as dots on the TV screen. As discrete facts, as dots, they make little sense and seem uninteresting. Grouped, facts become comprehensible and even engaging, a picture on the screen. In the second place, repetition that results from considering patterns several times, each time in a slightly different way, enhances learning. If a student does not grasp what an empire is in October with Sargon I, he may get it in November with the Chin, in January with the Guptas, in February with the Song or Yuan. He might then be able, in June, to examine what happened in the Soviet Union, before and after 1991, with intelligence and insight. In the third place, repeating patterns allows the teaching of history, no less than language or math, to be cumulative; and by that I do not mean just more facts to memorize. Students come to a period of history with previous understandings, and they must build on their earlier knowledge of both the patterns and what has already happened in a specific cultural area.

Applying the same pattern in various areas and at different periods of time highlights both the particular and the universal. Influences of culture and ethos become apparent if we note similarities and differences in the way groups react to similar events or challenges. For example, in the second millennium BCE, some nomadic invaders sacked the area they invaded (like Troy or Indus cities); some mixed and became very like the people they invaded (as in Sumer, Babylon, or the Middle Kingdom); some remained aloof and established rules of separation (in India, Sparta or Judea); some ultimately got thrown out (as the Hyksos in Egypt). Each area addressed the question of right action, but the Mediterranean world defined right action by laws; India defined it by *dharma*, and the people of Han offered *li* and *jen*. In addition, returning to the same area as we consider different patterns prevents students from concluding that worldviews do not change over time. Finally, and perhaps most importantly, since patterns appear to be "universal," but the applications of these patterns at a specific time or in a specific place is culturally specific, this organization models both universals in human experience and culturally specific realities, and students learn to appreciate both.

Let me illustrate concretely how patterning can work in conceptualizing World history. Think of the human past as a drama. As we "set the stage," human life is emerging. Our first pattern can be what it means to be human. Did humans evolve because two million year old Lucy-the-Lover, not man-the-tool-maker or weapon-maker, had the ability to bond and teach what she knew? Is the use of symbols what distinguishes human beings from other forms of life? Is it the ability to use tools and shape the environment? (The material/cultural dichotomy is already on stage.) At this point we have just a generic list of human characteristics, but we can test this tentative list against how various cultures, over time, define being human.

Act One of the human drama examines not "prehistory" but the thousands of years of human development in Africa and West Asia when humans established basic social institutions, and those institutions can be our second pattern. The agricultural revolution was not only a technological breakthrough but also a reordering of human interdependence. Farmers settled down and learned to share their produce so that some could specialize in other activities; and herders, constantly on the move, learned to cooperate to protect the herds and each other so that the tribe or clan survived. Our second pattern could also be the contrast between settled and nomadic ways of life, but we probably do not want to apply it in various areas at this point.

Characteristics of urban life is the pattern for Act Two that covers the third millennium BCE. The pattern includes a large diverse population, surplus, specialization and interdependence, uniform social control and government, a shared ethic and system of values and meanings, some way to keep records, and trade. Once we have an urban pattern, we can examine the large, relatively peaceful urban communities that emerged in Mesopotamia, Africa, India and Crete (and I sometimes add China although it falls in the second millennium). Families and tribes cooperated with strangers and produced enough surplus to allow for specialization and interdependence on a massive scale. Three of the urban breakthroughs centered around major rivers and one centered on maritime trade. Trading and meeting the challenge flooding rivers presented not only allowed people to produce larger surpluses but also taught people to cooperate on a grand scale, the primary requirement for interdependent urban life. People in Crete, India and Egypt, and later China, but not Mesopotamia, looked to natural barriers as their main lines of defense and relied on the priests and priestess's influence with divinity and not the warriors' use of spears for their safety.

Nomadic invasions is the pattern for Act Three that covers the second millennium BCE. Students plot possible reasons that Semitic and Indo-European nomads invaded, such as: climatic changes, increases in population, pressure from other nomads, inventions such as the chariot, famine, weakness within the urban communities, the lure of surplus on the plain, a charismatic leader, a possible collapse of the worldview or some combination of these factors. They then anticipate what nomads might do to areas and people they invade, including: invading and building an empire; invading, plundering or destroying and moving on; invading and mixing with the settled people; and invading, settling down but remaining separate from the settled people. Students can apply these possibilities to individual groups such as the Akkadians, Babylonians, Hittites, Achaeans, Hyksos, Hebrews, Assyrians, Scythians, Chaldaeans, Aryans, or Dorians, or, viewed from the urban perspective, examine what happened when nomads invaded Mesopotamia, the Indus, Nile and Yellow river valleys, or the Aegean world.

Characteristics of human society when the times are "out of joint" can be the pattern for Act Four that takes place in the middle of the first millennium BCE. Although nomadic military superiority allowed invaders to gain control over vast areas, settling down and mixing with urban and agricultural people did not bring a deep sense of meaning to either the conquered or the conquerors. Gods could not provide protection from invasions, and even good men experienced misfortunes. To complicate matters further, a gap widened between the rich and the poor in several areas, and the rising merchant class resented the power of hereditary landed aristocrats. People during this act often faced continuous war and violence as they struggled to find even minimal security and to forge new meanings out of their older

43

worldviews. The patterns includes questions like: In what can people believe? Why do good people suffer? How should one act? How can one keep from hurting others? How can people end wars? Who should lead? How can people build a sense of loyalty to the community?

In the midst of this crisis, during the hundred year period around 600 BCE, a host of significant thinkers ranging from Lao Tzu in China to Tales in Iona offered a variety of innovative ways to cope with life's insecurities. Karl Jaspers has identified this period as the Axial Age, and the Axial Age is the focus of the fourth act of the human drama. We examine, in the ongoing context of specific civilizations, the teachings of Confucius and Lao-tzu in the Middle Kingdom, of the Buddha and Mahavira in India, of Zoroaster and Hebrew prophets such as Amos or patriarchies like Job in Ancient West Asia, and Ionian philosophers like Pythagoras and democratic reformers such as Solon and Cleisthenes in Hellas. We can reprise the pattern from Act One about basic human institutions, and see what each Axial Age thinker suggested should be done with those institutions.

These thinkers struggled with, among other problems, how to tame the warrior. The *arete* the Homeric poets had immortalized celebrated excellence in war, and even Aeschylus wanted his tombstone to mention only that he had fought bravely at Marathon. The later Greeks offered warriors a different way to win honor—racing against one another at Olympia rather than killing one another on city ramparts—and political reformers redefined *arete* to include citizenship. The Hebrew prophets, trying to figure out why their God had allowed invaders to ravish first the northern kingdom of Israel and then the southern kingdom of Judah, said one must not only obey the law but that exploitation of the meek was unacceptable to God. In North India the Vedic texts had taught pregnant women to pray not just for sons, but for *vira*, brave warriors, but Mahavira turned the image of the hero upside down, calling himself the great *vira* because he conquered not others but his own desires. The Buddha also taught that one should control desire, and he encourage people to act with compassion, providing Brahminic ritualism and Upanishadic mysticism a social ethic, Living in the midst of almost constant war in the Middle Kingdom, Confucius advocated *li* and *jen* and suggested that the "chun-tzu"—the superior man—should never have to fight, and Daoists, identifying war as "ill omened," advised generals to treat victory as a funeral. Among Axial Age thinkers only Zoroaster in the West Asia advocated war as he spoke of a cosmic battle between good and evil that would result in the ultimate destruction of evil.

Empires is the pattern for Act Five that covers from about 500 BCE to about 200 CE. The pattern includes both what rulers and subjects of an empire want, and what makes an empire strong. Subjects want to feel safe; they should not be forced to fight in the army; demands for taxes and corvee must seem reasonable; laws should be public and appear fair; and the diverse population should be left alone to believe and worship as they please. Rulers want people to pay their taxes, fight in the army and obey the rules. In strong empires, people perceive that government demands are fair, there is a strong army, a sound tax base, and effective system of communication, the ruler has legitimacy with a system for the peaceful transfer of power, the bureaucracy is loyal and people identify with and are willing to fight for the empire.

During the period covered in Act Five, strong centralized control existed in west Asia, north India, north China, and in land around the Mediterranean, and the Maya rose in central America, so we might be tempted to stress universal aspects of human experience during this act. However, the empires that emerged were distinct, and various peoples looked at the world differently. In each area people made a synthesis out of insights from earlier values, values brought by the invaders and suggested by their Axial Age thinkers, and distinctive worldviews began to emerge. The western Asian worldview, resting on dualism, militarism and law, ultimately incorporated the ideal of citizenship and produced the Pax Romana. India's synthesis, a Hindu way of life rather than a vast political empire, rested on monism and transcendence, made *dharma* the basis for right action, and established caste as the organizing institution. The Han synthesis in the Middle Kingdom, retaining the organizational structure of the Ch'in and the Mandate of T'ien, incorporated the Taoist ideal of the harmony of opposites, offered *li* and *jen* as the basis for right action and affirmed the centrality of the family.

Trade and cultural diffusion, how ideas, people and goods are transmitted, is the pattern for Act Six that covers the first centuries of the Common Era, and the pattern here allows us to focus on material aspects of the human experience. Increased trade overland by camel caravan and across the seas by ship brought peoples of the Eastern hemisphere into more and more contact. Trade as well as the inundation of the Niger led to new cities such as Jenne. Trade connected west Africa with west Asia and brought east and west Africa into the wider drama. Trade linked the Middle Kingdom and Iberian peninsula.

Tracing patterns of trade and cultural diffusion, students examine not only methods of transportation but possible trade routes, examining wind patterns, climate and terrain. It means plotting existing trading centers through which goods passed. It involves plotting how particular goods and ideas travelled. Students can trace written languages including alphabets, foods such as rice, cotton, silk, oranges or, eventually, corn and potatoes, technology like the chariot, paper or printing. Some diffusion is limited to one region; much eventually becomes transcontinental.

People were also on the move. Besides traders carrying goods, nomadic warriors invaded (and we can review the patterns of nomadic invaders). Germanic tribes and Huns, like their cousins in Act Three, contributed to the breakup of Han, Roman and Gupta centralized control. Students already know that by and large nomads are "always on the borders," and they can ask to what extent internal disintegration or disease contributed to the nomads' successes. As the German nomads gradually settled down, chivalry, like the Olympic games a millennium earlier, would develop to keep soldiers in good condition without forcing them to kill one another.

The Jewish diaspora is another important aspect of the movements of people in this act. After the final destruction of the temple in Jerusalem in 70 CE, many Jews moved out around the Mediterranean, establishing significant communities as far away as the Iberian peninsula, the coast of the Indian sub-continent and in the Middle Kingdom.

Ideas also traveled in this period, and the transmission of ideas is an important aspect of this pattern as well. Ideas from the older, established ways of the mainlands influenced people on the Japanese archipelago and the British Isles, areas we might identify as "moonlight civilizations," reflecting much of what they learned. Perhaps most important, missionaries as well as merchants carried the teachings of the Buddha, Hindu philosophers, and the Christian "Good News."

A related pattern for this act could be the characteristics and spread of universal religions. Farmer, in his text on Asian regions in World history, identified characteristics of three universal religions, Mahayana Buddhism, Christianity and Islam, and we can use these as the pattern for this act. Each universal religion has a message meant for everyone, each is centered on divinity, offers salvation through an intermediary, guarantees immortality for believers in paradise, has written texts and is popularized so the average person can understand it. Students can apply this pattern to the developing beliefs of Christianity, Mahayana Buddhism and Islam and ask to what extent it compares with other faiths such as Hinduism, Zoroastrianism and Taoism. How these universal religions spread and become institutionalized is critical to this period of history and fits the pattern of cultural diffusion already established for this act.

The teachings of Jesus and the "Good News" of the Christians, influenced by ideas such as prophetic Judaism, Zoroastrianism and Platonic dualism, combined with the organizational structure of the Roman Empire and perhaps even some influence from the non-violence, mysticism and transcendence of India, to usher in the Age of Christendom. True to the environment that nurtured them, and to the German groups to which their message had to appeal, Christians became soldiers of Christ who eventually would attempt to spread their vision of world dominion by crusades, an idea not unrelated to the Islamic *jihad*. Christianity also spread south and east. King Ezana in Ethiopia tolerate and ultimately accepted Christianity at almost the exact time and with very much the same reluctance as Emperor Constantine.

Mahayana Buddhism spread north and east. In the Middle Kingdom it mixed with Taoism and Confucianism as people attempted to reconcile non-self and filial piety. The Hindu way of life spread south where, combining with south Indian devotional rituals and a commitment to ritual purity, it produced *bhakti* and the particular south Indian society organized around Brahmins and Untouchables. Hindu/Buddhist thought spread to Southeast Asia where people appropriated the Indian concept of ruler and began to develop "theater states." The king of Thailand still rules under the ideal of Ayodhya and is called Rama.

Identifying civilizational moods and motivations is the patter for Act Seven that covers from 350 to about 1200 CE and focuses on the spectacular cultural achievements in areas such as India, Byzantium, T'ang and Song China, Maya, Mali and the Islamic world. Students can recall what they already know about the unique worldviews, and see how these are moderated and revealed in this culturally rich period. The effervescences of these civilizations (to borrow McNeill's phrase) makes terms like "Dark Ages" or "Middle Ages" totally inappropriate.

Part of the reason for these cultural achievements was interaction among peoples (and we can consider again the diffusion of goods, ideas and people). Islam, a relative newcomer to the drama, built on the Hellenistic, Roman and Judeo-Christian worldviews, including the importance of law and the military. Nestorian monks used their hollow canes to smuggle silk worms out of China, and the resulting silk monopoly helped make Byzantium rich. Buddhist ideas animated the Neo-Confucianism of the Song. Chinese ideas bedazzled feudal lords on the Japanese islands and contributed to the cultural flowering of Nara and Hiean. Gold and other goods traded across the Sahara helped finance the emerging urban centers in Europe as well as enriching urban life in Ghana and Mali, and the Maya, who had incorporated the older Olmec civilization, built impressive monumental structures and independently invented the zero.

During Act Eight, the period from about 1200 CE to about 1400 CE, we recapitulate patterns such as nomadic invasions and the spread of goods and ideas. In Mesoamerica the nomadic Toltecs and Aztecs invaded and forcefully subdued the settled, if not wholly non-violent, groups they found in the Valley of Mexico. The Turks, another nomadic group on the move, converted to Islam, challenged Byzantium which claimed to be the legitimate heirs of the Roman Empire, and sent shock waves to the Western end of Eurasia. Mongolian nomads, another invasion from the steppes, bid for world dominance and created a Pax Mongolia that was probably no less peaceful than the Pax Romana a thousand years earlier.

Trade and cultural diffusion is important in this act, also. Although China had the technical prominence and could have become the leading trading power, Muslim merchants dominated trade in an ever-widening system that extended from Iberia to China. The plague, an invasion of another kind, reduced the population of Eurasia by between a third and a half, weakening the eastern empires. Many European survivors embraced the fleeting joys of this world and were not adverse to adopting values we like to identify with modernity. With the fall of (or conquest of) Constantinople, merchants and scholars, both Jewish and Christian, fled from Constantinople and gave Western merchants and rulers the wherewithal to outdo Islam, not by a frontal attack to the East with yet another Crusade, but by attacking from the West! Before the Aztecs could produce an Axial Age and tame their warriors, a group of European nomads invaded, coming not on horse and chariot but by ship and sea, as the ecumene expanded to embrace both the Eastern and Western hemispheres.

Act Nine, that covers the fifteenth to the seventeenth centuries CE, allows us to recapitulate the empire pattern from Act Five and the flower of human cultures from Act Seven. Empires like the Ming, Ottoman, Mughul and Inca display similarities but also significant difference both from one another and from their own earlier forms. The Ming find how difficult it is to reassert earlier Chinese values. Turkish, Islamic and Byzantine influences all contribute to Ottoman organization and power. India exhibits both a synthesis of Hindu-Islamic cultures and a withdrawal by many Hindus into their own cultural ethos. African kingdoms such as Songhai combine indigenous and Islamic characteristics, and, for a brief moment, Benin craftsmen and Portuguese merchants meet as equals. Residents of northern Italian cities, discovering Roman achievements and Hellenic humanism, and new northern European cities, supported by expanding trade, begin to formulate a uniquely European perspective. Aztec, Inca and other western hemispheric kingdoms try to prevail in spite of invaders that threaten them.

Act Nine brings us to the period identified by scholars like McNeill as the "rise of the West." Were we to give comparable time to the most recent five hundred years of the world's history, it would constitute, at most, three acts of the human drama. It is usually divided into a great many more. In each act, it is possible to apply some of these same patterns as well as to devise new ones that more exactly fit the most recent acts.

Extrapolating one major theme per time period and focusing on that issue leaves out a great deal of information and shapes what is included. The issue is not that this conceptual framework omits material, because any organization must do that, but rather to what extent it distorts our understanding of what happened in the past. Including a comparative approach to the development of systems of meanings among diverse people along with universal aspects of human experience can contribute to a more accurate study of World history and a fuller understanding of the past. It can also help students deal with tensions they now face in our own society.

When the reigning Chinese dynasty commissioned a history of the preceding ruling house, no one was surprised when the history reflected the present dynasty's values and worldview. Historians write from, as McNeill put it, "the moving platform of their own times." Herodotus wanted to celebrate Athenian greatness and the "otherness" of the Persians and Thucydides to teach that power corrupts. Whatever history we create in the 1990s cannot help but reflect our present concerns, biases, and values. At the present moment in the United States we are struggling with both the development of a growing global culture and the increased importance of primordial sentiments. Our students must deal with both realities in the contemporary world. The conceptualization of World history I have suggested reflects those concerns. However, I am aware that if people centuries from now considered this conceptualization, it may well tell them as much about American life and values at the end of the twentieth century as about the larger scope of World history we now seek to restructure.

Appendix

The Drama of World History

Act One: Origins of the Human Community: Learning to Cooperate (3500 BCE)
  A. Setting the Stage: Creation & Evolution
  B. Gathering and Hunting: Humans Share the Resources
  C. Settling Down: Revolutionary Changes brought by Agriculture
  D. Nomadic Herdsmen: An Alternate Lifestyle

Characteristic of humans

Act Two: Surplus, Specialization and Cities (3rd millennium BCE)
  A. Setting the Stage: What is so special about river valleys?
  B. Sumer: City-states in Mesopotamia
  C. Africa: The Nile River Valley Civilization
  D. India: The Harappan Civilization
  E. Aegean: Minoan Hegemony
  F. Summary: The Advantages of Cooperation, Trade & Interdependence

Urban life

Act Three: Nomadic Migrations and Invasions (2nd millennium BCE)
  A. Setting the Stage: The Nomadic Herdsmen on the Move
  B. Nomadic Invasions in Mesopotamia
  C. Nomadic Invasions into the Nile Valley
  D. Covenant and Conquest of the Hebrews
  E. The Aryans in India
  F. The Middle Kingdom under the Shang and Chou
  G. Achaeans and Dorians move into Hellas
  H. Who is peopling the Americas?
  I. Interaction and Change: Who conquered whom?

Nomadic invasions

Act Four: The Axial Age (1000 to 500 BCE)
  A. Setting the Stage: The times are out of joint
  B. The Axial Age in the Ancient Near East
  C. The Axial Age in India
  D. The Axial Age in the Middle Kingdom
  E. The Axial Age in Hellas

Facing reoccurring questions

Act Five: Establishing a Synthesis (500 BCE to 200 CE)
  A. Setting the Stage: Characteristics of Empires
  B. Persia: Empire Builder in the Ancient Near East
  C. The Hellenistic Synthesis
  D. The Hindu Synthesis: A Conquest of Ideas
  E. The Middle Kingdom defines itself as the People of Han
  F. Law and the Military triumph in the Mediterranean World
  G. Olmec civilization in Mesoamerica

Empire building

Act Six: Interacting Worlds (1st millennium CE)

   A. Setting the Stage: Cross-cultural trade & movement of peoples & ideas
   B. The Spread of Buddhism
   C. From Jesus to Christendom
   D. From Mohammed to Dar al-Islam
   E. New actors on stage
      1. Japan and British Isles reflect the mainland civilization
      2. Cities along the Niger; Trade along the East African coast
      3. Teotihuacan in Mesoamerica

Trading goods and spreading ideas; universal religions

Act Seven: The Flowering of Human Cultures (400 to 1200 CE)

   A. Setting the Stage: Make art, not war
   B. The Golden Age in India: Gupta & South Indian kingdoms
   C. The Flowering of the Byzantine Empire
   D. The Islamic Achievement
   E. Cultural and technological achievements of the T'ang and Song
   F. Reflections and innovation from the Japanese archipelago
   G. Achievements of the Maya in Mesoamerica
   H. Community Solidarity in Africa
   I. Church and Manor: A flowering of Christendom in Europe

Flowering of culture

Act Eight: The Afrasian World System (1200 to 1400 CE)

   A. Setting the Stage: New Waves of Invaders & New Patterns of Trade
   B. The Turks follow the pattern of invasion and conquest
      1. Seljuk victories
      2. Saladin and Islamic unity
      3. Sultanates in India
   C. The Mongols follow the pattern of invasion and conquest
      1. Genghis Khan and the Mongols on the Move
      2. The Yuan Dynasty
      3. Pax Mongolia
   D. A biological invasion: The Plague
   E. Invaders in the West
   F. Toltecs & Aztecs follow the pattern of invasion and conquest
   G. World Systems of trade
      1. Travelers & traders in West Africa
      2. Urban centers in Europe
      3. Trade through West Asia
      4. Trading centers in Asia

Nomadic invasions; spreading ideas and goods

Act Nine: The Expanding Synthesis (15 to 17th centuries CE)

   A. Setting the Stage: Nothing fails like success (Ross Dunn)
   B. Successful Kingdoms and Empires?
      1. All under heaven with the Ming
      2. Ottoman power & Islamic Hegemony
      3. Indo-Islamic Synthesis in Mughul India
      4. Songhai, Benin and other African kingdoms
   C. Nothing Succeeds Like Failure
      1. Europe Discovers a Classical Past
      2. So you couldn't find India?

Empire building

And Now for Something Completely Different: Gendering the World History Survey*

by Judith P. Zinsser

Professor Zinsser cautions that the "best intentioned 'add women and stir' approach high-lights only a few exemplars and leaves half of humanity isolated in some apparently peripheral section of the course that everyone can see 'will not be on the exam'." The author offers a practical remedy for removing gender blinders in building a viable world history course. Explaining how she organizes her course around a central question, Zinsser suggests books and films that may be effectively used to gender world history courses.

Judith P. Zinsser is a professor of history at Miami University (Ohio) and taught previously at the United Nations School. Her most recent publications are *History and Feminism: A Glass Half Full* (1993) and *A New Partnership: Indigenous Peoples and the United Nations System* (1995). She has been president of the World History Association.

As a high school teacher in the 1970s, I was proud of myself for changing my world history classes beyond recognition. I altered their European orientation by "including"—as we then described it, despite the paternalistic implications—units on Africa, the Americas, and Asia. You can imagine my shock when I discovered that in spite of these efforts I still had missed 51 percent of the world's population. This gender blindness—the fact that I could have simply overlooked so many millions of people throughout so much time and across so much space—remains the most frightening aspect of my training and of my early research and teaching. Women are clearly essential to every aspect of our experience, yet they were somehow made invisible.

It is not just the omission of women that is significant, but also the skewing of men's history. Men appeared unsexed and neutered as the "universal" for all human beings. The end result was a past less rich and less nuanced, only half discovered and half told. If we are to remedy this lack, how should we tell the history of men *and* women? What can we do to gender the world history survey?

First, one must remember that even more than other surveys, *any* course in world history will reflect an endless series of impossible and clearly subjective choices made by instructors, whether they teach high school, college, or graduate classes. Second, rarely will a world history course follow a simple linear narrative. Even the "marching civilizations across time" approach doubles back on itself as it describes first one cultural region and then another.

My course reflects, but does not follow, the traditional time breaks. In fact, I try to force myself and my students out of the familiar by using a big, open-ended "timeless" question as the frame for the entire course. I ask, and students answer, only one question. This year it was: What causes order in societies and what causes disorder? No culture or time period is favored with such a question. Instead, everyone's history becomes a potential case study, and traditional causal explanations like economic, social, and cultural factors become organizational devices rather than fixed answers.

Breaking old patterns also helps me honor my commitment to teach about women *and* men. I do not believe that the standard narrative organization for world, European, or U.S. history makes that possible. Even the best-intentioned "add women and stir" approach (or "don't stir" depending on your perspective) highlights only a few exemplars and leaves half of humanity isolated in some apparently peripheral section of the course that everyone can see "will not be on the exam." And, most important, the old frameworks and periodizations leave history,

*Reprinted from *Perspectives*, Vol. 34, No. 5 (1996), pp. 11-12.

and the men of that history, just as they have always been. No, in order to gender the survey one must rethink history in terms of actions, interactions, and reactions, by women and men, between women and men, by women, and by men.

To assure that my survey reflects gender I set three criteria for myself that I keep in mind as I write my lectures and plan discussions. These criteria influence the readings and films I choose and determine the oral and written assignments I require. My course must illustrate (1) joint actions by women and men in familiar events, (2) interactions between women and men, and (3) reactions by women and by men as separate experiences reflecting different perspectives.

To show how I use these self-imposed rules, I offer a range of examples from my course World History since 1500. In every class period, in order to indicate that the familiar events of world history consist of joint actions by women *and* men, I "sex the universal" in my lectures. That is, instead of referring to "Chinese peasants" I say "peasant women and men." Instead of "slave owners" I say "men and women slave owners." Students adopt this kind of phrasing without comment and apparently without realizing how different it sounds from what they usually hear.

The readings I assign fulfill one or more of my requirements. In my unit on 17th- and 18th-century China, students read *Emperor of China: Self-Portrait of K'ang-Hsi* (1988), which describes the thoughts of the powerful Qing emperor as constructed by Jonathan Spence. The book is very obviously about the reactions, separate experiences, and perceptions of a man. In contrast, *The Death of Woman Wang* (1979), also by Spence, offers a sense of women's *and* men's lives in rural China during the same time period. This book describes women and men as they relate to one another (Woman Wang is murdered by her husband) and as they exist as members of clans and of the village, as joint actors in familiar events. In our discussion of the "effectiveness of the imperial government in maintaining order" students comment on the differences in men's and women's experiences at K'ang-Hsi's court and in the isolated rural community described in *The Death of Woman Wang*. Without an impassioned speech on my part, they discover elite men's political power and women's vulnerability across class and culture.

The History of Mary Prince: A West Indian Slave, Related by Herself (1993), edited by Moira Ferguson, presents a description of enslavement in the early 19th century, but from a woman's perspective. Assigned books for the 20th century also follow by criteria. Zareer Masani, the creator of *Tales of the Raj* (originally a radio series, 1988), made a concerted effort to include both women's and men's accounts of life in the India of the 1930s and 1940s. Journalist Jane Kramer did the same in *Unsettling Europe* (1990), her account of immigrant families in 1970s Europe.

Each of the three films I show in my survey class vividly demonstrates interactions between women and men. All are international prizewinners with strong heroes and heroines. *Nine in Red Sorghum* (about a remote rural winery in 1930s China) and *Ma Tine in Sugar Cane Alley* (about Martinique in the same time period) are the principal influences in the lives of the young boys whose stories are portrayed. *Salaam Bombay* offers at least six different plots, each rich in the survival tactics of young boys and girls and of their male and female elders.

Lastly, I also mold my oral and written assignments to fit my three criteria. I formulate propositions for debates that require students to think about men *and* women as historical agents. For example, one of my propositions is "Men and women choose order over rights." And an essay assignment at the end of the term asks students to consider women and men as joint actors in familiar events, the interactions between women and men, and women's and men's separate perceptions and experiences. This year I have offered students a choice of auto-biographies by contemporary women political activists and I directed them to analyze "the roles women and men played in causing order or disorder." Two books are by Latin Americans (Domitila Barrios de *Chungara's Let Me Speak! Testimony of Domitila, a Woman of the Bolivian Mines* [1979] and *I Rigoberta Menchú—An Indian Woman in Guatemala*, edited by Elisabeth Burgos-Debary [1985]). Two other books are accounts of black and colored opposition to apartheid (Ellen Kuzwayo's *Call Me Woman* [1985] and *A Life's Mosaic: The Autobiography of Phyllis Ntantala* [1993]). Another choice is Le Ly Hayslip's *When Heaven and Earth Changed Places: A Vietnamese Woman's Journey from War to Peace* (1993) about the Vietnam War, and the last is Chen Xuezhao's *Surviving the Store: A Memoir* (1991), about events in China from the 1930s to the present.

Clearly, there is ample material available. For me, the difficulty was not selecting new readings, rather it was changing goals and priorities. I gave up the idea that there was a fixed body of information that had to be covered. I decided that vivid encounters with a few cultures were more important than learning names and dates from many cultures. I though about what I do as a historian and what of that experience I wanted by students to understand. The ability to imagine and think about history as both joint and separate enterprises by men and women is a key part of what I must pass on, not because I am a feminist, but because that's the way it happened.

Students at West Milford High School, West Milford, NJ. Photo by John Jordan

Toward Historical Comprehension: Essays and Examples of Classroom Activities

APPROACHES TO WORLD HISTORY

The National History Standards call for a minimum of three years of World History instruction between grades 5 and 12. They also advocate courses that are genuinely global in scope. Teachers may wish to explore a number of different conceptual and organizational approaches to curriculum design. How much time should be devoted to particular periods, regions, or historical issues? What subject matter should be emphasized and what topics excluded? What is the proper balance between generalization and detail? Different teachers and schools will arrive at different answers to these questions. The teaching examples presented here are compatible with and will enrich a variety of curricular frameworks. Among possible approaches, four are perhaps most widely used:

Comparative civilizations. This approach invites students to investigate the histories of major civilizations one after another. A single civilization may be studied over a relatively long period of time, and ideas and institutions of different civilizations may be compared. This framework emphasizes continuities within cultural traditions rather than historical connections between civilizations or wider global developments.

Civilizations in global context. This conceptualization strikes a balance between the study of particular civilizations and attention to developments resulting from interactions among societies. This approach may also emphasize contacts between urban civilizations and non-urban peoples such as pastoral nomads. Students are like to investigate the major civilized traditions in less detail than in the comparative civilizations model but will devote relatively more time to studying the varieties of historical experience world-wide.

Interregional history. Teachers have been experimenting with this model in recent years. Here students focus their study on broad patterns of change that may transcend the boundaries of nations or civilizations. Students investigate in comparative perspective events occurring in different parts of the world *at the same time*, as well as developments that involve peoples of different languages and cultural traditions in shared experience. This approach includes study of particular societies and civilizations but gives special attention to larger fields of human interaction, such as the Indian Ocean basin, the "Pacific rim," or even the world as a whole. In comparison with the other two models, this one puts less emphasis on long-term development of ideas and institutions within civilizations and more on large-scale forces of social, cultural, and economic change.

Thematic history. Here students identify and explore particular historical issues or problems over determined periods of time. For example, one unit of study might be concerned with urbanization in different societies from ancient to modern times, a second with slavery through the ages, and a third with nationalism in modern times. This approach allows students to explore a single issue in great depth, often one that has contemporary relevance. Teachers may want to consider, however, the hazards of separating or isolating particular phenomena from the wider historical context of the times. A useful compromise may be to choose a range of themes for emphasis but then weave them into chronological study based on one of the other three models.

A Note on Terminology

Bring History Alive! employs certain terms that may be unfamiliar to some readers. **Southwest Asia** is used to designate the area commonly referred to as the Middle East, that is, the region extending from the eastern coast of the Mediterranean Sea to Afghanistan, including Turkey and the Arabian Peninsula. **Middle East** is used only in the context of 20th-century history. The term **Afro-Eurasia** appears occasionally to express the geographical context of historical developments that embrace both Africa and Eurasia. The secular designations **BCE** (before the Common Era) and **CE** (in the Common Era) are used throughout the Standards in place of BC and AD. This change in no way alters the conventional Gregorian calendar.

Giuseppe Rosaccio's World Map, 16th century. National Archives

ERA 1

The Beginnings of Human Society

Giving Shape to World History

So far as we know, humanity's story began in Africa. For millions of years it was mainly a story of biological change. Then some hundreds of thousands of years ago our early ancestors began to form and manipulate useful tools. Eventually they mastered speech. Unlike most other species, early humans gained the capacity to learn from one another and transmit knowledge from one generation to the next. The first great experiments in creating culture were underway. Among early hunter-gatherers cultural change occurred at an imperceptible speed. But as human populations rose and new ideas and techniques appeared, the pace of change accelerated. Moreover, human history became global at a very early date. In the long period from human beginnings to the rise of the earliest civilization two world-circling developments stand in relief:

▶ **The Peopling of the Earth:** The first great global event was the peopling of the earth and the astonishing story of how communities of hunters, foragers, or fishers adapted creatively and continually to a variety of contrasting, changing environments in Africa, Eurasia, Australia, and the Americas.

▶ **The Agricultural Revolution:** Over a period of several thousand years and as a result of countless small decisions, humans learned how to grow crops, domesticate plants, and raise animals. The earliest agricultural settlements probably arose in Southwest Asia, but the agricultural revolution spread round the world. Human population began to soar relative to earlier times. Communities came into regular contact with one another over longer distances, cultural patterns became far more complex, and opportunities for innovation multiplied.

Why Study This Era?

▶ To understand how the human species fully emerged out of biological evolution and cultural development is to understand in some measure what it means to be human.

▶ The common past that all students share begins with the peopling of our planet and the spread of settled societies around the world.

▶ The cultural forms, social institutions, and practical techniques that emerged in the Neolithic age laid the foundations for the emergence of all early civilizations.

▶ Study of human beginnings throws into relief fundamental problems of history that pertain to all eras: the possibilities and limitations of human control over their environment; why human groups accept, modify, or reject innovations; the variety of social and cultural paths that different societies may take; and the acceleration of social change through time.

Essay

Is the Concept of Race a Relic?*
by Robert Lee Hotz

Are racial classifications a thing of the past? Robert Hotz examines contemporary scientific evidence on the theory of race and racial characteristics. The article explains how scientific investigation has moved beyond acceptance of traditional racial definitions, even though social scientists and public health experts "routinely make race-based comparisons of health, behavior and intelligence." The article stimulates debate on how we have thought about race and why it continues pervade contemporary society and politics.

Robert Lee Hotz is a science writer for the *Los Angeles Times*.

For centuries, Americans have classified themselves and their neighbors by the color of their skin. Belief in the reality of race is at the heart of how people traditionally perceive differences in those around them, how they define themselves and even how many scientists say humanity evolved. Today, however, a growing number of anthropologists and geneticists are convinced that the biological concept of race has become a scientific antique—like the idea that character is revealed by bumps on the head or that canals crisscross the surface of Mars.

Traditional racial differences are barely skin deep, scientists say. Moreover, researchers have uncovered enormous genetic variation between individuals who, by traditional racial definitions, should have the most in common. Some scientists suggest that people can be divided just as usefully into different groups based on the size of their teeth or their ability to digest milk or resist malaria. All are easily identifiable hereditary traits shared by large numbers of people. They are not more—and no less—significant than skin tones used to popularly delineate race. "Anthropologists are not saying humans are the same, but race does not help in understanding how they are different," said anthropologist Leonard Lieberman of Central Michigan University.

The scientific case against race has been building quietly among population geneticists and anthropologists for more than a decade. The American College of Physicians is urging its 85,000 members to drop racial labels in patient case studies because "race has little or no utility in careful medical thinking." But even if accepted, recent scientific findings on race cannot be expected to do away with centuries of social and political policies.

Many social scientists, medical researchers and public health experts routinely make race-based comparisons of health, behavior and intelligence—even though many of them acknowledge that such conclusions may be misleading. As a result, the creation of racial and ethnic categories for public health purposes is becoming increasingly contentious, experts say. U.S. census officials also are snarled in an effort to redefine how people can best be classified. "No one denies the social reality of race," said anthropologist Solomon H. Katz of the University of Pennsylvania. "The question is what happens to the social reality when the biological ideas that underpin it vanish."

"I find the term *race* pretty useless scientifically," said Luigi Luca Cavalli-Sforza. The Stanford Medical School scholar, one of the world's leading geneticists, is part of a global effort to identify the thousands of genes that make up the human biological blueprint and to explore its unique genetic variations. Cavalli-Sforza, 72, has compiled a definitive atlas of human genetic diversity. The "History and Geography of Human Genes," which draws on genetic profiles of

*Reprinted from *Los Angeles Times*, 15 April 1995.

1,800 population groups, is the most comprehensive survey of how humans vary by heredity. Fourteen years spent surveying the global genetic inheritance has convinced him and his colleagues that any effort to lump the variation of the species Homo sapiens into races is "futile."

"We have the impression that races are important because the surface is what we see," Cavalli-Sforza said. "Scientists have been misled this way for quite a while, until recently, when we had the means to look under the skin." What they did not find when they looked under the skin has been just as revealing as what they did find. Their work undermined an idea of race as old as the United States. Ever since the 18th century, when scientists first formally codified humanity into races by skin color, "humor" or temperament, and posture, most researchers have accepted the fundamental idea that people are divided into fixed racial types, defined by predictable sets of inherited characteristics.

If this concept of race had scientific validity, researchers would expect to find clusters of significant genetic traits arranged by skin color and population group. When scientists examined human genetic inheritance in detail, however, they found that inherited traits do not cluster and do not stay within any particular group, debunking the idea of homogeneous races. For example, the sickle-cell trait usually is treated as a hereditary characteristic of black Africans. As a single gene, it confers resistance to malaria, although if inherited from both parents, it can lead to sickle-cell anemia. But the trait appears wherever people had to cope with prolonged exposure to malaria. It is as prevalent in parts of Greece and south Asia as in central Africa. Even older traits such as blood type and tissue compatibility also do not correspond to any recognizable racial stereotypes, researchers said. Rather, they believe, the physical characteristics most people associate with race are the result of adaptations to climate, diet, and the natural selection of sexual attraction.

"The fact you have these differences for some genetic traits doesn't mean other differences follow with them," said anthropologist Michael Crawford of the University of Kansas. "Racial groups don't exist in nice discrete entities." Many scientists argue, however, that racial differences may be important vestiges of much earlier human evolution, and they point to ancient fossils and modern genes to bolster their case. "Based on fragmentary fossil evidence in Europe, African, and Asia, some scientists suggest that modern humans may have evolved simultaneously in different regions as scattered pre-human groups interbred to form a new species. Under that theory, racial differences not only are real, but could be a million years old or more.

But that idea was dealt a serious blow recently when experts at Emory University, the National Genetics Institute of Japan and Stanford University used the evidence provided by human genes to determine that modern humans originated in Africa and began to migrate as recently as 112,000 years ago. That means physical differences associated with race began to appear only a short time ago. In fact, new studies show that human genetic variation is really a measure of distance—how far people have migrated from the original African homeland, adapting gradually to new conditions.

There may be no better illustration of the misleading biology of race than the example of sub-Saharan Africans and Australian Aborigines. By the color of their dark skin they would seem to be closely related. In fact, they have less in common genetically than any other two groups on Earth. Meanwhile, scientific interest in the genetic diversity that underlies population differences around the worked has never been higher. Indeed, scientists who believe in the biology of race cite such small but significant genetic differences as evidence.

Today, scientists are discovering that a single flaw in the 100,000 human genes can cause cancer of mental retardation. Some researchers argue that the genetic differences responsible for racial variations in skin color, hair texture or body type—which account for no more than about 0.01% of a person's entire genetic inheritance—might be equally important. But the new research shows that such individual genes—which can exert an enormous effect on one's health and development—do not segregate themselves into the bundles of conspicuous, inherited traits normally associated with race.

People frequently seek biological reasons for what are in fact social differences, mistaking family ties and cultural values for evidence of racial differences. Prejudices about Jews show how misconceptions about biology have been used to buttress religious and ethnic hostilities, experts say. Anti-Semitic literature frequently treats Jews as a biological race, because they share religious beliefs and cherish certain customs as a matter of history, spiritual identity and family integrity. As a religion, however, Judaism encompasses many ethnic and racial groups. Nonetheless, some Jews of European ethnic origin—the Ashkenazi—do share a number of genetic traits, such as a high frequency of the gene responsible for Tay-Sachs disease. Is this then the evidence of a racial characteristic?

Experts at Yale University Medical School and the University of Washington in February used a similar, rare inherited disease among the Ashkenazi—idiopathic torsion dystonia—to reconstruct the group's lineage, by tracing it to a single mutation more than 350 years ago. Their work suggests that the modern Ashkenazi are descended from a few thousand families in medieval Eastern Europe who intermarried. So, the Ashkenazi are not a biologically distinctive race, but an extended family.

Questions about the biology of race are surfacing at a time when record immigration has revived public debate over racial identity, and second thoughts about affirmative action have led U.S. policymakers to grapple with a legacy of slavery and discrimination.

At its most extreme, scholars say, the concept of race encompasses the idea that test scores, athletic ability or criminality somehow are rooted in racial genetic chemistry. "Differences in skin color are often perceived as only the surface manifestations of deeper underlying differences, with respect to things like temperament, intelligence, sexuality...the stuff of which, common stereotypes are made," said Michael Omi, an expert on ethnic studies at UC Berkeley. Whenever researchers focus on race—whether polling political attitudes or seeking the roots of violent behavior—they encounter troubling ethical dilemmas, experts say. If racial labels indeed have no biological meaning, then issues of scientific accuracy, consistency and bias become even more acute. "In rejecting the biological conceptions of race, it opens up the way for us to debate how we have socially and politically thought about race and why it continues to have a hold on our imaginations," Omi said. "We will conduct a study about race and residential patterns, or race and arrest rates, or race and intelligence, without thinking about what social concepts of race we are using," he said.

Although it has been decades since anthropologists explicitly supported the idea that some races are superior, research on race is still emotionally charged. Geneticists whose work challenges traditional beliefs about racial biology find themselves accused of racism by people who worry that the research simply will reinforce the idea that *any* groups are different and that those hereditary differences are important. At the same time, some anthropologists whose work undercuts racial theories find their activities dismissed by many colleagues as politically motivated. Others contend that to deny the scientific reality of race is itself a form of racism.

Queasiness about the scientific study of race is understandable. In the past, scientists have done much to foster misguided ideas of racial biology and inherited inferiority. Biological concepts of race easily became tools of intolerance. Many scientists defend the idea that race matters—if only as a question of academic study. But even they cannot agree on how many races exist.

"Although it may be politically incorrect to talk about race as a concept, there is reality to race, in an evolutionary, biological and historical sense," said Craig Stanford, a biological anthropologist at USC. "But people are so quick to equate race with racism," he added. "The question...is, 'What does race mean?' Is there any useful concept that does not do more harm than good?" Although the study of race has traditionally been a tenet of anthropology, many of Stanford's colleagues simply avoid the debate because political sensitivities are so raw that to conduct serious research on racial biology is to risk public censure. "They are like astronomers who are afraid that the study of stars and planets makes them astrologers," he said.

When Lieberman at Central Michigan formally surveyed anthropologists, however, he found that slim majority now rejects the concept of biological races. "That marks an enormous degree of change in the discipline," he said.

As a matter of public health, racial labels still are the stuff of life and death. Infant mortality has been about twice as high for blacks as for whites since 1950; Native Americans have substantially higher rates of death from unintentional injuries than any other group, and compared to whites, native Hawaiians are more likely to die from heart disease, cancer, and diabetes. Blacks, Ashkenazi Jews, Chinese, Asian Indians, and other groups in America can have different—and potentially dangerous—reactions to common medication such as heart drugs, tranquilizers and painkillers, said Dr. Richard Levy, vice president of scientific affairs at the National Pharmaceutical Council.

But artificial racial categories can distort even the simplest public health statistics used to frame federal policy and allocate resources, medical authorities said. When scientists use racial designations—often created by others solely for census and other legal compliance purposes—as the basis for studies, they may unintentionally weaken their research and perpetuate racial stereotypes, health experts said. They can find an inherited, racial linkage where none exists, or overlook the medical effects of what people eat, where they live and how they are treated, said experts at the U.S. Centers for Disease Control and Prevention. Most medical researchers treat African Americans as a homogeneous group whose public health problems are linked to skin color, regardless of ethnic origin or family history.

In a finding often cited as evidence of inherited racial variation in health, several medical studies have determined that African Americans are at a higher risk of hypertension than whites. Other studies, however, suggest that high rates of heart disease among black Americans may be more a matter of diet and the stress of discrimination than genes.

Dr. Richard S. Cooper of Loyola University's department of preventive medicine and epidemiology says many black Americans are most closely related genetically to West Africans, yet West Africans do not share their higher rates of many major health problems such as heart disease and diabetes.

In all, experts have identified nine distinct black population groups in the United States that vary widely in history, economics, and social and environmental factors—all of which bear directly on health. U.S.-born black women and Haitian-born women, for example, have higher rates of cervical cancer than English-speaking Caribbean immigrants, while both immigrant groups have lower rates of breast cancer than U.S.-born black women. Even when groups are closely related, ethnic variation in diet can radically alter reactions to medications and other important medical characteristics. Researchers compared how villagers in India and Indian immigrants in England reacted to the same medications. They discovered that as immigrants adopted a new lifestyle their drug metabolism became more like the English.

When CDC medical anthropologist Robert A. Hahn in Atlanta started investigating infant death in the United States, he quickly discovered how misleading racial labels can be. Comparing birth and death certificates for 120,000 babies who died in 1982 or 1983, he found that many had been identified as one race at birth and another at death. In the absence of consistent scientific definitions, medical authorities and funeral directors relied on what their eyes told them. When Hahn double-checked the records, he discovered that infant mortality among Native Americans was twice as high as public health authorities had estimated. More black babies also had died than anyone had believed.

Many public health experts such as Hahn say racial categories can be such a misleading tool for monitoring public health that such labels should be abandoned. "I think it is important to analyze health care characteristics in terms of ethnicity, but it is important to realize what you are classifying is not race in a biological sense," Hahn said. "Public health people," he added, "have not paid sufficient attention to what the scientists have to say about race."

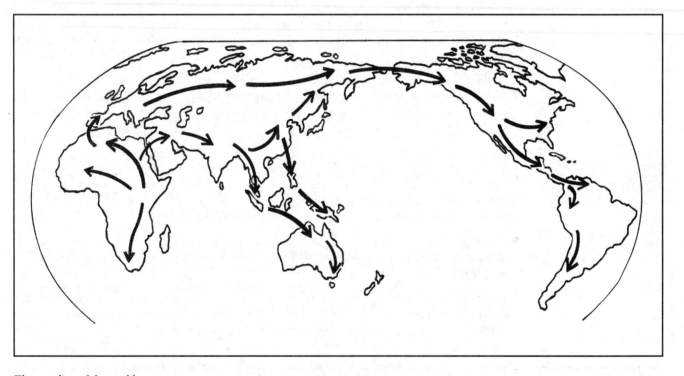

The peopling of the world

Sample Student Activities

I. The biological and cultural processes that gave rise to the earliest human communities.

A. Early hominid development in Africa.

Grades 5-6

▶ Explore the lives and practices of a variety of different animals, and compare their behavior with those of modern humans. *Which aspects of modern human culture—economics, food, clothing, shelter, politics, religion, communications, recreation, art, family and society—do other animals share? Which are uniquely human? What does it mean to be "human"?*

▶ Draw a map of Afro-Eurasia locating the Great Rift Valley/Olduvai Gorge, Beijing (Peking), Java and other sites of discoveries by Donald Johnson, the Leakeys and other paleoanthropologists studying hominid species.

▶ From historical evidence describe in drawing and writing the ways in which hunter-gatherers lived together in communities. *What do we know about early humans' "lifestyle"? How do we know it? How reliably do we know it?*

▶ Illustrate a mythological account of human origins. *What are the similarities and differences from the scientific explanation? What does the myth tell us about the values and beliefs of the culture from which it arose?*

▶ Assume the role of a carbon 14, fluorine, or DNA analyst and explain to a class on a field trip to your lab how this dating technique works. *How have these techniques helped us understand early human biological or cultural development?*

▶ Write job descriptions for an archaeologist, geologist, and anthropologist who might be working on a team studying hominid evolution in East Africa. *How do these scientists help us to understand early human history?*

Grades 7-8

▶ Read descriptions of the sites where early African hominids were found, and of the remains that were found there. *What inferences have scientists drawn about the behavior and way of life of early African hominids from this evidence? Which inferences are most reliably supported by the evidence, and what is the evidence that supports them?*

▶ Construct a description of the earliest known hominid-made tools. *What evidence do scientists use to support the hypothesis that they were deliberately manufactured, rather than merely found and used by early hominids?*

▶ Create a timeline to scale showing the most important points in the chronology of human evolution from the emergence of mammals to homo sapiens. Explain on what basis you have chosen what to show as "most important points' on your timeline.

Grades 9-12

▶ Draw on scholarly evidence and debate the question: *Were early hominid communities in East Africa hunters, scavengers, or collectors?*

▶ Classify pictures of skeletal remains such as skulls, jaws, and teeth as nonhominid primate, hominid, or Homo sapiens. Cite reasons based on evidence, and place them appropriately on a timeline. *How may such evidence assist us in understanding human evolution?*

61

◗ Write a plan to study a newly discovered site of hominid remains, explaining who would join your team and how and why various investigative techniques are to be used. *In what ways do recently-discovered sites affect the ways in which we study and understand our earliest history?*

◗ *Based on examination of a week's worth of household garbage, what could you infer about your own way of life?* Compare your conclusions with inferences you could make about an early hunter-gatherer community based on remains associated with it. *About what aspects of life are inferences drawn from common refuse most, and least, informative?*

◗ Using archaeological evidence, map the distribution and dates of Australopithecine, Homo erectus, Neanderthal, and the earliest Homo sapiens sapiens remains, along with the major features of flora, fauna, and climate associated with them. Based on this information, draw conclusions about the adaptability and success of hominids. *What new challenges did hominids have to meet as they moved from one climatic zone to another?*

B. How human communities populated the major regions of the world and adapted to a variety of environments.

Grades 5-6

◗ Using available resources such as *The Days of the Cave People, The Mammoth Hunt, Maroo of the Winter Caves*, and material from the Smithsonian's "Timelines of the Ancient World" or *Timeframe (Time-Life* series), compare and contrast life in hunter-gatherer communities in Africa, Eurasia, and the Americas. *How were earliest human communities and their life similar in different areas of the world?*

◗ Create a Paleolithic tool kit and explain the possible uses of each implement. *In what ways did humans develop tools to help control their environment?*

◗ Using sources such as *Timeframe (Time-Life* series), make a model of the Shanidar Cave in present-day Iraq and other such discoveries to describe the Neanderthal culture and community life.

◗ By investigating environments in which our early ancestors lived develop a set of criteria that establishes what factors made a particular geographic location an advantageous place for hunter-gatherers to live. *How do geography, climate, and other natural factors affect human life?*

Grades 7-8

◗ Analyze the story of the Piltdown Man hoax. *Why did people at first believe that the Piltdown Man fossils were genuine? What methods did scholars use to expose Piltdown Man as a hoax?*

◗ After reading accounts of hominid remains and environments, explain the survival advantages that language development would have given to early humans.

◗ Construct a series of map overlays to demonstrate the time-scale and geographical extent of human migrations from Africa to Eurasia and the Americas.

◗ Describe those features of Neanderthal burials from which inferences have been made concerning beliefs and feelings of Neanderthal peoples. *What arguments can be given in favor of, and against, the reliability of these inferences?*

◗ Examine illustrations of Late Paleolithic cave paintings found in Spain or France and discuss the possible social and cultural meanings of these paintings. *Can we infer the existence of religious beliefs from these cave paintings? Why or why not?*

Grades 9-12

▸ Explain what scholars have learned about the Neanderthals and assess theories about the biological and cultural relationships between this hominid and Homo sapiens sapiens.

▸ Based on the evidence of Neanderthal burials on the one hand and Cro-Magnon carvings and paintings on the other, infer answers to such questions as: *Were both these groups religious? How reliable is nonverbal evidence for peoples' thoughts and feelings?*

▸ Construct an account based on archaeological evidence of what differences would most strike a girl from a fishing camp who found herself in a mammoth hunters' camp. *What features of everyday life and relations between people were influenced by climate, geographic location, and economic specialization?*

▸ Hypothesize reasons why language developed as a way for humans to communicate. *How would language be useful to hunters who wished to trap and kill a mammoth? How might naming and classifying tools help in spreading technology from one community to another? How would language have helped communities make complex rules governing social relationships between men and women or adults and children?*

▸ Write an essay analyzing how humans populated the Americas in Paleolithic times. *What connections might there have been between migrations from Asia to the Americas and changing world climate? What kinds of evidence have scholars used to date early population movements in the Americas? How have their conclusions changed in recent years?*

II. *The processes that led to the emergence of agricultural societies around the world.*

A. How and why humans established settled communities and experimented with agriculture.

Grades 5-6

▸ Define wild and domestic plants and animals and make drawings illustrating differences between wild and domestic crops during the early agricultural period.

▸ Draw upon resources such as *Skara Brae* by Oliver Dunrea, the story of a prehistoric village in Scotland, in order to create illustrations or dioramas of early farming villages. *How did the practice of agriculture influence the way people led their lives?*

▸ Create a "you are there" travel brochure for the early agricultural era. Include information on geographic sites, food production, shelter, specialization, government, and religion.

▸ Write a diary entry expressing the personal conflicts you face as a hunter-gatherer being drawn into leaving your cave-dwelling to live in a permanent hand-built shelter. *What forces might draw you into such a move? What internal conflicts do all people face moving into new situations?*

Grades 7-8

▸ Write an account comparing the daily life of a hunter-gatherer and of an early farmer. *What problems and benefits are associated with each way of life?*

▸ Analyze illustrations of some of the new tools and other objects, such as sickles, grinding stones, pottery, blades, and needles) that appeared in the early era of agriculture. *In what ways are these objects likely to have affected daily life in early farming settlements?*

▸ Use a source such as Richard Leakey's *Dawn of Man* to describe how human communities might have domesticated wheat without being conscious that they were doing so.

▶ Map the areas in which evidence for early farming communities has been found, and identify the environmental features that would have favored the development of agriculture in those areas.

▶ Make a list of plants and animals domesticated during the "Neolithic Revolution," and construct a map showing where and when the domestication occurred.

▶ Construct a report about a new site that you, as its excavator, are convinced was inhabited by early agriculturalists. *What evidence would you cite to support your claim that the inhabitants of your site practiced agriculture?*

▶ Draw upon evidence developed by scholars to describe the role of fishing as a sedentary but nonagricultural way of life.

Grades 9-12

▶ Drawing evidence from scholarly sources, debate the questions: *Did human beings invent agriculture or discover it?*

▶ Examine archaeological reconstructions of hunter-gatherer and agricultural sites, including objects found there. Compare and contrast these sites posing questions such as: *Is the presence of permanent structures evidence for an agricultural community? Is the presence of tools such as grinding stones or sickles evidence for an agricultural society? Is a spear an indication of a hunter-gatherer society? Why or why not? What kind of evidence would reliably distinguish a hunter-gatherer from an agricultural site?*

▶ Debate questions such as: *What do historians mean by the "Neolithic revolution" and is the term "revolution" used here in a valid way? What does the term "Neolithic" mean? Is this term adequate to explain the complexities of early farming life? What better term than "Neolithic" can you come up with to express the complexities of early farming life?*

▶ Hypothesize ways in which hunter-gatherer societies could try to gain control over food supplies (such as fertility and hunting magic, protection of self-sown seeds, or confinement of a herd). *What part did the ability to store, as well as to control food supplies, play in the "Neolithic revolution"? Were gourds, baskets, and pottery integral or peripheral to the shift toward settled agriculture?*

▶ Construct historical arguments to assess the interconnection between agricultural production and cultural change (such as division of labor, change in concept of time, gender roles).

B. How agricultural societies developed around the world.

Grades 5-6

▶ Locate on a map the site of the ancient town of Çatal Hüyuk and describe the natural environment surrounding this town. Construct a model or illustration of Çatal Hüyuk and describe daily life in the community. *What problems needed to be solved that resulted from large numbers of people living together on a permanent basis?*

▶ Do research to compare the way of life of Neolithic hunter-gatherers, fishermen, and farmers. *What tools would these different groups need to make a living? How would they make these tools and where would they find materials for manufacturing them?*

▶ Write a diary entry describing a time in your village when a natural disaster has brought about long-term problems, including how it has affected as many aspects of your lives as possible. *What might people have done in anticipation that such natural disasters would commonly occur?*

◗ Using evidence on where different plants and animals were domesticated, create a menu for a meal that could have been eaten at a particular early agriculture site. Compare the range of choices with those you have today. *What factors contributed to the greater selection you have available?* Compare the nutritional content of this "early meal" with that of your last lunch or dinner. *Do you think people ate "better" then or do you eat "better" now? Why?*

Grades 7-8

◗ Make a chart comparing the positive and negative effects of agricultural life compared to hunter-gatherer life and debate the following question: *Did the emergence of agriculture represent an advance in human social development? What criteria would you use to evaluate whether or not it was an advance?*

◗ Construct a map demonstrating possible long-distance trade routes in Southwest Asia. *How does archaeological evidence support the routes in this map? What is obsidian, and why was it such an important item of trade?*

◗ Make a timeline tracing the emergence of agriculture worldwide up to about 4000 BCE, and identify on a world map both the major areas of agricultural production and the distribution of human settlements. *Why was it in these areas rather than elsewhere that agriculture became a way of life? What connections are there between the practice of agriculture and the pattern of settlement?*

◗ Construct stories, based on historical information, showing the most important steps in the transition from hunting and collecting to agriculture by different paths, whether as a result of a need for containers (such as gourds in Mexico), of habitual collection of wild grains leading to planting (as in Southwest Asia), or by confining rather than immediately killing animals.

◗ Identify those features of burials and of artistic remains from agricultural communities (such as Çatal Hüyuk) that suggest the existence of complex belief systems. *How do these compare with beliefs inferred from the burials and art associated with hunting-gathering groups?*

Grades 9-12

◗ Chart the probable differences between a hunting/gathering community of a few dozen people, a village of a few hundred, and a town of several thousand in relation to storage needs, sanitation, social hierarchy, division of labor, gender roles, and protection. Find evidence for your hypotheses.

◗ Map the distribution of sites where each of the following kinds of communities was found in the period of about 10,000-4,000 BCE: hunter/gatherers; wheat/barley/ cattle/sheep farmers; millet farmers; yam farmers; rice farmers; maize/squash farmers. List possible explanations why some groups developed or accepted completely sedentary agriculture, while others partly or fully kept to earlier patterns. *What evidence could you use to back up your hypothesis?*

◗ Make inferences based on scholarly evidence about specialization and political organization in such sites as Çatal Hüyuk and Jericho. *What features of settlement, such as fortification or crowding, would have had significant impact on inhabitants' ways of life?*

◗ Analyze scholarly evidence to explain the varied methods of crop cultivation. *How were methods of agriculture different in Southwest Asia as compared to West Africa and Southeast Asia?*

◗ Review scholars' explanations for the origins of agriculture. *What evidence has been presented for and against the various hypotheses about the development of plant and animal domestication?*

ERA 2

Early Civilizations and the Emergence of Pastoral Peoples, 4000-1000 BCE

Giving Shape to World History

When farmers began to grow crops on the irrigated floodplain of Mesopotamia in Southwest Asia, they had no consciousness that they were embarking on a radically new experiment in human organization. The nearly rainless but abundantly watered valley of the lower Tigris and Euphrates rivers was an environment capable of supporting far larger concentrations of population and much greater cultural complexity than could the hill country where agriculture first emerged. Shortly after 4000 BCE, a rich culture and economy based on walled cities was appearing along the banks of the two rivers. The rise of civilization in Mesopotamia marked the beginning of 3,000 years of far-reaching transformations that affected peoples across wide areas of Eurasia and Africa.

The four standards in this era present a general chronological progression of developments in world history from 4000 to 1000 BCE Two major patterns of change may be discerned that unite the developments of this period.

▶ **Early Civilizations and the Spread of Agricultural Societies:** Societies exhibiting the major characteristics of civilization spread widely during these millennia. Four great floodplain civilizations appeared, first in Mesopotamia, shortly after in the Nile valley, and from about 2500 BCE in the Indus valley. These three civilizations mutually influenced one another and came to constitute a single region of intercommunication and trade. The fourth civilization arose in the Yellow River valley of northwestern China in the second millennium BCE. As agriculture continued to spread, urban centers also emerged on rain-watered lands, notably in Syria and on the island of Crete. Finally, expanding agriculture and long-distance trade were the foundations of increasingly complex societies in the Aegean Sea basin and western Europe. During this same era, it must be remembered, much of the world's population lived in small farming communities and hunted or foraged. These peoples were no less challenged than city-dwellers to adapt continually and creatively to changing environmental and social conditions.

▶ **Pastoral Peoples and Population Movements:** In this era pastoralism—the practice of herding animals as a society's primary source of food—made it possible for larger communities than ever before to inhabit the semi-arid steppes and deserts of Eurasia and Africa. Consequently, pastoral peoples began to play an important role in world history. In the second millennium BCE migrations of pastoral folk emanating from the steppes of Central Asia contributed to a quickening pace of change across the entire region from Europe and the Mediterranean basin to India. Some societies became more highly militarized, new kingdoms appeared, and languages of the Indo-European family became much more widely spoken.

Why Study This Era?

▶ This is the period when civilizations appeared, shaping all subsequent eras of history. Students must consider the nature of civilization as both a particular way of organizing society and a historical phenomenon subject to transformation and collapse.

- In this era many of the world's most fundamental inventions, discoveries, institutions, and techniques appeared. All subsequent civilizations would be built on these achievements.

- Early civilizations were not self-contained but developed their distinctive characteristics partly as a result of interactions with other peoples. In this era students will learn about the deep roots of encounter and exchange among societies.

- The era introduces students to one of the most enduring themes in history, the dynamic interplay, for good or ill, between the agrarian civilizations and pastoral peoples of the great grasslands.

Excavation of a public drain at Lothal, Indus Valley. Archaeological Survey, Government of India

Essay

Collapse of Earliest Known Empire Is Linked to Long Harsh Drought*
by John Noble Wilford

What is the role of climatic change in the rise and fall of civilizations? Writer John Wilford reports on a scientific investigation that offers an explanation the fall of the Akkadian empire. Archaeologists, using historical archives and soil samples from the sites of three Akkadian cities, offer plausible theories for the fall of an early civilization.

John Noble Wilford has won two Pulitzer Prizes for his writing on science topics and on the Challenger disaster. He is the author of numerous books.

Under the renowned Sargon and his successors, the Akkadians of Mesopotamia forged the world's first empire more than 4,300 years ago. They seized control of cities along the Euphrates River and on the fruitful plains to the north, all in what is now Iraq, Syria and parts of southern Turkey. Then after only a century of prosperity, the Akkadian empire collapsed abruptly, for reasons that have been lost to history. The traditional explanation is one of divine retribution. Angered by the hubris of NaramSin, Sargon's grandson and most dynamic successor, the gods supposedly unleashed the barbaric Gutians to descend out of the highlands and overwhelm Akkadian towns. More recent and conventional explanations have put the blame on overpopulation, provincial revolt, nomadic incursions or managerial incompetence, though many scholars despaired of every identifying the root cause of the collapse.

A team of archeologists, geologists and soil scientists has now found evidence that seems to solve the mystery. The Akkadian empire, they suggest, was beset by a 300-year drought and literally dried up. A microscopic analysis of soil moisture at the ruins of Akkadian cities in the northern farmlands disclosed that the onset of the drought was swift and the consequences severe, beginning about 2200 B.C. "This is the first time an abrupt climate change has been directly linked to the collapse of a thriving civilization," said Dr. Harvey Weiss, a Yale University archeologist and leader of the American-French research team.

Such a devastating drought would explain the abandonment at that time of Akkadian cities across the northern plain, a puzzling phenomenon observed in archeological excavations. It would also account far the sudden migrations of people to the south, as recorded in texts on clay tablets. These migrations doubled the populations of southern cities overtaxed food and water supplies, and led to fighting and the fall of the Sargon dynasty. The new findings thus call attention to the role of chance—call it fate, an act of God or simply an unpredictable natural disaster—in the development of human cultures and the rise and fall of civilizations.

Among the drought's refugees were a herding people known as Amorites, characterized by scribes in the city of Ur as "a ravaging people with the instincts of a beast, a people who know not grain"—the ultimate put-down in an economy based on grain agriculture. An 110-mile wall, called the "Repeller of the Amorites," was erected to hold them off. But when the drought finally ended in about 1900 B.C., leadership in the region had passed from Akkad to Ur and then to the Amorites, whose power was centered at the rising city of Babylon. Hammurabi, the great ruler of Babylon in 1800 B.C., was a descendant of Amorites.

The correlation between drastic climate change and the Akkadian downfall also appears to complete the picture of widespread environmental crisis disrupting societies throughout the Middle East in the same centuries. Earlier studies had noted the effects of severe drought,

---

*Reprinted from *New York Times*, 24 August 1993

including abandoned towns, migrations and nomad incursions, in Greece, Egypt, Palestine and the Indus Valley. Until now, the connection between chronic drought and unstable social conditions had not been extended to Mesopotamia, the land between the two rivers, the Euphrates and the Tigris, often called "the cradle of civilization."

As to what caused such a persistent dry spell the scientists said they had no clear ideas, though they suggested that changing wind patterns and ocean currents could have been factors. A tremendous volcanic eruption that occurred in Turkey near the beginning of the drought, the scientists said, almost certainly could not have triggered such a long climate change.

Archeology's Sophistication

"This is a research frontier for climatologists," Dr. Weiss said in an interview. Dr. Weiss proposed the new theory for the Akkadian collapse at a recent meeting of the Society of American Archeology in St. Louis and then in a report in the current issue of the journal Science. His principal collaborators in the research were Dr. Marie-Agnes Courty, an archeologist and soil scientist at the National Center for Scientific Research in Paris, and Dr. Francois Guichard, a geologist at the same institution.

Other archeologists said the theory was plausible and appeared to provide the first logical explanation for the Akkadian downfall. Although he had not studied the report, Dr. Robert Biggs, a specialist in Mesopotamian archeology at the University of Chicago, said this was a good example of "archeology's growing sophistication in seeking reasons for serious political changes in the past."

In an article accompanying the report in Science, Dr. Robert McAdams, secretary of the Smithsonian Institution and an anthropologist specializing in Mesopotamia, cautioned that Dr. Weiss and his colleagues had not thoroughly established the link between climate and the empire's fall. He questioned whether such widespread and persistent drought could be inferred from local soil conditions at a few sites. "It will demand of other people in the field to either refute it or replicate it with their own work" Dr. Adams said of the theory. "And the only way to get people to pick up that challenge is for Weiss to stick his neck out. I applaud it." Dr. Weiss said the conclusions were based on tests of soils mainly at the sites of three Akkadian cities within a 30-mile radius places now known as Tell Leilan, Tell Mozan and Tell Brak in present-day Syria. Evidence of similar climate change was found in adjacent regions, and the archeologist said further tests of the theory would be conducted with the resumption of field work this week.

Land of Rainy Winters

The most revealing evidence has come from Tell Leilan, where Dr. Weiss has been excavating for 14 years and finding successive layers of ruins going back some 8,000 years. For several millennia, this was a small village established by some of the world's first farmers. Around 2600 B.C., it suddenly expanded sixfold to become the city of Shekhna, with 10,000 to 20,000 inhabitants. They lived in the middle of a land of rainy winters, dry summers and a long growing season for wheat and barley, much as it is today.

All the more reason the kings of Akkad, or Agade, a city-state whose location has never been exactly determined but is assumed to have been near ancient Kish and Babylon, reached out and conquered places like Tell Leilan about 2300 B.C. The region became the breadbasket for the Akkadian empire, which stretched 800 miles from the Persian Gulf to the headwaters of the Euphrates in Turkey.

Ceramics and other artifacts established the Akkadian presence there in Tell Leilan and other northern towns. And for years archeologists puzzled over the 300-year gap in human occupation of Tell Leilan and neighboring towns, beginning in 2200 B.C. It occurred to Dr. Weiss that since no irrigation works had been uncovered there, the region must have relied on rain-fed agriculture, as is !he case there today, in contrast to the irrigated farming in southern Mesopotamia. A severe drought therefore, could be disastrous to life in the north.

This idea was tested by Dr. Courty, using microscopic techniques she pioneered in a scientific specialty, soil micromorphology. By examining in detail the arrangement and nature of sediments at archeological sites, it is possible to reconstruct ancient environmental conditions and human activity.

One of the first discoveries was a half-inch layer of volcanic ash covering the rooftops of buildings at Tell, Leilan in 2200 B.C. All ash falls leave distinctive chemical signatures. An analysis by Dr. Guichard traced the likely source of this potassium-rich ash to volcanoes a few hundred miles away in present-day Turkey.

Migration From North

Since the abandonment of Tell Leilan occurred at the same time and the climate suddenly became more arid, volcanic fallout was first suspected as the culprit. Ash and gases from volcanic eruptions can remain suspended in the atmosphere for years, creating sun-blocking hazes and reducing temperatures. But from their knowledge of recent volcanoes, scientists doubted that the eruptions could have perturbed the climate over such a large area for 300 years. And there seemed no doubt about the drought lasting that long, Dr. Courty said. In the surrounding countryside at Tell Leilan and elsewhere, she examined a layer of soil nearly two feet thick and lying just above the volcanic ash. This layer contained large amounts of fine wind-blown sand and dust, in contrast to the richer soil in earlier periods. Another telltale sign was the absence of earthworm holes and insect tracks, which are usually present in soils from moister environments. This was strong evidence, the researchers reported, of a "marked aridity induced by intensification of wind circulation and an apparent increase" of dust storms in the northern plains of Mesopotamia.

It was during the 300-year desertification that archives of the southern cities reported the migration of barbarians from the north and a sharp decline in agricultural production, and showed an increasing number of names of people from the northern tribes, mainly the Amorites.

According to the evidence of the sediments, rain in more abundance returned to northern Mesopotamia in 1900 B.C. and with it the tracks of earthworms and the rebuilding of the deserted cities. Over the ruins of Shekhna, buried in the sands of the drought, rose a new city named Shubat Enlil, which means "dwelling place of Enlil," the paramount Mesopotamian god. The builders were Amorites.

In earlier excavations at Tell Leilan, Dr. Weiss discovered an archive of clay tablets showing that this was the lost capital of a northern Amorite kingdom often mentioned in the cuneiform writing of the period. This was the archive of Shamshi-Adad, the Amorite king who reigned from 1813 to 1781 B.C., containing the king's correspondence with neighboring rulers who concluded the ransoming of spies.

By then, the Akkadian kingdom of Sargon and Naram-Sin—the world's first empire—was long lost in the dust, apparently also the first empire to collapse as a result of catastrophic climate change. "Since this is probably the first abrupt climate change in recorded history that caused major social upheaval," Dr. Weiss said, "it raises some interesting questions about how volatile climate conditions can be and how well civilizations can adapt to abrupt crop failures."

AKKADIANS TO BABYLON

- Sometime before the third millennium B.C.: A tribe of Semitic-speaking herding nomads, perhaps originally from Arabia gradually settles down in northern Mesopotamia, which comes to be called Akkad.

- Middle of the third millennium B.C.: Akkadian names first appear in Sumerian documents.

- Around 2500 B.C.: Inscriptions written in Akkadian appear.

- 2340-2316 B.C.: Reign of Lugalzagesi, last of a line of Sumerian kings. It is a time of struggles among city-states for regional supremacy.

- Around 2300 B.C.: Rise of Sargon of Agade or Akkad, a Semitic-speaking ruler he defeats Lugal-zagesi and reigns for 56 years. The exact location of his city has never been found.

- 2278-2270 B.C.: Reign of his son Rimush, killed in a palace revolt.

- 2270-2254 B.C.: Reign of Rimush's brother Manishtushu also killed in a palace revolt.

- 2254-2218 B.C.: Reign of Manishtushu's son Naram-Sin thought to be the first to claim kingship as a divine right. His downfall was traditionally ascribed to divine retribution in the form of invading hordes from the east, called the Gutians. However, new research suggests complex internal problems and the beginning of a 300-year drought as the culprits.

- 2217-2193: Reign of his son Shar-kali-sharri, followed by a period of anarchy.

- 2200 B.C.: Volcanic eruption in Anatolia, after which many Akkadian settlements are abandoned.

- Around 2220-2120 : A Gutian dynasty is recorded, among others.

- 2123-2113: Rise of Utu-hegal who appoints-0r-Nammu as military governor at Ur. UrNammu overthrows his protector, assumes the title of King of Ur and founds a well-organized dynasty. The ziggurat, or stepped tower, prototype of the Tower of Babel, is first recorded in his reign. Ur falls gradually besieged by invaders like the Amorites and Elamites.

- 2028-2004: Reign of Ibbi-Sin ends with loss of empire. Some years later, a former underling Ishbi-Erra, expels the Elamites.

- 1984-1975. His son, Shu-ilishu; using the title King of Ur, continues a dynasty noted for peace and prosperity. Amorite influence remains strong and the desert sheiks who lead them are respected. An Amorite dynasty is founded at Larsa. Amorites are gradually assimilated into the Babylonian population.

- 1932-1906 B.C.: An Amorite king, Gungunum, claims titles of King of Sumer and Akkad and of Ur.

- Around 1894 B.C.: Emergence of an Amorite dynasty at Babylon. A city called Shubat-Enlil is built on the ruins of Shekhna abandoned in the drought.

- 1813-1781: Reign of ShamshiAdad, a powerful Amorite king. 1792-1750 B.C.: Reign of Hammurabi, famous king and lawgiver; toward the end of his reign, Babylon becomes a great military power and the seat of kingship.

- 1595 B.C.: Sack of Babylon by the Hittites, an Indo-European-speaking people from Asia Minor.

Sample Student Activities

> **I.** *The major characteristics of civilization and how civilizations emerged in Mesopotamia, Egypt, and the Indus valley.*

A. How Mesopotamia, Egypt, and the Indus valley became centers of dense population, urbanization, and cultural innovation in the fourth and third millennia BCE.

Grades 5-6

▶ Analyze some of the Indus valley seals. *What can you infer about life in the Indus valley from these seals?*

▶ Locate the Tigris-Euphrates, Indus, and Nile river valleys on a map. Compare the geographic features of these valleys using maps, photographs, and other appropriate pictorial sources. Identify common features that affect agriculture and food supplies. *Why did civilization develop near rivers that flooded?*

▶ From a list of technologies of our own time, identify those that had already been "invented" in some form by 1000 BCE. Debate the advantages and disadvantages of the technological developments that have been made since then. *Have we made "progress" since ancient times?*

▶ Experiment with a variety of materials to find those best used to write symbols of Mesopotamian (cuneiform), Egyptian (hieroglyphics) and Indus valley types. *How might the availability or scarcity of different resources affect cultural developments in a society?*

Grades 7-8

▶ Compare the characteristics of a Neolithic settlement such as Çatal Hüyuk or Jericho with those of an early city such as Ur or Mohenjo-Daro. *What characteristics suggesting the presence of civilization do the cities have that the Neolithic settlements lack? Which of these characteristics are also present at the sites of other early civilizations?*

▶ Research the technology for flood control and irrigation in the Nile and Tigris-Euphrates valleys. *How did irrigation ensure a reliable food supply? Why did large-scale irrigation projects require more complex political and administrative organization?*

▶ Create a skit entitled "A Day in the Life of Ur." Role-play characters such as ruler, priest, warrior, scribe, artisan, farmer, merchant, slave, mother, and father. Characters must explain why they are important to the overall economic and social welfare of the city.

▶ Read selections from the *Epic of Gilgamesh* and show how this story of a hero-king expresses ancient Mesopotamian religious and cultural values.

▶ Analyze a description of Mohenjo-daro. *What evidence is there that Mohenjo-Daro was a planned community?* Choose some features of the physical evidence at the site and suggest reasons for their development. Explain your reasoning.

▶ On a map plot the places where the Indus valley cities have been discovered. Compare the size of the Indus valley civilization with the sizes of Sumerian and Egyptian civilizations. *What other ways might they be compared? Why do we know less about government, society, and religion in Indus civilization than in ancient Mesopotamia or Egypt?*

Grades 9-12

▶ Draw upon selections from the Code of Hammurabi to analyze what it suggests about ethical values, social hierarchy, and relationships between men and women in Mesopotamia. *How does the Mesopotamian value system compare with modern American ethical and legal standards?*

▶ Using stories such as the Biblical account of creation in Genesis and the *Enuma Elish* from Babylon, compare and contrast the different beliefs these stories reflect.

▶ Draw on historical evidence to role-play a lesson given to a teenager by a Sumerian or Egyptian scribe to a teenager in their society and explain the principles of their script and why learning it is important.

▶ Construct a theory to account for Egypt's early unification under one ruler, whereas early Mesopotamia was a region of competing city-states. Find evidence to support the theory.

▶ Compare and contrast Mesopotamian ziggurats and Egyptian pyramids. *What economic and social preconditions had to exist to make their building possible? What motives impelled their building? What difference did they make to the lives of those who ordered them built and those who actually labored in the building process?*

▶ Examine the way the Indus people laid out and constructed their cities. *What does this evidence suggest about their government, political and economic organization, and values?*

B. How commercial and cultural interactions contributed to change in the Tigris-Euphrates, Indus, and Nile regions.

Grades 5-6

▶ Draw a map labelling the items Mesopotamia traded for and where they came from. *What products did Mesopotamians import, from where, and how were they imported? Compare Mesopotamian trade with Egyptian trade.*

▶ Locate on a map of northeastern Africa the cataracts on the Nile River, zones of agricultural settlement, the regions of Nubia and Kush, and the wind patterns in this part of Africa. From this information show how the geography and climate of the region affected trade in the Nile valley. *What items were traded? What evidence is there for cultural as well as commercial exchanges?*

Grades 7-8

▶ Trace on a map long-distance trade routes by land and sea connecting India, Mesopotamia, and Egypt. List goods traded along these routes and methods of record keeping and ownership. *Why were these goods important to the different societies?*

▶ Role-play a meeting of a king of Nubia with an Egyptian official detailing plans for trade. *What goods and tools will they trade? What will the methods of transport be?*

▶ Gather evidence that people in the Indus valley were in contact with other areas of the world. *What kinds of evidence are available? How wide was the Indus trading network?*

▶ Map the places of origin for the silver, copper, and tin used in Mesopotamia during the third millennium. *What exports did they have available to pay for the metals they imported? What peoples did importing these metals bring the Mesopotamians in contact with?*

Grades 9-12

▶ Investigate evidence for the hypothesis that Egyptian, Indian, and Mesopotamian societies borrowed from each other. *In what ways might such borrowing have taken place? What effects might cultural innovations have on a receiving society? Why are foreign innovations sometimes rejected? What are some modern examples of both cultural borrowing and rejection?*

‣ Prepare advice from an experienced Mesopotamian trader to his son in the third millennium BCE, including a map of trade routes, transport, dangers, information about merchandise known to have been carried by others, and possible religious or bureaucratic problems in the areas visited.

‣ Construct a chart showing the geographical features of Mesopotamia that encouraged trade with others (e.g., their lack of raw materials and access to the sea) and those features that inhibited trade (e.g., mountain barriers). Find evidence to decide whether the favorable features outweighed the unfavorable.

‣ Debate the relative importance of physical geography, demand for and available supply of specific resources, and centralized political power in the development of trade, using Egypt, Mesopotamia, and the Indus Valley during the third millennium BCE as case studies.

‣ Construct historical explanations for the shifting political relationship between Egypt and Nubia. *How would you account for Egyptian conquests in Nubia?*

II. How agrarian societies spread and new states emerged in the third and second millennia BCE.

A. How civilization emerged in northern China in the second millennium BCE.

Grades 5-6

‣ Hypothesize how people might have first discovered copper and later created bronze. Write a short story or series of journal entries on your hypothesis. *Why was the making and use of metal work important for humanity?*

‣ Research the writing tools and writing surfaces, as well as the nature and uses of writing in early Chinese society. Compare Chinese writing with writing techniques and functions in Mesopotamia and Egypt.

‣ Create a relief map illustrating the natural environment of the Huang He (Yellow River) civilization, including its natural resources. Analyze how the environment influenced the development of civilization there, comparing with Mesopotamia, Egypt and the Indus Valley.

‣ Look at pictures of Shang dynasty objects, then make a list of all you can tell about people living in that place and time based on this evidence. *What kinds of information about the lives of people who made and used the objects cannot be gained from the evidence of physical objects alone?*

Grades 7-8

‣ Examine illustrations of early Chinese inscriptions on oracle bones and accounts of what the inscriptions said. *Why did people write on these bones? How has the deciphering of these inscriptions enriched our knowledge of Chinese history during the Shang period? How reliable are these inscriptions as a source of information about Shang China?*

‣ Compare the climate and geography of the Huang He with that of the Tigris-Euphrates valley. *How did environmental factors affect the way early civilization developed differently in these two areas?*

‣ Examine maps illustrating the changes in the course of the Huang He. *What challenges would these changes present to the Chinese people and their government?*

‣ Examine early Chinese bronze vessels. *What inferences can be drawn about the ways they were made and used? About Chinese society at the time?*

‣ As an army leader speaking to a king of the time, present a persuasive case, consistent with historical information, in favor of switching to bronze weapons. *Who, and why, is most like to have been supportive of such a change? Who might oppose and for what reasons?*

Grades 9-12

‣ Look at a physical map of Eurasia and consider both geographical barriers and potential routes of communication between China and India or Southwest Asia. *What evidence is there for cultural contacts between China and these other centers of civilization in antiquity?*

‣ Compare the part that prevailing wind, current, and flooding patterns played in influencing features of the Nile, Tigris, and Huang He civilizations.

‣ Chart the similarities and differences between the military-religious leadership of the Shang kings and that of the kings of Egypt.

‣ Taking on the role of a Shang ruler, one of the king's noble vassals, a woman of the upper classes, a bonded peasant, or a slave, describe your rights and responsibilities and your relationship to those above and below you on the social scale.

‣ Construct a conversation, based on historical evidence, between a Shang priest and a Sumerian priest, comparing notes about religious beliefs and the uses of writing.

‣ Compare the kinds of information gained from inscriptions on oracles bones from early China, burials in early Egypt, and temple records in Sumer. *From which of them, and why, can modern scholars gain the most and least information about the society of its origin? How do differences in the reasons for making records, and in the survival rate of the records made, influence our knowledge of early societies?*

B. How new centers of agrarian society arose in the third and second millennia BCE.

Grades 5-6

‣ Using pictorial evidence and historical resources hypothesize how the invention and use of the plow, the weaving loom, and pottery may have changed the lives of humans and affected human populations. *What unforeseen effects may arise from people's development of new technologies?.*

‣ Compare the technologies used in ancient agricultural societies with those used today in industrialized and agricultural settings. *What are the advantages and disadvantages of the newer technologies?*

‣ Create an illustrated Venn diagram comparing the use of bronze in early civilizations with its use today. *What metals serve as substitutes for bronze today?*

‣ Research the archaeological work of Sir Arthur Evans at Knossos and study a reconstruction of the palace and city. *What do we learn of Minoan culture from Evans's endeavors?*

Grades 7-8

‣ Compare the relative importance of the introduction of pottery, bronze-working, and the plow. *What areas of life did these new technologies influence? What impact did they have on politics, warfare, wealth disparities, and gender roles? What evidence can you find to support your hypotheses?*

‣ Play the role of a craftsman of Syria who is expert in making bronze swords. Explain to a group of apprentices the technological procedures for making these weapons. *In what ways were bronze weapons superior to those made from stone?*

- Prepare a plan for the building of Stonehenge based on evidence about conditions at the time of its building. *How are the stones to be obtained, transported, and erected? How are the laborers to be recruited, provisioned for, and supervised? How will the enterprise be financed? How will the structure be used?*

- Drawing upon illustrations of Egyptian and Minoan murals and pottery, develop hypotheses on the nature and extent of cultural contact between these two civilizations.

- Create an account as though by a Mesopotamian trader in Crete, explaining ways that Minoan society differed from that of Hammurabi's state politically, economically, religiously, militarily, and in terms of gender roles. *How were the differences noted related to geography and resources?*

- Read the legend of Theseus and the Minotaur. *What finds from Minoan Crete have scholars suggested might have given rise to the story, and to some of its details?*

- Drawing on pictures and descriptions of Minoan "bull-leaping," role-play a Minoan diplomat explaining to a foreign visitor the significance of this.

Grades 9-12

- List objects found on Minoan sites that are known to have come from elsewhere, and Minoan wares found outside of Crete. On the basis of this list indicate on a map the places that were in contact with Minoan civilization, and hypothesize the influence of trade on the development of Minoan civilization.

- Create a map indicating the most important urban centers of Southwest Asia, Egypt, and the Aegean basin as of about 2000 BCE. *What has archaeology revealed about the development of cities along the eastern Mediterranean coast, notably Byblos and Ugarit? In what ways did these cities form a commercial bridge between the networks of Southwest Asia, Egypt, and the eastern Mediterranean?*

- From historical sources create a chart of important technological advances such as the bow and arrow, pottery, the wheel, weaving, the sail, bronze casting, the plow, etc., showing their possible places of origin, approximate time of introduction, and uses. *What impact did these technologies have on the lives of the people who used them? On the social organization and on the political or economic power of the groups who used them?*

- Research pictorial and archaeological evidence on agriculture and agricultural societies in tropical West Africa. *In what ways did agricultural developments stimulate the growth of societies in this part of Africa?* Compare this development with that occurring in Southeast Asia at the same time.

- Gather evidence for the hypothesis that rice was first domesticated in Southeast Asia, and trace the spread of rice cultivation throughout Asia. *What promoted, and what limited, this spread?*

- Drawing on illustrations of Minoan art, infer characteristics of relations between men and women in Crete. *What evidence would you look for to validate your inferences? Is such evidence available?*

III. *The political, social, and cultural consequences of population movements and militarization in Eurasia in the second millennium BCE.*

A. **How population movements from western and Central Asia affected peoples of India, Southwest Asia, and the Mediterranean region.**

Grades 5-6

▶ Define the term "kinship." *How could social groups, even large ones, be organized on a basis of kinship? What role does kinship play in American society today?*

▶ Research the climate and geography of Central Asia. *How would this kind of climate and geography be compatible with the formation of pastoral societies? What are the characteristics of this kind of society?*

▶ Read stories from ancient sources about relationships between agricultural and pastoral peoples (e.g., Cain and Abel) and explain how the two groups might have viewed each other. *In what ways were pastoral and agricultural peoples dependent on each other, and how/why might they have come into conflict?*

Grades 7-8

▶ Describe the climate and geography of the land mass of Central Asia and hypothesize why animal breeding enabled successful human adaptation to the steppe.

▶ Make charts of some of the major languages of the world today, including languages from Indo-European and Afro-Asiatic families. *How can linguists tell that languages are related to one another? If two languages are related, does that mean that the speakers of those languages will necessarily share other aspects of culture?*

▶ Research Indo-European languages, and create a language tree with Indo-European as the "trunk" of the tree. *Where are English and Spanish placed on this tree in relation to other languages?* Name some languages spoken in the United States today that would not be on this tree.

▶ Role-play a conversation between people from a pastoral and an agrarian society, exploring differences and similarities in their ways of life and ideas.

▶ Research the lifestyle of early pastoral peoples in Eurasia or Africa. *What animals did their economies depend on? What other resources besides food did these animals offer them? What was their means of transport, shelter, and warfare? What features of their society were directly influenced by the demands of pastoralism?*

▶ Construct a map showing the locations of pastoral nomad societies and of settled agricultural societies during the second millennium BCE. *In which areas of contact is there historical evidence for conflict between the two kinds of societies? For conquest of one by the other? For transformation from one way of life to the other?*

Grades 9-12

▶ Construct a map showing the migrations of Indo-European language speakers from their homeland, showing approximate dates for arrivals in new locations, and adding an overlay map showing the distribution of Indo-European language speakers today. *How might a language be introduced to a new area?*

▶ Drawing historical information, construct a chart showing advantages and disadvantages of life in a pastoral and an agrarian society of the second millennium BCE.

▶ Debate the hypothesis that, for pastoralists, a nomadic way of life is a necessity rather than a preference. *What information can you present to serve as evidence for your arguments?*

▶ Compare pastoralists and settled agriculturalists in terms of the problems and opportunities presented by their sources of food, their ownership of food-producing resources, the way that food could or had to be stored, and the tools needed for processing it. *What was the impact of the food sources used in each society?*

▶ Drawing on historical information, create a conversation between a pastoral nomad woman and a man from a village of agriculturalists about what is expected of women and men in each of their societies.

▶ Draw on scholarly evidence to describe the characteristics of the relations between early herders and farmers. *In what ways could relations between pastoral peoples and agrarian societies involve both conflict and mutual dependence?*

B. The social and cultural effects that militarization and the emergence of new kingdoms had on peoples of Southwest Asia and Egypt in the second millennium BCE.

Grades 5-6

▶ Draw on visual data and written sources to explain how the invention of chariots affected transportation in Southwest Asian societies. Investigate the development of chariot warfare. *In what ways were chariots both effective and ineffective weapons of war?*

▶ Assume the role of an archaeologist exploring King Tutankhamen's tomb. Compare the findings to those from other archaeological sites. *What do the treasures from the tomb indicate about Egypt? What conclusions can be drawn about the life of the pharaoh?*

▶ Role-play a scene from a New Kingdom Egyptian marketplace showing how life there was affected by contacts with other parts of the world (including goods traded, stories of traders, etc.). *How is life in any society influenced by its connection to other peoples?*

Grades 7-8

▶ Write entries in the "Who's Who" of Egyptian history describing the political and cultural achievements of Thutmose III, Ramses II, and Queen Hatshepsut. Based on their achievements, debate the question: *Who should get "top billing"? On what basis should "top billing" be assigned?*

▶ As a military commander of the Hittite army, write an argument in favor of spending more of the revenues on chariots. Justify the argument with reasons historically known to be valid.

▶ Write epitaphs for Hatshepsut, outlining her achievements during the New Kingdom. Display epitaphs on a homemade obelisk.

▶ Develop a chart that graphically shows Egyptian expansion during the Old, Middle, and New kingdoms. These graphic representations can take the form of an illustrated timeline, transparency overlay, or relief map and should include the factors that made expansion possible.

▶ Create a set of instructions on chariot warfare for use by a commander of Hittite or Egyptian armies.

▶ Create a series of maps showing the migrations of the Hittites and the expansion of their empire. *What peoples did the Hittites come into conflict with, and with what results?*

Grades 9-12

▶ Draw a map of the major states existing in Southwest Asia, Egypt, and the eastern Mediterranean in the later second millennium, and consider why the wars and diplomatic relations among these states probably represent the first era of "internationalism" in world history.

▶ Survey visual and written sources (e.g., *The Iliad*, Egyptian wall paintings, and Assyrian bas reliefs) and describe the effects of introducing chariot warfare onto the battlefield.

◗ Compare the accomplishments of Sargon and Akhenaton (Amenhotep IV), and evaluate which of them had a greater historical impact, giving reasons to justify the assessment.

◗ Create a chart showing the main features of Egyptian religious beliefs during the New Kingdom; Akhenaton's beliefs; and Hebrew monotheistic beliefs. Then determine to what extent it would be accurate to describe Akhenaton as a "monotheist."

◗ Playing the role of an adviser to one of the Hittite kings, outline the factors that made Egypt a dangerous rival to the Hittites in Southwest Asia.

C. How urban society expanded in the Aegean region in the era of Mycenaean dominance.

Grades 5-6

◗ Investigate how geography influenced the development of Mycenaean society.

◗ Draw upon selections from the *Iliad*, the *Aeneid*, and pictures of jars and red-clay portraits to retell the story of the siege of Troy.

Grades 7-8

◗ Draw up a chart giving all the evidence in favor, and against, the hypothesis that warfare was the leading value of Mycenaean society.

◗ Create an "eyewitness account" of a burial in a Mycenaean beehive tomb. *Who was being buried? What was the tomb like? What grave-goods were buried with the corpse?*

◗ Draw up a chart comparing Minoan and Mycenaean government and economy. *What reasons can you give for the differences and similarities? What evidence can you give to support your reasoning? Given the choice, and taking into account historical information, would you have preferred to live in Minoan Crete or Mycenaean Greece? Explain your reasoning.*

◗ As the excavator of a Mycenaean site, what evidence would you cite to document your claim that your site shows Egyptian, Southwest Asian, and Minoan influences? *What actual evidence exists that would support such a claim?*

Grades 9-12

◗ Drawing on the physical evidence in Mycenaean shaft tombs, write a description of society, government, and trade in the second millennium BCE.

◗ Compare Mycenaean with Egyptian royal tombs. Hypothesize what these tombs suggest about social classes and the nature and role of government.

◗ Using descriptions by archaeologists, ground plans based on excavations, and pictures of remains and reconstructions, compare Mycenaean fortresses with Minoan palaces. *What conclusions about their respective societies may be drawn from this evidence? How does investigation of other available evidence support, modify, or negate your conclusions?*

◗ Read passages from the *Iliad* about the Mycenaeans and the Trojan War. Locate Mycenaean and Trojan areas on the map. Having investigated archaeological evidence for trade and warfare in these areas, and the successive levels of occupation at the site of Troy, write a critique of Homer's account in the *Iliad*. *How do the descriptions of the Greeks given compare with what can be inferred about the Mycenaeans from archaeological evidence?*

◗ Create a timeline showing the timespan of Minoan civilization, the start and expansion of Mycenaean civilization, and the relationship of these to Egyptian and Hittite history. *What part did migrations and technological innovations play in the events shown on the timeline?*

D. The development of new cultural patterns in northern India in the second millennium BCE.

Grades 5-6

- Look at slides or photos of the ruins of Mohenjo-daro and research reasons why this city disappeared. *What are some of the possible causes of the decline or disappearance of cities in history? How could changes in the environment have contributed to the fall of Mohenjo-daro and other Indus cities?*

- Read, or view a filmed version of, a segment of the Indian epic "The Mahabharata." Describe what this story tells us about the values of the people who created it. *What can myths tell us about the society and culture from which they come?*

Grades 7-8

- Drawing upon books such as A. K. Ramanijan's *Folktales from India,* examine the values that governed Indian society. *How is the varna system reflected in these folktales?*

- Develop a presentation of possible climatic, demographic, technological, or social changes that might have caused Aryan pastoral peoples to leave Central Asia. *What might have pushed them from the steppes? What might have attracted them to the Iranian plateau and into the Indus valley? What evidence would support your hypotheses?*

- Analyze *Rig Veda* 10.90 to determine what the Aryans believed were the ideal divisions of society. *What is the significance of the term "varna"? What privileges and restrictions were placed on the various varna?*

- Read odes from the Vedas that praise the major Vedic gods—Indra, Varuna, Soma, and Agni. *What do these writings suggest about important Aryan values?*

- Retell the story of the conflict between the Pandavas and Kauravas in the *Mahabharata. What does it suggest about tensions among Aryan tribes as they began to settle down in the Indo-Gangetic plain? About rulership and the bases of a ruler's legitimacy?*

- Construct a series of overlay maps, showing the chronology of Indo-Aryan peoples' movements from Central Asia into India and the Eastern Mediterranean. *What peoples did the Indo-Aryans conquer or displace?*

Grades 9-12

- Examine photographs and descriptions of excavations of Indus cities such as Mohenjo-daro to determine what happened to these cities. *What explanations could there be for a decline in trade, overcrowding, and people being left unburied in the streets? What evidence is there for any of these explanations?*

- Analyze various Vedic hymns. *What do they suggest about people's beliefs?*

- Research the origins of the word "Aryan" and the peoples who came to be called Indo-Aryan. *Based on works such as the* Vedas *and* Mahabharata, *what was Aryan culture in India like? How did Nazi use of the term "Aryan" in the 20th century differ from the way historians of early India use the term?*

- Compare linguistic (shared vocabulary), literary (*Vedas*), and archaeological evidence for the way of life and beliefs of India's Aryan immigrants in the second millennium BCE, and assess what information is most reliably known.

- Hypothesize from historical information what factors (disease, famine, environment, invasion, etc.) led to the collapse of the Indus valley civilization. *How does this decline compare with that of other peoples such as Sumerians?*

◗ Assess how reliable the *Iliad* and *Odyssey* and the *Mahabharata* and *Ramayana* are as sources of historical information about this period. *How might historians determine to what extent these epics reveal information about the time period when they were first written down or the earlier period in which the stories were set?*

IV. Major trends in Eurasia and Africa from 4000 to 1000 BCE.

Major trends in Eurasia and Africa from 4000 to 1000 BCE.

Grades 5-6

◗ Research the location of agricultural communities and urban settlements in Eurasia and Africa at three different points in time between 4000 and 1000 BCE. Create a map showing your findings. *What is the connection between the spread of agriculture and the development of the first cities?*

◗ Write a series of diary entries from the perspective of a village-dweller who has just encountered a traveler from a distant place and been exposed to a new product, idea, or technique. Describe how that encounter changed that person's life. *How do you respond to new things you encounter through contact with people of different cultural backgrounds?*

◗ On a map use arrows to show how products were exchanged within the broad region surrounding Mesopotamia. *What does the map tell you about interdependence of groups resulting from trade?*

◗ Investigate the climate and physical geography of Southwest Asia, the Nile valley, or the Mediterranean basin. *How important was geography to the development of that region? How did geography influence economic life and trade? Do you think that societies in that region would have developed differently if the climate were different?*

Grades 7-8

◗ *What characteristics would you claim for your society if you wanted to convince someone from another society that yours was a "civilization"? How do your criteria for "civilization" compare with scholars' definitions?*

◗ Make a timeline showing the most important inventions, discoveries, techniques and institutions that appeared during the third and second millennia BCE. *On what basis did you choose what were the "most important"?*

◗ Role-play bronze-age women and men of different countries, occupations, and social classes, such as a Mycenaean warrior, a Minoan trader, a Danubian peasant woman, an Egyptian slave. For each, explain what difference the availability of bronze has made in your life.

◗ Debate the questions of which was the more decisive transformation in human history: the Neolithic revolution, or the emergence of civilization. *On what bases can the decisiveness of such a transformation be judged? What evidence can you present to support your argument?*

◗ Show the areas in which urban civilizations existed on a map of the world about 1000 BCE. *What geographic, ecological, demographic, economic or other explanations can you come up with to explain why civilization did or did not emerge in different regions of the world? What evidence would support your explanations?*

◗ Write a "biography" for one of the significant inventions, techniques, ideas or institutions that appeared during this period (such as pyramids, chariots, iron working, rice-cultivation). *Where was it born? How was it nurtured? Where did it travel to, how was it received, and what difference did it make to the lives of those among whom it appeared?*

◗ Debate the question of whether peasants, traders, craftspeople, or soldiers were most important in sustaining the power of rulers in the third or second millennium BCE, drawing on evidence from various societies of the time.

◗ Hypothesize what caused Aryans and Greek-speaking peoples to move into India and the eastern Mediterranean. *In what ways may these migrations be seen as a part of the pattern of movement of all Indo-European peoples? Should these movements be called a "chariot revolution"?*

Grades 9-12

◗ *If you were a historian studying an early society, what features of that society would lead you to label it "patriarchal"? What evidence would you expect to find that would support such a label? Which of the societies of the third and second millennia most, and which least, closely fits the model of a "patriarchy"? What specific differences between them lead you to this conclusion?*

◗ Choose a city of the third or second millennium, and, taking conditions at the time into account, construct a convincing proposal to submit to the ruler in favor of abandoning the use of forced labor and freeing all slaves. Then craft the arguments most like to be used by those wishing to convince the ruler to reject your proposal. *What part did political, social, religious and ethical ideas play in the arguments for and against?*

◗ Compare the lives of women of the upper and lower classes, of men of the upper and lower classes, and of men and women of the same class in Mesopotamia or in Egypt during a particular period of time. *Did social class or gender make the greater difference in the lives of people at the time?*

◗ Construct maps of successive periods during the third and second millennium, showing the location of agricultural populations and of cities. *What evidence is there during this period for increasingly dense populations? How well do your maps support a hypothesis of accelerated population growth? What other evidence would support such a hypothesis?*

◗ Construct a grid with the various types of society such as hunter-gatherer, pastoral nomad, neolithic agricultural, and urban civilization along one axis, and categories such as government, social classes, methods of food and tool production, religious beliefs, and art forms along the other axis. Fill in the boxes of the grid, drawing on historical information of the third and second millennia BCE. *Which of the categories serves most clearly to distinguish the various types of society from each other?*

◗ Create parallel accounts, based on historical information, of pastoral peoples' reasons for conflict with agrarian societies, and vice versa. *What reasons were there for mutual dependence in spite of reasons for conflict?*

◗ Drawing on historical information, construct a list of the characteristic features of pastoral nomadism. *What archaeological remains would lead the investigator of a site to conclude that those who had lived there were pastoral nomads? What remains would lead the investigator to question such an identification? What remains would suggest the site almost certainly could not have been occupied by nomad pastoralists?* Explain your reasoning.

ERA 3

Classical Traditions, Major Religions, and Giant Empires, 1000 BCE-300 CE

Giving Shape to World History

By 1000 BCE urban civilizations of the Eastern Hemisphere were no longer confined to a few irrigated river plains. World population was growing, interregional trade networks were expanding, and towns and cities were appearing where only farming villages or nomad camps had existed before. Iron-making technology had increasing impact on economy and society. Contacts among diverse societies of Eurasia and Africa were intensifying, and these had profound consequences in the period from 1000 BCE to 300 CE. The pace of change was quickening in the Americas as well. If we stand back far enough to take in the global scene, three large-scale patterns of change stand out. These developments can be woven through the study of particular regions and societies as presented in Standards 1-5, below.

▶ **Classical Civilizations Defined:** The civilizations of the irrigated river valleys were spreading to adjacent regions, and new centers of urban life and political power were appearing in rain-watered lands. Several civilizations were attaining their classical definitions, that is, they were developing institutions, systems of thought, and cultural styles that would influence neighboring peoples and endure for centuries.

▶ **Major Religions Emerge:** Judaism, Christianity, Buddhism, Brahmanism/ Hinduism, Confucianism, and Daoism all emerged in this period as systems of belief capable of stabilizing and enriching human relations across much of the world. Each of these religions united peoples of diverse political and ethnic identities. Religions also, often enough, divided groups into hostile camps and gave legitimacy to war or social repression.

▶ **Giant Empires Appear:** Multi-ethnic empires became bigger than ever before and royal bureaucracies more effective at organizing and taxing ordinary people in the interests of the state. Empire building in this era also created much larger spheres of economic and cultural interaction. Near the end of the period the Roman and Han empires together embraced a huge portion of the hemisphere, and caravans and ships were relaying goods from one extremity of Eurasia to the other.

Why Study This Era?

▶ The classical civilizations of this age established institutions and defined values and styles that endured for many centuries and that continue to influence our lives today.

▶ Six of the world's major faiths and ethical systems emerged in this period and set forth their fundamental teachings.

▶ Africa and Eurasia together moved in the direction of forming a single world of human interchange in this era as a result of trade, migrations, empire-building, missionary activity, and the diffusion of skills and ideas. These interactions had profound consequences for all the major civilizations and all subsequent periods of world history.

▶ This was a formative era for many fundamental institutions and ideas in world history, such as universalist religion, monotheism, the bureaucratic empire, the city-state, and the relation of technology to social change. Students' explorations in the social sciences, literature, and contemporary affairs will be enriched by understanding such basic concepts as these.

▶ This era presents rich opportunities for students to compare empires, religions, social systems, art styles, and other aspects of the past, thus sharpening their understanding and appreciation of the varieties of human experience.

Olmec stone head, Mexico

Essay

From the Axial Age to the New Age:
Religion as a Dynamic of World History*

by Carlton H. Tucker

Historians have long recognized the pivotal role of religion in the study of world history from prehistory to contemporary times. The following article describes the course of study the author initiated at San Francisco University High School. The class focuses on religion as the central organizing principle for exploring cultural transformation, interaction, and diffusion. The author includes a detailed description of the course, including recommended texts and thinking skills.

Carlton Hayes Tucker is a veteran high school history teacher and currently Head of Upper School at Princeton Day School. He has traveled extensively in China and India.

From the paleolithic to the neolithic age and from the Axial Age to the New Age, religion has been a key dimension of human societies. Thus, it should be essential to the teaching of a World history course, particularly at the precollegiate level. Often World historians, such as William McNeill and Leften Stavrianos, have posed other dynamics of World history such as trade and technology, but religion needs to be an integral part of any such course. If history is the study of change and continuity of human societies and ecological systems over time, religion has helped preserve and sustain coherence of societies, maintain connection between civilizations, provide a sense of human progression, induce change—renewal, regeneration, transformation—in cultures, and render insights into the human, natural and supernatural worlds.

The thinking and behavior of both individuals and civilizations are often shaped by religious beliefs and values, creating what might be termed a worldview. History, our own nation's pluralism, and contemporary events provide ample evidence that religion is a significant cultural value and powerful motivating force. Needless to say, religion has also inspired much of the world's beautiful art, architecture, literature, and music.

If one assumes that history attempts to make the present intelligent, and without being a Whig historian, one need only look at recent events to see the importance of religion in understanding contemporary affairs. A recent picture and caption in the New York Times, highlighting a rarely practiced ritual from Jainism, "a pacifist religion that arose in the sixth century BCE as an offshoot of Hinduism," begged for a World history context with a religious explanation. Another example is the meeting of the Parliament of the World's Religions in 1993, commemorating a similar meeting at the Chicago World's Fair a century ago, which launched the serious system study of world religions in the West. Lastly, one can city an article in the *New York Times*, entitled, "Holiday Dilemma at Schools: Is That a Legal Decoration" that raised questions about the attempt of the United States to accommodate various religious traditions at the Christmas holiday season.

For students to have any understanding of contemporary religious conflicts, which range from Bosnia and Northern Ireland in the West to India and East Timor in the East, a historical perspective, which includes the religious dimension, is paramount. With the ending of the Cold War, new paradigms in which religion figures prominently are emerging to explain foreign affairs. Harvard's Samuel P. Huntington predicts that the next "clash of civilizations" will be the world conflict of the West and the Islamic world. This is parallel to University of

*Reprinted from *The History Teacher*, Vol. 27, No. 4 (Aug. 1994), pp. 449-464.

California, Santa Barbara's Mark Juergensmeyer's "new cold war," which he feels will involve a confrontation between the zealots—religious fundamentalists—and Western secular societies. Thus, to encourage a broader historical understanding of complex current events we need a deeper sensitivity to the role of religion. In doing this it is important to pose key questions to students.

The educational reformer, Theodore Sizer, has proposed that schools in general and teachers in particular raise the essential questions of their discipline. For religion in World history one might have to begin with the basics: "What is religion? How did it originate? What does religion have to do with family, aging, death?" A study of religion in World history would definitely advance such major historical questions as to whether religion played a role in the rise of science, capitalism, and individualism in the West, or whether Confucianism is a religion or not. Moreover, this type of study would pride some other essential understandings for American high school students, whether it be artistic renderings of religious figures, or political concepts such as theocracy, religious law, and divine right/heavenly mandate, or economic concepts such as usury.

There are a few models for the incorporation of religion into World history. For one historian, the same central question is asked for almost all civilizations, "What can I do to be saved?" A World history course in this case would explore how each of these civilizations has answer this fundamental question. This represents what might be termed the constant theme approach. While perhaps the phrasing of this particular question indicates a western conceptual framework, it raises the question about similarities and differences among religions. Some students of religion believe there is a transcendent unity to all religions, some see the cultural and specific distinctions, while still a third group sees some combination, like a mosaic of elements of unity and distinction. Even with this debate about the particular or universal nature of religion, this thematic approach provides a useful comparative methods.

Another innovative thematic approach, has been utilized by Kevin Reilly in his textbook, *The West and the World*. Here such thought-provoking themes are presented as "Age and Family: Religion and Cultural Change," "Violence and Vengeance: Religion and the State," and "Ecology and Theology: Religion and Science." Reilly's companion book of readings also helps elucidate these themes. Steve Gosch has also collaborated on a book of documents, which has a section devoted to religion among the arrange "topical contents."

My own approach is perhaps more eclectic, borrowing from all the World historians, while still working within a somewhat traditional paradigm. The World history course that I formerly taught for a decade until this year at San Francisco University High School is a self-designed, two-semester course with a common syllabus and a series of introductory lectures; it has seven class sections and four teachers. The course loosely follows the California framework for history and social studies, particularly with regard to religion. Also, the course satisfies the newly instituted, entrance requirement to the University of California system, namely a year's study of World history, culture and geography.

In this course, there are six major units, beginning with prehistory and paleolithic times, and continuing through to contemporary cultures. Focusing exclusively on the African-Eurasian landmasses, the course selects major "golden ages" of particular civilizations and examines the process of their initial development and the later cultural diffusion. The course is both thematic and comparative in orientation but moves through historical time in a conceptual "post-holing," rather than in an actual chronological manner. Though comprehensive, the goal of the course is not maximum coverage. We choose key facets of a historical period that raise questions, challenges, or problems, as well as illustrating archetypal patterns of development. Comparisons are made of major civilization as a whole, often using religion as the key factor. While there are compromises and choices made, the course has its own integrity, combining a World history, World cultures, and World religions course. In different semesters the course has been complemented by interdisciplinary connections with the biology, English, art, or community service programs.

The course is nevertheless committed to using religion as the main organizing principle. This commitment is ensured by the fact that the only survey textbook that we use throughout the entire year is devoted to religion, Living Religions. Generally using a single history textbook is problematic, especially for high school freshmen, but we have found that this book is an exception. Students are fascinated by different religions, various worldviews, and elaborate rituals. Nevertheless, because of students' general antipathy for textbooks, my colleagues and I decided to use only one book per unit, supplemented with a reader of primary and secondary sources, which we compiled ourselves. (See course outline.) This reader helps provide the World history context as well as reinforcing this commitment to understanding religion's role in World history. This commitment is also ensured by the questions asked, specifically on semester examinations, and the journals which the students keep. These journals are almost exclusively devoted to having students find news articles about the religion we are studying and reflect and comment on it based on the reading.

As the title of the text, *Living Religions*, indicates, it offers more of a contemporary orientation than a history of World religions. It nevertheless serves to ground students in the basic tenets of the major faiths of the world. Its weakness is its strength in that it captures the essence of the religion, highlighting the basic developments of each, but not giving an extensive analysis of its historical role. The general structure of the book, beginning with indigenous sacred ways and moving from non-Western to Western religions, might also be another model for a World historical inquiry.

Our approach to religion is not theological, but rather phenomenological and historical, with a particular emphasis on the cultural, anthropological, and sociological aspects of tradition. Our working assumption is that religion is seen as a belief system that informs and shapes a culture, which in turn establishes a certain worldview. Religion is also more than just a worldview; it has an important spiritual dimension as well. One World historian even describes religion as "expressing the inexpressible...an encounter with the numinous—divine power...a sense of the presence of something 'wholly other,' something totally different in kind from all the material realities of everyday living." However, in order to express this sometimes indescribable experience, one has had to turn to metaphors. This has led, however, to religious discourse moving from "the level of the universal down to the historically conditioned realities of a particular time and place."

The first semester of the course examines three historical developments: precivilization—paleolithic to neolithic age of cultures, early civilization (neolithic to 1000 BCE), and the ancient, classical civilizations of Hellenic and Hellenistic worlds (1000 BCE to 100 CE). The spring term explores three Asian civilizations: Hindu Indian in South Asia, Confucian and Buddhist China in East Asia, and the Jewish-Christian-Islamic Mediterranean world in West Eurasia. This format introduces students to the people, religious cultures, and historical events at the dawn of, and throughout the development of, the major Western and non-Western civilizations. Religion is the central organizing principle for this exploration of cultural transformation, renewal, interaction, and diffusion. The religious dimension serves to inform the students about various religious experiences and worldviews, cultural values and diffusion, civilizational tensions and progression. The course also provides the sense of historical continuity; it specifically exposes students to the religious people, ideas, and teachings that became enduring influences in World religious-thought systems across the centuries to the present day.

We begin the course with an examination of paleolithic to neolithic cultures, using a case study approach specifically looking at one culture, the BaMbuti tribe, "the Pygmies," of the African rainforest. Their culture is both historical and contemporary, from which we extract generalizations about indigenous peoples and cultures. While this approach is not without its problems, it nevertheless is useful, practical, and almost necessary for ninth graders. Two assumptions are made with this approach. First is that indigenous peoples had and, in fact still do have a religious worldview; and second, that there are some similarities between these ancient tribal peoples and other indigenous peoples, particularly with regard to religious ways. There are important questions and debates about these assumptions. On the one hand, there is the position of Carl Jung, who has asserted that "all primitive societies have always had religion." Then there are World historians, such as Hugh Thomas, who raise doubts: "naturally, there is no certainty that there was religion, yet it is easy to imaging hunting men enjoying a primitive worship of sun and moon...." However, we prefer to follow Anthony Esler's argument: "there is at least some evidence that some sort of supernatural belief—the seeds of religion—existed as far back as 100,000 BCE. We conclude this section with an investigation of the influence of the neolithic revolution on the religious dimensions of early civilized humans.

In the next unit, we focus on the ancient riverine civilizations of Mesopotamia and Egypt. Here, the students explore the relationship of religion to the environment, specifically the Tigris-Euphrates and Nile rivers. There are also comparisons made between Egyptians and Mesopotamian views of religion. Students become acquainted with such concepts as theocracy and priestly classes; furthermore, they see the architectural manifestations of religious beliefs in these civilizations with the ziggurats and pyramids. An important context for understanding the nature of this religious experience is provided by one World historian when he said, "if the religious vision that resulted seems strange to us, it is perhaps safer to attribute the differences to the civilization that shaped that vision, rather than to any crucial difference in the religious experience itself." In addition to general historical background reading, the students read the *Epic of Gilgamesh* to give a Mesopotamian worldview and to compare the Mesopotamian flood story with the later Biblical one. This is in part to anticipate the rise from this geographic area of one of the world's first universal faiths, Judaism, "a religion independent (however) of an geographic or cultural focus." In further anticipation of Judaism as well as in preparation for comparing various views of life after death students read excerpts from the Egyptian *Book of the Dead*. Finally, anyone familiar with the 104th Psalm in the Hebrew Scriptures will have no trouble recognizing its antecedent in the Song to Aton, during Ikhnaton's reign.

The last unit of the first semester is an investigation of the ancient classical civilization of the Hellenic and Hellenistic worlds (1000 BCE to 100 CE). As most historians would agree, religion in classical Greece was an integral part of polis life and accordingly affected every aspect of that life. It was evident everywhere, in mythology, art, architecture, literature, rituals, and ceremonies. The Greeks, however, didn't feel that their sole human existence was to be slavishly dutiful to their religious nature. Along with the extraordinary florescence of religious expression the students explore the rise of rational philosophical thought.

In studying this classical period, we use Karl Jaspers' model of the Axial Age, a time from ca 600 BCE to 600 CE in which many of the world's great religions and/or philosophical thinkers arose. This was a moment on a grand scale and a historical breakthrough from earlier traditional religions. Perhaps no other era in World history has contributed so much to spiritual and rational thought as this time period with these great traditions—the Hellenic Platonists and the Hebrew prophets, Persia's Zoroaster and India's Buddha and Mahavira (Jainism), China's Confucius and Lao Tzu, all arose during this period. Why and how this occurred are fascinating questions for World historians to investigate. This unifying period of World history and World religions is foundational for later unity, development, and diffusion. In fact, this unique period, in and of itself, prides a wonderful, tripartite model for examining World history: 1) a foundational moment for a civilization inspired by religion; 2) the unfolding of religion and its infusion into a civilization; 3) the diffusion of the religion and civilization. In this unit we invite students to take an artistic license with history by having them develop, through role playing, imaginary dialogues among or between such religious luminaries and historical contemporaries as Socrates, Jesus, Zoroaster, Buddha, and Confucius.

There are many implications of the Axial Age perhaps for a better understanding of today's contemporary, "New Age" world. As one popular World history text states,

> the late twentieth century is reminiscent of the initial encounter of the West and East in the Hellenistic Age. Then, the rationalistic, humanistic Greeks encountered the eastern mystery religions and were profoundly influenced by them. Now, various strains of mystical thought again appeared from the East and from "primitive" peoples. It could be said that the non-Western world was providing intellectual repayment for the powerful secular ideologies it had borrowed in the nineteenth century.

Religion does go hand-in-hand with Hellenic rationality. Fordham University professor, Ewert Cousins goes a step further, however. He calls the contemporary age "the second Axial Age." Whereas the first Axial Age was an emergent moment of these classical religious traditions, the second one—the contemporary age—is another breakthrough moment because of the meeting of World religions on such a vast scale. As a result of this meeting, traditional religions themselves are changing through their response to each other and to the challenge of the global environment crisis.

Even when one explores the major Hellenic inter-civilizational conflict with the Persians, one has the opportunity to introduce the religious culture behind the Persian empire—Zoroastrianism. An important World history question for students is why this religion didn't circle the world. One would think that a religion which placed so high a value on the individual, so logically separated good from evil, and saw a symbiotic relationship with God would not remain almost exclusively a Persian possession and privilege.

As part of this Axial Age, the classical Hellenic era and the expansive Hellenistic age also serve as models for examining other civilizations' developments, both toward a classical stage and then toward the process of cultural diffuison. This model of analysis anticipates many of the other World religions and their development and diffusion throughout the Eurasian landmass. These included Buddhism, Confucianism, Christianity, and much later Islam. Furthermore, the campaigns of Alexander the Great helped bring about a significant Hellenic influence in the artistic renderings of the Buddha.

It is actually with Alexander the Great, as a personification of cultural diffusion across the Eurasian landmass, that we end one semester and begin another. This concept of the Axial Age also links the two semesters of the course. Here again, we explore one of the great schisms of history which occurred in the sixth century BCE. During this time religious reformations challenged age-old religious and social systems previously accepted in Eurasia. Both Buddhism in Indian and Confucianism in China emerged and had profound impacts on their respective civilizations, and later on others. In order for students to appreciate the significant effect of these religious traditions, it is necessary to establish the historical and cultural setting for both.

Thus, in the first unit of the spring semester we examine the ancient, classical civilization of India, with a major focus on Hinduism. It is important to begin with the historical background of the development of Hinduism as one of the first religions with an established set of "scriptures." A natural comparison might be between these "peoples of the book" and others, such as the Hebrews. At the same time, however, Indian civilization is also rich in oral traditions. One major goal of this unit is to explore the religious ideas, cultural values, and worldviews as expressed in the great epic, The Ramayana. Through close textual reading, dramatic performances, and art work, the students may begin to understand how central this epic has been in the development of Indian civilization. We also explore some of the reasons that might have led to the religious reformation and cultural transformation of the Hindu Indian worldview by Buddhism. Buddhism then becomes our focus, both for an understanding of the religious and civilizational dimensions and for its trans-civilization linkage—indeed its Hellenistic quality.

The biography of the Buddha's life is central to understanding the basis of this religious tradition. Two of the key questions that are also explored are why Buddhism no longer exists in India and how and why it was transmitted to other cultures. Or phrased differently, what characteristics about either the religion or the new cultures allowed it to be so transportable and to develop elsewhere? Conversely, why did it leave India and not become a central part of its religiously heterogeneous civilization? Generally, some of the most lively class discussions occur about the religious dimensions and worldview of Buddhism. It is here that we try to make some appropriate intellectual connections to the students' community service work. The biography of the Buddha resonates win what students view and experience as some of the social ills of the contemporary world. This experiential component of community service has its own philosophical integrity. However, linking it with another worldview might help provide a context for the students' own questions about their community service experiences, as well as about the Buddhist tradition itself.

Similar to the Hellenic civilization's rise to a classical stage, we analyze the rise of the Indian civilization to one of its classical stages, the Gupta era (300-500 CE). Just as the Hellenistic tradition helped create artistic renderings of Buddhism, the religion itself also inspired wonderful art. In fact, some of the best surviving Gupta era sculptures and paintings are Buddhist inspired in the Ajanta and Ellora caves. Within India some other areas of religion that might be worth including in a World history survey are the role of Ashoka and his proclamation of religious tolerance, the intriguing *bhakti* devotional movements, and the influence of Jainism. My survey course is not able to include these areas, however. At this stage of the survey and at this time of the year, the course turns next to China.

It is through the dynamics of trade, transportation, and technology that we move geographically along the silk road from the Indian to Chinese civilizations. These trade routes, which were both overland and by sea, connected not just India and China but actually the whole Eurasian landmass. Material exchange and cultural borrowing became lively activities along these trade routes. It is during the Axial Age that these routes also fostered the diffusion of religious ideas, particularly Buddhism from India to China. During this section of the course, while studying Buddhism's migration, students generate projects, particularly about the "silk roads," as they come to understand many aspects of cultural diffusion, Eurasian geography, and trade.

When presenting China, some World history surveys offer a comparative study of the Han and Roman civilizations. This is a fruitful model, given that they were historical contemporaries and, in fact, had cross-cultural interaction. Perhaps an equally interesting model might be to focus within Chinese civilization itself, particularly looking at the T'ang dynasty China (618-907 CE). This "golden age," cosmopolitan dynasty shifted the world's center of gravity to East Asia, and for the next millennium China was truly the "middle kingdom." During this almost "inter-civilizational" dynasty, three new religious traditions flourished in China—Buddhism, Nestorian Christianity, and Islam, which intermingled with both indigenous religions and cultural aspects. In fact, this "hellenic and hellenistic-like" dynasty also serves as an interesting laboratory for examining these Axial Age religious traditions blending within China, and later, for some religions and civilizations aspects diffusing throughout the Eurasian world. This diffusion process renewed the Han-Roman world axis, as well as established a new East Asian cultural axis, particularly with Japan and Korea.

It was during this legendary dynasty that trade, technology, and religion converged to produce the world's first printed material—the Buddhist sutras. Here, the oral aspects of Indian traditions give way to a Chinese civilization steeped in writing and the written textual tradition. This new printing technology, while enhancing the already strong commitment to the written word, made these new religious traditions more accessible in a written form. The great Chinese classic, *Journey to the West*, a fantastic, "Wizard of Oz"-pilgrimage-like story, highlights this process of returning to India to retrieve the great Buddhists texts and bring them to China. Now with this new technology there was a renewed emphasis placed on texts, and similar to other religious traditions, a strong hermeneutical tradition arose around the texts of both Confucianism and Buddhism.

Students studying China ought to focus on this textual tradition, and the World history survey should acknowledge this significant civilizational contribution. In the course, after preliminary background readings on geography, traditional family life, and the T'ang dynasty, students read selections from Confucius' *Analects*, *T'ang, Dynasty Stories*, and Buddhists scriptures. Each of these readings renders insights into the human, natural, and supernatural worlds, comprising part of the Chinese worldview. It was during the T'ang dynasty that Confucianism, having developed and flourished for a millennium, now underwent a regenerative press. This renewal and transformational process into a neo-Confucian tradition helps undermine the ever-present assumption that Confucianism is exclusively a static, monolithic system. Neo-Confucianism is very important to connect with the Chinese goal of moral governance, the implementation of a civil service examination system, and key Chinese cultural values. Some of the significant questions to ask in a World history class are: does Confucianism have a religious dimension and how would we compare Buddhism and Confucianism?

The last unit of the course returns along the silk routes to Western Eurasia. Here, we focus on the birth, development, and diffusion of the three monotheistic religions—Judaism, Christianity, and Islam. We begin by using very specific readings concerning the origins of each of these traditions, especially readings from sacred texts. Then we attempt to provide a context for these religions by using selective historical examples to illustrate their development and later diffusion throughout the Eurasian world. We focus more particularly on this diffusion process, drawing on Ross Dunn's model for analysis. He suggests that the major factors that have helped diffuses these major religions have been immigration, force, and missionary work.

This helpful model of analysis may be used with the diffusion of other religions, such as Buddhism.

A major assumption governs this last unit, however. Many of our students lack significant understanding about religion in general, and few have had any formal religious training. This course assumes that of the three religions—Judaism, Christianity, and Islam, they know the least about Islam. Thus, while providing an introductory overview of Judaism and Christianity, we focus more on Islam. Besides reading *Living Religions* and selections from the Koran, we read Elizabeth Fernea's *Guests of the Sheik*. While dealing with contemporary (1960s) village life in Iraq, it raises interesting issues, particularly about gender as well as historical continuity and change for Islam.

Our course ends here, but I have a few thoughts about other ways to approach this last unit. One model might be to compare the religious diffusion of Christianity through the roman empire with Islam's rapid spread across the Eurasian world in the eighth century CE. Also, a parallel model to the historical analysis of the T'ang dynasty would be to focus on medieval Spain and the interactions of the three religious traditions of Judaism, Christianity, and Islam. This model provides a different perspective on 1492 and the "Reconquista." The diffusion of Christianity to the new world and the impact of the Sephardic Jews would also be an interesting comparison. Another fruitful comparison between Christianity and Islam might be their different reactions to the fourteenth century Black Death.

In conclusion, for our own understanding of the contemporary age, which Cousins calls "the second Axial Age," it is necessary to look back into history. Even in the struggle for new paradigms for the post Cold-War world religion figures prominently. The World history survey course needs to consider religion as more than an integral part, but almost as a vehicle through which history moves. Religion has been both a stabilizing and destabilizing force throughout history; cultures and people have been transformed by and, in turn, have transformed religion. Certain religions have remained largely in one geographic area, while others have migrated to other parts of the world, bringing with them new characteristics, values, and worldviews. Much has been inspired by and created in the name of religion. Religion has both encourage d and retarded change in cultures. If one uses Karl Jaspers' very provocative "Axial Age" model then one can see some breakthrough moments in history. Whereas the first Axial Age was an emergent moment of these classical religious traditions, the second one—the contemporary Axial Age—is another breakthrough moment because of the meeting of world religions on such a vast scale. As a result of this meeting, traditional religions themselves are changing through their response to each other and to the challenge of the global environmental crisis. From the Axial Age to the New Age, religion has been a central focus, and the world history survey course can profitably reflect this dynamic.

Appendix A

The Course

History I introduces you to a chronological, cross cultural survey of the historical and cultural experiences of mankind. The study of indigenous peoples is followed by an examination of Ancient Near Eastern civilizations (Egypt and Mesopotamia), and then the classical civilizations of the West (Hellenic Greece) and East (Indian and China). Taught in a thematic manner, the course examines the roles of religion, law, social structure, geography, and climate in shaping cultural development and interaction. The course concludes with a study of three monotheistic religions: Judaism, Christianity, and Islam.

A variety of texts is used in this course, from a work of anthropology (*The Forest People*) to an epic poem (*The Epic of Gilgamesh*) to works of philosophy (Plato's *Apology* and *Crito*). Students are encouraged to appreciate the many different ways in which history can be learned.

History I is also integrated with the other core freshman courses—English I, Biology, Study Skills, and Community service—in both thematic content and the teaching of skills.

The Books

The Living Religions	Mary P. Fisher and Robert Luyster
The Forest People	Colin Turnbull
The Epic of Gilgamesh	Herbert Mason (trans.)
Classics of Western Thought	S. Nulle (ed.)
The *Apology* and *Crito*	Plato
History I Reader	History department (ed.)
The Ramayana	R. K. Narayan
The T'ang Dynasty Stories	Xang Xianyi and Glady Yang (trans.)
Guests of the Sheik	Elizabeth Fernea

The Cultures

1. *Prehistoric*
   Paleolithic to neolithic
   hunter-gathers
2. *Ancient Near East*
   Mesopotamia and Egypt
3. *Western Classical*
   Hellenic and Hellenistic Greece
4. *South Asian Civilization*
   Hindu India
5. *East Asian Civilization*
   Confucian and Buddhist China
6. *West Asian—Middle East*
   Judaism, Christianity, Islam

Themes/Approaches

Human, Environment, and Culture
(Anthropological/Sociological/
Religious)
Human, Civilization, and Religion
(Literary/Historical/Religious)
Human, Religion, and Politics
(Historical/Religious/Philosophical)
Human and Religion
(Literary/Religious/Legal)
Human, Religion, and Law
(Literary/Religious/Legal)
Man, Woman, and Religion
(Literary/Religious)

The Skills

History I hopes to develop good habits of mind—study habits—in order for you to be a successful student at UHS. Some particular ones on which the course concentrates are:

1. Careful Reading
2. Clear and Organized Writing
3. Note-taking: both in class and in your reading
4. Articulate Speaking and Discussion Skills
5. Careful Listening
6. Organization and Concentration Skills
7. Research Skills
8. Map/Geography Skills

Appendix B:
An Example Showing How the Course Deals With India

<u>Week 1</u>	<u>February 8-12</u>	<u>Introduction to China</u>
Monday	February 8	Classes Begin (2nd Semester); introduce India, and read in class.
Wednesday	February 10	Geography of India. Slide-lecture Introduction. Read *History I Reader*, pp. 1-17; **Terms:** Ganges River, Brahmaputra River, Indus River, monsoon, Sanskrit, Dravidian. *Write:* 5 generalizations about the geography and culture of India.
Thursday	February 11	Hinduism: Read *Living Religions*, pp. 58-65; *Reader*, pp. 17-22. **Terms:** Mohenjo-Daro, Harrappan Civilization, Aryans, Dravidians, Siva, Vedas, Rig Veda, Brahman (the Concept), Sanskrit, Vishnu, 5 castes.
Friday	February 12	Later Hinduism: Read *Living Religions*, pp. 65-74; In class, "Karma." **Terms:** Upanishads, atman, reincarnation, karma, dharma, samsara, moksha, puranas, Ramayana, Mahabharata, Bhagavad-Gita, bhakti, yuga, Kali, Yuga, Krishna, maya.
<u>Week 2</u>	<u>February 15-19</u>	<u>India's Golden Age and Castle System</u>
Monday	February 15	No School. Presidents' Holiday
Wednesday	February 17	India's Golden Age: Gupta Empire. Read in *Reader*, pp. 23-28. In class collect questions for the Swami.
Thursday	February 18	Caste System, Read in *Reader*, pp. 29-35; 45-48, "Dharma of Kings and Tailors." **Terms:** varna, jati, names of castes, dharma; 50 min. blocks:C.S.L.
Friday	February 19	Guest Lectures in L-4 by Swami Prabudhandanda, S. F. Vendanta Society. read in *Reader*, pp. 48-53; "Maya" and "Parade of the Ants."
<u>Week 3</u>	<u>February 22-26</u>	<u>Women in India: "Dadi" and Ramayana</u>
Monday	February 22	QUIZ on key terms in Hinduism
Wednesday	February 24	Swami, "Maya," "Parade of the Ants" discussion. Work on <u>Journal</u>.
Thursday	February 25	Meet in L-4. *Film, "Dadi."* Read in *Reader*, pp. 36-39; Do Journal. Identify the main tensions in a Hindu joint-family, especially for women.
Friday	February 26	Ramayana: Read Introduction, Prologue and Chap. 1. <u>Journal due</u>. Question: Why is this chapter titled "Initiation"?

<u>Week 4</u>	<u>March 1-5</u>	<u>Ramayana</u>
Monday	March 1	Marriage of Rama and Sita. Read *Ramayana*, chpt. 2
Wednesday	March 3	Moral "dharmatic" dilemmas. Read *Ramayana*, chpt. 3. Write: What dilemmas are present in this chapter?
Thursday	March 4	Rama in love and Sita stolen. Read *Ramayana*, chpts. 4-5.
Friday	March 5	More moral "dharmatic" dilemmas. Read *Ramayana*, chpts. 6-7. Question: Why did Rama kill Vali? Introduce Essay.
<u>Week 1</u>	<u>February 8-12</u>	**Introduction to China**
Monday	March 8	Siege of Lanka. Read *Ramayana*, chpts 8-11. Question: Did Kumbakarna or Vibishana follow dharma?
Wednesday	March 10	Rama's Victory. Finish *Ramayana*, chpts. 12-14. Begin working on essay
Thursday	March 11	Work on *Ramayana* essay. Special Event: Classical Indian Dance Performance in Auditorium-1 pm.
Friday	March 12	*Ramayana* essay due.

Coptic Christian Church, Cairo, Egypt. Photo by Ross Dunn

Sample Student Activities

> **I.** *Innovation and change from 1000 to 600 BCE: horses, ships, iron, and monotheistic faith.*

A. State-building, trade, and migrations that led to increasingly complex interrelations among peoples of the Mediterranean and Southwest Asia.

Grades 5-6

● Locate on a map of the Mediterranean Sea the major Phoenician port cities and colonies such as Carthage, and show the trade routes that linked these cities. *Why did the Phoenicians establish cities throughout the Mediterranean? With whom did they trade? What items were traded?*

● Make a relief map showing the mountainous Greek peninsula and the major Greek city-states. *How did geography influence the location and development of city-states?*

● Construct a model or describe a typical Greek polis, including such features as an acropolis, the temple of the patron deity, gymnasium, and agora. Construct a dialogue with a friend in another city, each of you describing your polis and why it is so important to you.

Grades 7-8

● Explain the importance of iron weapons and cavalry in the rise of the Assyrian empire. *What were the consequences of this new technology? How do the consequences compare to the consequences of adopting chariot warfare earlier?*

● Locate the Assyrian and New Babylonian empires on a map of Southwest Asia. *What are the geographic features of these two empires? Why were the river valleys so important to these empires?*

● Analyze Assyrian bas reliefs and answer the questions: *How do these depict hunting, warfare, and the use of weapons? What do these art forms and their subject matter tell us about Assyrian culture and society?*

● Write a manual for smiths wishing to change from bronze to iron technology, outlining differences in methods of obtaining and working the metals, advantages and disadvantages in making the change, and advice on how to increase demand among the smith's clients for products of the new technology.

● Create a series of maps showing the migration, settlements, and trade contacts of the Phoenicians during the second and first millennia BCE. *Who were the Phoenicians' rivals and enemies during this period? What contributed to the growth of Phoenician power?*

● Prepare a map showing the location of the important Greek city states and colonies established in the Black Sea, northern Africa, and the western Mediterranean basin. *Why did the Greeks establish colonies in the Mediterranean and Black Sea basins? Did these colonies together constitute a Greek empire?*

● Compare the Phoenician or Greek system of writing to Egyptian hieroglyphics and Mesopotamian cuneiform. *What were the underlying principles of the various systems? Which was easiest to learn, and why? What other systems of writing are known from this period?*

Grades 9-12

▶ Research the laws of Hammurabi and of lawmakers such as Draco and Solon. *How do their perspectives suggest differing views on the role of law in society? How did the differences in the societies they lived in influence their views?*

▶ Examine the early Phoenician, Greek, Hebrew, and Etruscan alphabets. *How would you account for similarities? What evidence can you give to support your argument?*

▶ As a 7th- or 6th-century BCE Greek tyrant, compose a proclamation justifying your rule to the inhabitants of the city.

▶ Debate the hypothesis that it was Assyrians' cruelty in war that was responsible for their rapid, successful take-over of the old centers of power such as Mesopotamia and Egypt. *What other factors contributed to Assyrian success?*

▶ Write an obituary for one of the famous statesmen of pre-classical Greece, such as Pisistratus, Solon, Draco, Cypselus, Cleomenes, or the legendary Lycurgus. *What characteristics and actions of these famous people were admired by their contemporaries? For which of their actions were they blamed and by whom?*

▶ Compare Greek city-states (such as Athens, Sparta, Corinth) in the pre-classical period with Sumerian city-states (such as Ur, Kish, Uruk) and with empires (such as the Minoan, Egyptian, Assyrian). *What were the distinctive characteristics of the Greek polis?*

▶ Explain the reasons for tension and conflict between social classes in Greek city-states in the 8th-6th centuries, using Athens and Sparta as case studies. *What different solutions to the tensions and conflict did the two city-states adopt?*

▶ Construct a chart comparing the different types of government in Greek city-states of the pre-classical era, and debate the advantages and disadvantages of each.

▶ Explain basic ideas of Afrocentric writers regarding the importance of ancient Egypt in world history. *In what ways have some classical historians challenged these ideas? Why did Afrocentric writings about the ancient Nile valley and Mediterranean region become subjects of public controversy in the U. S. in the 1980s and 1990s? What kinds of historical evidence have Afrocentric writers and their critics drawn on to support their cases?*

B. The emergence of Judaism and the historical significance of the Hebrew kingdoms.

Grades 5-6

▶ Construct a timeline tracing important periods in ancient Hebrew history from the earliest times through the Babylonian captivity. Illustrate the timeline with drawings depicting events in Hebrew history. *In which of the events you show did religion play an important part?*

▶ Construct a model of King Solomon's temple. *What are the central features of the temple complex? What is the role of the temple in Jewish history?* Compare Solomon's temple and a Greek temple of the same period. *What similarities do you see, and how would you explain them?*

▶ Read selections from the Hebrew Scriptures such as stories about the Creation, Noah, the Tower of Babel, Abraham, the Exodus, the Ten Commandments, David, and Daniel and the Lion's Den. Explain the ethical teachings shown in the stories and compare them to those you've studies in other ancient societies.

Grades 7-8

▸ Write an account describing the political and social structure of Israel during the reigns of Kings Saul, David, and Solomon. *What political role did the judges play? What were the reasons for discontent during the rule of King David? What were the foreign influences in the kingdom during Solomon's reign? Why did the kingdom split into the kingdoms of Israel and Judah?*

▸ Create a map showing the probably route of Hebrews escaping from Egypt, and their spread across Palestine until King Solomon's time. *What peoples did the Hebrews have to defeat in order to achieve Solomon's kingdom?*

▸ Role-play a Hebrew parent at the time of the Babylonian captivity explaining to your children the importance to them of their religion. *What would you tell them about oral and written accounts of their history and traditions?*

▸ Choose the person you feel was most important in Hebrew history between the times of Abraham and Solomon. Compose a brief biography, explaining why you feel your choice was good.

▸ Assume the role of a religiously observant Jewish man or woman and write a series of daily diary-entries including the Sabbath, noting each action from getting up to going to sleep that is prescribed by the Jewish religion. *What entries would you make about actions, feelings and thoughts that were influenced by your religious beliefs? How do Jewish religious prescriptions concerning women and men differ?*

Grades 9-12

▸ Read selections from the books of Ezra and Nehemiah and prepare a presentation explaining how the Hebrew people were able to preserve their identity during the Babylonian captivity. *What effect did the captivity have on the subsequent history of the people and their beliefs?*

▸ Read selections from the Hebrew Scriptures. Based on your reading, write an essay on Hebrew culture focusing on its ethical aspects. *What values are reflected in Hebrew prescriptions for personal behavior? In what ways did belief in monotheism support ethical behavior?*

▸ Trace the dispersion of Jewish communities on a map. Explain the reasons for and the consequences of the Hebrew diaspora. *What are the modern implications of the diaspora?*

▸ Chart the differences between the characteristics of Yahweh and his relationship to the Hebrew people on the one hand, and the characteristics of Southwest Asian nature deities and their relationship to their worshipers on the other. Construct a historical argument to account for the differences.

▸ Read selections from the Hebrew Scriptures, including the Torah and Psalms, and analyze basic teachings and practices of Judaism: its basis in ethical monotheism; its historic belief in the Covenant between God and the Jewish people; the role of prophecy; the Torah as the source of Judaism's beliefs, rituals, and laws; and the Torah's ethical injunction, "Do justice, love mercy, and walk humbly with thy God."

▸ Trace the changes in the political organization of the Hebrews from a loose confederation of nomadic tribes with the Ark of the Covenant as their focus, to the centralized territorial state under King Solomon. *What were the costs of the process?*

▸ Compare Jewish monotheism with Akhenaton's Atonism. *What did they have in common? What were the differences in the ideas about the deity, about the relationship between deity and worshipers, the ethical components of the religion, and the breadth of participation in the religion by the people?*

C. **How states developed in the upper Nile valley and Red Sea region and how iron technology contributed to the expansion of agricultural societies in Sub-Saharan Africa.**

Grades 5-6

▶ Locate Egypt and Kush on a map and draw in the geographic features that either assisted or hampered communication between these two kingdoms. Assume the role of a trader from Kush to Egypt and plan an itinerary for your voyage, allowing for the barriers you'll face.

▶ Analyze pictures of the pyramids in Kush. *What do these pyramids seem to suggest about the relationship between Egypt and Kush? What questions would you need to ask to find out whether the relationship suggested really did exist?*

▶ Assume the role of an iron smith in Kush and explain the process of making iron to a new king. *What uses of iron were most important in Kushite society?*

Grades 7-8

▶ Write an account of the Kushite conquest of Egypt from the point of view of both a Kushite and an Egyptian. *In what respects would two such accounts be most likely to differ?*

▶ Assume the role of an artist commissioned to commemorate the conquest of Egypt by the Kushites. Draw a series of pictorial representations of the conquest for a public building in Thebes, the city adopted by the victorious Kushites as their capital.

▶ Make a list of the goods traded between Egypt and Kush, and explain what favored and what hindered trade between them.

▶ Draw a map showing the physical geography of Africa and Eurasia. Locate on the map users of iron technology and centers of iron production from its beginnings to about 500 BCE, and hypothesize how each came to be such: by separate invention, conquest by iron users, trade, spread of ideas. *What evidence can you find to support your hypotheses?*

Grades 9-12

▶ Analyze the social and political consequences of economic contacts between Kush and Egypt.

▶ Debate the question: *Was Kush a cultural satellite of Egypt, a distinctive civilization in its own right, or both? What archaeological or other evidence might be used to argue either side of the question?*

▶ Evaluate current theories about the spread of iron technology in Sub-Saharan Africa. *By what routes and from where is the technology likely to have reached West Africa? What evidence might support the theory of independent development of iron technology in East Africa?*

▶ Analyze illustrations of Nok terra cotta figures and metal implements. *What can be inferred from these physical remains about the culture and society of the West African people who created them?*

▶ Brainstorm what kinds of archaeological or other evidence you might expect to find for the impact of foreign conquerors on a conquered society in the period on either side of about 1000 BCE. *Having looked at Egyptian sculpture, painting and architecture before and after the Assyrians' and the Kushites' conquests of Egypt, what can you infer about the impact of these conquests on Egypt? What other sources do you wish you could consult to answer this question, and why?*

D. How pastoral nomadic peoples of Central Asia began to play an important role in world history.

Grades 5-6

♦ Construct a map showing the location and range of pastoral nomadic peoples in the first millennium BCE. *How did nomadic groups travel and move their belongings and herds?*

♦ Create a story, a song, or a poem relating the importance of the horse to the pastoral nomadic peoples of Central Asia.

♦ Write a story from the perspective of an Eastern European village-dweller seeing a Scythian warrior, riding a horse, for the first time. *How can an encounter with something new affect one's view of the world?*

Grades 7-8

♦ Write an account of a day in the life of a pastoral nomadic person of Central Asia. *For which parts of your account did you have the most, and the least, abundant and accurate evidence? How would you account for the differences in the availability of evidence?*

♦ Label on a map of the Eastern Hemisphere the great chain of arid regions extending from the Sahara Desert to the Gobi Desert of China. *Where did major river valley civilizations exist in relation to this arid belt? How were human communities able to adapt to the environments of these desert and steppe lands? What was the relationship between peoples of the "steppe and the sown"?*

♦ Evaluate the importance of the horse in nomadic life including its use with the chariot, as a cavalry mount, and as a beast of burden. *How did the horse change life on the steppes?*

♦ Describe the technology involved in using the horse to pull vehicles, carry riders, and fight. *From where, and how early, are harness, bridle, bit, saddle, horse armor, stirrup, and so on known? Which of these is most important in using the horse for transport? Which for war?*

♦ Construct a chart comparing the domestication of the sheep and the horse in terms of the changes each produced in the lifestyle of nomad pastoralists. *In which areas of life was the difference between the kinds of changes the greatest?*

♦ Create one or more maps showing the movements and territorial extent of Scythians, Hsiung-nu and their immediate neighbors in the period of about 800-300 BCE. *What is known about both peaceful and warlike interactions between the nomads and their neighbors? What evidence is there for each?*

Grades 9-12

♦ Analyze drawings or pictures of remains in the royal Scythian tombs and research archaeological accounts to explain Scythian society and culture.

♦ Compare Herodotus's account in *The Histories* of a Scythian burial with archaeological evidence from the excavations of Scythian tombs. *What parts of Herodotus's documentary account are confirmed by the physical evidence? What are the advantages and disadvantages for a historian of verbal and of non-verbal evidence? Using both kinds of evidence, what can be inferred about life in Scythian society from the disposal of their dead?*

♦ Drawing on historical evidence, role-play a Scythian or Hsiung-nu leader giving advice to his son about what his behavior as leader should be towards members of his own tribe, other pastoral nomad groups, and settled agricultural peoples encountered in their wanderings. *What difficulties would have to be faced when trying to conquer (as opposed to raid) other nomads? Settlements of agriculturalists? Which would be easier, and why? What such conquests appear in the historical record?*

♦ Use Scythian and Hsiung-nu nomads as case studies to explain how the horse facilitated territorial expansion and changed leadership roles. *In what ways did leadership among pastoral nomads such as these differ from leadership in settled agricultural communities?*

♦ Construct a chart showing what pastoral nomadic peoples had to offer that was of value to major agrarian states and vice versa. Hypothesize under what circumstances reciprocal needs and wants would lead to economic interdependence and what other circumstances would lead to conflict. Find information about contacts such as those of the Hsiung-nu with China and assess how well it supports your hypotheses.

♦ Drawing on historical evidence, role-play a Chinese ruler threatened by the appearance of a large number of Hsiung-nu close to his borders. *What actions would you take? What resources could you mobilize? What weapons and tactics would you use? What would be your greatest strength and weakness?*

> **II.** *The emergence of Aegean civilization and how interrelations developed among peoples of the eastern Mediterranean and Southwest Asia, 600-200 BCE.*

A. The achievements and limitations of the democratic institutions that developed in Athens and other Aegean city-states.

Grades 5-6

♦ Assume the role of either a citizen, a merchant, a foreign resident, or a slave in both Athens and Sparta. Describe your life in each of these city-states. Compare the rights and responsibilities of a citizen in each city. After the class shares their findings, answer the question: *How did life differ depending on social class?*

♦ Construct a comparative chart that graphically depicts similarities and differences between Athenian democracy and the military aristocracy of Sparta.

♦ *If you were a woman in the 6th or 5th century BCE, would you rather have lived in Sparta or in Athens?* Give reasons based on historical evidence for your decision.

♦ Create a map of the Aegean area and depict each of the major Greek city-states. Delineate each city-state as to its form of government (democracy, oligarchy, tyranny, aristocracy, monarchy) by a symbol or color. *How many other Greek city-states followed the political lead of Athens or Sparta, and how many followed neither?*

♦ Participate in a debate between Athenians and Spartans (including those of different classes, men and women) on any of several issues: Should the right to vote be granted to women? Should slavery be abolished? Should the two city-states form an alliance to defend against foreign invasions? Take into consideration the values of your city-state as you debate.

Grades 7-8

♦ Prepare a chart listing the major political systems of Greek city-states in the 6th and 5th centuries BCE and explain the evolution of these governmental systems. *What are the advantages and disadvantages of each system?*

♦ Construct a chart showing the major changes in Athenian political organization from the initial monarchy to the forms under Solon and Cleisthenes. *What innovations did Cleisthenes make?*

◗ Drawing on historical evidence, describe the differences in the lives of citizens, resident foreigners (metics) and slaves in Athens, and of citizens, "dwellers about" (perioiki) and helots in Sparta. *If you were a citizen in the sixth or fifth century, would you have preferred to be a citizen of Athens or of Sparta? Why? What if you were legally free, but not a citizen? If you were unfree? If you were a woman? Would social class make a difference in your preference if you were female?*

◗ Describe the typical social roles that women had in Athenian society and women's rights under the law. Hypothesize why democracy was limited to males only. *What kinds of evidence would you look for to help support your hypotheses?*

◗ Compare how, and to what extent, the ideal of political equality was fulfilled in Athens and Sparta of the sixth and fifth centuries. *What about economic and social equality?*

◗ Analyze Pericles' *Funeral Oration* to discern Athenian values during the 5th century BCE. *In what ways and to what extent did daily life in classical Athens reflect these ideals?*

Grades 9-12

◗ Describe the Greek concept of the barbarian as set forth in the works of Aristotle and other writers, and explain the position of "barbarians" in Greek city-states. *Could a "barbarian" become a Greek? How could the Greek concept of "barbarian" provide a foundation for greater communication between Greeks and outsiders? What is ethnocentrism? Are all modern societies and nations ethnocentric to some degree?*

◗ Analyze selections from *The Republic*. Prepare a report on how Plato's ideal polis has influenced political thought in the modern world.

◗ Explain the social strata in Athens and Sparta in the 5th century BCE. Choose one of the two, and compare its social structure to that of another Greek city-state such as Corinth or Thebes. *How would you account for similarities and differences?*

◗ Draw evidence from Thucydides's *Melian Dialogue* to examine the concepts of political freedom, national security, and justice. Appraise Pericles's "Funeral Oration" from the perspective of a Melian following the Athenian conquest.

◗ Support or refute the statement: "Athens was the laboratory of democracy and democratic law."

◗ Construct a historical argument to explain why Sparta developed into a military aristocracy and Athens into a democracy.

◗ Read Athenian philosopher Plato's ideas about women as guardians in *The Republic* and/or his student Aristotle's ideas about women in his *Politics*. *To what extent, and in what ways, do the ideas about women in these passages support or contradict what is known from other sources about the realities of fourth- and fifth-century BCE women's lives in Athens? In Sparta? When there is conflicting evidence from different sources about conditions or events in the past, how do historians deal with the contradictions?*

B. The major cultural achievements of Greek civilization.

Grades 5-6

◗ Participate in a role-play of the trial of Socrates. *What does the story of Socrates tell us about his values?*

◗ Find local examples of art and architecture that reflect the influence of Classical Greece. Make drawings and label the features that show that influence.

◗ Study photographic evidence of Greek pottery and explain how the images on the pottery reflect life in ancient Greece. With this reference construct a replica of a piece of Greek pottery and illustrate this with scenes from life in your community. *How can art reflect culture and values?*

◗ Analyze illustrations of classical Greek sculpture and evaluate them for evidence of social ideals of manhood, womanhood, and athletic prowess.

◗ Compare representations of humans in Egyptian and in classical Greek art. *In what ways did each express the society in which it was produced?*

◗ Research and make a model of one of the seven wonders of the ancient world as described by the Greeks. *What does the selection of these achievements as "wonders" by the Greeks tell you of their values? What would you consider to be the "seven wonders of the modern world"? The "seven wonders of your neighborhood"?*

◗ Read or view a dramatic presentation of a Greek play, and create a mask that represents a certain character in the play. *What purposes do plays have for a society?*

Grades 7-8

◗ Read and compare several Greek myths using a source such as Charles and Rosalie Baker's *Myths and Legends of Mt. Olympus* or Ingri and Edgar Parin d'Aulaire's *Book of Greek Myths. How are gods and goddesses depicted in Greek mythology? What is anthropomorphism in relation to Greek mythology and how do Greeks and their gods and goddesses relate in these myths? How did Greek gods and goddesses compare to those of other societies you've studied?*

◗ Read selections from Greek dramatists such as Sophocles, Euripides, and Aeschylus and discuss what evidence they offer of ancient moral values and civic culture.

◗ Summarize the stories told about major women characters (such as Clytemnestra, Medea, Antigone, Lysistrata) by Greek dramatists and describe the kind of people these women are portrayed as being. *How accurately do Greek dramatists reflect Greek attitudes towards women known from other sources?*

◗ Drawing on information about the ideas of Greek philosophers such as Thales, Anaximander, Pythagoras, Democritus, explain what their views were about the shape, composition, and movement of the earth, and the development of living things. *In what ways can they be called scientists? Which later ideas about nature did they foreshadow?*

◗ Compare creation myths from Sumer, Egypt, Babylon, and Greece. *What images of the gods are presented in these myths? What human characteristics do they show? What similarities and differences in world view do these myths suggest?*

◗ Examine photographic and other evidences of Greek art and architecture and read selections from Greek literature to determine how the arts reflected cultural traditions and values.

Grades 9-12

◗ Present dramatic readings from selections of Greek tragedies and comedies, such as Sophocles's *Antigone* and Aristophanes's *The Clouds. What are the lessons transmitted through Greek tragedy and comedy? How does drama reflect values?*

◗ Compare Egyptian and Sumerian deities with the Greek gods and goddesses. Draw upon visual evidence of deities and humans as depicted in bas reliefs, statues, and monuments to discover how these societies saw themselves in relation to their gods and goddesses. *What do depictions of goddesses suggest about attitudes toward women? Is there other evidence in Egyptian, Sumerian, and Greek life to support inferences about attitudes of women based on their depiction of goddesses?*

‣ Read excerpts from the introductory sections of the works of Herodotus and Thucydides that reveal their methods as historians. *What would you praise or criticize about them as historians, and why?*

‣ Compare the ideas of Plato and of Aristotle about the most desirable form of government. *How closely did the government they considered the best resemble the one they themselves lived under?*

‣ Compose a volume retelling several myths from Greece on a common theme, such as those focusing on origins (the Titans, Uranus, Gaia and Kronos, the three races, Pandora, Deucalion); on relationships between male and female deities (Zeus, Hera, Athena, Demeter, Hades and Persephone); or story cycles connected with heroes such as Theseus, Odysseus, Achilles, Herakles. *What influences from outside Greece can be traced in Greek myths? To what extent, and in what ways, do the myths reflect the nature of Greek society and culture? How have Greek myths been incorporated into modern language, literature, and other forms of cultural expression?*

‣ Socrates was condemned to death on the charges that he had corrupted the youth, introduced religious innovations, and did not worship the gods of the state. *If you were the prosecutor, what evidence consistent with known facts could you present to substantiate your case? If you were arguing for the defense, what information would you want to present? What aspects of Socrates' teaching would not be covered during his trial on these grounds?*

C. The development of the Persian (Achaemenid) empire and the consequences of its conflicts with the Greeks.

Grades 5-6

‣ Create a map of the eastern Mediterranean and Aegean, and indicate the location of the major Greek city-states. Using colored pencils or other delineations, show the growth of the Persian state from the time of Cyrus I through the wars with Greece.

‣ Write a series of diary entries of a Persian warrior who fought in one of the Persian Wars, describing the events he witnessed and his feelings about the war. *How would a Persian's views of the wars have differed from that of a Greek warrior?*

‣ Create maps of the four famous battles in the Persian Wars—Marathon, Thermopylae, Salamis, and Plataea. Use different colors for the Spartans, the Athenians, and the Persians. Include a key to indicate what each color means. Use the maps to tell the story of the war.

‣ Write a letter from an Athenian woman to her husband fighting against the Persians, including a description of how people at "home" feel about the war and how it is affecting their lives. *How can the actions of people "at home" affect the conduct of a war being waged afar?*

Grades 7-8

‣ Devise a plan for the governing of an ethnically diverse empire such as that of the Persians. *How effectively did the Persians deal with specific problems related to the vast size of their empire?*

‣ Tell the story of the struggle between the Persians and Greeks from different perspectives. Use conflicts such as the battles of Marathon, Thermopylae, or Salamis. *How were Greeks and Persians likely to have differed in telling this story?*

‣ Compare and contrast the basic ideas and teachings of Zoroastrianism with religious beliefs of the Greeks, Hebrews, and Egyptians.

▶ Read accounts of the Persian Wars such as Jill Paton Walsh's *Persian Gold* and *Crossing to Salamis. Based on these accounts and others, what are we able to infer about the changes these wars wrought on the lives of the peoples of the Persian empire? Of Greece?*

▶ Brainstorm all the things you can think of that contributed to the failure of the Persians to conquer the Greeks. *What events and conditions contributed most decisively to Greek victory? If you were to pick the single most decisive factor, what would you pick? Why?*

Grades 9-12

▶ Construct a map showing the arrival of Indo-European speakers in Iran, and the extent of Cyrus the Great's, Darius's, and Xerxes's empires at various periods of time. *What peoples did each conquer? What was the internal organization of their empire like? How did the Persian Empire compare with the earlier Assyrian and Babylonian ones?*

▶ Read selections from Herodotus's *History* describing key events of the Persian Wars. Debate the accuracy of his reports. *What might indicate a bias in Herodotus's story? What questions would you ask to help decide how reliable his account is?*

▶ Analyze various accounts and histories of Persian rule such as Herodotus and the Book of Esther. *To what extent did the Persians respect the cultural traditions and religious beliefs of peoples living within their empire?*

▶ Analyze the basic tenets of Zoroastrianism, the relationship of religion to political entity, and the place of religion in Persian society.

▶ Compare and contrast the Greek city-states' military organization with that of the Persians at the time of the Persian Wars. *In what ways did the political makeup of the two antagonists dictate their military organization? What were the overall strategies of these antagonists, and in what ways is this a reflection of their political and military organizations?*

▶ Debate the statement that "It was not so much Greek military superiority as Persian weakness and demoralization that caused the Persian defeat in these wars." *How were the Greek city-states able to defeat the Persian armies and navies?*

▶ Explain how the victories over Persia led to a restructuring of the Greek political balance, and ultimately, the ruinous internecine Peloponnesian Wars. *How do writers such as Thucydides explain the rise and fall of Athens and the Delian League? What connections can be made to the Persian Wars?*

D. Alexander of Macedon's conquests and the interregional character of Hellenistic society and culture.

Grades 5-6

▶ Retell the story of *The House of Pindar*, the Poet of Thebes. *How does the story portray Alexander?*

▶ Construct a map tracing the route of Alexander's army through the Persian Empire to India. Indicate major battles that his army fought and cities he founded. *How do Alexander's conquests compare in size to that of the original Persian Empire?*

▶ Assume the role of a soldier in Alexander's army and write a letter to a friend describing the peoples, sights, and events you encounter during your conquest of the Persian Empire.

▶ List Hellenistic achievements in astronomy and measurement of the earth. *How accurate were these early scientists?*

Grades 7-8

▶ Explain how Alexander of Macedon came to power and built a vast empire. *How did the career of Alexander's father, Philip II, pave the way for his imperial expansion? How did Alexander's empire differ from that of the earlier Assyrian, Egyptian, and Persian empires? What methods did Alexander use to unite his empire?*

▶ As one of Alexander's successors—Seleucus, Antigonus, or Ptolemy—develop a dialogue to justify ruling part of Alexander's empire.

▶ Analyze city building and architecture to assess the extent of Greek and Macedonian influence in southwest Asia and Egypt after the conquests of Alexander.

▶ Draw up a balance sheet, assessing the benefits and costs of Alexander's conquests.

▶ Examine images of the Buddha from Gandharan school of art in India. *What evidence is there of Persian or Greek influences on these images?*

Grades 9-12

▶ Draw from the teachings of Socrates, Zeno, Epicurus, and other Greek philosophers to debate the question: *What makes for a "good life"?*

▶ Research the relationships between men and women during the Hellenistic era. *What new opportunities were open to women during this period?*

▶ Construct an explanation of the cultural diffusion of art and architecture through assimilation, conquest, migration, and trade. *How did Hellenistic themes influence art and architecture in northwest India or the western Mediterranean?*

▶ Analyze the major achievements of Hellenistic mathematics, science, and philosophy. In an oral report or written essay, explain the significance of these achievements. *What were Indian contributions? What impact have these achievements had on the modern world?*

▶ Examine evidence from Indian, Egyptian and Middle Eastern cultures of the first (last?) three centuries CE and identify Hellenistic influences (for example, in Egyptian depictions of the Zodiac). *Do you think peoples of these other lands welcomed or resisted such influences?*

▶ Research Hellenistic religions. Assess the impact of Greek thought and language on Judaism and other religions in this period.

▶ Explain the achievements in mathematics and measurement of such Hellenistic scientists as Euclid, Archimedes, Eratosthenes. *In what ways did their interests and methods differ from those of pre-Socratic Greek philosophers? From Plato and Aristotle?*

▶ Draw up a timeline showing the most significant of Alexander's actions in his empire. *On what bases did you decide which of his actions were most significant?*

III. *How major religions and large-scale empires arose in the Mediterranean basin, China, and India, 500 BCE-300 CE.*

A. The causes and consequences of the unification of the Mediterranean basin under Roman rule.

Grades 5-6

▶ Retell the legends of the founding and early history of Rome such as the fable of Romulus and stories from the *Aeneid*. *What do legends tell us about the beliefs and values of the ancient Romans? How do historians use myths and legends in describing ancient civilizations?*

▶ Draw a map locating the different ethnic groups and city-states of the Italian peninsula ca. 509 BCE. *Who were the Etruscans and what influence did they have in early Roman history? Where were the Greek settlements located? What influence did they have on the Latins?*

▶ Draw on evidence from David Macaulay's *City* to reconstruct a typical Roman city and explain the function of the public areas and buildings. Include diagrams of Roman residences and sketches of Roman aqueducts. Find examples of public buildings that use Roman architectural styles. Compare a Roman city to a modern U.S. city. *How are these cities different and similar?*

▶ Develop short biographies and sketches of famous Romans such as Cincinnatus, Scipio Africanus, Tiberius Gracchus, Cicero, Julius Caesar, Augustus, Nero, Marcus Aurelius, and Constantine for a class magazine entitled, "Roman Stars." *What do the lives of these famous people tell about Roman values? What changes in values can be determined from the early Republic to the last years of the empire?*

▶ Draw on stories such as Ellis Dillon's *Rome under the Emperors* and Chelsea Yarbro's *Locadio's Apprentice* to write diary entries describing what life was like for common people living in Rome and Pompeii.

Grades 7-8

▶ Create a series of maps showing the location of Etruscan, Roman, Phoenician, and Greek settlements in the eighth to sixth centuries BCE. *What relationships of trade, conquest, rivalry, borrowing, influence did the Etruscans have with these peoples? What other areas did the Etruscans trade with by land and by sea?*

▶ Develop an account reporting the conclusion of the Punic Wars. Include interviews with important participants, a summary of each war, and an explanation of the importance of these wars to Rome.

▶ Read selections from Plutarch's *Lives of Famous Greeks and Romans* on Tiberius and Gaius Gracchus. *What were the reforms championed by the Gracchi? How did these measures arouse hostility among the great landowners? How did the Senate deal with the Gracchi brothers?*

▶ Construct a comparative study of the legal and social positions of women in different classes in Rome and the earlier Greek city-states. Prepare a debate between a Roman woman and one from Periclean Athens in which they discuss their positions in society.

▶ Develop a set of overlay transparencies or charts to describe the major phases of Roman expansion.

▶ Use information from sources such as Rosemary Sutcliff's *Song for a Dark Queen* to explain the Roman occupation of Britain. *What was the nature of the conflict between the British and the Romans?*

▶ Compare the military leadership of famous generals in ancient history such as Alexander of Macedon, Hannibal, and Julius Caesar.

Grades 9-12

▶ Compare innovations in ancient military technology such as the Macedonian phalanx, the Roman legion, the Persian cataphract, the Chinese crossbow, and the Greek trireme, and explain how they affected patterns of warfare and empire building.

▶ Compare Latin and Greek as universal languages of the Roman Empire. *What political, cultural, and commercial purposes did these two languages have?*

▶ Read selections from Polybius's treatment of the Roman Constitution. Identify those elements in his description that influenced the American political system.

▶ Examine the reign of Augustus and analyze its significance in the transition from Roman Republic to imperial government. Compare the Roman Republic with Imperial Rome. Assess the relative merits of the two types of government. *How did one form of government turn into the other? What were the causes and consequences of the change?*

▶ Explain the cultural influence of Hellenistic arts and architecture on the Romans. *What major Roman artistic and technological achievements were influenced by Hellenistic traditions?*

▶ Describe the "silk roads" connecting the Chinese and Roman empires in trade, and assess their impact on these societies and on peoples of Central Asia.

B. The emergence of Christianity in the context of the Roman Empire.

Grades 5-6

▶ Tell the story of the life of Jesus of Nazareth. *What did he teach?*

▶ Analyze several of Jesus's parables such as "the good shepherd," "the good Samaritan," or "the prodigal son." *What message do these parables illustrate?*

▶ Prepare a short biography of Paul the Apostle and explain how he helped spread Christian teachings and practice.

▶ Analyze accounts from the New Testament that describe early Christian principles. *What moral and spiritual values are expressed in these teachings?*

▶ Compare in chart form Roman polytheistic values and beliefs to those of early Christianity. *What do you think would have drawn people to Christianity?*

Grades 7-8

▶ Examine the moral and spiritual teachings expressed in Jesus's "Sermon on the Mount" (Matt. 5-7). *In what ways did his teachings both confirm the prohibitions of the Ten Commandments in the Hebrew Torah (e.g., you shall not kill, bear false witness, covet your neighbor's possessions) and expand upon them?*

▶ Construct a map locating the centers of the early Christian church in the 1st century CE and the extent of the spread of Christianity by the end of the 4th century CE.

▶ Examine illustrations of early Christian religious art such as mosaics and paintings. *What stories are told in these art works? What values do they express? How do they compare to the religious art of other ancient civilizations?*

▶ Compare the impact that each of the following emperors had on Christianity, and explain the reasons: Nero, Constantine, Julian, and Theodosius.

▶ Construct a list of those ideas and acts of Paul that most influenced the history of Christianity after him. *On what bases might he be called the "second founder of Christianity"?*

Grades 9-12

▶ Analyze the similarities and differences between Judaism and Christianity in their respective beliefs concerning the Deity.

▶ Read selections from the lives of early Christian martyrs, such as the *Martyrdom of St. Polycarp*, and construct an account explaining the role of the martyr in the spread and ultimate success of Christianity in the Roman Empire.

▶ Compile a listing of the fundamental teachings and practices of early Christianity. *Which of these teachings is distinctive to Christianity and no other faiths? In which way has the development of Christianity been affected by Hebrew, Greek, Persian, or other influences?*

▶ Map the areas in which there were recorded Christian communities by the end of the 1st century CE, and the areas that were predominantly Christian by the end of the 4th century CE. *Who were the people, and what were the events and circumstances that helped the spread of the Christian religion from its location of origin to other parts of Asia and to Africa and Europe during this period?*

▶ Read Romans, Chapter 8, and write an essay discussing what you think are the most important Christian themes in Paul's message.

▶ Explain the impact of Christianity on the Roman Empire. *Why did the Romans attempt to destroy Christianity? How did Christians respond to the persecutions? What was the significance of Constantine's conversion to Christianity and of Theodosius's antipagan legislation in the late 4th century?*

C. How China became unified under the early imperial dynasties.

Grades 5-6

▶ Make drawings of the contents of Shi Huangdi's tomb and the building of the first Great Wall and label evidence that shows the achievements of the Qin period.

▶ Retell a Chinese folktale to explain what life was like for ordinary people in ancient China.

▶ Write a diary entry as a person working on the Great Wall under order of Emperor Qin, expressing your views of the value of the work you are doing and your feelings about working under harsh conditions. *What reasons do people have for submitting to "greater authority"?*

▶ Use excerpts from Marilee Heyer's *The Weaving of a Dream* to describe Chinese values and belief systems.

▶ Define the Mandate of Heaven and the idea of virtuous rule. *How does this compare to how other cultures you've studied confer authority on their rulers?*

▶ Use the following three passages expressing the "Golden Rule" and explain how Confucius, Aristotle, and Jesus sought to promote harmony in society. Confucius: *"What you do not want done to yourself, do not do to others."* Aristotle: *"We should behave to our friends as we would wish our friends to behave to us."* Jesus: *"So whatever you wish that men would do to you, do so to them."* Create a poster illustrating one of the three passages, incorporating the artistic aesthetic of that religious or moral culture.

Grades 7-8

▶ Use overlays or a series of maps to trace the lands controlled by the Shang, Zhou, Qin, and Han dynasties. Compare the extent of the Han empire to that of Alexander the Great and the Roman Empire at the time of the emperor Trajan. *How would you account for the success and limit of Han expansion?*

▶ Diagram the social hierarchy in China including scholar-officials, farmers, artisans, merchants, soldiers, women, and slaves. Compare the stratification of Chinese society with that of other ancient societies. *What gave people status in China? How was the composition of Chinese society similar to or different from that of other ancient societies?*

▶ Explain how the Zhou used the concept of the "Mandate of Heaven" to justify the overthrow of the Shang dynasty. *How does this concept compare with ideas about the power and legitimacy of rulers in other ancient civilizations?*

▶ Create a graphic organizer of Chinese achievements in science, technology, the arts, and practical methods of farming and irrigation. *How did these achievements compare with those of the Greeks and Romans?*

▶ Summarize the most important teachings of Confucius in a set of ten guidelines for human conduct. *How do these Confucian guidelines compare with the Ten Commandments?*

▶ Construct a manual for use by those wishing to take the civil service examinations during the time of the Han empire. *Who could take the examination? How long would it take to prepare for it, how difficult would it be, what should be studied, what were the arrangements for taking the examination, could it be re-taken in case of failure, and what advantages did passing it confer?*

▶ Drawing on historical information, create an account of your travels as though written by a Han merchant using the "silk road" in his trading ventures. *What goods do you trade in? How are those goods transported? What peoples do you encounter on the way? Where is the end-point of your trade route? What difficulties and dangers do you have to anticipate, and how do you try to minimize them? What new ideas and products have you brought home with you from your trading trips? How were they received?*

Grades 9-12

▶ Stage a debate among a Confucianist, Daoist, and Legalist over which philosophy would end the era of warring states.

▶ Read selections of Qin laws on penal servitude and debate history's verdict on Shi Huangdi. *Was he a cruel tyrant or a great builder?*

▶ Prepare a museum display using illustrations from Chinese art up to the end of the Han dynasty. *How does the art reflect the history and philosophy of China during this period?*

▶ Research the legal and social position of women of different classes in the Confucian tradition. Compare the Confucian definition of women's roles with those of Ban Zhao (ca. 45-120 CE) as recorded in *Lessons for Women.*

▶ Participate in a debate on a modern legal issue of interest to students where you assume the role of a Confucianist, a Daoist or a Legalist. *Which of these belief/value systems do you find to be closest to your own? Why?*

D. Religious and cultural developments in India in the era of the Gangetic states and the Mauryan Empire.

Grades 5-6

◆ Retell in your own words an excerpt from the *Jataka* tales. *What do the* Jataka *tales reveal about Buddhist teachings?*

◆ Tell the story of the life of Siddhartha Gautama. *Why is he called the Buddha? What are the "four truths" of Buddhism? What values did Buddha teach? How did these values compare to those of Brahmanism? To the teachings of Jesus?*

◆ Assume the role of Ashoka being interviewed by a traveler. Tell you life story and explain the code of laws you have established to govern your empire. *How would Ashoka advise people to treat one another? What laws might Ashoka recommend? How do you think Buddhism influenced Ashoka's ideas?*

◆ Examine selections from Brian Thompson's *The Story of Prince Rama* and describe how Indian epic stories reflect social values.

Grades 7-8

◆ Analyze several animal stories from the Panchatantra. *What advice do they offer people with little power? Which of these strategies did Chandragupta Maurya use? How does the advice compare with morals in Aesop's fables?*

◆ Describe basic features of social relationships in India during this period. *How was membership in social groups important? How did this affect such institutions as marriage and one's choice of occupation? How did the belief in dharma, one's fundamental duty in life, affect social behavior?*

◆ Read selections from the rock and pillar edicts of Ashoka. Analyze what evidence they yield concerning Indian society, religion, and history in the Maurya period. Construct a chart listing the achievements of Ashoka and evaluate his accomplishments. *How do these accomplishments compare to those of other ancient leaders such as Alexander of Macedon and the Han emperors of China?*

◆ Map the spread and extent of Buddhism up to about 300 CE. Explain the role played by such factors as royal favor, missionary activity, monasticism's appeal, expansion of trade in its spread.

◆ Trace the expansion of Buddhism and Christianity on an outline map of Eurasia and Africa. *What are similarities and differences in the successful expansion of these religions?*

◆ Read the story of Shvetaketu from the *Chandogya Upanishad*. How do these teachings compare with the Buddhist teaching about *nirvana*. *What does Shvetaketu's father teach his son about Brahman and moksha?*

Grades 9-12

◆ Draw evidence from literature to compare gender relations in India, China, and Greece. Use literary works such as the *Ramayana*, the Chinese *Book of Songs*, and the plays of Sophocles. *How accurately do they reflect the status of women in ancient India, China, and Greece?*

◆ Debate the statement: *"Women were better off as Buddhists than they were in Brahmanic society."*

◆ Explain how Buddhist teachings challenged the Brahmanic social system, especially caste, dietary practices, language usage, and the role of women. *Which of Buddha's reforms contributed to its appeal and promoted the spread of Buddhism in India and beyond?*

▶ Interpret selections from Kautilya's *Arthashastra* as a source of knowledge of Indian political thought and culture in the Maurya period. *According to Kantilya, what must a ruler do in order to be successful in foreign relations and domestic policy? How accurately does what he says reflect conditions in India in this time?*

▶ Research how Ashoka's support for Buddhism affected the spread of that religion in India. Compare with the effects of the Roman emperors' tolerance for and support of Christianity on the spread of that faith in the empire. *How important was imperial support? What other factors influenced the spread of each religion?*

▶ Examine the religious ideas associated with the *Upanishads. How did these later books of the Vedas reflect Brahmanic teachings? How do Brahmanic teachings compare with Buddhist teachings about such ideas as reincarnation, the self, salvation, and how life should be lived?*

IV. The development of early agrarian civilizations in Mesoamerica.

The achievements of Olmec civilization.

Grades 5-6

▶ Construct a topographical map of Mesoamerica. *How did various features of geography influence Olmec civilization?*

▶ Research the land of the Olmec, including the nature of the soil, and plant and animal life. Become "A Farmer for a Day," and describe in words and/or pictures your experiences. *What plants do you cultivate, and how? What animals are part of your daily life? What problems do you have, and what solutions to them do you try? How is it that information about the daily life of an Olmec farmer is known to American students today?*

▶ Examine illustrations of the large sculptured stone heads dating to the Olmec times. *How might the Olmec have moved rocks from source points to where the heads stand? What do archaeologists think the heads signify?*

Grades 7-8

▶ Construct a ground plan or a model of an Olmec city, such as La Venta or San Lorenzo. Explain what the ground plan of the buildings and ball courts might reveal about the Olmec people. *What questions do you have about the Olmec that could not be answered based on the evidence of ground plans alone?*

▶ Explain the importance of maize to the Olmec civilization. *What methods of farming were used? How did farming in Mesoamerica differ from that of other agrarian societies in the ancient world?*

▶ Suppose that archaeologists found a stone sculpture in a new site all by itself. *What features would lead them to label the sculpture as "Olmec"?*

▶ Make posters of Olmec farming methods. Evaluate their demographical and environmental impact. *What connections can you make between Olmec agriculture and the development of Olmec society? In what ways are agricultural strategies such as the chinampas (floating gardens) sound ecologically? Are they still used? Why or why not?*

▶ Examine pictures of the Olmec monumental stone heads. *What can you infer about the type of political and economic control needed to produce this monumental sculpture? Why did people ritually mutilate these heads?*

♦ List the conditions you consider had to be present in order for the Olmec civilization to develop. *When and where did these conditions first make their appearance in Mesoamerica?*

Grades 9-12

♦ Using archaeological and historical information, explain the political, economic, and social structure of Olmec society. *How can we give an accurate record of the development of the Olmec civilization without having deciphered their written records?*

♦ Research the archaeological or pictorial evidence available to support the hypothesis that the Olmecs had cultural influences on the development of Zapotec and Mayan civilizations. *What role can trade play in the diffusion of aspects of culture? In what other ways can one society influence another?*

♦ Plan a museum exhibit of Olmec archaeological finds. Write labels for the various objects you include in the exhibit and explain how they reflect how people lived and worked in Olmec communities. *What can be inferred about Olmec beliefs from the objects in your exhibition? How would you change the exhibition if your aim was to show "the development of Olmec civilization"?*

♦ Debate the validity of the statement that the Olmec were the "mother civilization" of Mesoamerica.

♦ Create a map showing the location of Olmec sites, and of Olmec-influenced remains on sites of other groups contemporary with the Olmecs. Brainstorm all the methods that might have led to the finding of Olmec artifacts on non-Olmec sites. *What kinds of evidence would you look for that would help you to decide which of the hypotheses you generated was the most likely to be correct?*

♦ Compare the Olmec civilization with the Indus valley one, whose writing modern scholars have also not yet deciphered. *About which of the two do we know more? Why?*

V. *Major global trends from 1000 BCE-300 CE.*

Major global trends from 1000 BCE-300 CE.

Grades 5-6

♦ Draw a map identifying the major trading centers along the Silk Road and showing the major products exported from those centers. *How would the establishment of such international trade routes have changed life for people throughout Afro-Eurasia?*

♦ Participate in a debate among slave owners, government leaders, and free common people in Han China, Maurya India, classical-era Greece, and imperial Rome over a proposition to abolish slavery in each place. Include information about the forms slavery took, its advantages and disadvantages to each group, and alternatives to slave labor. *Why do you think slavery and other types of coerced labor existed over such a long period of human history?*

♦ Create a collage or poster for one of the major classical civilizations presenting images of its most important cultural developments in politics, economics, art, architecture, literature, and religion. Make a shield or flag incorporating a central symbol that best represents to you the distinctive cultural style of this civilization. *How would you compare your flag or shield to one you might make to represent American culture today?*

Grades 7-8

▶ Trace the connections between the introduction of iron technology, economic and military considerations, and political change. *Why has iron been called the "democratic metal"?*

▶ List the major civilizations that flourished in the period of 1000 BCE to 300 CE. For each, give a brief description of their institutions, systems of thought, and cultural styles that best qualify them to be called "classical" civilizations. *Would you add any of the earlier civilizations to the ranks of the "classical" ones? If so, which, and on what basis? If not, why not? Which of the classical civilizations' legacies are still influential today?*

▶ Identify the problems of keeping a very large territory inhabited by many different kinds of peoples united under one government. *Drawing on the history of empires during this period, what advice would you give to a would-be builder and maintainer of a new empire at this time about the roles of the military bureaucracy, communications, trade, and other aspects of developing an empire?*

▶ Based on historical evidence, create a travel log recording the routes and impressions of a traveller visiting all the areas where Greek or Hellenistic ideas and styles have spread by 300 CE. *What places have you visited? What traces of Greek influence have you found in each?*

▶ Create a map showing the main trade routes at several periods during the 1000 BCE-300 CE timespan. Use symbols placed next to the routes to indicate the main items traded. Show, and label, the location of centers of both trade and production. Indicate the location and extent of the major countries that traded. *Which areas of Afro-Eurasia seem to have been least involved in long-distance trade? Most involved? What explanations can you come up with for these differences?*

▶ Construct a conversation between a slave from the Han dynasty in China, and one from the Roman Empire, exchanging information about what it is like to be a slave in their respective countries. *How does a person become enslaved, and how might he or she be freed? What kinds of jobs do slaves do, where do they live, how are they treated? What does the law have to say about slaves? On what sources did you draw for information to construct your dialogue?*

▶ Keep a log for one week, recording every instance you can find of something you see, read, hear, think or believe that is a legacy in the present from one of the classical civilizations. To get you started, look at a penny. *How many legacies from classical civilizations can you identify?*

Grades 9-12

▶ Create an overlay map, showing the areas where the population was predominantly Jewish, Hindu, Buddhist, Confucian, Daoist, and Christian during various periods between 1000 BCE and 300 CE. Indicate some of the diverse political and ethnic groups that shared the same beliefs. *By 300 CE, what had happened to earlier religions such as Atonism, worship of the divine Pharaoh, worship of the Great Mother, ancestor worship, the Greek and Roman gods, Zoroastrianism?*

▶ Compare the nature and uses of unfree labor in the Han, Maurya, and Roman empires, and in the Greek city-states. *How would you explain the widespread use of such labor in the ancient world? How did slavery fit in with other social hierarchies such as those based on class, caste, gender? What differences were there between chattel slaves and other kinds of unfree labor? What forms did slavery take in the different societies? What connections did slavery have with militarism?*

▶ Using one of the classical civilizations as a case study, trace through time the endurance of some of its characteristic traditions. *What explanations can be given for cultural and social persistence? How would you account for the continued importance of Confucian ideas in China, while Legalism lost influence? For the tenacity of Judaism in the diaspora? For the steadfast adherence of Greeks to ideals of freedom?*

◗ Compare the roles of the priesthood and of monasticism in Judaism, Christianity, Hinduism and Buddhism as means to religious continuity. *Why was neither institution a part of Confucianism? What institution helped preserve Confucian continuity instead?*

◗ Compare the methods used by Christianity and Hinduism to bind together large numbers of people from very different traditions into a unified religious and cultural tradition. *How did each handle dissenting religious traditions? How important to their success was political support? What institutions did each develop that helped in welding their followers together?*

Roman ramparts at Caesarea, Israel. Photo by Ross Dunn

ERA 4

Expanding Zones of Exchange and Encounter, 300-1000 CE

Giving Shape to World History

Beginning about 300 CE almost the entire region of Eurasia and northern Africa experienced severe disturbances. By the seventh century, however, peoples of Eurasia and Africa entered a new period of more intensive interchange and cultural creativity. Underlying these developments was the growing sophistication of systems for moving people and goods here and there throughout the hemisphere—China's canals, trans-Saharan camel caravans, high-masted ships plying the Indian Ocean. These networks tied diverse peoples together across great distances. In Eurasia and Africa a single region of intercommunication was taking shape that ran from the Mediterranean to the China seas. A widening zone of interchange also characterized Mesoamerica.

A sweeping view of world history reveals three broad patterns of change that are particularly conspicuous in this era.

▶ **Islamic Civilization:** One of the most dramatic developments of this 700-year period was the rise of Islam as both a new world religion and a civilized tradition encompassing an immense part of the Eastern Hemisphere. Commanding the central region of Afro-Eurasia, the Islamic empire of the Abbasid dynasty became in the 8th-10th-century period the principal intermediary for the exchange of goods, ideas, and technologies across the hemisphere.

▶ **Buddhist, Christian, and Hindu Traditions:** Not only Islam but other major religions also spread widely during this 700-year era. Wherever these faiths were introduced, they carried with them a variety of cultural traditions, aesthetic ideas, and ways of organizing human endeavor. Each of them also embraced peoples of all classes and diverse languages in common worship and moral commitment. Buddhism declined in India but took root in East and Southeast Asia. Christianity became the cultural foundation of a new civilization in western Europe. Hinduism flowered in India under the Gupta Empire and also exerted growing influence in the princely courts of Southeast Asia.

▶ **New Patterns of Society in East Asia, Europe, West Africa, Oceania, and Mesoamerica:** The third conspicuous pattern, continuing from the previous era, was the process of population growth, urbanization, and flowering of culture in new areas. The 4th to 6th centuries witnessed serious upheavals in Eurasia in connection with the breakup of the Roman and Han empires and the aggressive movements of pastoral peoples to the east, west, and south. By the seventh century, however, China was finding new unity and rising economic prosperity under the Tang. Japan emerged as a distinctive civilization. At the other end of the hemisphere Europe laid new foundations for political and social order. In West Africa towns flourished amid the rise of Ghana and the trans-Saharan gold trade. In both lower Africa and the Pacific basin migrant pioneers laid new foundations of agricultural societies. Finally, this era saw a remarkable growth of urban life in Mesoamerica in the age of the Maya.

Why Study This Era?

▶ In these seven centuries Buddhism, Christianity, Hinduism, and Islam spread far and wide beyond their lands of origin. These religions became established in regions where today they command the faith of millions.

▶ In this era the configuration of empires and kingdoms in the world changed dramatically. Why giant empires have fallen and others risen rapidly to take their place is an enduring question for all eras.

▶ In the early centuries of this era Christian Europe was marginal to the dense centers of population, production, and urban life of Eurasia and northern Africa. Students should understand this perspective but at the same time investigate the developments that made possible the rise of a new civilization in Europe after 1000 CE.

▶ In this era no sustained contact existed between the Eastern Hemisphere and the Americas. Peoples of the Americas did not share in the exchange and borrowing that stimulated innovations of all kinds in Eurasia and Africa. Therefore, students need to explore the conditions under which weighty urban civilizations arose in Mesoamerica in the first millennium CE.

Mont St. Michel monastery,
France. Photo by Ross Dunn

The Experiences of Christian Missions to the East and West*
by Jerry H. Bentley

Professor Bentley examines the success of propagating Christianity in Europe and analyzes the contrasting experience of conversion to Nestorian Christianity in central Asia and China. The essay explains the differences in Catholic and Nestorian beliefs and focuses on the spread of Christianity after the collapse of the Roman empire. Bolstered by the papacy and the sponsorship of newly converted kings, Roman Catholicism spread throughout western and northern Europe. Although Nestorian Christianity initially extended across central Asia to China, it experienced more difficulty in incorporating prevailing cultural and religious forms and could not rely on the political support that helped promote Catholicism in Europe. This excerpt from Bentley's book Old World Encounters *models a cross-cultural approach to teaching world history.*

Jerry H. Bentley is Professor of History at the University of Hawaii and editor of the *Journal of World History*. He has published widely on early modern Europe, Renaissance humanism and world history. His works include *Humanism and Holy Writ: New Testament Scholarship in the Renaissance*.

Constantine and his successors ensured for Christianity an opportunity to establish itself in the Roman empire. But the Christian emperors could not guarantee that their faith would penetrate, and still less that it would dominate the culture of the western world. The collapse of the Roman empire and its displacement by Germanic successor states could conceivably have resulted in the disappearance of Christianity as an important cultural force. At the least, it looked as though the Arian Christianity favored by Germanic peoples might very well prevail over the Catholic faith embraced by the emperors and bishops of Rome.

As in the case of other religious and cultural traditions that attracted large followings in foreign lands, Christianity succeeded largely because of syncretism—its willingness to baptize pagan traditions and its capacity to make a place for them within a basically Christian framework. But the survival of Roman Catholic Christianity and its eventual domination of western culture depended also on two other especially important developments: the emergence of a strong source of authority and agent of organization in the papacy, and the alliance of the popes with Germanic rulers of the northern lands who could provide political and military support for the Roman church. The importance of these developments is clear not only from the success of Catholic missions in Europe but also from the ultimate failure of Nestorian missions in Asia. A dual process of syncretism and conversion induced by pressure established Christianity as the dominant cultural tradition in Europe. In Asia, however, Christian syncretism did not enjoy the benefits of strong organizational leadership or state sponsorship. Christians there were unable to maintain distinctive communities, and eventually they themselves underwent conversion by assimilation to indigenous cultural traditions. The following pages will briefly examine the expansion of Catholic Christianity in western and northern Europe, then analyze the contrasting experience of Nestorian Christianity in central Asia and China.

In most parts of the world, merchants figured prominently as bearers of culture. In early medieval Europe, however, missionaries came mostly from the monasteries. Among the most effective of them were Celtic monks of the fifth and sixth centuries who preached their faith and established new communities throughout Ireland, Wales, Cornwall, and Brittany. Some of

---

*Reprinted from *Old World Encounters: Cross-Cultural Contacts and Exchanges in Pre-Modern Times* (New York: Oxford University Press, 1993), pp. 100-110.

them ventured into northern England and Scotland; others traveled south to Gaul, Switzerland, and Italy. All of the Celtic missionaries worked independently of the church and bishop of Rome. They differed from the Romanists in their more pronounced asceticism, looser institutional discipline, and method of calculating the date of Easter, among other points. Their popularity and sincerity, however, enabled them to establish Celtic Christianity as a powerful cultural force in lands beyond the reach of the Roman church.

Beginning in the sixth century, however, the Roman church took the cultural initiative in Europe. Pope Gregory I (590-604)—sometimes called Gregory the Great—brought energy and determination to his office, which he fashioned into a powerful tool of cultural leadership. Gregory provided guidance on Roman Catholic observances and institutional discipline. He established relationships with Franks, Lombards, Visigoths, and other Germanic peoples who threatened the Roman church. So far as the expansion of Christianity goes, his most important project was the evangelization of Britain. In the year 596 he dispatched a group of forty missionaries under the leadership of St. Augustine of Canterbury (not to be confused with the more famous theologian, St. Augustine of Hippo). They soon won a prominent patron with the conversion of King Ethelbert of Kent, who helped them to establish churches, monasteries, and episcopal sees in southern England. The tight organization and strict discipline observed by this outpost of Roman Christianity—along with the sponsorship of King Ethelbert and his successors—enabled it to grow at the expense of the Celtic church. By the mid-seventh century it had become plain that in order to avoid fruitless competition, the English church needed to decide in favor of either Roman or Celtic observances. At the synod of Whitby (664) English clerics opted for the Roman alternative, and the Celtic church entered a period of decline that led ultimately to its complete disappearance. The revived papacy of Gregory I thus developed as a powerful source of authority and cultural influence, one capable of organizing missionary efforts and attracting religious allegiance over very long distances.

Quite apart from the reinvigoration of the Roman church's leadership, alliances with Germanic rulers also promoted the spread of Christianity in Europe. The Roman church did not necessarily benefit immediately from all Germanic conversions. Beginning about the late fourth century, for example, the Visigoths had turned increasingly to Arian Christianity—rank heresy from a Roman point of view. In fact, from a modern, analytical point of view, their conversion to Christianity of any variety reflected the Visigoths' progressive assimilation into the society and culture of the late Roman empire. This subtlety provided little comfort, however, for representatives of the Roman church eager to preserve the purity of its doctrine.

More important and far more useful for the Roman church were the Franks. Some of them had lived within the Roman empire since the third century and very likely had converted to Christianity at an early date. Not until the conversion of Clovis, however, did Frankish policy favor specifically Christian interests. A combination of personal and political motives seems to have brought about Clovis's conversion. His wife, Clotilda, was Roman Catholic and constantly urged Clovis to accept her faith. The turning point, however, came only after Clovis had defeated the Alamanni in the year 496, a victory that he attributed to intervention by the Christians' God. He delayed his baptism—perhaps until as late as 508, twelve years after his victory over the Alamanni—but eventually joined a large number of his fellow Franks in officially converting to Roman Catholic Christianity.

The entry of the Frankish ruling elite into the Roman Catholic community set the stage for the process of conversion induced by political pressure in northern Europe. Royally sponsored missionaries and monks spread the Christian message to rural communities throughout the

Frankish realm. They scorned pagan customs and beliefs and strenuously argued the superiority of the Christian God over pagan deities and fertility spirits. They also attacked pagan morality, which they sought to replace with their own more stringent code. They even destroyed temples and shrines, replacing them with churches and monasteries.

The significance of the Frankish conversion to Christianity became most clear during the reign of Charlemagne (768-814), whose many services not only enabled the Roman church to survive but also helped it to establish a presence in previously pagan lands. On several occasions Charlemagne protected the papacy from threats posed by Lombards and other Germanic peoples, and he sponsored educational programs designed to prepare priests for their work. Perhaps most important of his services for present purposes was his long, intermittent campaign of more than thirty years to impose order in Saxony. Both Charlemagne and his adversaries clearly recognized religion as an important element of their conflict. Thus Widukind, an especially fiery and effective Saxon leader, sought to overthrow Frankish authority, destroy Christian churches, expel missionaries, and restore pagan ways. Besides establishing garrisons and leading armies against rebel forces, Charlemagne used his faith as an ideological weapon against the pagan Saxons. In a moment of temporary superiority in 785, he forced Widukind to accept baptism along with other prominent Saxons, and he imposed on their land a famous and especially harsh ordinance providing the death penalty for those who forcibly entered a church, violated the Lenten fast, killed a bishop or priest, cremated the dead in pagan fashion, refused baptism, plotted against Christians, or disobeyed the Frankish king. Charlemagne's efforts of course did not result in immediate and enthusiastic conversion of the Saxons to Christianity. Nonetheless clearly, however, they enabled the Roman church to establish a secure presence that over the long term brought about the Christianization of Saxony.

Charlemagne's difficulties with the Saxons serve as an effective reminder that Christianity met with stiff resistance as missionaries promoted their faith across cultural frontiers. In the Saxon case, of course, resistance to Christianity reflected political as well as cultural conflict. But even in the Frankish heartland, culture-based resistance to Christianity continued for a very long time indeed. In the middle of the seventh century, for example, St. Eligius, bishop of Noyon, preached zealously against pagan drunkenness and dancing in his diocese. According to his biographer, he received a straightforward and unambiguous response: "Roman that you are, although you are always bothering us, you will never uproot our customs, but we will go on with our rites as we have always done, and we will go on doing so always and forever. There will never exist the man who will be able to stop us holding our timehonoured and most dear games." Only after many decades of preaching by monks and missionaries did the Frankish realm gradually become a Christian land.

Throughout Europe, the process of social conversion to Christianity proceeded the more effectively when missionaries agreed to honor established cultural traditions and to absorb them into a syncretic but fundamentally Christian synthesis. To some extent this policy of accommodation continued the practice of the earliest Christians, who endowed pagan festivals and heroes with Christian significance, turning them into holy days or saints, in order to bridge the gap between established pagan culture and the new Christian alternative. In like fashion, later missionaries baptized pagan beliefs and customs concerning fertility and health; they built churches and shrines on sites traditionally recognized as having special power or cultural significance; and they associated Christian saints with the virtues and powers ascribed to local heroes. In a famous letter, Pope Gregory the Great instructed St. Augustine, his missionary in England, that the idol temples of that race should by no means be destroyed but only the idols in them. Take holy water and sprinkle it in these shrines, build altars and place relics in them. For if the shrines are well built, it is to the service of the true God. When this people see that their shrines are not destroyed they will be able to banish error from their hearts and be more ready to come to the places they are familiar with, but now recognizing and worshipping the true God.

The syncretic approach thus helped to establish lines of continuity between pagan and Christian traditions, thereby easing the process of conversion to foreign cultural standards. When bolstered by the leadership of the revived papacy and the sponsorship of newly converted kings, syncretism helped Roman Catholic Christians to spread their faith to all corners of Europe. Their religious cousins, the Nestorian Christians, did not enjoy the advantages of organizational energy and political sponsorship, at least not over the long term. Nestorians spread their faith to Mesopotamia, Persia, central Asia, and even to China. Nestorian communities in Mesopotamia add Persia survived for more than a millennium, although the expansion of Islam deprived them of their vitality and severely reduced their numbers after the seventh century. In central Asia and China, however, Nestorians had an even more difficult experience. In some ways they lost their distinctively Christian identity: they did not remain in communication with other Christian communities, and they dropped a large amount of specifically Christian doctrine. Their beliefs and values inclined over time toward those of Buddhists, Daoists, and Muslims, and indeed most Nestorians eventually became absorbed into one or another of those cultural alternatives. The Nestorian experience thus differed markedly from the Roman Catholic, and a comparative analysis of the two throws particularly interesting light on the dynamics of cross-cultural encounters.

Nestorian doctrine arose out of Christological debates of the late fourth and early fifth centuries. In combatting the teachings of Arians and other early Christian heretics, the patriarch of Constantinople, Nestorius, advanced the idea that two distinct natures, divine and human, coexisted in Jesus' person. Because of his arrogance and difficult personality, Nestorius had many enemies, and they gleefully attacked his teachings. Some of them argued that Nestorius overemphasized Christ's human nature; others held that his distinction between human and divine natures implied a belief in two Christs. In the year 430 Pope Celestine excommunicated Nestorius, and in 431 a church council at Ephesus deposed him and banished him to his monastery. Yet Nestorius's ideas survived and for two centuries even flourished in the east. By the late fifth century, Nestorians had become solidly entrenched in Mesopotamia and Persia, where their hostility to Byzantine and Roman churches worked to their advantage, endearing them to Christian communities already established in those lands. The Sassanian kings persecuted Nestorians and Manichaeans in their efforts to favor officially approved Zoroastrianism. The arrival of Islam presented even greater difficulties for Nestorians in the Middle East. Islamic rulers allowed Nestorians to keep their faith, and the Abbasid caliphs permitted a Nestorian patriarch to reside at Baghdad and to govern his church, under close supervision of the caliphate. But taxation undercut the economic foundations of Nestorian church and society, and most Nestorians eventually converted to Islam.

Already, however, the Nestorian church had begun to spread its influence even further to the east. Nestorian merchants traded actively not only throughout Mesopotamia and Persia but also in India, Ceylon, central Asia, and China. Because the Mesopotamian and Persian churches had already gone into eclipse during the early days of Islam, Nestorians in central Asia and China had at best sporadic contact with their patriarch and other cultural authorities. They attracted limited political support, so that their tradition led a precarious existence in

Asia. They exhibited the same inclination toward syncretism that marked Roman Catholic missions in Europe. Absent large populations and political support, however, the Nestorians' syncretism in Asia did not attract many converts from local cultural traditions. Instead, it served as a bridge for the Nestorians themselves to undergo conversion by assimilation to Asian traditions. Several writings of high interest survive, mostly from the libraries and scriptoria of Dunhuang, to represent the experiences of Nestorian communities in central Asia and China.

Nestorians had entered China by the early seventh century at the very latest. The first identifiable Nestorian there was the missionary Alopen, who visited Changan and was received by the Emperor Tang Taizong in the year 635. Alopen brought with him Christian scriptures and other writings, which he had translated into Chinese. The emperor himself read and approved the works, as indicated in a remarkable decree of the year 638:

> The Way had not, at all times and places, the selfsame name; the Sage had not, at all times and places, the selfsame human body. Heaven caused a suitable religion to be instituted for every region and clime so that each one of the races of mankind might be saved. Bishop Alopen of the Kingdom of Persia, bringing with him the sutras and images, has come from afar and presented them at our capital. Having carefully examined the scope of his teaching, we find it to be mysteriously spiritual, and of silent operation. Having observed its principal and most essential points, we reached the conclusion that they cover all that is most important in life. Their language is free from perplexing expressions; their principles are so simple that they "remain as the fish would remain even after the net of the language were forgotten." This teaching is helpful to all creatures and beneficial to all men. So let it have free course throughout the empire.

As a result, in spite of Buddhist and Daoist opposition, Nestorians established a monastery for twenty-one monks in Changan.

During the early years of their community's life in China, Nestorians taught a recognizably Christian doctrine. This is clear from several doctrinal statements, attributed to Alopen, from the midseventh century, which outline the basic story and ethical teachings of Christianity. The "Jesus-Messia Sutra," for example, briefly relates Jesus' birth, life, teachings, and death. The "Discourse on Monotheism" and "Discourse on the Oneness of the Ruler of the Universe" both emphasize the Christian God as sole creator of all things. The "Lord of the Universe's Discourse on Alms-Giving" paraphrases Jesus' Sermon on the Mount. The fundamentally Christian character of the Nestorians' faith emerges clearly also in the inscription of a famous Nestorian monument, erected in the year 781 at Changan. The inscription began by recognizing the existence of one triune God, the creator of the world and of pure humankind, unstained by sin. Satan then corrupted God's human creatures and introduced evil into the world. One person of the divine trinity thereafter arrived on earth as both mortal man and messiah. He set an example of perfection, destroyed the power of Satan, opened the road to human salvation, then returned to his heavenly abode. His ministers preach equality, practice asceticism, and promote holiness.

Unlike Buddhists and Manichaeans, however, the Nestorians never negotiated the leap from the diaspora community to the host society. To some extent, their failure to attract large numbers of Asian converts was due to the difficult language and alien concepts that they presented. Buddhists had employed Daoist and Confucian vocabularies when they entered China, and Manichaeans skillfully appropriated Buddhist and Daoist terminology. The Nestorians also relied heavily on Buddhist and Daoist vocabularies in their documents, but some of their doctrines were so specific to Christianity that they could not convey them very well with borrowed terminology. Nestorians called their treatises "sutras," in the Buddhist manner, and they used terms like "buddhas" or "devas', as synonyms for saints or angels. But the early Nestorians made little effort to accommodate Asian tastes in certain other respects. Whereas Manichaeans had referred to Mani as the "Buddha of Light," using a term that resonated nicely in both Sanskrit and Chinese, Nestorians devised an awkward and unpolished transliteration when they represented the name of Jesus in Chinese as "Yishu"—which could be interpreted to mean "a rat on the move." And Nestorians persistently emphasized concepts like the corporeality of Christ and the physical resurrection of individual bodies, which Asians found alien and unattractive.

Quite apart from the difficulty of attracting Asian interest in their doctrines, the Nestorians also faced hostility and persecution from established political authorities. As a part of its attack on foreign religions in the ninth century, the Tang dynasty targeted Nestorians for suppression, alongside Buddhists, Manichaeans, and Zoroastrians. An imperial edict of the year 845 ordered some three thousand Zoroastrians and Nestorians out of their monasteries, returning them to lay society with the stipulation that "they shall not mingle and interfere with the manners and customs of the Middle Kingdom." The policy worked its- effects gradually but nonetheless effectively. This is clear from the work of al-Nadinl, a Persian encyclopedist of the late tenth century, who reported the findings of a Nestorian monk who had traveled from Baghdad to China with instructions to oversee the church there. The monk returned with the news that "the Christians who used to be in the land of China have disappeared and perished for various reasons, so that only one man remained in the entire country."

Only vestiges of Nestorian Christianity survived the Tang persecutions. It is true that the church reappeared: the next chapter will show that Nestorians successfully propagated their faith in China a second time during the thirteenth and fourteenth centuries. Between the tenth and thirteenth centuries, though, Nestorians presumably either departed from China or became absorbed by Buddhist and Daoist communities. In a way, the Nestorians' willingness to accommodate their message to a Chinese audience—by employing Buddhist and Daoist concepts to represent Christian doctrine—eased the process by which they themselves adopted different beliefs and values. A document of the early eighth century illustrates in striking fashion how accommodation could lead Christians to esteem and even to adopt the values of other cultural traditions.

The document in question is the "Sutra on Mysterious Rest and Joy," attributed to Bishop Cyriacus, a Persian missionary and head of the Nestorian church at Changan during the early eighth century. The treatise portrays Jesus teaching Simon Peter and other disciples, but the doctrines advanced there are specifically and almost exclusively Daoist. To attain rest and joy, according to the Jesus of this sutra, an individual must avoid striving and desire but cultivate the virtues of nonassertion and nonaction. These qualities enable an individual to become pure and serene, a condition that leads in turn to illumination and understanding. Much of the treatise explains four chief ethical values: nondesire, or the elimination of personal ambition; nonaction, the refusal to strive for wealth and worldly success, nonvirtue, the avoidance of self-promotion; and nondemonstration, the shunning of an artificial in favor of a natural observance of these virtues. The treatise in fact does not advance a single recognizably Christian doctrine but offers instead moral and ethical guidance of the sort that Daoist sages had taught for a millennium. The Jesus of the treatise even likened himself explicitly to Laozi, the legendary founder of Daoism, by mentioning ten streaks on his face—marks traditionally associated with the ancient's age. In the light of the "Sutra on Mysterious Rest and Joy," it is not difficult to understand how Nestorians in China could make a relatively easy transit from Christianity to Daoism through a process of conversion by assimilation.

Culture, Religion, and the Spread of Civilization

A double dynamic—long-distance trade and imperial expansion—drove the process of cross-cultural encounter during the period 600 to 1000. Merchandise crossed central Asian steppes and the waters of the southern seas in quantities vastly larger than earlier times had seen. As a result, cultural traditions also gained wider exposure than earlier conditions had permitted. The spread of Hinduism and Buddhism best exemplify the capacity of religions and values to travel the roads of traders. Meanwhile, the restoration of imperial unity to China and the establishment of an Islamic empire inevitably brought about encounters between peoples of different cultural traditions. Western Eurasia experienced similar developments, though on a smaller scale, as Franks and other Germanic peoples attempted to fill the political vacuum created by the collapse of the Roman empire. The various empire builders of this period occasionally used culture as a political tool and insisted that subjugated peoples adopt the beliefs and values of their conquerors. More commonly, though, a combination of political, social, and economic incentives led to gradual acceptance by subject peoples of cultural traditions, without need for conquerors to order conversion by main force.

In light of the traditional characterization of this period from 600 to 1000 as a dark age, one point bears special emphasis; the seventh to tenth centuries without doubt witnessed more political and imperial expansion, more commercial and cultural exchange than any previous period of human history. Expansion and exchange in turn brought about the spread of literacy and technology of faiths and values, and indeed of civilization itself. Cross-cultural encounters of necessity played a prominent role in promoting these developments. By no means did all efforts at cultural expansion succeed; many of them lacked the political, social, or economic support necessary for long-term survival, and others faced such stiff resistance from indigenous traditions that they could not survive the crossing of cultural boundaries. By no means, either, did efforts at cultural expansion result in the replication of a given tradition in a new region; when crossing cultural boundaries, beliefs and values necessarily adapted and made accommodations to the political, social, and economic, as well as cultural traditions of different peoples. Thus, when it occurred on a large scale, crosscultural conversion followed a process of syncretism rather than wholesale cultural transformation, or the refashioning of one people according to the cultural standards of another. Nevertheless, cross-cultural encounters of the period 600 to 1000 left rather deep impressions whose outlines remained visible for a long term, continuing in many cases even to the present day.

Sample Student Activities

> **I.   Imperial crises and their aftermath, 300-700 CE.**

A.   The decline of the Roman and Han empires.

Grades 5-6

▸ Construct a timeline showing major historical milestones in the period from the late Roman empire through the rule of Justinian. Make a parallel timeline showing milestones reached during the Han empire. *What inferences can be made from the information in your timeline about possible causes of the decline of the Roman and Han empires? What other possible causes can you think of that would be hard to show on a timeline?*

▸ Construct a map showing the migratory movements of the Hsiung-nu, Germanic tribes, Huns, and Slavs. *What ecological, economic, or political factors might have motivated these groups to move in the directions they did?*

▸ On a chart or Venn diagram list the causes for the decline of the Han and Roman empires. From your chart determine similar and differing problems. *Do all empires suffer from similar problems and failures that lead to their decline and fall?*

Grades 7-8

▸ Write an account of the nomadic invasions of the Roman Empire in the 5th century CE, including information derived from primary sources such as Orosius, Tacitus, Ammianus Marcellinus, and Priscus, and from secondary sources. *Why did the Romans call these invaders "barbarians"?*

▸ Create a timeline labeling major battles, events, and political changes that occurred from the 3rd through 7th centuries in China and Europe. Delineate the division of the Roman Empire and the incursions of invaders into the Han and Roman worlds.

▸ Draw on historical evidence to write a "state of the empire" speech as it might have been given by one of the late Roman emperors, outlining the strengths and weaknesses of the empire in his time.

▸ Write an essay comparing the strengths and weaknesses of the Roman and Han empires. Infer from your comparison why each declined and fell and why one lasted longer than the others.

Grades 9-12

▸ Identify key trends or events in the weakening and decline of the Han and Roman empires, such as internal corruption, overextension of political capacity to rule, generals setting themselves up as rulers, or the settlement of previously hostile nomads within the borders. Analyze the relative significance of these factors. *How were political, military, social, and economic causes of imperial decline linked to one another?*

▸ Drawing evidence from the writings of the Roman historian Tacitus regarding the Germanic peoples, analyze the way in which he represents Germanic family life. *What does Tacitus say about relations between men and women? How did the status of Germanic women compare to that of Roman women?*

♦ Construct a chart with Europe, China, and India as headings and list the characteristics of each of these regions that changed after the arrival of the invading and conquering nomadic peoples. Based on the chart, write an essay assessing the relative impact of the barbarian movements on the regions of Europe, China, and India by the close of the 7th century.

♦ Research the history of Byzantium before it was chosen by Constantine to become the second capital of Rome. *What was its population? What role did the city play in the Roman empire prior to 330 CE? Why was it an ideal site for a second capital?*

♦ Construct a "balance sheet" or chart delineating the differences between the Western and Greek parts of the empire in the 4th century CE. Show the strengths and weaknesses of each, and hypothesize as to why the empire broke up in one region but not the other.

B. The expansion of Christianity and Buddhism beyond the lands of their origin.

Grades 5-6

♦ Compile a chart showing the basic beliefs of Buddhists and Christians. *Which aspects of each religion might appeal to people of the 3rd-5th centuries CE and why?*

♦ Draw a map of Europe, the Mediterranean world, Southwest Asia, India, Southeast Asia, and China. Using colored pencils delineate the extent of the spread of Buddhism, Christianity, Hinduism, and Confucianism. Indicate with alternating colors areas where they overlap.

♦ Write an article for an investigative journal explaining the ways in which Buddhism and Christianity spread to new areas and new peoples. *What role did monks play?*

♦ Participate in a debate or write a dialogue between Buddhist and Christian followers trying to explain reasons for their conversions and their attraction to their particular religious beliefs and practice.

Grades 7-8

♦ Locate on a map and illustrate the emerging centers of Christian and Buddhist teachings. Trace the routes used by believers to spread their faith.

♦ Compare and contrast the roles that Ashoka and Constantine played in spreading Buddhism in India and Christianity in Europe.

♦ *"Times of trouble lead to an increased interest in religion."* Investigate this statement with regard to the demise of the Han and Roman empires and the commensurate growth of Buddhism and Christianity. *How important was the concept of universal salvation in preaching these two religions? Did the growth of these religions hasten the fall of the Han and Roman empires or did the decline and fall of these empires stimulate the spread of Buddhism and Christianity?*

♦ Compare the methods and routes used to introduce Christianity to both Ethiopia and Ireland. *How was this religion received in these parts of the world?*

♦ Research the issue of relations between men and women in Buddhist and Christian teachings. *How did Buddhist and Christian teachings approach these issues differently?*

Grades 9-12

♦ Read and analyze selections from the letters of the Apostle Paul on the subject of marital relations. Explain how these views informed early Christian theology and social practice.

♦ Compare and contrast the spread of Daoism and Buddhism in China.

♦ Investigate the relationship between the growth of international trade and the spread of Christianity and Buddhism in the 3rd-6th centuries CE. *Did commercial enterprise follow or precede the extension of these new religions? What was the relationship between teachers and traders?*

◆ Read Buddha's sermon at Benares (Varanasi) and Jesus's *Sermon on the Mount.* Compare and contrast the messages delivered by these teachers.

◆ Discuss the relationship between "patronage" and the advancement of religion in the context of the spread of Buddhism and Christianity during this era. *What was the role of kings and princes in the promotion of religion? How and why did the concept of "peace" appeal to the rising commercial class?*

◆ *If you were a woman in late imperial Rome, how would the ruling that made Christianity the official religion affect your life? Would your social class and marital status make any difference?*

◆ Research the history of Manicheanism as a religion that spread from Persia to both the Roman Empire and China beginning in the 3rd century CE. *What did the Prophet Mani teach? How were Manichean teachings different from those of Christianity?*

C. The synthesis of Hindu civilization in India in the era of the Gupta Empire.

Grades 5-6

◆ Construct a diorama based on an episode from the *Ramayana. How does the story present dharma as the primary social value? What is the dharma of the ideal king, husband, wife, brother, and friend?*

◆ Recreate pictures of the cave structures at Ajanta and Ellora. *To whom are these sanctuaries dedicated? What does the art and architecture suggest about the relationship among various religions in India during Gupta times? What can primary sources like these teach us about a people?*

◆ Write a poem showing an understanding of the fundamental beliefs of Hinduism including Brahma, dharma, the caste system, ritual and sacrifice, reincarnation, and karma.

◆ Make a long-division calculation using Roman numerals, then Indian/Arabic numerals. *Why is the first way harder than the second?* Imagine a world without zero and explain the difficulties this would cause.

Grades 7-8

◆ Construct a physical map of India and label the Gupta Empire. Draw the path from China to India that the Chinese pilgrims Fa Xian and Xuan Zang might have followed. *What gifts might these pilgrims have taken back to China?*

◆ Read selections from *Shakuntala* by Kalidasa and discuss the ways in which this play represents gender relationships in Gupta India. *How reliable a source is drama for the actual beliefs and behaviors of people?*

◆ Assume the roles of different castes and role-play an episode in the daily life in an Indian village. *Did affiliation with an unprivileged caste provide any advantages? What were some disadvantages? What were the criteria for ranking castes?*

◆ Explain in an essay the causes of the Gupta empire's rise in India, the collapse of the Mauryan-Buddhist power, and the reinstatement of the Brahmans under the Guptas. *Was it a political move on the part of the Guptas to ally themselves with the Brahmans?*

◆ Read the account of Gupta India by the Chinese monk Fa Xian. *What impressed him about life in India?*

◆ Identify the major achievements of scholars in technology, mathematics, astronomy, and medicine during the Gupta period. *What import did some of these achievements have in later centuries in other parts of the world?*

Grades 9-12

▶ Make a chart comparing the Gupta golden age during the reign of Chandragupta II to that of Athens during the Age of Pericles.

▶ Trace the route of the Hun invasion of India and explain its consequences for Indian society. *What was the impact of the invasion on India? How similar were its consequences in India to invasions of Europe at the end of the Roman Empire?*

▶ Since the Guptas did not write history, assess how contemporary historians use art, literature, archaeology, temple inscriptions, and foreign travelers' accounts as a basis for knowledge of Gupta India.

▶ Explain how Buddhist monks influenced education, literature, and higher learning in India during the Gupta era. *What were the famed centers of learning in India in the 4th and 5th centuries, and what did they teach? What comparable educational centers existed in the world at this time?*

▶ Explain how the development of South Indian temple architecture such as the temple at Madurai reveals the resurgence of Hinduism in India and the spread of Hinduism to South India. *What were the various functions carried out in the temple complex? How did temple towns stimulate urban and economic growth?*

D. The expansion of Hindu and Buddhist traditions in Southeast Asia in the first millennium CE.

Grades 5-6

▶ Look at pictorial evidence depicting gods and goddesses of India, Malaysia, and Southeast Asia and note similarities. *In what ways may these depictions indicate a relationship between Buddhism and Hinduism?*

▶ Research the monsoon and the ocean currents, and construct a model of a seaworthy boat of this era. Map a voyage from southeastern India to a destination in Southeast Asia. *How would a knowledge of the monsoons and ocean currents affect ship construction? How did the ocean currents promote cultural diffusion?*

▶ Prepare shadow puppets like those from Southeast Asia. Put on a shadow puppet play based on a story you find from a Southeast Asian society. *What are the subjects of these puppet plays? What do they reveal about contact between India and Southeast Asia? What other evidence is there of contact between these two areas?*

Grades 7-8

▶ Draw a map of Southeast Asia and, using different colors, indicate those countries that were influenced by Buddhism and those influenced by Hinduism. *Which countries were influenced by both beliefs?* Draw an overlay map of long-distance trade routes. *How significant a connection does there seem to be between the spread of religions and trade? What questions would you ask to help establish a connection more reliably?*

▶ Study the history of Southeast Asia and note the presence or absence of Hinduism and Buddhism in various parts of this area by the end of the first millennium. *Did Hindu and Buddhist clerics precede or follow trade between India and Southeast Asia?*

▶ On a map of East, South, and Southeast Asia, trace lines of known or potential sea routes. Discuss the geographic problems that a sea merchant might encounter sailing between Southeast Asia and either India or China. *How did the monsoon winds affect sailing routes and schedules?*

Grades 9-12

▸ From evidence of art and architecture, such as temple sculpture and adornment and tower-temple structures, explain the spread of Hindu and Buddhist faith and thought in Southeast Asia. Make a drawing of one of the Indian temples such as Borobudur in Java, noting in written form the similarities between Indian and Southeast Asian temple architecture. *What do the temple sites tell about the spread of Indian influence? What were the functions of the temples?*

▸ Find a devotional poem or prayer directed to a particular deity, such as Vishnu, Shiva, Krishna, or Devi, and analyze attitudes (bhakti) toward divinity. *Does this same form appear in the adaptations of the Buddhist-Hindu culture of Southeast Asia?*

▸ Examine Hindu-Buddhist architecture, such as stupas, cave structures at Ajanta and Ellora, and temples at Angkor Wat and Borobudur. From your examination hypothesize the influence of Indian religions on Southeast Asia.

▸ Write an essay examining the evidences of Hinduism and Buddhism in Southeast Asia. From your examination determine the influence of Indian culture on this area, the acceptance of these religions by the rulers and peoples of the area, and the ways in which Southeast Asians adopted and adapted these religions.

▸ Research the history of the Pandyas and Pallavas in South India. Map their trade relationships with West Asia, Greece, Rome, and Southeast Asia. *How did the Pallavas help spread Hindu and Buddhist ideas to Southeast Asia?*

II.   *Causes and consequences of the rise of Islamic civilization in the 7th-10th centuries.*

A.   The emergence of Islam and how it spread in Southwest Asia, North Africa, and Europe.

Grades 5-6

▸ Explain the effects of geography on the lifestyle of nomads and town-dwellers of the Arabian peninsula. Describe the conditions that led to the growth of trade. *Why were the oases important to trade? What goods were traded, and where did they originate?*

▸ Write a diary entry from the point of view of a disciple describing the life of Muhammad and his devotion to God. *What basic beliefs and values did Muhammad proclaim?*

▸ Identify and explain the importance to Islam of the Qur'an, the Hegira (Hijra), the Ka'ba, the Sunna, the Hajj, the daily prayer (Salat), alms (Zakat), and Ramadan. *How did these pillars of faith affect the daily life of Muslims?*

▸ Draw evidence from art, architecture, and poetry to illustrate Muslim influence on the Iberian peninsula. *How did Muslims come to exert an influence in this area?*

Grades 7-8

▸ Read accounts of the story of Abraham, Moses, and Jesus in the Old and New Testaments and in the chapter of the Qur'an entitled "The Cow" (2:40-96; 2:124-136); and "Maryam" (19:1-58), and make a chart showing the differences between each version.

▸ Read selections from the short chapters at the end of the Qur'an and describe the morals and values they express. *What made Islam attractive to new converts and what actions by Muslims aided the process of increasing the number of adherents?*

♦ Describe the campaigns that brought areas from Spain to India under Muslim rule. *Who were the important individuals and groups who participated? What kind of military tactics did the conquerors use?*

Grades 9-12

♦ Compare the Byzantine and Sassanid empires. *How different were their political institutions? To what extent did their economies depend on trade? How did their social structures differ? What factors weakened these empires in the 7th century?*

♦ Read excerpts from the Qur'an that deal with women. *What can you infer from these excerpts about the position of women in Islamic communities? How did the statements of the Qur'an and the actions and sayings of the Prophet change women's position from what it had been in these communities before Islam?*

♦ Describe a typical mosque (masjid) and explain how its layout reflects the relationship between people, their spiritual leaders, and God in Islam. Compare this to an early Christian church and Jewish synagogue.

♦ Write an historically valid account of the battle of Tours in 732, and explain its significance from the perspectives of a Frankish Christian chronicler and an Arab Muslim scholar of Iberia, both writing in the 9th century. *How do the accounts agree and differ? What conclusions may be drawn from the differing accounts? What are the changing views of this event in modern historiography?*

♦ Discuss the process by which Arabic became a widely spoken language and the main medium of written communication in the early Islamic centuries. *What was the importance of Arabic in the Islamic religion? In what regions of Africa and Eurasia was Arabic an important language in the 8th century as compared with the 6th century? Why did Muslim converts in such regions as Egypt and North Africa learn to speak and write Arabic? Why did many Christians and Jews in Southwest Asia learn Arabic? Where is Arabic spoken in the world today?*

♦ Prepare a chart showing steps taken by early Muslim leaders and scholars to record and transmit the Qur'an and Hadith. Show what branches of scholarship developed from study and compilation of these documents, and compare the importance of oral and written transmission.

B. **The significance of the Abbasid Caliphate as a center of cultural innovation and hub of interregional trade in the 8th-10th centuries.**

Grades 5-6

♦ Chart the trade routes that converged on Baghdad. *Why was Baghdad a center of trade and commerce? What items were traded? How did trade promote cultural exchanges?*

♦ Role-play a conversation between a Muslim and a non-Muslim in the Abbasid era, with the Muslim pointing out to the other person the benefits of conversion.

♦ Investigate military slavery as a form of social bondage in early Islamic society. *Why did rulers want to recruit military slaves? Where did these slaves come from? Why have they been called "slaves on horses"? What differences were there between military slavery and domestic or agricultural slavery?*

Grades 7-8

◗ Compose a letter from a scholar in Muslim Spain to a colleague in Baghdad, describing economic and cultural conditions in his city. *How did the use of Arabic language promote cultural exchange among Muslims in various regions?*

◗ Read excerpts such as *Sura IV* from the Qur'an to discover what kind of family life and gender relations were prescribed in Islamic society. *How do these compare to prescriptions concerning men, women, and families in the Old and New Testaments?*

◗ Examine how the Abbasids promoted learning and advanced science, mathematics, and medicine. Research individuals such as Ibn Sina (Avicenna), Abu Hanifa, Hunayn, or al-Biruni, and explain how they advanced scientific knowledge.

◗ Research the treatment of non-Muslims in the Abbasid empire. *What was the legal status of Christians and Jews living in the empire? In what ways did they contribute to the achievements of Abbasid society?*

Grades 9-12

◗ Research the lives of prominent women such as scholars, philanthropists, poets, and artists during the Abbasid period. *What factors in Muslim society enabled them to reach prominence?* (Resources: N. Abbot, *Two Queens of Baghdad* and E. W. Fernea and B. Q. Bezirgan, *Middle Eastern Muslim Women Speak*)

◗ Explain the social roles and relative status of government bureaucrats, landowning notables, scholars, peasants, urban artisans, and slaves within the Abbasid empire. *What influence did religion have on social roles and social standing? What advantages did conversion to Islam confer?*

◗ Role-play the part of an adviser to an Abbasid ruler, and review Sassanid Persian and Byzantine government and military institutions in comparison with Abbasid ones. *What are the strengths and weaknesses of each?*

◗ Make a list of the effects that the Muslim practice of veiling and seclusion of women on the one hand, and the Muslim law giving women control over their own property, income, and inheritance even after marriage on the other, are likely to have had on women's lives.

◗ Assuming the role of an Arab merchant, write a letter to a fellow merchant in Baghdad describing your voyage from the Persian Gulf to the city of Guangzhou (Canton) on the South China coast. *What was the voyage like? What sort of relations do you have with the Chinese government? What goods are you trading in? Why did you travel such a long distance to trade?*

C. The consolidation of the Byzantine state in the context of expanding Islamic civilization.

Grades 5-6

◗ Construct a map showing the expansion of Orthodox Christianity in Eastern Europe and Russia.

◗ Draw and label typical weapons of this period such as the compound bow and arrow, lance, body armor, and Greek fire. *How valuable were these weapons in the defense of the Byzantine Empire? Why was Greek fire a closely guarded secret?*

◗ Write a letter from a citizen of the Byzantine state expressing your support to Theodora in her efforts to lead your people against Arab Muslim attacks. *What role does public support play in maintaining a government's effectiveness, especially in times of war?*

◗ Research an important cultural or political achievement made during this period in Byzantium. Create a mosaic to illustrate this achievement.

Grades 7-8

▶ Research and make models of various military and merchant ship designs of the 9th century such as the Mediterranean galley, the dhow, and Viking ships. *What accounts for the differences in these designs? To what uses were each of these kinds of ships put? What was the relative importance of the army and the navy in Byzantine defense against Arab Muslim attacks?*

▶ Assuming the role of a Byzantine military official, describe the weapons, fortifications, and military preparedness of the Byzantine Empire and explain how it was able to withstand Bulgar and Arab attacks.

▶ Assume the role of a foreign traveler and describe your impressions of Constantinople and the imperial government of the Byzantine emperor. *How would your impressions differ if you were a traveler to Baghdad describing that city and the Abbasid imperial government?*

Grades 9-12

▶ Describe the spread of Greek Orthodox Christianity into the Balkans, Ukraine, and Russia between the 9th and 11th centuries. *What explains the acceptance of Greek over Latin Christianity in part of the Slavic world?*

▶ Construct an appeal to the Byzantine emperor on the importance of preserving the works of the ancient Greek and Hellenistic scholars. *What arguments would you use to convince the emperor of the necessity of maintaining Greek learning?*

▶ Compare and contrast Constantinople and Baghdad as centers of manufacturing and long-distance trade. *How did economic power translate into military and political power in each?*

▶ Draw evidence from the legends in the Russian Chronicle regarding Vladimir of Kiev and his conversion to Eastern Orthodox Christianity. *Why was Vladimir inclined to accept the Greek Orthodox Church rather than Judaism, Islam, or Latin Christianity? What do the stories reveal regarding the relationship of church and state in Kievan Russia?*

III. *Major developments in East Asia and Southeast Asia in the era of the Tang dynasty, 600-900 CE.*

A. China's sustained political and cultural expansion in the Tang period.

Grades 5-6

▶ On a map of China, show the physical features of the land, locate the network of canals, and indicate the greatest extent of the Tang dynasty. *How did China's geography affect farming techniques? How did the Grand Canal change life in China?*

▶ Assume the role of a diplomat or traveler from Constantinople or Baghdad to one of the cities of Tang China, and write accounts to government officials back home of what you have observed. *What could your empire learn from Tang China?*

▶ Describe the development of cities in Tang China. *Where did major cities develop? Who went to live there? What caused people to migrate to cities?*

▶ Write a letter from a city planner in Tang China explaining to a fellow planner what made a success of his development. Include a plan of the development showing the major geographical advantages and factors that attracted people to migrate there.

Grades 7-8

▶ Assuming the role of an adviser to a Tang emperor, argue for the development of a network of roads and canals in the empire. *How would you justify the cost of these public works? How might you raise the money needed? How would you organize the building project? How would they benefit the state and the public?*

▶ Explain how Buddhism was introduced from China to Korea and Japan. Tell the story of how the Korean emperor encouraged Japan to adopt Buddhism. *Why did the Soga clan advise the Japanese emperor to accept Buddhism?*

▶ Map the extent of the Tang empire and mark the major trade routes used. *What products were exchanged?*

▶ Analyze Tang landscape painting and examples of Tang pottery. *What ideas and values about everyday life are expressed?*

Grades 9-12

▶ Research living conditions in China and compare urban with rural society during the Tang dynasty. *How did life differ in rural areas from urban communities?*

▶ Research and discuss the story of the journey of the Tang monk Xuan Zang to India in quest of Buddhist scriptures. *What part did the "Monkey King" who accompanied Xuan Zang play? Journey to the West,* the novel chronicling the journey, was written much later, in the Ming Dynasty period. *Is the novel likely to tell us more about Tang times or Ming?*

▶ Summarize the technologies developed during the Tang dynasty and how they were used. *What impact did these technologies have on China? By what routes might knowledge of these technologies have spread?*

B. Developments in Japan, Korea, and Southeast Asia in an era of Chinese ascendancy.

Grades 5-6

▶ Construct a map of the Japanese islands showing elevation and the proximity of the islands to Korea and the Chinese mainland. *What role did geography play in the development of Japan? How did it influence Japan's relations with China and Korea?*

▶ Draw upon evidence from diaries to write a poem describing the lives of women in the court of the emperor. *What was the position of women in Heian Japan?*

▶ Research how wet rice is cultivated and drawn an outline of the agricultural cycle associated with it. *What role did the family play in rice cultivation in Japan? How did the family accommodate the rice cycle? How are popular festivals in Japan related to the agricultural cycle? What role did rice play in the economy of Japan?*

Grades 7-8

▶ Reading selections from the *Kojiki* in *Sources of Japanese Tradition,* explain the legends of the creation of Japan. Explain the differences between history and legend. *What do these stories tell you about ancient Japanese history?*

▶ On a timeline, trace the development of the early cultures of Japan from the Jomon, ca. 10,000 BCE, through the "tomb culture," ca. 200 CE. *What did each of these cultures introduce to the islands of Japan?*

▶ Explain the basic beliefs of Shinto. Using works of art and literature, describe the impact of Shinto on Japan.

▶ Investigate how the Chinese language was used as a written "lingua franca" for government throughout East Asia at this time. *How does this compare with the use of Latin in the West?*

▶ Describe courtly life and the search for beauty in Heian Japan. *Why was calligraphy so important in pottery?*

Grades 9-12

♦ Examine how the Tang dynasty extended its influence in East Asia. *To what extent did Korea and Vietnam adopt Chinese traditions? To what extent did Korea and Vietnam resist Chinese political domination? What was the relationship between Tang China and Japan? Why do you think a historian who has studied the influence of Confucianism and Chinese government on Vietnam referred to the latter as a "smaller dragon"?*

♦ Analyze Prince Shotoku's "Constitution" for evidence of borrowing and adapting Chinese ideas in ancient Japan. *If the Taika reforms had endured, how might Japan's imperial government have changed?*

♦ Read selections from the *Diary of Murasaki Shikibu* and *The Pillow Book* by Sei Shonagon. Discuss the importance of women as authors at the Japanese court of the Heian period. *Who were these women? How did their writings reflect social roles and values of the imperial court?*

♦ Examine the difference between spoken language and writing systems. *How many writing systems are there in the world? What is unique about the Chinese writing system?* Explain how the Japanese adapted the Chinese writing system to fit the spoken language of Japan.

♦ Select poems from the *Kokinshu*. *What is distinctive about the* waka (*or* tanka) *form that developed in Japan at this time?*

♦ Research the history of the commercial state of Srivijaya in Southeast Asia. Studying a map of the region, explain why the Strait of Malacca was such a strategic waterway for interregional trade. *How did the pattern of the monsoon winds make Srivijaya a "hinge" of trade between China and India? Why do you think Srivijaya became a rich and powerful kingdom?*

IV. The search for political, social, and cultural redefinition in Europe, 500-1000 CE.

A. The foundations of a new civilization in Western Christendom in the 500 years following the breakup of the western Roman Empire.

Grades 5-6

♦ Write a biography of Clovis including his conversion and its results, and map the lands he conquered. *What part did his wife Clothilde and other royal women of the time play in the Christianization of Frankish and Saxon peoples? What part did conquest play?*

♦ Explain the function of monasteries in western Europe during the early medieval period and sketch a plan for a monastery that reflects those functions. *What services did monasteries perform? How did monasteries preserve ancient learning? Why did monks become missionaries? Did monks and nuns fulfill the same functions?*

♦ Read the description of Charlemagne given by his friend and biographer Einhard, and an account of Charlemagne's government, laws, and conquests in a secondary source. *What can you infer from this information about his values and aims? About the difficulties he had to overcome? About his successes in achieving his aims?*

Grades 7-8

♦ Map the Carolingian world, including the tributary peoples. *How did the Carolingian influence expand, what were its greatest acquisitions, and why did it contract?*

◆ From illustrations and written accounts (Einhard), describe the coronation of Charlemagne. *At his coronation what did Charlemagne expect of his people and himself? What were his expectations and perhaps his goals? How were they fulfilled?*

◆ Research and compare the lives of Charlemagne, Harun al-Rashid, and the Empress Irene. *How did each of these leaders influence the political order in Europe?*

◆ Discuss the usefulness of the term "Dark Ages" to characterize medieval Europe, and consider the factors that might make for a "dark age" in any society.

◆ Examine the Rule of St. Benedict. *Why did St. Benedict prescribe times for prayer and meditation? Was this rule harsh? Why were men and women willing to live by this rule? What importance did this rule have for monks, nuns, and missionaries?*

Grades 9-12

◆ Compare Charlemagne's empire with Byzantium, the Abbasid empire, and the Islamic caliphate of Iberia in regard to their size, wealth, and political organization.

◆ Construct a chart showing several significant similarities and differences in the governance and worship in the Latin Catholic and Byzantine churches. *How did the "governors" of these churches seek to promote conversion in eastern and western Europe?*

◆ Relate the life of the Anglo-Saxon missionary Boniface. *How did he represent "the romanization of Europe"? In what ways did he serve as an exemplar for other monks and missionaries?*

◆ Read excerpts from *The Song of Roland*. Evaluate it as a factual account of Charlemagne's military campaign in 778. *What other purposes might the document have had? How did the campaign change the relationship between the Roman Church and western Europe? How does it express the growing relationship between the secular and religious leaders of Western civilization?*

◆ Write an account of the relationship between the popes and Carolingian rulers on the other. *What interest did the popes and rulers have in common? In what ways did they further each other's interests? In what ways did their interests conflict?*

B. The coalescence of political and social order in Europe.

Grades 5-6

◆ Sketch a Viking ship and, on a map, locate major Norse settlements. Trace Viking travel routes to the North Atlantic, Russia, western Europe, and the Black Sea. *Where did the Vikings come from? Why did peoples of England or northern France fear them so much? Why do you think the Viking settlement in North America (Newfoundland) did not endure?*

◆ Write a biographical report on King Alfred of England. *Why was he called Alfred the Great? How did he defend his lands against the Vikings?*

◆ Make a poster comparing Norse mythological characters to Greek and Indian figures. *How does this mythology affect Western culture to this day (names of days, etc.)?*

Grades 7-8

◆ Keep two journals, one for a day in the life of an early medieval noble woman and one for a peasant woman. Include subjects such as marriage, family, food, work, household organization, and religion. *How were the roles of women in differing social classes similar and varying? What burdens affected a peasant woman who was a serf? What legal rights and protections did women have in the feudal order?*

♦ Construct a map of major Norse settlements and routes of communication in the region extending from North America to Russia and the Black Sea. *What contributions did Vikings make to long-distance trade? Should they be credited with the European "discovery" of America? Why did Norse settlements in Newfoundland and Greenland fail to survive?*

♦ Read selections from *The Saga of the Volsungs*, the Norse epic of Sigurd the Dragon slayer. *What might the saga tell us about folk like in northern Europe between the 5th and 11th centuries?*

Grades 9-12

♦ Research the status of peasants in 9th- and 10th-century Europe. *Were peasants better or worse off in these centuries than they had been under Roman rule? How did the political fragmentation of Europe after Charlemagne affect the lives of peasants?*

♦ Research reasons why the Carolingian empire did not endure after the death of Charlemagne. Draw a political map of western and central Europe in the 10th century. *Why were European nobles able to assert independent power? What connection may have existed between Viking and Magyar invasions and the political fragmenting of large areas of Europe?*

♦ Construct a chart comparing how the Magyar cavalry and the Viking longboat gave an advantage to invaders. *How did Norse invasions of Britain affect Christian culture and learning? What happened to the Magyar invaders after the 10th century?*

V. The development of agricultural societies and new states in tropical Africa and Oceania.

A. State-building in Northeast and West Africa and the southward migrations of Bantu-speaking peoples.

Grades 5-6

♦ Create a relief map of West Africa illustrating the topography of the regions. Use symbols to locate agricultural products, settlements, and trade items. Include a legend and brief explanation interpreting the display.

♦ Draw a Venn diagram comparing Jenne-jeno with earlier river valley civilizations such as Mesopotamia. *What influence did the natural environment have on agriculture, settlement patterns, and trade in each case?*

♦ Create a travel guide that highlights the basic survival skills, supplies, and means of transport necessary to cross the Sahara Desert around 1000 CE. *How did the difficulties faced in making such a trip affect trade between the Mediterranean region and West Africa? What were the most important goods traded? Why were camels superior to wheeled transport in making the crossings?*

Grades 7-8

♦ Identify a person in your family who is the family historian, the "keeper of tales." Interview this person for a family story and share it with the class. *What functions did the griot have in West African society? What sources are there for West African history during this era? In what different ways do oral traditions and other kinds of evidence, verbal and physical, give historians access to the past?*

♦ Write a traveler's guide to the routes taken by the salt-gold trade. Include a description of Jenne-jeno. *How did the salt-gold trade promote urbanization in West Africa?*

▶ View slides or pictures that portray the physical and cultural diversity of West Africa and write a few words describing each. Compile the descriptions in a paragraph beginning with "West Africa is...."

▶ Drawing on archaeological evidence for the growth of Jenne-jeno, interpret the commercial importance of this city in West African history. *How did the commercial importance of Jenne-jeno in this era compare with that of contemporary western European commercial centers such as early Venice?*

▶ Describe the royal court in Ghana and how the monarch ruled. *How might belief in the king's divinity have contributed to Ghana's imperial success?*

▶ Read Ethiopian legends of the introduction of Christianity to that land. *By what routes do you think Christianity might have reached Ethiopia in the 4th century? What importance do Solomon and Sheba have in Ethiopian accounts of their past? Where was the kingdom of Aksum, and why did its location favor international trade?*

Grades 9-12

▶ Locate the region occupied by Ancient Ghana on a modern map of Africa. *How did the geographic location of the Soninke contribute to their ability to exploit trade to and from the Sahara? What was the role of grain production in the establishment of the empire?*

▶ Construct an abstract model of an empire using comparative information from the Ghana and Carolingian states. *What characteristics must a state have to be considered an empire? What were some major differences between the Ghana and Carolingian empires? What similarities and differences do you find in these two empires in agriculture, trade, standard of living, expansionary tendencies, and the role of religious ideas?*

▶ Discuss the unique characteristics and strengths of oral tradition and the role of the griot in West African society. Compare this to the role of the monk in medieval Europe in keeping knowledge alive. Assess the strengths of each method of recording history.

▶ Design a room for an exhibit in an archaeological museum for West African artifacts. Choose the items you would display and label them in a way that would contribute to understanding of reasons for the development of Ghana into a large-scale empire.

▶ Read selections from the *Periplus of the Erythraean Sea*, the Greek shipping manual of the 1st century CE, for evidence of the importance of trade in the African state of Aksum. *What are some of the goods that passed through Adulis, the Aksumite Red Sea port? How was Aksum well situated to play a large role in long-distance trade? What reasons do historians give for the decline of Aksum in the 8th century?*

▶ Map the spread and pattern of settlement of Bantu-speaking farmers and herders in eastern, central, and southern Africa up to 1000 CE. *In what ways did knowledge of ironworking, the introduction of bananas from Southeast Asia, and the presence of the tsetse fly influence settlement patterns?*

B. The peopling of Oceania and the establishment of agricultural societies and states.

Grades 5-6

▶ Make a model of a simple ocean-going vessel that would have been used by early migrants in Oceania to populate the islands. *How might patterns of ocean currents and wind have facilitated or hindered such migrations?*

▶ Drawing upon myths, legends, long-ago experiences, and histories of early Hawaiians, draw pictures illustrating daily life on the islands in distant times.

▶ Compare and contrast how life in Hawaii today differs from life there before the eighteenth century.

Grades 7-8

▶ Research sources on the history of Southeast Asia and the Pacific islands of Polynesia and New Zealand. From your reading discern aspects of the cultures of these peoples that indicate that there is a "link" between these areas. *Did the islanders have ancestors who came from Southeast Asia? How did they get to these islands?*

▶ Research and prepare a map with icons showing plants and animals introduced by Polynesian settlers. *Where did these plants and animals come from? How did these introductions affect the existing island flora and fauna?*

▶ On a map of the Pacific areas trace lines of known or potential trade routes. Discuss the geographic problems that a trader would encounter traveling to the Pacific islands.

Grades 9-12

▶ Report on the Maori, a people of New Zealand. *When did they arrive in New Zealand? Where did they originate? What evidence is used by anthropologists to determine their place of origin?* In your report include information about the religion, art, class structure, and government of the Maori.

▶ View the film "Rapa Nui," about Easter Island. Research the work of archaeological and anthropological studies done that speculate on the cause of the collapse of the social order there. Include studies done by Alfred Metreaux and Thor Heyerdahl. *Which study does the film support?*

▶ Compare and contrast the art of Oceanic societies. *What materials were used? What seemed to be the purpose of the art? What was not depicted?* Choose art objects representing several oceanic cultures and tell what is known about these items. Using a map of Oceania, locate the origin of the art you have chosen.

▶ Compare and contrast the different types of boats and related navigational skills developed in several regions of the world in the first millennium CE and decide what advantages each design offered the sailors. *How did sailors/shipbuilders adapt their vessels to the particular areas to be sailed and the needs of trade?*

> ## VI. The rise of centers of civilization in Mesoamerica and Andean South America in the first millennium CE.

A. The origins, expansion, and achievements of Maya civilization.

Grades 5-6

▶ Locate Maya city-states on a map of Mesoamerica using symbols to indicate roads and sea routes. Hypothesize reasons for the development of urban societies in these locations.

▶ Select a Maya deity and construct a clay figure or a mask depicting its attributes. Explain the importance of religion and religious beliefs in Maya society.

▶ Compare the Maya pok a tok (a ceremonial ball game) with our modern sports. *Which modern sport is pok a tok most like?* Illustrate the similarities on a double drawing. *Were the reasons for playing the games also similar?*

▶ Make medals to compare Mesopotamian ziggurats with the Maya pyramids. *In what ways are they similar? In what ways are they different? Were the purposes they served similar or different?*

Grades 7-8

◗ Draw a map illustrating the exchange of trade items, commodities, and luxury goods such as cacao, salt, feathers, jade, and obsidian. *What conclusions may be drawn from the extent of Maya trade? How important was trade to the Maya economy?*

◗ Use visual data, such as graphs and charts, to illustrate how the Maya altered their methods of farming depending on topography and climate. *How important was agricultural production to the development of the Maya empire?*

◗ Construct a model or visual representation of a Maya city-state such as Palenque. Estimate the number of people who are likely to have lived in such an urban settlement. *What conditions had to be met to allow such numbers to live together?*

◗ List the major achievements of Maya civilization and explain their relationship to everyday life. *How did achievements in astronomy affect Maya society? How valuable to farmers were mathematical innovations and the calendar to farmers?*

◗ Research interpretations why classical Maya society declined, and prepare an oral presentation analyzing and evaluating these factors.

◗ Read excerpts from Douglas Gifford's *Warriors, Gods and Spirits from Central and South American Mythology* to examine the ways in which Maya myths reflect social values and daily survival skills.

Grades 9-12

◗ Select two contrasting Maya deities and compare with two Hindu deities. Make an illustration showing comparisons.

◗ Using methods of an archaeologist and historian, explain how we have knowledge of Maya civilization from deciphered hieroglyphics. *How has the Maya "Long Count" calendar served as a tool for learning about Maya civilization? How might Spanish destruction of Maya books hamper our understanding of Maya culture? How have recent historical interpretations altered our knowledge of Maya political organization and warfare?*

◗ Create a schematic design including a temple/pyramid, cave, ball court, and planetarium, and explain their relationship to each other and to Maya religious beliefs.

◗ Create a mural using glyphs integrated into the design, illustrating social organization, ritual practices such as blood letting and warfare. Explain the mural, relating it to historical evidence of Maya society and religious beliefs.

◗ Read excerpts from the *Popul Vuh*. Compare it with Christian notions of creation and beliefs.

B. The rise of the Teotihuacán, Zapotec/Mixtec, and Moche civilizations.

Grades 5-6

◗ On a map of the Western Hemisphere, locate the Zapotec, Teotihuacán, and Moche civilizations. *In what modern countries would you find archaeological sites of each of these civilizations?*

◗ Construct a model of Monte Albán based on pictorial representations and site plans. *What does the model tell about the Zapotec civilization?*

◗ Locate Monte Albán and Teotihuacán on a topographical map. Write a short description of each environment and discuss the ways that they might be similar or different.

◗ Construct and decorate clay pottery using symbols that are important to you. *How can pottery help us learn about societies such as the Moche who left no written records? What can we learn from the Moche pottery and clay figures?*

Grades 7-8

♦ Examine Maya and Teotihuacán murals, and speculate on reasons for their differences. *What inferences may be drawn from these murals about the societies that produced them? Why do you think the Teotihuacán murals lack battle scenes?*

♦ Research *ayllus* (kinship groups) and explain how they regulated family and community life in Andean societies.

♦ Examine Moche art and artifacts to determine patterns of daily life among the people. *What do these artifacts tell about the interests, occupations, and religious concerns of the people?*

♦ Make a map showing the different types of agriculture practiced in the Moche/Andean area.

♦ Using photographs and illustrations, construct a model of the Grand Plaza at Monte Albán. *How long may it have taken to build the plaza? What functions did the buildings on the plaza have? What does Monte Albán tell us about the organization of Zapotec/Mixtec society?*

Grades 9-12

♦ Compare religion and ritual practices of Moche, Teotihuacán and Maya civilizations. *Based on the 1988 discovery of the tomb of a Moche warrior priest, what is known about religion and ritual practices in Moche society? How does this compare to what is known about the Maya or Teotihuacán?*

♦ Construct a two-layer calendar using a 360-day year, 30-day month, and overlay with a different Mesoamerican calendar. *What accounts for the differences in these calendars?*

♦ Research the cultures of the Moche, Tihuanaco, Chimu, or other Andean societies, exploring such aspects as textile production, gold metallurgy, burial practices, and social relations between men and women.

♦ Develop a hypothesis to assess possible methods of contact between Mesoamerica and the Andean world. Use examples of agriculture, societal structure, and artisan crafts to consider cultural diffusion.

♦ Present a report on the Moche using maps and other visuals. Choose a contemporary civilization in Afro-Eurasia and compare the Moche's accomplishments to other civilizations of that time period. Select one European, one Asian, and one African society.

VII. *Major global trends from 300-1000 CE.*

Major global trends from 300-1000 CE.

Grades 5-6

♦ Draw a wall-size map identifying the major overland and maritime trade routes linking Africa, Europe, and Asia. Use symbols to show the major goods that were carried along those routes. *How were ideas and religious beliefs spread along trade routes? What in your own life has been brought to where you live from some other part of the world?*

♦ List the factors that led to the weakening of empires in Africa and Eurasia by the end of the 10th century CE. *How are these factors similar to those that weakened empires of the ancient world? What can we learn from this that would apply in our world today?*

♦ On a map of Eurasia and Africa indicate the distribution of major religions at about 300 CE. *Make another map for 1000 CE. What accounts for differences in the two maps? How did advocates of different religions spread their ideas?*

Grades 7-8

▶ Choose a period some time between 800 and 1000 CE and write a handbook, based on historical information, for Muslim merchants doing business at that time. Describe trade routes, commercial goods, peoples, and other information, as well as problems likely to be encountered along the routes.

▶ Choose several specific items known to be transmitted long distances in the last quarter of the first millennium CE, including both intangibles (such as the concept of zero) and tangibles (such as paper or oranges). For each, trace its transmission from its point of origin to other regions. *What part did Muslims play in the transmission of ideas and goods during this period?*

▶ Map major maritime and overland trade routes in Africa and Eurasia near the beginning and the end of the 300-1000 CE period. For each period explain which people dominated each of the major routes, what people were served by the routes, and what major items were exchanged. *What impact did the changes in trading patterns have on the societies involved?*

Grades 9-12

▶ Based on historical evidence pertaining to the first millennium CE, write a speech to an audience of potential converts to Buddhism, giving reasons why they should make this change. Write other speeches appealing to them to become Muslims or Christians. *What characteristics of the audiences you are appealing to need to be taken into account? How will your appeal to the different groups need to differ?*

▶ Construct a grid indicating on one axis empires such as the Roman, Han, and Gupta that collapsed during the first millennium CE. List on the other axis possible causes of the collapse such as nomadic invasions, failings of rulers, and social and economic conditions. After filling in information for each box of the grid, debate whether the causes of decline of these empires were more similar than different. *What factors might account for the similarities and differences?*

▶ Using a set of overlay maps, compare the temporal and geographical movements of pastoral peoples from the Arabian Peninsula with those from Central Asia in the first millennium CE. Assess, in each case, the part that environmental change, religion, military technology, and other factors might have played in animating these movements.

Bas relief at Mahabalipuram, South India. Archaeological Survey, Government of India

ERA 5

Intensified Hemispheric Interactions, 1000-1500 CE

Giving Shape to World History

In this era the various regions of Eurasia and Africa became more firmly interconnected than at any earlier time in history. The sailing ships that crossed the wide sea basins of the Eastern Hemisphere carried a greater volume and variety of goods than ever before. In fact, the chain of seas extending across the hemisphere—China seas, Indian Ocean, Persian Gulf, Red Sea, Black Sea, Mediterranean, and Baltic—came to form a single interlocking network of maritime trade. In the same centuries caravan traffic crossed the Inner Asian steppes and the Sahara Desert more frequently. As trade and travel intensified so did cultural exchanges and encounters, presenting local societies with a profusion of new opportunities and dangers. By the time of the transoceanic voyages of the Portuguese and Spanish, the Eastern Hemisphere already constituted a single zone of intercommunication possessing a unified history of its own.

A global view reveals four "big stories" that give shape to the entire era.

▶ **China and Europe—Two Centers of Growth:** In two regions of the Eastern Hemisphere, China and Europe, the era witnessed remarkable growth. China experienced a burst of technological innovation, commercialization, and urbanization, emerging as the largest economy in the world. As China exported its silks and porcelains to other lands and imported quantities of spices from India and Southeast Asia, patterns of production and commerce all across the hemisphere were affected. At the opposite end of Eurasia, western and central Europe emerged as a new center of Christian civilization, expanding in agricultural production, population, commerce, and military might. Powerful European states presented a new challenge to Muslim dominance in the Mediterranean world. At the same time Europe was drawn more tightly into the commercial economy and cultural interchange of the hemisphere.

▶ **The Long Reach of Islam:** In this era Islamic faith and civilization encompassed extensive new areas of Eurasia and Africa. The continuing spread of Islam was closely connected to the migrations of Turkic conquerors and herding fold and to the growth of Muslim commercial enterprise all across the hemisphere. By about 1400 CE Muslim societies spanned the central two-thirds of Afro-Eurasia. New Muslim states and towns were appearing in West Africa, the East African coast, Central Asia, India, and Southeast Asia. Consequently, Muslim merchants, scholars, and a host of long-distance travelers were the principal mediators in the interregional exchange of goods, ideas, and technical innovations.

▶ **The Age of Mongol Dominance:** The second half of the era saw extraordinary developments in interregional history. The Mongols under Chinggis Khan created the largest land empire the world had ever seen. Operating from Poland to Korea and Siberia to Indonesia, the Mongol warlords intruded in one way or another on the lives of almost all peoples of Eurasia. The conquests were terrifying, but the stabilizing of Mongol rule led to a century of fertile commercial and cultural interchange across the continent. Eurasian unification, however, had a disastrous consequence in the 14th century—the Black Death and its attendant social impact on Europe, the Islamic world, and probably China.

▶ **Empires of the Americas:** In the Western Hemisphere empire building reached an unprecedented scale. The political styles of the Aztec and Inca states were profoundly different. Even so, both enterprises demonstrated that human labor and creative endeavor could be organized on a colossal scale despite the absence of iron technology or wheeled transport.

Why Study This Era?

▶ The civilizations that flourished in this era—Chinese, Japanese, Indian, Islamic, European, West African, Mesoamerican, and others—created a legacy of cultural and social achievements of continuing significance today. To understand how cultural traditions affect social change or international relations in the contemporary world requires study of the specific historical contexts in which those traditions took form.

▶ The modern world with all its unique complexities did not emerge suddenly in the past 500 years but had its roots in the developments of the 1000-1500 era, notably the maturing of long-distance trade and the economic and social institutions connected with it.

▶ To understand both the history of modern Europe and the United States requires a grasp of the variety of institutions, ideas, and styles that took shape in western Christendom during this era of expansion and innovation.

The Cambodian city of Angkor Thom, 12th century. Library of Congress

Essay

Islam as a Special World-System*
by John Obert Voll

John Voll analyzes the shared sources of the Islamic experience that brought together urban and pastoral societies and transcended international boundaries. Voll contents that even in the context of the political fragmentation of the Muslim world the "great network of teachers and students provided one of the most important vehicles for the expansion of Islam...." The article stresses the importance of studying Islam as a world-system based on a community of discourse.

John Voll is on the faculty of the Center for Muslim-Christian Understanding and the History Department at Georgetown University. He is a past-president of the Middle East Studies Association and has written extensively on Islamic, Sudanese, and world history.

Islam is identified as a religion, a civilization, a way of life, and many other things. Some of this is simply a result of the confusion created by using the same term for different phenomena. As Marshall Hodgson noted twenty years ago, the terms *Islam* and *Islamic* are used "casually both for what we may call religion and for the overall society and culture associated historically with the religion." ' Confusion is also created by attributing to Islam the characteristics of terms that are thought to be generic but in fact have distinctive cultural or historical referents. This is sometimes clear in discussions that speak of Islam as a "religion" and may also be the case when we speak of "Islamic civilization." It may be useful to ask whether the complex of social relations that is often called Islamic civilization can be most effectively conceptualized for purposes of world historical analysis as a civilization or whether there are more useful identifying terms.

The current transformation of major social formations on a global scale provides the opportunity to reexamine our understanding of the nature of some of the basic units. In particular, it opens the way for examining the large-scale networks of relations that are the major units of contemporary global interactions. I propose to start with a well-known reconceptualization of global interactions, the world-system concepts that have been articulated by Immanuel Wallerstein, and to see if this framework can help define the global Islamic entity more usefully and clearly.

World-system theory is not a simple, monolithic explanation of global human history and society. Even as initially defined by Wallerstein, it was a complex cluster of approaches to understanding a wide variety of experiences. The world-system conceptualization has now become the basis for many different perspectives and interpretations, as the articles in issue after issue of the *Review* of the Fernand Braudel Center illustrate. Recent articles in that journal by Samir Amin and Andre Gunder Frank and a thought-provoking retrospective by Wallerstein all suggest the luxuriant productivity of this perspective.

Within this very broad field of concepts, it is difficult in a short discussion to do justice to the full relevance of world-system theory to an understanding of the Islamic historical experience. Therefore, I take one aspect of the early formulations of Wallerstein and explore its implications for the study of Islamic history. At the same time I consider the implications of Islamic history for world-system theory, because I think that the Islamic experience represents a special case that suggests a different way to formulate a world-system analysis.

*Reprinted from *Journal of World History*, Vol. 5, No. 2 (Fall 1994), pp. 213-226.

In his early presentation of the world-system approach, Wallerstein argued that

thus far there have only existed two varieties of such world-systems: world-empires, in which there is a single political system over most of the area...and those systems in which such a single system does not exist over all, or virtually all, of the space. For convenience and for want of a better term, we are using the term "world-economy" to describe the latter.... Prior to the modern era, world-economies were highly unstable structures which tended either to be converted into empires or to disintegrate. It is the peculiarity of the modern world-system that a world-economy has survived for 500 years and yet has not come to be transformed into a world-empire.... This peculiarity is the political side of the form of economic organization called capitalism.

This general presentation of the differences between modern and premodern world-systems is appealing both for its clarity and for what we know about the history of the major world civilizations. The alternations between grand imperial unifications and politico-economic disintegration in China, India, the Middle East, and Western Europe are important parts of the world historical narrative. The pattern described by Wallerstein of incipient world-economies that result either in imperial unifications or disintegrations seems to fit the history of the Middle East in the Islamic era. There is the period of the great imperial unification begun by the Arab-Muslim conquests in the seventh century and continued by the Umayyad and Abbasid caliphates. This imperial unification is part of the long line of great world-empires that brought the Middle Eastern and Mediterranean world-economy (or world-economies) under the control of one or two major imperial systems. This series began as early as the Phoenician-Greek-Persian network of the seventh century B.C.E. and stretched through the Hellenistic state system created by the conquests of Alexander the Great to the later Parthian-Sasanid and Roman-Byzantine empires.

The standard account notes the disintegration of the Islamic imperial system under the Abbasid rulers of the tenth and eleventh centuries C.E. and its replacement by a decentralized network of smaller states ruled by military commanders, or sultans, who replaced the imperial caliphs as the effective rulers of Muslim areas by the twelfth century. The final act in this process of disintegration was the destruction of Baghdad, the Abbasid capital, by Mongol forces in 1258. Journalistic accounts speak of the era of "backwardness and stagnation that afflicted the Muslim world between the fall of Baghdad...and the renaissance of the twentieth century." In the scholarly terms of his influential book, *The Arabs in History,* Bernard Lewis notes that at this time took place the "transformation of the Islamic Near East from a commercial, monetary economy to one which, despite an extensive and important foreign and transit trade, was internally a quasifeudal economy, based on subsistence agriculture "

This gloomy picture is correct in some very specific and limited ways. The imperial political unity of the Islamic world was irretrievably destroyed by the middle of the thirteenth century and in many areas the effectiveness of the urban-based commercial monetary economy was significantly reduced. In the terms of Wallerstein, in the absence of an effective world-empire, the old world-economy of the Middle East seems to have disintegrated. At this point one might simply state that the history of the premodern Islamic world-system appears to bear out Wallerstein's formulation.

However, the standard gloomy picture of the Islamic world following the Mongol conquest of Baghdad is not the only possible picture, as the works of scholars like William H. McNeill Marshall G. S. Hodgson, Ira Lapidus, and others show. The gloomy picture does not prepare the observer for the actual world situation at the beginning of the sixteenth century. As McNeill has noted,

> We are so accustomed to regard history from a European vantage point that the extra-ordinary scope and force of this Islamic expansion [in the period 1000-1500 C.E.], which prefigured and overlapped the later expansion of western Europe, often escapes attention. *Yet an intelligent and informed observer of the fifteenth century could hardly have avoided the conclusion that Islam rather than the remote and still comparatively crude society of the European Far West, was destined to dominate the world in the following centuries.*

In this so-called era of stagnation, the size of the Islamic world virtually doubled from what it had been in the days of the glories of the Abbasid caliphs. By the middle of the sixteenth century major Muslim imperial states had been established in the Mediterranean world, Iran, South Asia, Central Asia, and sub-Saharan Africa. The power and glory of the Ottoman, Safavid, Mughal, Uzbek, and Songhai empires more than matched the emerging Iberian empires of the day and outshone the smaller dynastic states of Western Europe. In addition, Islam was actively winning converts beyond the boundaries of these empires in Southeast Asia, southeastern Europe, and elsewhere.

The world of Islam was, in fact, dynamic and expanding, not static and stagnating, or disintegrating. As a global unit, however, it is difficult to define in the standard terms of world-systems theory. It stretched from the inner Asian territories of the Manchu empire in China and the small sultanate of Manila in the Philippines to the Muslim communities growing in Bosnia and sub-Saharan Africa. Whatever the unit was, it was not a world-empire and had no prospect of becoming one. At the same time, it was not disintegrating and collapsing. Neither of the alternatives posed by Wallerstein for premodern world-systems seems to be applicable to the Islamic entity in world history in the period just before modern times.

Part of the problem may lie in the way we look at this Islamic entity as it emerged in the centuries following the collapse of effective Abbasid imperial power in the tenth century. The term most frequently used is *civilization,* as in "classical (or medieval) Islamic civilization." This is an awkward term because it implies a civilizational coherence similar to other historic civilizations. As long as the Muslim community was primarily or exclusively Middle Eastern, it could be thought of as the most recent phase of the long-standing tradition of civilization in the Middle East. In the half-millennium after the Abbasid collapse, however, Islam became an important component in many societies outside the Middle East. Some, like India, themselves represented significant traditions of civilization, and this civilizational identity was not eliminated by the introduction of Islam. As a result, by the sixteenth century, the Islamic entity was an intercivilizational entity, not an autonomous "civilization." Further, this expanding Islamic entity now included areas where the complex urban structures characteristic of traditions of civilization were not the dominant modes of social organization. The Islamic entity included both urban-based and pastoral nomadic communities.

This Islamic entity was a vast network of interacting peoples and groups, with considerable diversity and yet some sufficiently common elements so that it is possible to speak of these diverse communities as being part of "the Islamic world." I hasten to add that the problem of understanding the "unity and diversity" found within the Islamic world is a major and continuing one for scholars of Islam.' It is tempting to think of this Islamic world as a premodern world-system. In terms of Wallerstein's early definition, it is possible to see this vast network of interacting peoples and groups as "a social system...that has boundaries, structures, member groups, rules of legitimation, and coherence."

The real foundation of this world-system does not appear to be a world-economy in the precise sense of the term as used in the analyses of Wallerstein and others. The primary sense of a self-contained identity and the meaning of the boundaries and legitimations do not lie predominantly in the world of trade, production, and exchange. In the current debates over the nature of world-systems and such issues as whether or not there is one world-system extending over 5,000 years, as Frank argues, most people engaging in the discourse of world-systems theory are speaking about the material world and economic forces.

Perhaps a foundation of economic ties does bind the Muslim communities of West Africa, Central Asia, the Middle East, and Southeast Asia. Unfortunately, there has been little examination of the trade patterns within the Muslim world in the centuries following the Abbasid collapse. Recent research by Janet L. Abu-Lughod shows how important such studies can be. She presents a picture of "a long-standing, globally-integrated 'world-system,' to which Europe had finally attached itself." She notes that this world-system of the thirteenth century had three or four core areas and states that "no single cultural, economic, or imperial system was hegemonic. Indeed, a wide variety of cultural systems coexisted and cooperated, most of them organized very differently from the West."' It is noteworthy that the trade of the three major "core" zones in Abu-Lughod's analysis (the Middle East Central Asia and China, and the Indian Ocean basin) tended to be dominated by Muslim-controlled groups or Muslim communities. However, it was not trade or economic exchange that gave this Islamic entity its identity or basic cohesion.

In a recent article, Wallerstein noted that scholars dealing with world-systems analysis face the challenge of "elaboration of world-systems other than that of the capitalist world-economy."' I suggest that to understand the premodern entity of the Islamic world as a world-system, it is necessary to define world-systems in ways that are not as closely confined to the economic and material dimensions of history as the conceptualizations of almost all world-systems scholars. For example, Wallerstein insists that the networks and boundaries that define a world-system must be related to material exchanges and the economic dimensions of social systems.'

The Islamic world had a dimension of social legitimation and boundary definition that made it possible for someone like the great Muslim traveler, Ibn Battuta, to journey in the fourteenth century from North Africa to China and yet remain largely within "the cultural boundaries of what Muslims called the Dar al-Islam or Abode of Islam." This Dar al-Islam can be seen as a special example of a large-scale human group, using the definition of William H. McNeill: "What is common to all groups, surely, is a pattern of communication among members, sufficiently frequent & and sufficiently standardized as to minimize surprises and maximize congruence between expectation and experience so far as encounters within the group itself are concerned."' This pattern of communication in the Islamic world is not primarily based upon exchange of goods, coordination of means of production, or a large network of economic activities. Instead, it is built on the shared sources of the Islamic experience, which provide the basis for mutually intelligible discourse among all who identify themselves as Muslims within the Dar al-Islam.

One can view the world of Islam as a large, special type of "community of discourse," in the sense in which that term is used by Robert Wuthnow: "Discourse subsumes the written as well as the verbal, the formal as well as the informal, the gestural or ritual as well as the conceptual. It occurs, however, within communities in the broadest sense of the word: communities of competing producers, of interpreters and critics, of audiences and consumers, and of patrons and other significant actors who become the subjects of discourse itself. It is only in these concrete living and breathing communities that discourse becomes meaningful." This pattern of communication or discourse provides the basis for identifying Dar al-Islam as a social system or human group possessing boundaries, structures, coherence, and rules of legitimation.

The Islamic discourse was able to cross the boundaries between urban-based and pastoral agrarian societies and those between the different major traditions of civilization in the Afro-Eurasian landmass. Networks of personal and organizational interaction created at least a minimal sense of corporate, communal identity in the vast emerging world-system. The modern world-system described by Wallerstein is the "capitalist world system," identified by a distinctive structure of production and exchange. Similarly, the Muslims might be said to have created the "Islamic world-system," identified by a distinctive set of sociomoral symbols for the definition of proper human relationships. I am *not* saying that the capitalist world-system is an "economic" system and the Islamic world-system is a "religious" one. Rather, I am suggesting that both are relatively comprehensive social systems that can qualify as world-systems, even though the primary identifying characteristics are drawn from different dimensions of the social system as a whole.

The emerging Islamic world-system of cat 1000-1800 presents some interesting problems of definition, which may be helpful in the effort to elaborate world-systems other than that of modern capitalism. I suggest that the early Islamic community—the imperial community of the Umayyads and the Abbasids from the seventh to the mid-tenth century—followed the standard pattern of world-system development. The classical Muslim caliphate was an important successor state to the "universal empires" of the tradition established by the Persians and Alexander the Great. As the world-empire system disintegrated, the collapse of the Middle Eastern world-economy seemed to be following suit.

If the premodern world-systems model held true, one would expect to see the disintegration of factors providing a systemwide sense of cohesion or shared identity. In political terms, this was clearly the case, as a variety of dynasties claimed the title of caliph, and even the fiction of loyalty to a single "successor to the Prophet" disappeared. However, although the sense of community-connectedness changed its form and organizational expression, it did not disappear. New-style organizations of legitimation and identity emerged, which were not directly dependent upon the political structure or state system. These were elaborations in concrete social forms of Islamic concepts and symbols providing a sociomoral foundation for transregional communal identity.

This transformation of the Islamic world-system can be described by paraphrasing Wallerstein's words concerning the distinctiveness of the modern world-system. He noted: "It is the peculiarity of the modern world-system that a world-economy has survived for 500 years and yet has not come to be transformed into a world-empire—a peculiarity that is the secret of its strength." I suggest that a similar statement can be made about the Islamic world-system since 1000 C.E.: It is the peculiarity of the Islamic world-system that a world-society survived for almost 1000 years and yet has not become transformed into either a world-empire or a world-economy—a peculiarity that is the secret of its strength and ability to survive.

The new Islamic world-system of the post-1000 era had distinctive organizational characteristics that contrast with the traditional Islamic world-empire. In the world-empire state, personal piety took many forms but tended not to become institutionalized. Respected figures led exemplary lives and established what is now called Sufism. For the first five hundred years of Islamic history, Sufism was a mood of pious and often ascetic devotion reflecting the lives and teachings of highly respected individuals. Not until the effective collapse of imperial unity, however, did this devotional tradition come to be manifested in the great social organizations called the *tariqahs,* which are the brotherhoods of every Muslim society.

In the twelfth century, the great *tariqah* organizations began to take shape.' In the context of the political disintegration of the Muslim world, the *tariqahs* assumed increasing importance as the vehicle for social cohesion and interregional unity. The "sufi movement was based on its popular appeal, and its new structure of religious unity was built on popular foundations.... While many *tariqahs* had only local significance, the greatest orders...spread over the whole or a large part of Islamic territory. Thus they contributed...to maintain the ideal unity of all Muslims....Teachers and disciples journeyed from end to end of the Muslim world, bearing the seeds of interchange and cross-fertilization within the sufi framework.'"

This great network of teachers and students provided one of the most important vehicles for the expansion of Islam in sub-Saharan Africa and Southeast Asia. The *tariqahs* gave people an identity that could be recognized throughout the Islamic world. Thus, a member of the Naqshbandiyyah Tariqah from northwest China could find brothers all along the road to Mecca. For example, in the eighteenth century this was the path followed by Ma Ming Xin, who studied with Naqshbandi *shaykhs* in Central Asia, India, Yemen, and the Holy Cities. On his return to China, his new approach led him into revivalist revolution that had ties with *tari*qah-related holy wars in many other parts of the Islamic world of the time. These *tariqah* networks provided an important foundational bond for the postimperial Islamic world-system.

In addition to shared teachings and identity, the *tariqahs* also provided physical support for travel throughout the Islamic world. After the development of the major widespread *tariqahs,* the wandering Sufi could turn to fellow members of the *tariqah* for spiritual support and also for shelter in the buildings of the order. Most *tariqah* centers had facilities for long-term students and more temporary travelers as well as areas for the practice of pious ritual. The visitors' facilities were known by various names throughout the Islamic world, such as *zawiyah, khanqah,* and the like, but they all performed comparable functions in making pious travel possible.'

Wandering scholars provide a similar vehicle for systemwide interactions. Muhammad is reported to have said, "Seek knowledge, even unto China," and Muslim scholars were great travelers. These were not simple sightseeing adventurers. Their goal was to gain greater knowledge within the framework of Islamic understanding. Travel for the sake of religious scholarship became "a normative feature of medieval Muslim education" and an important part of the definition of scholarship. The great traditions of legal opinion became the great "schools of law," with standardized texts to be taught and passed on. Study of the texts of law and traditions *(hadith)* of the Prophet and the other major disciplines provided the program for the travelers. By the twelfth and thirteenth centuries, a standard set of works defined the major schools of law and the accepted collections of traditions of the Prophet, and these provided a common "canonical syllabus of learning" for scholars anywhere within the postimperial Islamic world-system.'

The changing organization of travel in search of knowledge reflects the postimperial institutions of the Islamic world. The development of instructional centers went from individualized instruction, especially in particular mosques *(maslids)* that were not mosques for the Friday congregational prayers, to *masjids* with accompanying structures specifically for lodging out-of-town students and travelers (usually called *khans)*. These were followed by formal institutions of Islamic learning, called *madrasahs,* which emerged by the eleventh century in Southwest Asia, especially in the Seljuk domains, but rapidly spread throughout the Islamic world. It was in these *madrasahs* that the "canonical syllabus" was presented to scholars traveling in search of knowledge.

The vocabulary underwent a parallel evolution. The Arab terms for "travel" *(rihla)* and "seeking knowledge" were used almost interchangeably in early writings. Later they were separated, with *rihla* applying to pilgrimage and the other terms keeping the basic meaning. "This change may reflect the institutionalisation of the *madrasa* system in place of the formerly more individualized, orally-oriented relationships which prevailed between students and teachers in the early medieval centuries of Islamic history. Thus, Ibn Battuta [in the fourteenth century] usually looks for buildings—i.e., colleges of Islamic law and Sufi convents—rather than the solitary but renowned scholar here and there on his itinerary."

How the networks of Sufi teachers and itinerant scholars were related to the flows of economic goods is not clear. These people followed the same paths as wandering merchants, and Muslim merchants and Sufi teachers are frequently mentioned together as important elements in the nonmilitary expansion of Islam in many regions. It is clear, for example, that the two worked together in the Islamization of what is now the northern Sudan in the seventeenth and eighteenth centuries. In some cases, different branches of great families combined with *tariqahs* to provide a basis for networks of exchange of knowledge, political influence, and trade goods. For example, by the sixteenth century the Aydarus family of south Yemen had established a far-flung network of trade contacts, *tariqahs,* and scholarly centers throughout the Indian Ocean basin. Notables in this family held high positions in the courts of Indian princes and also acted as *tariqah* leaders and scholars of *hadith.*

Clearly, people who traveled in the Islamic world of the postimperial era—whether they were Sufi disciples, students of law, or merchants—were moving within a comprehensible unit that transcended the boundaries of regional traditions of civilization. Many were in the same situation that Sam Gellens notes for Ibn Battuta: "Ibn Battuta may not have known the local languages of the places he visited, but he did know the cultural language of Muslims and hence felt at home." They were moving within the framework of a hemispheric community of discourse, or discourse-based world-system.

This sense of community is symbolized and emphasized in the belief system through the general requirement of the pilgrimage to Mecca. Every year a large gathering of believers from throughout the Islamic world assembles in the central sanctuaries of Islam on the holiday of the pilgrimage. This requirement to travel and come together has had enormous significance in giving professing Muslims a sense of belonging to an entity that transcends particular civilizations or societies. It provides a way of communicating across boundaries that might exist within the community of Muslims. In Mecca during the pilgrimage it is possible to have a sense of a shared discourse that affirms the authenticity of the Islamic message, much like what Ibn Battuta experienced as he traveled in the various parts of the Islamic world. In contemporary times, the account of the pilgrimage by Malcolm X shows the continuing vitality of this experience of a special community of discourse.

The strength of this Islamic world-system is reflected in the fact that even at the peak of the hegemonic power of the modern capitalist world-system, Sufi teachers, merchants, and scholars continued to be successful in winning converts to Islam in Africa and Southeast Asia. Dutch commercial and imperial interests may have controlled the islands of Southeast Asia for centuries, but this control did not prevent the steady advance of Islam in those same islands. A similar situation can be seen in both West and East Africa, where the modern colonial state established an institutional framework that provided "new possibilities of expansion" for Sufi orders and Muslim teachers and traders.

This double level of world-system operation, even in the nineteenth and twentieth centuries, suggests the need for a broader conceptualization of *world-system*. World-systems may compete and also may operate in different dimensions of a social system in ways that force a changing definition of *hegemonic*. Wallerstein has suggested that the world-system perspective needs to be "unidisciplinary" and not just "interdisciplinary" or "multidisciplinary" in method and approach, but he recognizes the difficulty of this task.

The issues raised by considering the Islamic world-system may help in developing a broader approach. I suggest that the modern capitalist world-system was not the first long-lasting world-system without a world-empire. The Islamic community had already developed such a world-system in the centuries following the collapse of the Abbasid state by the tenth century C.E. This nonimperial world-system was not based on a world-economy. Instead it was a discourse-based world-system tied together by interactions based on a broad community of discourse rather than by exchange of goods. The capitalist world-system strongly influenced this Islamic world-system, but it did not destroy it. The interpretation of the capitalist and Islamic world-systems represents a subject of study that tests even the most talented unidisciplinary scholars of modern history.

Ruins of Sijilmasa, Muslim caravan city of the northern Sahara. Photo by Ross Dunn

Sample Student Activities

> **I.** *The maturing of an interregional system of communication, trade, and cultural exchange in an era of Chinese economic power and Islamic expansion.*

A. China's extensive urbanization and commercial expansion between the 10th and 13th centuries.

Grades 5-6

▶ Assume the role of an ambassador to Song China and write an account of Chinese innovations in warfare. Describe the use of gunpowder in crossbow arrows, bombs, and guns. *What were the consequences of these weapons?*

▶ Map the expansion of China's external trade with Southeast Asia and the lands rimming the Indian Ocean. *What effects did this trade expansion have on China? On other parts of Asia and on Africa?*

▶ Investigate the use and spread of wood-block book printing, and make a wood block print of your own. *For what kinds of purposes were prints first used in China? Once printing spread, how did it change gentry life? What are the advantages and limitations of this technology compared to hand printing?*

Grades 7-8

▶ Explain the factors that led to the development of a merchant class in Song China. *How did the expansion of trade and commerce influence the growth of cities? What were traditional social attitudes in China toward merchants and commercial activity?*

▶ Write an essay comparing the city of Hangzhou (Hangchow) with London or other cities of the 10th-13th centuries.

▶ Write a personal journal entry of a young Chinese man who has just taken the state civil service examination. *What social class was this man a member of? What did he have to do to prepare for the exams? What was a typical exam day like?*

▶ Make a three-section chart on the basic beliefs of Confucianism, Daoism, and Buddhism. *How did Zhu Xi blend these into a new synthesis called neo-Confucianism?*

Grades 9-12

▶ Study reproductions of Song art. *How do Song paintings reflect Confucian, Daoist, and Buddhist ideas?*

▶ Research Chinese achievements in alchemy, astronomy, and medicine during the Song dynasty. *How did Chinese advances in science and medicine compare with those in Europe and Southwest Asia during the 500-1500 CE period?*

▶ Investigate arguments and political conflicts during the Song dynasty over how the government should deal with rapid social change and a growing economy. *What were the main positions? Which position won out for the long term in China?*

▶ Describe footbinding of women as a social practice in Song China and analyze ways in which this practice expressed patterns of relationship between men and women.

▶ Investigate the life of a typical Chinese gentlemen. *What might his attitudes have been toward (a) family structure and values, (b) servants or tenant farmers; (c) the imperial government?*

- Discuss the basic ideas of Neo-Confucianism. Analyze how these ideas affected Chinese society, government, and education.

- Write a story depicting at least two aspects of economic changes in China during the Song dynasty. Compare and contrast the impact of economic changes from the point of view of a person of the landed gentry and from the point of view of a city dweller.

- Debate the question: Did China nearly achieve an industrial revolution between the 10th and 13th centuries?

B. Developments in Japanese and Southeast Asian civilizations.

Grades 5-6

- Write an account or make a comic book of the daily life of a boy in training as a Japanese warrior. *How would your training change as you grew older?*

- Assume the role of a news reporter to write or tell the story of the Mongol invasions of Japan in 1274 and 1281 and how the Japanese defeated the invaders. *What part did the "divine wind" (kamikaze) play in the defeat of the Mongols and how was this depicted by the Japanese? Why do you think a ruling power in China might want to invade Japan?*

- Research the art of Japanese screens and paper-making and describe the values they represent. Make a Japanese screen painting based on designs of the period, or compare a tanka poem on paper you make with recycled materials.

- Make a diagram illustrating the relative social status of warriors, peasants, women, nobility and others in feudal Japanese society.

Grades 7-8

- Study a physical geography map of mainland Southeast Asia. Locate the Red River and the states of Champa, Dai Viet, and Angkor. *Why do you think Dai Viet and Angkor were both strong agricultural societies? Why did Champa's prosperity depend heavily on maritime trade?*

- Describe the system of feudalism that developed in Japan. *What led to the development of feudalism? How powerful were the daimyo? What are the similarities and differences between the institutions of feudalism in Japan and medieval Europe?*

- Construct a timeline showing the important political events of the Kamakura period of Japanese history.

- Read excerpts from *The Tale of Heike*. *Why were military tales of particular importance at this time?* Discuss how political and military developments affected the lives of common people.

- Read excerpts from *The Ten Foot Square Hut* by Kamo no Chomei and discuss the life of the author. Analyze how his decision to become a monk reflected political, social, and religious developments of the time.

Grades 9-12

- Construct a table analyzing how women's experiences in feudal Japanese society were affected by social class and stage of life.

- Research Noh drama and compare Noh to Greek tragedy. *How does each demonstrate philosophical values and traditions?*

- Examine the development of Buddhist sects in Japan and explain the appeal of each of these communities. *How was Japanese society affected by Zen Buddhism? Why did Zen Buddhism have wide appeal among the samurai? What accounted for the popularity of Jodo ("Pure Land") Buddhism?*

▶ Research different art forms of the Kamakura and Ashikaga periods such as painting, pottery, literature, dance, flower arranging, and rock gardens. *How do the arts reflect Buddhist and Shinto values?*

▶ Draw evidence from art and literature to examine the lives of common people in Japan.

▶ Study pictures of the temple of Angkor Wat that was built in Cambodia beginning in the 12th century. *Why was this enormous temple built? How does it combine Indian and Southeast Asian art and architecture? Why has this temple been called one of the most impressive structures ever built?*

C. How pastoral migrations and religious reform movements between the 11th and 13th centuries contributed to the rise of new states and the expansion of Islam.

Grades 5-6

▶ Create a chart listing the scientific achievements of Islamic civilization between the 11th and 13th centuries. *How did new discoveries encourage communication among different peoples of the Islamic world?*

▶ Put on a skit based on an excerpt from *A Thousand and One Nights. How do the tales reflect the multiethnic character of the Islamic state? What do the tales teach us about life in the 11th-13th centuries?*

▶ Create an artistic design for a public plaza based on Islamic architectural forms and designs.

Grades 7-8

▶ Research the kind of life that students led in an Islamic college in Cairo, and compare it with the lives of European university students in this period.

▶ Write a tourist's guide to Cairo in the age of the Fatimids. *Under what circumstances did Cairo become an international center of trade and Islamic culture in that age? What are the geniza documents, and what have historians learned from them about the life of Jewish and Muslim communities in Egypt and the Mediterranean in the Fatimid period?*

▶ Develop overlay maps showing Turkic migrations, Islamic expansion, and the retreat of the Byzantium empire.

▶ Read excerpts from Ibn Jubayr's account of his travels between Spain and Mecca (1183-1185). *What was the purpose of his journey? What characteristics of Muslim society does he find worth writing about?*

Grades 9-12

▶ Compare the way of life of Turkic peoples such as the Seljuks with that of earlier peoples of the steppes such as the Huns, or the early Germanic tribes.

▶ Discuss basic ideas of Sufism and the meaning of mysticism as an aspect of religious belief and practice. *How did Sufi organizations contribute to the spread of Islam? What social, cultural, or political roles did Sufi orders play in Muslim cities and rural areas?*

▶ Compare the origins and growth of the Seljuk and Ghaznavid empires as Turkic military states.

▶ Interpret selections from Muslim chronicles and literary works regarding Muslim military, political, and cultural responses to the Christian crusades in Syria-Palestine.

▶ Read excerpts from Ibn Jubayr's account of Cairo, Damascus, and Sicily during the Crusades. *What interactions does he describe among Muslims and Christians in these places, and how is society affected by the Christian campaigns?*

◆ Read selections from the *Rubaiyat* of Omar Khayyam and the writings of al-Ghazali, and discuss ways in which these writings exemplify Sufi ideas. *What other aspects of Islamic society do these writings express?*

◆ Investigate the life and writings of a religious or intellectual figure such as Maimonides, al-Biruni, Ibn al-Arabi, al-Tusi, or Firdawsi. Present the accomplishments of one of these figures in a first-person oral report.

◆ Research the origins of the North African Islamic reform movements. *How did the reform message of the Almoravids transform rival clans into a unified force? How did the Almoravid and Almohad states boost the trans-Saharan gold trade?*

D. How interregional communication and trade led to intensified cultural exchanges among diverse peoples of Eurasia and Africa.

Grades 5-6

◆ Using an outline map of the Eastern Hemisphere, identify the chain of seas that stretches from East Asia to Scandinavia; then draw routes sea travelers might have taken to sail across the major regions extending from the South China Sea to the Baltic Sea.

◆ Identify the major commercial cities involved in Indian Ocean trade and use icons to indicate their trade goods.

◆ Draw on annotated illustrations showing why a camel is the best mode of transportation across the desert. *Are camel caravans still used in long-distance trade across Central Asia and the Sahara Desert?*

Grades 7-8

◆ Construct a chart showing the pattern of the seasonal monsoon winds in the Indian Ocean basin. *What climatic factors account for this pattern? How did the monsoon winds affect the possibilities and limitations of seaborne navigation and trade in the Indian Ocean? What importance did products such as gold, silks, woolens, pepper, ivory, cowry shells, and slaves have for economies of Asian, African, or European societies?*

◆ Construct a chart or illustrations of the architecture of caravansaries and khans in Central Asia and the Middle East. Describe their functions and the sort of people you might meet there. *Why did they become gathering places for local people as well as travelers?*

◆ Make a model or drawing of a typical lateen-rigged sailing craft of the Indian Ocean. *How did this type of vessel take advantage of the monsoon winds?* Describe positive and negative aspects of making a long voyage on a lateen-rigged ship. *How did the large Chinese junks that plied the China seas and Indian Ocean differ in construction and technology from lateen-rigged vessels? What technology enabled Chinese ships to be so large?*

Grades 9-12

◆ Debate the proposition: The economic and commercial expansion of Song China was the single most important factor in the intensification of interregional communication and trade across Eurasia.

◆ Analyze the relationship between Indian Ocean trade and the rise of city-states along the East African coast. *What cause-and-effect relationship may there have been between the spread of Islam and expansion of trade routes?*

◆ Write a reaction paper to the following statement: Ideas are carried along trade routes together with goods and products. Therefore, the direction of trade routes can affect the course of history in very important ways. Suppose trade caravans had been unable or traders unwilling to cross the Sahara. *How might African society be different today? What effect might such a barrier have had on the spread of Islam?*

II. *The redefining of European society and culture, 1000-1300.*

A. Feudalism and the growth of centralized monarchies and city-states in Europe.

Grades 5-6

▶ Study a map of medieval Europe showing the extent of kingdoms and location of city-states. Compare this map to a political map of Europe today. *What kinds of historical developments might be inferred from the changes?*

▶ Prepare a report on William the Conqueror and explain how he was able to win control of England after the Battle of Hastings. *Why did William invade England? What sort of changes did William make in governing England?*

▶ Construct a map of a medieval English manor showing the major structures and identifying where peoples of different social classes lived. *What benefits did the manorial system provide for each group of people who lived on a manor? In what way did a free peasant's and a serf's life differ?*

▶ Construct a model of a European castle of the 12th or 13th century and explain daily activities in and around the castle. *What were the purposes of castles? In what ways did the life of the castle depend on the work of serfs? In what ways did serfs depend on the castle and its inhabitants?*

Grades 7-8

▶ Using the Bayeux Tapestry write an account of the conflict between William of Normandy and Harold of England. *Why did the Normans invade England? What factors contributed to William's success at the Battle of Hastings? Which kind of political changes did William initiate? How did England change culturally and socially in the two centuries following the Norman Conquest?*

▶ Investigate events leading to Runnymede (1215). Analyze the Magna Carta from the perspective of a serf, free man, noble, or cleric. *Did this event give the serf or free man any rights or privileges?*

▶ In an essay discuss the changing position and power of the papacy from the Early Middle Ages to the High Middle Ages. *What stimulated this change? How did the relationship between popes and feudal rulers change?*

▶ Assume the role of a serf on the manor and describe your daily activities, your rights, obligations, legal and economic position, and relationship to freemen, slaves, and lords. *In what ways was manorialism an economic system? How did it promote economic growth and the accumulation of wealth?*

Grades 9-12

▶ Discuss those common features or activities that allowed city-states such as Genoa, Venice, and Bruges to become commercial, financial, and economic leaders of Europe. *How did they maintain their independence? In what ways did their political structure differ from that of the centralizing monarchies?*

▶ Prepare an oral report evaluating the relative importance of mercenary armies, bureaucracies, and earlier feudal options such as marriage alliances and the building of fiefs in the growth of centralized royal power. *In what ways did these institutions assist monarchs in assuming greater powers?*

- Make a diagram showing the structure of the English and French governments, and compare and contrast the workings of the English Parliament and the French Estates-General. *To what extent did these institutions involve popular participation in government? How much real power did these representative bodies have in how their nations were run?*

- Based on reading Christine de Pisan's advice to princesses and other elite women in *Treasure of the City of Ladies* and the Parisian manual *The Good Wife*, analyze relations between women and men in 14th-century political and family life.

- Discuss the evolution of elective monarchies in eastern Europe as compared to hereditary states in western Europe. *What prevented the creation of hereditary monarchies in eastern Europe?*

- Write an essay analyzing in what way the Magna Carta was a product of the feudal system. *How did this document foreshadow later developments in the English political system?*

- Compare the western European feudal system with the Byzantine or Abbasid political systems. *How did the systems differ? Which system offered the greatest security to ordinary people? What is political legitimacy? How did kings in western Europe exercise legitimacy in comparison with the Byzantine emperor or Abbasid caliph?*

B. The expansion of Christian Europe after 1000.

Grades 5-6

- Construct a map tracing the route of the First Crusade and write a letter from a crusader describing where he traveled and what he did along the way. Compare his experiences to those of later crusaders. *What caused the Crusades? What were the goals of the popes and those of kings?*

- Investigate the legend of El Cid and explain why he is a legendary Spanish hero. *How much of the legend is based on historical evidence? How would you regard El Cid if you were a Muslim? a Castilian? What was the Almoravid empire and why was El Cid opposing it?*

- Role-play a meeting between representatives of King Richard the Lion Heart and the Muslim ruler Saladin. *How might each representative have explained why Christian and Muslim armies were fighting in the Levant? Why was control of Jerusalem so important to both sides?*

Grades 7-8

- Explain how the development of agricultural technologies such as the iron plowshare and the wheeled plow stimulated greater agricultural production in Europe. *How did increased agricultural production lead to increased economic development and the growth of population?*

- Using bar graphs, compare the increase in population and agricultural production in Europe ca. 1000-1300. Infer from these graphs the relationship between population and agricultural production.

- Assume the role of a young adult from a noble family in training for knighthood and give an account of the training he would receive. *What responsibilities and rights did this squire learn? How might he approach his relationship to his lord, his church, noblewomen, and serfs?*

- Drawing on sources such as Scott O'Dell's *The Road to Damietta*, discuss the role that saints played in the spread of Christianity.

- Draw a recruiting poster for the Crusades for either the Christian or Muslim armies. *How did the Christian and Muslim leaders entice common soldiers and knights to commit so much of their lives to the Crusades? What benefits might be derived from such service? How does the concept of Muslim* jihad *compare to the concept of "crusade"?*

Grades 9-12

▶ Drawing on literature such as Rudyard Kipling's *Puck of Pook's Hill*, describe what daily life was like as feudalism was developing in the last century of the first millennium CE. *How were the lives of serfs, knights, and lords interrelated? What difference does it make to learn about daily life under feudalism from a novelist like Kipling, from a history textbook, or from looking at the actual tools used by people living in feudal times, the plans of their homes, and legal documents listing their possessions?*

▶ Compare and contrast the population growth, economic growth, and urbanization in Europe, Abbasid Southwest Asia, Song China and West Africa after 1000 CE. *What similarities and differences may be found in the causes for this development?*

▶ Develop a series of letters exchanged between merchants and bankers describing the developing financial institutions of North Italian cities. Analyze the relationship between banking, trade, and the power of feudal aristocrats.

▶ Research attitudes of Latin Christian crusaders towards Jews and Greek Christians. *Why did crusaders ravage Jewish communities in western Europe on their way to fight the Muslims? Why did Latin crusaders seize Constantinople in 1204?*

▶ Analyze why Latin Christian states and maritime cities achieved commercial and naval dominance over Muslim power in the Mediterranean and Black Sea basins between the 11th and 13th centuries. *What caused these European states to develop naval power? What is the relationship between commercial and naval development and political strength?*

▶ Define the term "guild" and describe the rise of guilds as economic and social institutions. *What was a guild? How did a guild work? How effective were guilds in promoting economic growth, product quality, and the rights of workers?*

C. The patterns of social change and cultural achievement in Europe's emerging civilization.

Grades 5-6

▶ Collect pictures that demonstrate the architectural differences between houses of worship of this period, for example a Romanesque church, a Gothic cathedral, and a mosque of the Fatimid or Mamluk period in Egypt. Look at your community and locate buildings illustrating architectural elements from this period. Prepare an album of pictures or drawings and explain how these designs relate to the medieval period. Speculate on why modern builders chose to use them.

▶ Define the term "university" and on a map of Europe locate the cities that were home to the major universities of later medieval times. *What was the purpose of the university in medieval Europe? Who did it educate and why? How did people of that time view the university? Why were universities founded in certain cities? Which country had the most universities?*

▶ Make an annotated illustration of a Jewish community in Europe. *What jobs or professions did Jews typically engage in? What part did the synagogue play in community life?*

Grades 7-8

▶ Examine photographic evidence of interior decorations of Gothic churches and Spanish mosques. *How do these designs express cultural and religious beliefs and values?*

▶ Use evidence from David MacCaulay's video, *Cathedral: The Story of Its Construction*, to explain the cultural importance of Gothic cathedrals. *What role did the craft guilds play in the building of cathedrals? What did these structures indicate about the place of religion in society?*

◆ Read excerpts from literature on courtly love such as Ibn Hazm's essay "The Dove's Neck-lace" and examples of Andalusian poetry. Compare these works with troubadour poetry and medieval European works on chivalry. *What do they tell about women's lives? What musical influences accompanied this literature?*

◆ Research the origins of Christian universities of Europe and describe their organization and studies. *What were cathedral schools, and how did they serve as a foundation for universities? By what means did Muslim scholarship become available to Europeans?*

Grades 9-12

◆ Construct a grid to analyze the degree to which women's experiences in feudal European society were determined by social class, area, time, and stage of life. *What life choices were available to women of various classes and marital status in medieval Europe? What was the basis for women's "education"?*

◆ Compare the political and social influences of Orthodox and Latin Christianity in eastern and western Europe. *How did the religious authority of the papacy differ from that of the patriarch? How did the political influence of the patriarch in the Greek Orthodox church differ from that of the pope?*

◆ Trace the ways in which classical works such as those of Aristotle and Plato became a part of medieval philosophy in western Europe. *Was philosophy a part of the offerings of the university? What role did Thomas Aquinas play in reconciling ancient learning with Christian teaching?*

◆ Describe the kinds of contact that took place between Spanish and other European Christians and the Muslims of Spain. *How did these contacts allow the diffusion of ideas and culture from Muslim Spain into other parts of Europe?*

◆ Compare medieval women's lives as they appear in excerpts from the 12th-century *Art of Courtly Love* verses of *Women Troubadours*, the late 14th/early 15th-century Pisan's *Treasure of City of Ladies*, and Dati's diary in *Two Memoirs*. *What do these sources reveal about women's social status? How did the ideals of courtly love affect them? How did social class influence their experience?*

III. The rise of the Mongol empire and its consequences for Eurasian peoples, 1200-1350.

A. The world-historical significance of the Mongol empire.

Grades 5-6

◆ Drawing on accounts of his life, dramatize major events in the career of Chinggis Khan. *On what basis did you decide what was a "major" event?*

◆ Construct a map showing the extent of Chinggis Khan's conquests. *What factors contributed to his success as a conqueror? Consider his use of horses, bows and arrows, new military tactics, and strategies of terrorizing populations.*

◆ Create costumes representative of what would have been worn by Mongol warriors and construct models of the weapons used in the conquest of China, Southwest Asia, and Russia.

◆ Using an Arno Peters map projection of the world, illustrate the size of the Mongol empire at its greatest extent. Make overlays to compare the empire's size with that of the United States or other modern countries.

Grades 7-8

▶ Write a short story as told by someone your age about the siege of his or her home city in Persia by a Mongol army. *How would the story differ if it were told by a Mongol warrior?*

▶ Explain the differences in social, political, and economic organization between Mongol steppe nomads and sedentary populations such as those of China and Russia. *What were the relative strengths and weaknesses of each? Why did the Mongols prevail?*

▶ Use the reported remarks of Chinggis Khan—"Man's highest joy is in victory: to conquer one's enemies, to pursue them, to deprive them of their possessions, to make their beloved weep..."—to examine the record of Mongol conquests. *Is this an accurate appraisal of Mongol warriors?*

▶ Create a map of the trade routes that emerged under Mongol domination; explain why these routes were located where they were, and illustrate the commodities exchanged. *How do we know about the existence and location of these trade routes?*

Grades 9-12

▶ Examine the Mongol conquests between 1206 and 1279, and construct a historical argument explaining the relationship between military success and Mongol army organization, weapons, tactics, and policies of terror.

▶ Read the report of John of Piano Carpini, the 13th-century papal emissary, on the Mongol threat. Analyze his social and cultural biases about the Mongols.

▶ Prepare a schematic diagram explaining the system of succession followed by Mongol rulers after the death of Chinggis Khan. *How important were the disputes over succession, the absence of a bureaucracy, and increasing divisions between those favoring traditional steppe ways and those adopting the ideas of conquered urban cultures, in the division of the Mongol empire and its eventual decline?*

▶ Compare selections from the travels in Asia of Marco Polo and Ibn Battuta. Using the descriptions of their travels, account for the flourishing city life under the areas of Mongol domination.

▶ Debate the concept of the "Pax Mongolica," comparing it to the Pax Romana. *Is it worth the cost of terror to have an enforced peace?*

B. The significance of Mongol rule in China, Korea, Russia, and Southwest Asia.

Grades 5-6

▶ Conduct a conversation between two Chinese people under Mongol rule, one approving and the other complaining about the current political situation. *What might each one have to say?*

▶ Construct a family tree of Mongol rulers. *What was the family relationship between Chinggis Khan and Khubilai Khan? Who were some famous European contemporaries of these men?*

Grades 7-8

▶ Research the accomplishments of Batu and explain what is meant by the "Golden Horde." *How did the Mongols gain control in Russia? Describe their rule.*

▶ As a member of the Golden Horde, write a letter to Khubilai Khan describing your rule in eastern Europe and Russia.

▶ Construct a graphic organizer to show characteristics of Mongol society and culture, of Muslim society and culture, and of contacts between Mongols and Muslim peoples. *Why do you think the rulers of the Golden Horde and the Khanate of Persia-Iraq converted to Islam?*

Grades 9-12

- Use historical information to debate the accuracy of the statement by Chinggis Khan's adviser that "the empire was won on horseback but it will not be governed on horseback" when applied to Mongol rule in China.

- Construct a museum exhibit using illustrations of selected works of art from the Yuan Mongol dynasty and explain the relationship of Chinese artists to the Mongol court. *To what extent did the Mongols support the arts? What can be discerned about Chinese history from the art of the period?*

- Compare the consequences of the Great Khan Ogodei's death for Mongol rule in eastern Europe with the consequences of the Great Khan Mongke's death for Mongol invasion plans of Egypt. *What Mamluk strengths helped to bring about their defeat of the Mongols?*

- Debate from the points of view of Chinese, Russians, or Persians the advantages and disadvantages of living under Mongol rule. Evaluate the impact of technological advances, political and fiscal policy, foreign trade, warfare, and military domination on these regions.

- Trace the extent of Mongol control in Europe and Southwest Asia on a map. Research reasons for the success of the Mamluk in halting Mongol advance into Egypt.

IV. *The growth of states, towns, and trade in Sub-Saharan Africa between the 11th and 15th centuries.*

A. The growth of imperial states in West Africa and Ethiopia.

Grades 5-6

- Draw visual portrayals of desert, semi-arid steppe, savanna, and rain forest climatic zones, and hypothesize how life in each area may be similar and different. *Why is there no permanent settlement in extreme climatic zones?*

- Read the story of Solomon and Sheba in the Old Testament and Ethiopian legends of Solomon's role in founding the first dynasty there. *What evidence is there to show that the queen of Sheba was a monarch of southern Arabia?*

- Research military technology of Mali, Bornu, and Songhay as a factor in their success. *Why were horses important in the development of these empires? Why did horses have to be continually imported from North Africa.?*

- Draw a map of Africa showing the outline of major kingdoms such as Ghana, Mali, Songhay, Kanem-Bornu, and Ethiopia and identify major centers such as Walata, Timbuktu, Mogadishu, and Kilwa. *Was trade important to these peoples of Africa? How did it move?*

- Look at photography of the bronze works of Benin and Ile-Ife and explain how these may have been created. *What might these art works tell us about the life of peoples who lived in this part of West Africa?*

Grades 7-8

- Diagram one of the rock-hewn churches of Lalibela in Ethiopia. *What policies and achievements was King Lalibela noted for?*

- Compare the political, economic, and social structure of Mali and Songhay. *How important was trade to the two empires How did the wealth and power of Mansa Musa or Askia Muhammad compare with that of Christian and Islamic rulers? What roles did Muslim scholars play in governing the cities?*

♦ Read Ibn Battuta's and Leo Africanus's accounts of travels in Mali and Songhay and evaluate their reports. *What did they admire about these empires? What did they criticize? Why did Ibn Battuta disapprove of the social relations between men and women in Mali?*

♦ Investigate the Mali Kingdom of Mansa Musa and accounts of his pilgrimage to Mecca in 1324. *What can you discover about the wealth, power, and capability of this monarch and his kingdom?*

Grades 9-12

♦ Compare and contrast the West African Sudan and the East African coast in terms of political, social, economic, and religious developments between the 10th and 13th centuries. *How were these areas of Africa affected by outside influences? What role did commerce play in their development?*

♦ Draw on E.W. Bovill's *The Golden Trade of the Moors* to explain why trans-Saharan slave trade developed in medieval times. *Why was there a market for slaves from West Africa in the Mediterranean region and Southwest Asia? Under what circumstances were people likely to be enslaved in West Africa? Why were the majority of slaves transported across the Sahara women? What did Islamic teachings have to say about slavery and the treatment of slaves?*

♦ Evaluate the achievements of the Zagwe dynasty of Ethiopia as patrons of Christian art and architecture and explain Ethiopian decorative art. *How did Ethiopians construct rock-hewn churches? What are some of the characteristics of painting in Ethiopian art?*

♦ Construct a chart comparing Ethiopian, Latin, and Eastern Orthodox Christianity. In your chart include role of clergy, hierarchy, ritual, art, role of women in the church, language, and role of government. *In what ways do Ethiopian Christians appear to have adopted Northeastern African traditions to Christian practice?*

♦ Select several bronze sculptures and other art forms from Ife and Benin to present an oral report on the role of the ruler, class and gender differences and level of technology. Contact several museums that have exhibits of the art of Ife and Benin and include in your report the late 20th-century value of these items.

B. The development of towns and maritime trade in East and Southern Africa.

Grades 5-6

♦ As an Indian merchant trading in Kilwa, write a letter home about a visit to Great Zimbabwe. Include your reasons for going there, what you saw, and the advantages you will derive from the visit.

♦ Construct a vocabulary chart of Swahili words. *What are the advantages of a "trading language"?*

Grades 7-8

♦ Locate the site of Great Zimbabwe on a modern map of Africa. *What geographical features made this a good place to control the long distance trade between the gold fields of the western plateau and the Swahili coast? What caused the Shona people to abandon this site?*

♦ Construct a model of the "Great Enclosure" at Great Zimbabwe and develop hypotheses about the purpose of this building. *What questions would need to be answered to help check the validity of your hypotheses? What types of evidence have historians used to reconstruct the history of Bantu-speaking peoples?*

♦ After watching a film on the Khoisan hunter-gatherer peoples of southwest Africa, discuss what sort of encounters are likely to have occurred between the Khoisan and southward-moving Bantu farmers in the second millennium CE. *Why is the territory of Khoisan peoples so restricted today?*

- Assume the role of a Muslim immigrant from the Persian Gulf and Oman to one of the eastern African islands of Zanzibar, Mafia, Pemba or Kilwa. *What events transpired in the Persian Gulf to cause you to emigrate during the 11th and 12th centuries?* Describe the ship you would have travelled on and the time of year you would have left the Arabian Peninsula. Describe the life you would establish on the East African island. Include a few Swahili words and Arabic words to make your journal even more authentic.

Grades 9-12

- Make a simplified chart of the family of Bantu languages. Make a list of basic words in Swahili, Zulu, or other Bantu languages and compare these words for similarities and differences. *What can the relationships among the Bantu languages tell us about the migrations of Bantu-speaking peoples? What major cultural or social differences were found among Bantu-speaking groups? What part did Swahili play as a lingua franca of trade?*

- Explain the role of gold in the trade patterns of East Africa during this period. *Where did the traded gold come from and who controlled its source? What else was traded besides gold?* Map the trading network of the Indian Ocean basin, including East African commercial cities such as Kilwa.

- Read excerpts from Ibn Battuta about his visit to East Africa and secondary sources on the Swahili-speaking commercial towns there. From them, construct an account of the class structure and Arab or Persian influences in these towns. *Who were the ruling elites?*

- Create a children's story based on the lives of three children living in the 11th century in the Zimbabwe plateau area: child of a laborer in the gold mines, merchant's child, and a child of the royal family. Make your story rich in detail about the geography and rituals of these ancient people.

V. *Patterns of crisis and recovery in Afro-Eurasia, 1300-1450.*

A. **The consequences of the Black Death and recurring plague pandemic in the 14th century.**

Grades 5-6

- Describe what might happen to the daily life of a Southwest Asian or European town suddenly afflicted with plague.

- Write a short story or script a play about families in Europe, North Africa, and Southwest Asia during the height of the Black Death. Include information on topics such as: *Did people know the causes of the plague? How did they respond to the plague? Was the response different in Christian and Muslim areas? How did the plague change the lives of those who survived?*

Grades 7-8

- Map the origin and spread of the 14-century plague on a physical relief map. Hypothesize about the connection of the spread of the disease to the flow of goods along the Silk Route. *What areas were spared the ravages of the plague?*

- Draw evidence from primary source documents and visual materials to infer how villagers in western Europe and Southwest Asia responded to the Black Death. Write an account describing how you would have reacted if you were a villager and a deadly mysterious disease was threatening your village. Record whether or not your reactions would have been the same as those shown in the sources, explaining why or why not.

◆ Drawing information from books such as Ann Turner's *The Way Home*, and Ann Cheetham's *The Pit*, discuss the impact of the plague on young people. *What options were available to them? What evidence would the authors have had to draw on to construct their accounts?*

Grades 9-12

◆ Read and discuss accounts of the effects of the Black Death by Boccaccio or other 14th century European writers. Read Ibn Battuta's accounts of its effects on Syria and Egypt. Compare these accounts. *What aspects of the disease and its effects did contemporaries focus on?*

◆ Examine primary sources and secondary sources of scapegoating during the Great Plague. *How did the pogroms affect Jewish communities in the Holy Roman Empire? Why did Jews flee to Poland and Russia in the mid-14th century?*

◆ Describe the medical, administrative, and psychological measures taken in attempts to cope with plague in the 14th century. *What other measures might have been taken under 14th-century conditions had the transmission of plague through fleas and rats, as well as by direct human-to-human transmission, been known?*

◆ Make a list of what you consider to be the likely social and cultural consequences of the high mortality, prolonged fear and social dislocation that accompanied recurrent pandemics in the 14th and 15th centuries. Check your hypotheses against historical evidence. *What impact did the Black Death have on economic, political, and religious life?*

◆ Assess the impact of climatic change on European agriculture and population in the early 14th century. *What was the "little ice age"? What effects could long-term climate change of less than 3% increase or decrease in global temperature have on the United States in the 21st century?*

B. Transformations in Europe following the economic and demographic crises of the 14th century.

Grades 5-6

◆ Look at examples of Greek and Roman and then of Renaissance art and architecture. *How did the former influence the latter?*

◆ Study peasant uprisings such as that of Wat Tyler in 1381 to understand what led the peasants to rebel. Plot on a map and create a timeline for the major rebellions in Europe between 1300 and 1500. *Were these rebellions due to the same causes?*

◆ Write short biographies of persons involved in the Hundred Years War such as Edward III and Henry V of England, Charles VII of France, and Joan of Arc. Focus on their part in the war.

◆ Drawing on an assortment of picture books, discuss and compare examples of Italian Renaissance art. *What is appealing about Renaissance painting or sculpture? What differences of composition can be seen in comparing a Renaissance painting with one from an earlier period in European history?*

Grades 7-8

◆ Use examples from European history to explain why a major decrease in population raised the price of labor following the Black Death. Analyze possible social and economic effects of both population decline and increase of wages. *What effects do historians think the Black Death may have had on serfdom in Europe?*

◆ Assume the roles of an English and a French chronicler and debate the causes of the Hundred Years War.

▶ Develop a role-play activity or write a skit about the conflict between King Philip IV of France and Pope Boniface VIII. *How do you think Holy Roman Emperor Henry IV or King John of England would have responded to the conflict if they were alive at that time? How would Pope Gregory VII or Innocent III have responded? What does the conflict between Philip and Boniface indicate about the power of the papacy in the early 14th century?*

▶ Write short biographical sketches of prominent figures of the late Medieval and early Renaissance periods, such as Dante, Petrarach, Boccaccio, Giotto, Botticelli, Donatello, Dürer, Brunelleschi, and Isabella d'Este. *Did these individuals share similar values and attitudes? How did writers and artists portray life in the early Renaissance? What is meant by Renaissance Humanism? Why did wealthy or powerful persons become patrons of the arts?*

Grades 9-12

▶ Compare the power and prestige of the papacy at the time of the Babylonian captivity and Great Western Schism to the papacy of Innocent III, a century and a half earlier. *How might the conflict between the popes at Avignon and Rome have stimulated reform movements within the Catholic Church? To what extent did the problems within the Catholic Church stimulate kings and princes to challenge papal authority? Did the Great Western Schism pave the way for the Protestant Reformation?*

▶ Read the accounts of the trial of Joan of Arc from the official report of the proceeding. *Why was Joan tried in a church court? What was the charge brought against her? What accounts for the Catholic Church's review of her trial a quarter of a century later? Why is Joan revered as a patron saint of France?*

▶ Develop a list of the characteristics of 15th-century Italian humanism. *What reasons can you give for its emergence in this time and place? Which segments of the population were most significantly influenced by Italian humanism?*

▶ Research the European role of gunpowder in weaponry, compared to traditional weaponry (mounted knights with lances, longbow, etc.). *What social and political effects did the use of gunpowder have? How did it strengthen royal power?*

▶ Write a set of educational recommendations in accordance with humanist ideals. *Who should be educated and what should they learn?*

C. Major political developments in Asia in the aftermath of the collapse of Mongol rule and the plague pandemic.

Grades 5-6

▶ Write a biography of Osman. *How did his achievements lay the foundations of the Ottoman empire?*

▶ Using overlays, map the expansion of the Ottoman state during the first century and a half of its existence. *How important do you think the bosphorus and the Dardannelles were as a barrier to military expansion?*

Grades 7-8

▶ Research the empire of Timur the Lame (Tamerlane) and assess the impact of his conquests on Southwest Asia and India. *What part was played in Timur's successes by mobility, opponents' weakness, and a strategy of terror? How would you compare and contrast Timur and Chinggis Khan as conquerors, destroyers, and empire builders?*

▶ Compare Samarkand under Timur and his successors with Florence under the Medicis. *How did rulers contribute to the flourishing cultural life in each? How important was governmental support of the arts and sciences?*

♦ Write a series of letters from an Ottoman *ghazi* warrior to a European knight. Your letters should reflect the similarities and differences in terms of duties, experiences, dress, and manners.

Grades 9-12

♦ Produce a European newspaper "special edition" dated at the time of the collapse of the Mongol rule in China. Include interviews of several persons who speculate what caused the downfall. Review the threat the Mongols once posed to eastern and central Europe. Interview several merchants and traders for their reaction to the possible end of Pax Mongolia.

♦ Compare the conquests of Timur with those of Chinggis Khan. *How did their treatment of resisting and submitting peoples contribute to their successes? What were the benefits and disadvantages of their rule for their Mongol followers and their subject peoples? To what extent was each influenced by values or ideas of the cultures with which he came in contact?*

♦ Compare and contrast Timur's patronage of scholars, artists, and scientists at Samarkand with the patronage taking place in Italian city-states at the same time. *To what extent was the "Republic of Letters" a widespread phenomenon in the civilized world during this period? What evidence is there for communication among scholars and artists across cultural and religious lines?*

♦ As a panel of experts, present to the class an account of the rise of the Ottoman empire from its beginning in Anatolia under Osman to the conquest of Constantinople by Sultan Mehmed II. *What accounts for the success of the Ottoman empire?* Include maps and other visual aids in your presentation.

VI.   *The expansion of states and civilizations in the Americas, 1000-1500.*

A.   The development of complex societies and states in North America and Mesoamerica.

Grades 5-6

♦ Make a mural illustrating the different types of sources (archaeological, artistic, written, etc.) that can be used to tell us about life in the Americas before the coming of the Europeans.

♦ Construct a model or draw a plan of Tenochtitlán and label the most important buildings in the city. *Why did the Aztecs call this city the "Foundation of Heaven"?*

Grades 7-8

♦ Compare and contrast the ways in which the natural environments of the North American plains, the southwestern deserts, and the tropical forests of Yucatan affected the organizations of societies in these regions.

♦ Demonstrate a knowledge of the Aztecs by constructing an example of an artifact such as a royal robe, the Aztec calendar, or a floating garden (chinampa). Describe its use and relationship to Aztec culture.

♦ Read excerpts from Bernal Diaz's *True History of the Conquest of Mexico* comparing Tenochtitlán to European cities. *What were the unique qualities of Tenochtitlán as described by Bernal Diaz?*

Grades 9-12

♦ Locate on a map the territory occupied by the Aztecs in their early nomadic warrior period (to 1325), the settlement at Tenochtitlán about 1325, and the city's emergence to a dominant positions over other city-states of Mexico by the late 15th century.

- Write an account from the point of view of residents of Tenochtitlán or Spanish soldiers or priests of Aztec economy and technology. Include descriptions of the complex organization of markets providing food and luxury goods to the population, intensive agriculture in chinampas in the lake; fishing in the lake; well-engineered causeways; canals; dikes to separate salt water from fresh water; and the central temple and palace complex.

- Draw upon slides or pictures of the mound center located at Cahokia in Illinois. Research the archaeological findings that have led to the reconstruction of Mississippian society and culture as it may have existed between 1000 and 1500 C.E. Consider the evidence for this center being a city comparable to cities of the same period in Eurasia or Africa. Develop arguments for and against the proposition that a major civilization developed in the Mississippi valley after about 1000 AD.

- Analyze why the Aztecs practiced human sacrifice on a large scale. *How might human sacrifice have been linked to religious beliefs, warfare, and the power of the state? In what other societies, premodern or modern, has human sacrifice been practiced?*

B. The development of the Inca empire in Andean South America.

Grades 5-6

- Draw graphic diagrams comparing the structure of Inca and Aztec societies indicating the roles of groups such as family, class, priests, warriors, and governors.

- Make a list of the different food plants that were the basis of Inca and Aztec agriculture. Prepare a menu describing a meal an inhabitant of the Aztec or Inca empire might have eaten. *What food might a South American or Mesoamerican have had that a European or West African could not have had before the 16th century?*

- Construct a mural showing various aspects of Inca society, and explain what the illustrations reveal about the structure of society. *What was everyday life like for the common people living in the empire?*

Grades 7-8

- Construct a three-dimensional map of the Inca empire, using different colors to show the expansion of the empire over time (ca. 1230 to 1525). *What problems did the geography of the empire present? What were the variations in climate within the empire? How did altitude and terrain affect Inca agriculture?*

- Describe the Inca communication system and consider how it contributed to both effective central government and long-distance trade.

- Compare Inca and Aztec temples. *What do Inca and Aztec artistic styles in metalwork, textiles, and pottery reveal about their cultural achievements?*

- Describe the discovery of Machu Picchu, and explain what the site can tell us about the Inca civilization.

- In an oral report describe and present illustrations of the Inca communication system and consider how it contributed to both effective central government and long-distance trade.

Grades 9-12

- Analyze gender roles in the Caribbean, Mesoamerican, and Andean societies using visual source material such as religious images and myths. *Which of the qualities of the gods seem to fit descriptions of roles expected and admired in men and women?*

- Compare the Inca capital of Cuzco and Inca engineering of roads, bridges, and irrigation systems with the Aztec capital of Tenochtitlán and its attendant technology.

♦ Evaluate the argument by some historians that the Inca empire was an early "welfare state." *How did Inca government compare with that of the Aztecs?*

♦ Explain how Inca rulers overcame problems of governing an enormous, geographically and climatically diverse group of territories. *What impelled Inca conquests and expansion?*

VII. *Major global trends from 1000 to 1500 CE.*

Major global developments from 1000 to 1500 CE.

Grades 5-6

♦ Make a collage illustrating the influences of Islamic civilization on major regions of Afro-Eurasia from the 11th to the end of the 15th centuries. *How extensive was the spread of religion, science, and the arts? Which of these areas are predominantly Muslim today and which are not?*

♦ Write a series of diary entries for a Muslim merchant traveling from the Arabian Sea to Southeast Asia in the 13th or 14th centuries. Include descriptions of ports, production centers, merchant communities, and traders different from yourself. Write a second diary for an Italian merchant traveling from Venice to Alexandria. *In what ways might the cultural backgrounds and experiences of the two merchants be similar or different?*

Grades 7-8

♦ Describe or make drawings of weapons used by the Mongols, the Chinese army, and the knights of the Holy Roman Empire in the 13th and 14th centuries. *What connections can be made between the weapons used and the societies that used them, including such factors as social divisions, technological developments, and cultural values? Up to about 1450 what part did gunpowder play in warfare?*

♦ Drawing on historical evidence, role play a meeting between a Japanese and a Western European noble warrior sometime during the 12th century. Construct a dialog regarding their relations with those above and those below them in the political and social hierarchy, their rights and obligations, and the character of feudalism in the two societies.

Grades 9-12

♦ Write two entries for an "Encyclopedia of Science and Technology," one on China and one on Western Europe for the 1000-1500 period. In each entry discuss the following: *What were dominant attitudes to science and its basic theories? Who were the practitioners of science and mathematics? Which sciences flourished? What were the most significant scientific and technological advances of the period?*

♦ Based on historical evidence, produce a "survivor's eye-witness account" of the mid-14th century Black Death. Take the role of a person living in Central Asia, Egypt, France, or England. *What were the short-term economic, social, and other consequences of the plague in your area?*

♦ Draw a map showing Mongol military movements in the 13th century. Pick several countries or regions significantly affected by Mongol military operations in this period. Compare the consequences of Mongol invasion and rule in these different regions. *In what ways might geography, regional government, religion, social structure, and the personalities of Mongol rulers have affected the encounter between the Mongols and those they conquered and ruled?*

ERA 6

The Emergence of the First Global Age, 1450-1770

Giving Shape to World History

The Iberian voyages of the late 15th and early 16th centuries linked not only Europe with the Americas but laid down a communications net that ultimately joined every region of the world with every other region. As the era progressed ships became safer, bigger, and faster, and the volume of world commerce soared. The web of overland roads and trails expanded as well to carry goods and people in and out of the interior regions of Eurasia, Africa, and the American continents. The demographic, social, and cultural consequences of this great global link-up were immense.

The deep transformations that occurred in the world during this era may be set in the context of three overarching patterns of change.

▶ **The Acceleration of Change:** The most conspicuous characteristic of this era was the great acceleration of change in the way people lived, worked, and thought. In these 300 years human society became profoundly different from the way it had been in the entire 5,000 years since the emergence of civilizations. Five aspects of change were especially prominent. Though American Indian populations declined catastrophically in the aftermath of the first European intrusions, world numbers on the whole started their steep upward curve that continues to the present. The globalizing of communications produced intensified economic and cultural encounters and exchanges among diverse peoples of Eurasia, Africa, and the Americas. Capitalism emerged as the dominant system for organizing production, labor, and trade in the world. Innovations in technology and science multiplied and continuously built on one another. European thinkers, drawing on a worldwide fund of ideas, formulated revolutionary new views of nature and the cosmos, ideas that challenged older religious and philosophical perspectives.

▶ **Europe and the World; the World and Europe:** Europeans came to exert greater power and influence in the world at large than any people of a single region had ever done before. In the Americas Europeans erected colonial regimes and frontiers of European settlement that drew upon various European traditions of law, religion, government, and culture. Europeans seized relatively little territory in Africa and Asia in this era, but their naval and commercial enterprises profoundly affected patterns of production and interregional trade. The trade in human beings between Africa and the Americas to provide a labor force for European commercial agriculture was a particularly catastrophic aspect of the expanding global economy. Closely linked to Europe's far-reaching global involvement was its own internal transformation—political, social, economic, and intellectual. In this era peoples almost everywhere had at some time to come to terms with European arms and economic clout, but as of 1750 Europe by no means dominated the world scene.

▶ **Empires of Eurasia:** Indeed, the greater share of the world's peoples, cities, agrarian wealth, and land-based military power were in this era and still concentrated in the region stretching from the eastern Mediterranean to China. Between the late 14th and early 16th centuries four huge empires arose to dominate the greater part of Eurasia and Northern Africa. Effectively employing artillery and other firearms to expand territorially and maintain law and order among diverse populations, the Ming, Ottoman, Mughal, and Safavid states have sometimes been called "gunpowder empires." They unified such large areas of Afro-Eurasia—politically, economically, and culturally—that they contributed much to processes of globalization.

Why Study This Era?

▶ All the forces that have made the world of the past 500 years "modern" were activated during this era. A grasp of the complexities of global interdependence today requires a knowledge of how the world economy arose and the ways in which it produced both enormous material advances and wider social and political inequalities.

▶ The founding of the British colonies in North America in the 17th century took place within a much wider context of events: the catastrophic decline of American Indian populations, the rise of the Spanish empire, the African slave trade, and the trans-Atlantic trade and migration of Europeans. The history of colonial America makes sense only in relation to this larger scene.

▶ Any useful understanding of American political institutions and cultural values depends on a critical grasp of the European heritage of this era.

▶ The great empires of Eurasia—Ottoman, Persian, Mughal, and Ming/Qing—all experienced cultural flowerings that paralleled the Renaissance in Europe. These achievements are an important part of our contemporary global heritage.

A Banker and his Wife
by Flemish painter
Quentin Matsys Alinari.
Art Resources Bureau

The Potato Connection*
by Alfred W. Crosby

Crosby urges the reader to examine the biological and ecological impact of the Columbian exchange. The botanical revolution of the sixteenth century introduced new crops, resulting in dietary changes in Europe, Africa, and Asia. The importance of the exploration and conquest of the Americas was readily recognized by sixteenth-century Europeans; however, they had no comprehension of the value of the food crops they took home. Imagine feeding the ever-growing population of the world today without the extraordinarily hardy and productive crops that originated in the Americas!

Alfred Crosby has written extensively on post-Columbian medical and ecological history. His publications include *The Columbian Exchange* and *Ecological Imperialism*.

In the sixteenth century, Francisco López De Gómara, biographer of Hernán Cortés and historian of Spain's new empire, declared that the European discovery of the New World was one of the two most important events since Creation—the other being the incarnation of God. To Gomara's fellow Europeans, the Americas did indeed provide golden opportunities for conquest and evangelization. But they had no idea that their most influential acquisitions would be the food crops they took home, chiefly maize and the white potato.

For those of us who live Hemisphere, the importance Columbus's landfall in 1492 is self-apparent. But what difference did it make for the peoples on the other side of the Atlantic Ocean?

For some, the impact of contact was undoubtedly negative. The forced migration of millions of Africans to America's plantations, for example, was to Europe's advantage, but certainly not to Africa's. Most Asians, until the mid-nineteenth century, were indifferent to the discovery of the Americas.

But in Europe the fallout from Columbus's find was immense. Europeans extracted enormous sums—in Spanish dollars, French livres and British pounds—from the New World's mines, soils and waters, capital that may have spurred the Industrial Revolution in Europe. And what would European history, plagued by riot and war, have been like without America to receive fifty million or so people? How would modern science have developed if the unknown plants, animals and peoples of America had not exploded old concepts? The authorities of antiquity had known nothing of America's existence. They had envisioned one-legged men, phoenixes and griffins, which could not be found anywhere; but they had not written of animals with pockets (opossums), birds that fly backwards (hummingbirds) or snakes that rattle—all of which awaited discovery in the New World. Never had they dreamed of the variety of peoples native to America, whose very diversity inspired the invention of anthropology, a scientific outlook many Europeans could not yet embrace, reverting instead to the ancient concept of the subhuman heathen or creating new fictions like Jean Jacques Rousseau's "noble savage." Both concepts still stalk our scholarship and popular culture today.

While such examples of America's shaping influence on Old World *thought* are impressive, they do not reflect direct influence in the way that the transfer of plants and animals do.

Biologically, America was indeed a new world to Europeans, Africans and Asians. It had been separate from the Old World for an immense stretch of time, except for connections in the frigid north, and free from even that frosty link for the past 10,000 years. It had been

---

*Reprinted from *World History Bulletin*, Vol. XII, No. 1 (Winter/Spring 1996), pp. 1-5.

independent for long enough to have raccoons, skunks, chipmunks, hummingbirds and rattlesnakes, and for Americans to have developed their own distinct civilizations. Politically, America may have become a satellite of the Old World—specifically of Europe—after 1492, but biologically the Old and New Worlds were near equals. The Old World proffered its distinctive flora and fauna—smallpox virus, malaria plasmodia, horses, cattle, sheep, house cats, starlings, wheat, rice, barley, turnips, peas and so on. The New World's most influential contributions were food crops.

A few other life forms—largely valueless exports—made their way over. Turkey crossed the Atlantic early but never replaced any of the Old World's domesticated fowl; North American gray squirrels have largely displaced the indigenous red squirrels in Great Britain, and American muskrats have spread from central Europe beyond the Urals. But the impact of such transplants has been minimal. The exception may be the spirochete of syphilis, which many scientists and historians claim is as American as the rattlesnake. Europeans first recognized the disease in the mid-1490s, shortly after Columbus's return from America. Voltaire vested his pie-in-the-sky Pangloss with the infection. Pangloss caught it from Paquette, who caught it from a monk and so on back to an early Jesuit, who had caught it from one of Columbus's companions. Did the real Columbus, as many have insisted for the last half millennium, transport the disease across the Atlantic?

The scientific record is frustratingly unclear. Syphilis is one of a close-knit family of diseases, or perhaps one manifestation of an ancient and widely distributed infection. Proving that a given lesion on an ancient bone was caused by syphilis and not by a similar infection is a shaky proposition. In fact, the disease has provoked far more literature than more important illnesses—tuberculosis or malaria, for instance. (Sin is catnip for scientists and scholars alike.) Certainly it has had a decisive influence on the lives of particular individuals—including Gustave Flaubert and Lord Randolph Churchill, Winston's father. But syphilis has not deflected the course of human history—American crops have.

A mention of the important American food crops immediately reveals their significance for Old World agriculture and diet. Who can imagine Italian cooking without the tomato, Indian curries without the chili pepper, or an Irish stew without potatoes to mop up the gravy? Protein-rich American beans (kidney, navy, string, lima, butter, pole, French, haricot, snap, frijol, but not the soybean) have served as "poor man's meat" in Europe, Africa and Asia. These, along with the peanut and fruits like the guava, papaya, squashes, avocado and pineapple, have fed Old World peoples for centuries, but their effects on the course of history are negligible compared with those of America's four abundant sources of carbohydrates: manioc, maize and the two potatoes.

Potatoes, white and sweet, are related not botanically, but only by an accident of comprehension. The Taino Indians of the Greater Antilles and Bahamas used the word "batata" for sweet potato; in the sixteenth century, the Spanish mistakenly transferred the word to the Andean tuber, and their names have been confused ever since. (The fact that Old World yams are also often called sweet potatoes does not help.)

Manioc, maize, sweet potatoes and white potatoes are extraordinarily hardy and more productive than the staples of Old World agriculture, except for rice. Their cultivation requires human labor, of which the Old World had a surplus, plus a stick, some sort of spade and perhaps a knife. American Indians, who had few beasts of burden and no metal farming equipment, had bred crops that required neither. Their needs adapted these crops for the peasants and poor of the Old World.

Most inhabitants of the temperate zones know manioc only as tapioca, the bulk element of certain desserts. Since its transfer (probably by Portuguese slavers) from Brazil, it has become one of Africa's most basic staples and is often considered a native plant. More than three times as much manioc root is now produced there as in South America. Often known as cassava, it is one of the developing world's great staples. Tropical peoples eat its tender shoots and leaves but value it chiefly for its starchy roots, which can weigh as much as eleven pounds. It is an amazingly hardy plant, resistant to pests and infections, thriving from sea level to 7,000 feet in poor soils, both in flood and drought. In Indonesia, it flourishes where thirsty rice cannot, in the hills and mountains.

The sweet potato probably arrived in the seventeenth century in New Guinea (brought over by Chinese and Malay traders), where its generous productivity in the highlands may have triggered a population explosion—just as the white potato did in Ireland during the same period. In warm lands the sweet potato (which, like manioc, was first seen by Europeans in the West Indies) also does well on marginal ground. It is important as a staple and particularly as a backup crop or famine food in Africa, China and regions of Indonesia where rice won't grow. Unlike manioc, it thrives in frostless temperate zones; it carried thousands of Japanese through the famines of 1832, 1844, 1872 and 1896 when other crops failed.

But more important than manioc and sweet potatoes for feeding the masses of the Old World were maize and the white potato. Their distributions overlap, with more of the grain in warm lands, more of the tuber in cooler. The one spurred population growth in Africa, the other in northern Europe.

The scientific name, *Zea mays*, and the common "maize" were both derived from the Taino word for the crop, whose fields of it were the first ever seen by Europeans. But somehow English speakers of North America tagged the American cereal "corn," the generic term used in Britain for all cereals (which is incidentally what the word refers to in the King James version of the Bible—Abraham, Joshua, David, Solomon, Jesus and St. Paul never saw an ear of the American grain).

The Maya and a number of other American Indian peoples had maize gods—and no wonder. It provides for more of humanity's needs than any other crop. It is one of the most versatile, thriving in climates as diverse as torrid Nigeria and the cool plains of northern China. In times of need, it can be eaten green. In times of war, it can be left on the stalk after it ripens, protected at least for a while from weather, birds and rodents by its husk. Once harvested and dried, it can be stored for years without spoiling. Its grain makes as good feed for livestock as for humans, and its leaves, unlike those of the other grains, make good fodder. Huts and sheds can be built of its stalks, and smoking pipes from its cobs. In 1498, according to Columbus, maize was already growing in Castile, but Europeans hesitated before adopting it. Northern Europe was too cool, and in much of the south the crop required irrigation during dry Mediterranean summers. Iberian Jews and Muslims, fleeing Christian persecution, may have brought it to the eastern Mediterranean, where population pressure was greater than in Western Europe in the sixteenth century, and maize was recorded in the 1570s growing "six, seven or eight cubits high" in fields along the Euphrates and around Jerusalem and Aleppo.

The slave trade, which placed a premium on cheap food that would survive the heat and damp of equatorial passage, was what brought maize to Africa (although linguistic evidence suggests that the grain also came down the coast from the Middle East). West Africans were cultivating maize at least as early as the last half of the sixteenth century, and ship-wrecked Portuguese saw fields of it on the coast of South Africa's Indian Ocean as early as 1630. By the

173

latter half of the nineteenth century, maize was one of the most widely cultivated of all foods in Africa.

Indonesian chroniclers paid little attention to the arrival of maize (food tends to receive much less attention than kings and battles), but like maios, the crops grew in countryside unsuitable for paddy rice, such as the lofty interior of Java. It proved a boon to China, where in the sixteenth century almost all the level, wet land for rice was already under cultivation, and the Chinese had few crops that would do well in hilly, drier and colder lands. Today China is second only to the United States as a producer of this American grain, and in China, unlike the United States, it is used almost entirely to feed humans.

The potato is to the temperate zone what rice is to the tropics. Given plenty of water, this Andean plant will produce more calories per unit of land in a cool climate than any alternative. Its tuber (a fleshy part of the underground stem) is a rich source of starch and provides some protein and even vitamin C, which was often in chronic shortage in northern winter diets. One can almost live on a diet of potatoes alone, which the Irish proved: A man with no more than a spade, even a wooden one, and an acre and a half of land in potatoes could, with a few supplements such as buttermilk, keep a family of five healthy. Adam Smith, the Scottish economist, recognized the potato's increasing value in this backhanded compliment to it and the Irish:

> The chairmen, porters, and coalbearers in London, and those unfortunate women who live by prostitution, the strongest men and the most beautiful women perhaps in the British dominions, are said to be, the greater part of them, from the lowest rank of people in Ireland, who are generally fed with this root [sic]. No food can afford a more decisive proof of its nourishing quality, or of its being peculiarly suitable to the health of the human constitution.

The potato's disadvantage is that it does not keep well, and before modern refrigeration those who relied on it were always dependent on the success of the next harvest.

The Old World was slow to take to the potato. European farmers already had the early turnip and parsnip, and the fact that the leaves of the potato plant are toxic did not encourage its wholesale cultivation or consumption. But the potato had another appeal: Europeans considered it (like the tomato) an aphrodisiac. That's why when Shakespeare's Falstaff sees the object of his affection approaching in *The Merry Wives of Windsor*, he lustily shouts, "Let the sky rain potatoes."

The plant arrived in Europe—as an ornamental—in the sixteenth century. In the seventeenth century the Irish, pushed off the most fertile land by the English after siding with the Stuart kings against Parliament, adopted the American tuber for its caloric productivity—more than twice that of any alternative in Ireland's climate. In the next century the French and Prussians, driven by war, did likewise. (Not only does the potato fill soldierly bellies cheaply, but when soldiers requisition food, they may leave potatoes in the ground while they trample crops in the field and cart off grain in the bare.)

Eighteenth-century Russians paid little attention to Catherine the Great's suggestion that her subjects plant potatoes, but the failures of the traditional crops in the nineteenth century convinced them. In the last 40 years of the century, potato production went up 40 percent in the dominions of the czar. Today, the former Soviet Union is the biggest producer of potatoes in the world.

Maize and potatoes were undoubtedly the New World's most precious gifts to the Old World, more valuable than all the silver from Potosi or gold from the Sacramento Valley, but gifts, like swords, can be double edged. The wide spread of maize cultivation in southern Europe, Hungary and the Balkan provinces of the Ottoman Empire made it *the* cash crop for growing cities. But lacking the vitamin B complex constituents, especially niacin, a diet exclusively of maize causes pellagra, the disease of the three D's: dermatitis, dementia and death. In 1755, a medical journal described just such an illness common in Spain's province of Asturias. Soon northern Italian physicians recognized the same symptoms, and by 1856 more than 37,000 cases were reported in Lombardy. Today, with the benefit of vitamin supplements, only in the Third World and in South Africa do maize farmers suffer from the disease.

Too great a dependence on maize eased people into the grave. Too great a dependence on white potatoes killed them swiftly. Many northern Europeans, notably the Irish, bet their lives on the unvarying productivity of the potato. But as the nineteenth century progressed and steamship technology reduced the number of days' voyage between America and Europe, American parasites caught up with the plant.

Between 1750 and 1841 the potato-loving population of Ireland had grown from three million to more than eight million, making it one of the most densely populated countries in Europe. In the 1840s ("the hungry 40s") an American parasite, *Phytophthora infestans*, arrived, reducing the tuber to black slime. Between 1841 and the next census, a generation later, Ireland's population dropped by half because of famine, disease and emigration. Ireland became, for its size, the chief exporter of humans on earth; the northeast coast of the United States took on a Celtic cast; and Patrick and Bridget Kennedy, great-grandparents of the first Catholic President of the United States, set sail across the Atlantic (and so did two of my great-grandparents).

The most important change of the last few centuries, more important than the propagation and shriveling of Marxism, or the Industrial Revolution, is the population explosion. Between the mid-eighteenth century and the present, the total number of humans on this planet rose from fewer than 800 million to 5.5 billion. Among the various causes of that increase is the nourishment associated with the cultivation of American crops overseas. In some places the connection is undeniable. In China, for example, where the population has grown from 330 million to more than a billion, people depend on a supply of food of which about 37 percent is American in origin.

With little prospect of worldwide population control, we need every productive variety of food plant whose requirements of climate, soil or space differ from our staples. We need strains of maize and potatoes resistant to the insects, worms, rusts, and blights that threaten our popular strains. We need plants that will prosper in seasons when we leave the land fallow. We need to squeeze two and three harvests into a single year. We must use the odd corners of land too steep, too dry, too wet, too acidic or too alkaline for our current crops. We need species that will preserve the land's fertility rather than diminish it.

In short, we need another descent of the sort of vegetable manna that Columbus inadvertently introduced to the Old World. Fortunately, we have only begun to exploit the pre-Columbian larder. When Europeans first arrived, the agriculturists of Mesoamerica were cultivating some sixty-seven species of plants (for food and other purposes), those of the Inca region about seventy. And this does not include plants first domesticated by the farmers of the Amazon and Orinoco basins. Native American crops account for about one-fifth of the world's crops.

Most of us, except botanists and anthropologists, are ignorant of all but a few of these plants and will remain so, because they do not fit our immediate needs. Other plants will soon be familiar, because they are productive despite saline soils and can survive overabundance or shortage of water, and so on. They make good insurance policies for our uncertain futures. For instance, which of our staple crop is especially tolerant of ozone? None, I suspect; but what about the Andean cereal quiona, which produces great quantities of starch and protein at 13,000 feet, an altitude at which it is subject to high levels of ozone?

Another neglected crop, amaranth, was cultivated by American Indians all the way from the desert borderlands of the southwestern United States to the southern Andes. It was one of the most ancient of Mexico's crops: The Aztecs collected half as much of this cereal in tribute as they did of their staff of life, maize. But cultivation fell off sharply soon after the European arrival, probably because the Spaniards saw that it was intricately involved in the old religious practices: images of gods were made from its dough, which was even called the "bones of god." (Amaranth is available today in Mexican markets as blocks of candy—seeds bound together with honey or molasses—called *alegna*, joy.)

Yet the crop is a nutritional marvel. Its stems and leaves are as edible as spinach and richer in iron; its prolific seeds are a source of a good grade of starch and are 16 to 18 percent protein of a quality comparable to that of cow's milk. Amaranth flour mixed with wheat or maize flour is about as protein-rich as eggs.

The plant does well at various altitudes in different soils, even tolerating salinity (the curse of irrigated land) better than many cereals. It weathers droughts and cold, though not frosts, and is now being grown in China, Nepal, India and Kenya.

Few Europeans, Africans and Asians know about amaranth—or quiona, achira, ahipa, oca, maca, kaniwa, lucuma, pepino or tarwi, among scores of other native American crops—but how many Americans knew about China's soybean seventy-five years ago? Very few indeed. Yet it is now a major crop, nutritionally and economically, in the United States and Brazil, both of which produce far more soybeans than China. And if Europeans, Africans and Asians continue to be as smart about importing crops as American farmers have recently been about soybeans, New World crops will continue to make history in the Old World.

Terrestrial globe, Gerhard Mercator, 1541. National Maritime Museum, Greenwich, England

Sample Student Activities

> I. *How the transoceanic interlinking of all major regions of the world from 1450 to 1600 led to global transformations.*

A. Origins and consequences of European overseas expansion in the 15th and 16th centuries.

Grades 5-6

▶ Trace the routes of Zheng He, Díaz, Vasco da Gama, Columbus, and the Polynesians on a world map and explain how they used prevailing wind currents to reach their destinations. Select two locations to travel between by a sail boat and use information from maps and wind currents to chart the best route.

▶ Research an invention useful for navigation such as the compass, astrolabe, or quadrant. Find out where it originated and how it was used. Demonstrate, using visuals, its impact on exploration and trade. *How did mariners navigate before these inventions? What is used today for the same purpose?*

▶ Compare diagrams of a Portuguese caravel, Indian Ocean dhow, and Chinese junk of the 15th or 16th centuries to assess their sailing abilities. *What advantages for long-distance travel did each type of vessel have? What advantages did innovations such as the stern-post rudder offer?*

▶ Construct a picture story of the life of Columbus. Use a map to locate the routes of his voyages to America. *How might you have viewed Columbus if you were one of the sailors during the first voyage to America? What might you have thought about Columbus's arrival if you had been one of the Taino "Indians" on the island of Guanahaní (San Salvador) in 1492?*

Grades 7-8

▶ Create a poster, diorama, or three-dimensional model of a rudder, smooth and clinker-built hulls, compass, astrolabe, and types of sails as used in navigation and ship-building in the latter part of the 15th century. *Where did these technologies originate? How did they affect trade?*

▶ Construct a historical argument or debate on such questions as: *Were the voyages of Columbus a "discovery"? How should Columbus be characterized: conqueror, explorer, missionary, merchant?*

▶ Role-play interviews with Jewish and Muslim scholars and artisans to determine their contributions to Iberian culture. Theorize and draw conclusions about the effects on Iberia of the loss of the talents of Jews and Muslims after they were expelled. *Where did Jews settle? Where did Muslims go? What did these groups contribute to their new home states?*

▶ Construct a map of the world indicating the major trading nations of the 15th century, the trade routes that existed at the beginning of the era, and those that were developed during this period. Students should denote the nations and trading routes by color.

Grades 9-12

▶ Analyze Chinese naval and commercial activities in the Indian Ocean in the early 15th century. *What do Chinese fleets reveal about technology and wealth at this time? How did the Chinese use a tribute system as a means of trade?*

▶ Examine the work of Prince Henry the Navigator, the navigational instruments that were available in his time, and the "school" of navigation developed to improve navigation. Students should look at the type of "course work" that would have been studied at this time. *Were such innovations limited to the European world or were advances in navigation being made in other parts of the world?*

▶ Assume the role of an adviser to King João II of Portugal and develop a position paper outlining Portugal's trade goals and potential routes to attain these goals. *Why did the Portuguese monarch reject Columbus's scheme to reach the Indies by sailing west?*

▶ Write an illustrated essay on how the lateen sail, the sternpost rudder, or the magnetic compass contributed to the technology of shipbuilding and navigation in 15th-century Portugal. *Where are these three inventions likely to have been first used? How did the magnetic compass, which was in use in earlier centuries in China, give mariners of the Mediterranean or Atlantic greater confidence in sailing out of sight of land during the winter months? What are the advantages and disadvantages of a "fore-and-aft" sail like the lateen in comparison with a square sail?*

▶ Taking the point of view of a Spanish general and a Muslim court official of Granada, debate the likely consequences of the Spanish conquest of Granada in 1492. Taking the point of view of a Spanish bishop, explain the forced conversion or exile of Jews and Muslims from Spain.

▶ Analyze the Iberian states' organization for overseas trade and colonization. Assess the influence of the Reconquista campaigns. *What role did the central governments play in these enterprises?*

▶ Analyze the socio-political structures of Iberian and other European states in comparison with those of China and the Muslim states. *Was there a relationship between social and political stability and the development of economics and trade?*

B. Encounters between Europeans and peoples of Sub-Saharan Africa, Asia, and the Americas in the late 15th and early 16th centuries.

Grades 5-6

▶ Research and write an account of King Affonso II of the Kongo and his relations with the Portuguese.

▶ Investigate the lives of Montezuma, Malinche, Cortés, Atahualpa, or Pizarro. Sketch pictures of the encounters between the Spaniards and the Aztecs or Incas.

▶ Research the life of Bartholomew de las Casas and explain why las Casas has been called the defender of the Indians. *Does he deserve that title?*

▶ Map Cortés's journey into Mexico and examine both indigenous and European depictions of the conquest of Tenochtitlán. Evaluate the point of view of the sources.

▶ Using books such as Scott O'Dell's *The King's Fifth*, discuss the motivations behind Spanish conquests in the New World.

▶ As a reporter describe and comment on the first contacts between the Amerindians and the early European explorers. *How did each appear to the other? What were they expecting of the people they met and what were they looking for in their meeting?*

Grades 7-8

▶ Research the possible reasons that the Inca empire fell to Pizarro. *What caused the Inca empire to delay in defending itself against the Spaniards? What strategies did the Spaniards use to capture Atahualpa?*

▶ Construct a map identifying the major ports and enclaves held by the Portuguese in Africa and Asia in the 16th century. Explain how the Portuguese succeeded in dominating seaborne trade in the Indian Ocean basin for several decades. *How much military or political influence did the Portuguese have over the states and empires of Africa and Asia? How did the leaders in these areas view the Portuguese?*

▶ Conduct a debate among las Casas, Sepúlveda, the Quakers in North America, and the Jesuits in Paraguay over the treatment of Amerindians. Evaluate the role of religions in the treatment of the Amerindians.

▶ Drawing on books such as Scott O'Dell's *The Amethyst Ring, The Captive,* and *The Feathered Serpent* and Gloria Duran's *Malinche: Slave Princess of Cortez,* discuss the impact of Spanish conquest on the day-to-day lives of Aztec, Maya, and Inca peoples.

▶ Evaluate the impact of the first Iberian explorers on the Amerindian societies and cultures of South and Central America. *What did the contact with the Europeans mean to the Indians and their lives?*

Grades 9-12

▶ Examine the causes and explain the consequences of the conflict between Portuguese and Ottoman Turkish military power in the Red Sea, Arabian Sea, and Ethiopia in the early 16th century.

▶ Compare the Portuguese impact on West African and East African peoples in the late 15th and the 16th centuries. *Did the presence of Portuguese naval vessels and merchants have any impact on the kingdom of Benin? What consequences did the coming of the Portuguese have for the maritime trade of the East African city-states? Why did the Portuguese settle in the Zambezi River valley and how did they affect African trade and politics?*

▶ Investigate the impact Christian missionaries had on Sub-Saharan Africa and Asia during the 16th century.

▶ Construct a comparative balance sheet of early Iberian colonialism in the Americas and Asia. *How did the European military impact on these two regions differ?*

▶ Research the role of the Catholic Church in the colonial administration of Spanish America. *How did the Church become both the defender and oppressor of Indians?*

▶ Compare the strategies, tactics, and assumptions of Turks, Indians, Japanese, and Chinese in dealing with foreign merchants in the 16th century. *In what ways did they underestimate the threat posed by European naval power?*

▶ Research the Japanese reactions to activities of the Portuguese and Spanish. *In what ways were Hideyoshi's invasions of Korea a response to Spanish takeover of the Philippines?*

▶ Assess the means by which Spain and Portugal ruled their colonial empires in the Americas. Compare Iberian organization of labor and social stratification in the Americas with the system of labor in a European manorial community. *What effect did the encomienda system have on the local people? How was military and civil authority exercised? What role did the Church play?*

C. The consequences of the worldwide exchange of flora, fauna, and pathogens.

Grades 5-6

▶ Research a plant or domestic animal that was transported by sea from one part of the world to another in the 16th century. On a large outline map of the world, graphically represent its route.

▶ Keep a journal of foods you eat for a day. Cross out those items that would not be available in North America had the worldwide exchange not taken place. Diagram on a map where the various foods you are eating were first grown.

▶ Research the effects of the horse, sheep, and pig on life in the Americas. *How did they change farming and ranching?*

Grades 7-8

▶ Construct graphs of estimated population trends in the Americas, Europe, and East Asia in the 16th and 17th centuries. *Why did populations drastically decline in parts of the Americas but rise in Europe and East Asia?*

▶ Draw a map and placing items of flora and fauna exchange at their points of origin. Illustrate on the map the global dispersions of these items. Select a place in Africa, Asia, Europe, or the Americas and plan a menu for two banquets, one before "the exchange" and the other after.

▶ Draw evidence from primary and secondary source materials to describe the effects of disease on the Amerindian population. Examine possible psychological effects of catastrophic mortality on Amerindians. *Why was it possible for so few Europeans to dominate indigenous peoples? How may the spread of disease have made it easier to make converts to Christianity?*

Grades 9-12

▶ Trace the "travels" of one item from the flora (sugar, coffee, cassava, corn, potato) and one from fauna (horse, cattle, chicken, pig) from one part of the world to another between the 16th and 18th centuries. Analyze the impact of these on world economic change.

▶ Develop a chart classifying the major diseases that were transferred as a result of transoceanic travel in the 16th and 17th centuries. Include the areas they would affect, the means by which they were spread, the immunities of native populations to these diseases, and the impact that the spread of disease had upon individual societies, world trade, and political expansion and control. *How did Amerindian societies combat disease?*

▶ Selecting a specific native population such as Aztec, Inca, Zuni, Tuscarora, Powhatan, or Iroquois and, using primary and secondary sources, describe demographic changes that occurred in e 16th and 17th centuries. Hypothesize the effects disease-driven demographics change might have had on society and culture.

▶ Draw on sources such as *Seeds of Change: A Quincentennial Commemoration* to analyze the impact of worldwide exchange of people, flora, fauna, and pathogens on contemporary ecology, economy, and culture.

▶ Assess how the encounter with Amerindian civilizations affected European ideas regarding the image of the "noble savage," systems of ethno-racial classification, natural history, cartography, and human origins.

II. *How European society experienced political, economic, and cultural transformations in an age of global intercommunication, 1450-1750.*

A. Demographic, economic, and social trends in Europe.

Grades 5-6

▶ Research one of the social classes of early modern Europe and construct a project that illustrates occupations, a typical home, and the roles of men, women, and children.

- Research what factors reveal a woman's social and legal status in Europe in the period 1450-1750. Determine the relative changes in status among women in different social classes from earlier periods and during these centuries. Role-play a conversation among women representing various classes, discussing how their positions in society have changed and why.

- Locate on a map the major cities of Europe at the beginning of the 17th century. On an overlay indicate the major urban areas toward the end of the 18th century. *How do the maps differ? Why and how do cities grow?*

Grades 7-8

- Research the Spanish silver trade from America and its effect on the world economy.

- Explain the "agrarian revolution." *What factors caused the "revolution?" How did the it change society? What were its effects on western and eastern Europe?*

- Create a chart showing population growth in major European nation/states during the 15th and 16th centuries. Students should indicate the nation, the year, and the population. From this information they should analyze the causes for such demographic growth, and the potential impact of such growth on the state.

- Explain the factors that may have stimulated population growth and those that may have deterred it.

Grades 9-12

- Define the "price revolution" in terms of 16th-century Europe. *How does this relate to the rise of capitalism? What is the evidence that the "price revolution" took place?*

- Using data from the period 1550-1700, graph the increase of agricultural production and population in Europe. Relate these developments to to demographic and technological changes during the period.

- Assume the role of a merchant and prepare a rationale for engaging in international trade in the 16th century. *What products would you select to trade? What are the existing markets and what markets need to be created? How would you finance, transport, and market goods? What problems are peculiar to each market item? What role would you expect the state to take in trade and commerce?*

- Research how Dutch and English merchants amassed enough capital to explore and make significant investments in overseas areas. Create a brochure aimed at attracting investors.

- Using historical evidence, draw a chart showing changes in men's and women's work options resulting from developments such as the increased division between capital and labor, and the increasing emphasis on wages as a defining characteristic of "work." *What effect did family roles, class, and geographical location have on women's work in this period? In what ways did their work situation remain unchanged?*

B. The Renaissance, Reformation, and Catholic Reformation.

Grades 5-6

- Research the development of linear perspective in art in 15th-16th-century Europe and make a camera obscura.

- Keep a record of the time it takes to copy a page of a textbook by hand. Multiply this by the number of pages in the book to determine how many hours it might take to reproduce one book by hand. Discuss how the printing press increased the spread of knowledge.

▶ Research the life of a leading figure of during the Renaissance and Reformation such as Sofonisba Anguissola, Benvenutto Cellini, Cervantes, El Greco, Rabelais, Sir Philip Sidney, or Zwingli. Assemble information about the person using illustrations to help explain his or her contributions to society.

▶ Write a letter from a young man to his parents explaining his attraction to the ideas of the Protestant reformers.

Grades 7-8

▶ Compare the Gutenberg printing press with that used by Benjamin Franklin and with a modern printing press. *How has the technology changed? How has the new technology influenced learning and communication?*

▶ Research changing gender roles during the Renaissance and Reformation. Using a television panel show format, interview a cross section of women about their lives and interests. *Did the status of women change during this period of time? Who were the leading women of the period?*

▶ Construct a map showing the geographical patterns of religious affiliation in Europe in the early 17th century. *What factors might have contributed to the conversion of specific populations to Protestant faiths?*

▶ Study examples of Renaissance architecture and examine local buildings, churches, and homes to determine the influence of Renaissance architecture. Collect photographs of public buildings in the United States and display them with pictures of Renaissance buildings that might have inspired them.

▶ Analyze the art forms and artists of the Renaissance. Use one particular artist to show how the artist affected the society of his or her era. Reconstruct or copy the work of a particular artist or architect.

▶ Select illustrations to display in a classroom "museum" showing changes in art and architecture from the Middle Ages through the High Renaissance. Describe these changes and draw conclusions about how the points of view of artists changed.

Grades 9-12

▶ Read excerpts from *The Prince* and compare Machiavelli's understanding of "realpolitik" with that of Kautilya in *Arthashastra*.

▶ Examine excerpts from Renaissance writers such as Petrarch, Boccaccio, Cervantes, Erasmus, More, and Shakespeare. *How did authors reflect the spirit of Renaissance humanism in their works?* Compare and contrast northern humanism with that of the Italian Renaissance.

▶ Assess the impact of the rediscovery of Greco-Roman antiquity in the 15th century and its role in the development of new forms of art and scholarship. *Who were the leading figures in the revival of Classical architecture and sculpture? What factors stimulated the rediscovery?*

▶ Analyze the theological views of leading reformers of the Reformation such as Luther, Calvin, and the Anabaptists. *How did their central beliefs challenge the practices and authority of Catholicism? What were the consequences?*

▶ Assume the role of a Protestant woman writer, such as Katherine Zell, and respond to Luther's assertion, *"The rule remains with the husband, and the wife is compelled to obey him by God's command....The woman...should stay at home and look after the affairs of the household."*

▸ Examine the major political, social, and economic consequences of the religious wars in Europe in the 16th and 17th centuries. *What were the political consequences of these conflicts? To what extent does the map of Europe today reflect the consequences of these struggles?*

▸ Use books such as Irving Stone's *The Agony and the Ecstasy*, Claudia Van Canon's *The Inheritance*, and Barbara Willard's *A Cold Wind Blowing* to discuss social and political conflict in Europe during the Renaissance. *How did such conditions conflict with prevailing humanist principles?*

C. Rising military and bureaucratic power of European states between the 16th and 18th centuries.

Grades 5-6

▸ Explain the impact gunpowder had on European warfare and collect pictures to show how fortifications changed after the introduction of gunpowder.

▸ Working within small groups, examine the lives of leading European political figures such as Henry VIII, Elizabeth I, Philip II, James I, Oliver Cromwell, Louis XIV, or Peter the Great. Incorporate pictures and sketches with information regarding the life and accomplishments of the selected leader.

▸ Develop a list of freedoms that an English citizen would have realized as a result of the Revolution of 1688.

Grades 7-8

▸ Research Elizabeth I's reign and explain her accomplishments as queen of England. *How effective was Elizabeth's leadership? To what extent did her actions contribute to the development of a strong national state?*

▸ Trace the spread of gunpowder from China to Europe, and assess the role of gunpowder in establishing and maintaining the power of leaders of the European states during this period.

▸ Assume the role of Catherine the Great and prepare a manual for leadership to advise future Russian rulers on how to govern.

▸ Research the founding of St. Petersburg. *Why was St. Petersburg called the "window on the West"?*

▸ Drawing on books such as E. M. Almedingen's *The Crimson Oak* and Erik Christian Haugaard's *Cromwell's Boy*, describe what life was like for people living in European states. *How were conditions in various countries different?*

▸ Identify three characteristics of an "absolute" monarch and debate the extent to which James I of England, Louis XIV of France, and Peter I of Russia were absolute monarchs. *Which other rulers would you characterize as absolute? How does their authority compare with that of the emperors of China or the Ottoman sultans?*

▸ Identify the long-range and immediate causes of the English Revolution of 1688. Debate in what ways this revolution was "Glorious." *What were the effects of English ideas of popular resistance and liberty upon the development of self-government in the American colonies?*

▸ Develop a comparison of the capital cities of Europe during this century. *How were they similar and how did they differ?* Look at the architecture, leadership, societies, and other factors in each city.

Grades 9-12

▶ Compare the pressures for building and maintaining a large army today with those of states in the 17th and early 18th centuries. *What was Machiavelli's advice regarding the use of mercenaries? Was this advice followed in early modern Europe?*

▶ Write a defense of your position during the English Civil War from the perspective of a Cavalier or Roundhead.

▶ Write a biographical sketch of the Louis XIV, emphasizing ways in which royal pomp and ceremony were used to represent absolutist power.

▶ Construct a map of Russia with overlays showing the expansion of territory from the close of the 16th century through the end of the 18th century. *What appear to be Russia's goals in territorial expansion? What lands did Russia acquire during the reigns of Peter the Great and Catherine the Great?*

▶ Research the reigns of Frederick the Great, Catherine the Great, and Joseph II. *Which of these monarchs best deserves the title "Enlightened Despot"?*

▶ Compare the characteristics of the Dutch Republic with the characteristics of other states during this period. *What role did commerce play in determining who exercised political power? What were the results of Dutch government attitudes toward various religious groups? How did such a small state come to play such an important role in world trade and international affairs?*

▶ Write an essay explaining how Amsterdam gained commercial supremacy from the northern Italian city-states in the latter part of the 16th century. Compare Amsterdam's ascendancy with the decline of Venice.

▶ Contrast English political development with the development of one or more absolutist monarchies. *What were the long-term effects of these differing patterns of development?*

D. How the Scientific Revolution contributed to transformations in European society.

Grades 5-6

▶ Define the word "revolution" and explain what is meant by the Scientific Revolution.

▶ Research one of the great thinkers and scientists of the Scientific Revolution such as Copernicus, Vesalius, Galileo, Bacon, or Newton. Use information gathered through research to construct a short essay, poem, or play emphasizing what was new about his ideas and how his discovery was made.

▶ Define the term "astronomy," and explain ways in which this science may affect our lives today. *How did astrology, as practiced in Medieval Europe, differ from astronomy?*

Grades 7-8

▶ Using the scientific method, chart the major constellations and note the position of the sun as it rises and sets over a period of two to three weeks. *Does such a chart indicate that the stars and planets revolve around the earth or that the earth revolves around the sun?* Debate the statement: *Superstitions prevented people from accepting the scientific method.*

▶ Investigate the concepts of scientific method advanced by Francis Bacon and René Descartes. *What other scientists influenced these thinkers?*

▶ Research the trial of Galileo. Assuming the roles of defense and prosecution, conduct a simulated trial presenting evidence of Galileo's innocence or guilt. Evaluate the arguments presented in the context of 17th-century thought and values.

♦ Construct a chart or a timeline showing important events of the Scientific Revolution and the person or persons associated with each. Write a biography of one person for a science "hall of fame." Select from major fields of endeavor such as astronomy, mathematics, biology, earth science, physics, chemistry, botany, and medicine.

Grades 9-12

♦ Analyze one of Shakespeare's plays such as *Macbeth* or *Hamlet* and cite examples of references to ghosts, witches, or spirits. *What do such references tell us about 16th- or 17th-century belief in the supernatural? What consequences resulted from those beliefs? Were such beliefs considered scientifically sound at the time?*

♦ Draw evidence from Galileo's letter to the Grand Duchess Christina (1615) to explain his ideas about the solar system. Discuss Galileo's points in light of religious conservatism and the Scientific Revolution. *Why does Galileo feel it is dangerous to apply scriptural passages to science-related problems?*

♦ Research the titles of some important books translated from non-European languages like Arabic and Chinese that were found in the libraries of European universities and scientists during this period. *Who undertook these translations? How might these works have influenced European science and mathematics?*

E. The significance of the Enlightenment in European and world history.

Grades 5-6

♦ Define the terms "enlightenment" and "enlightened." *What image does the term "enlightenment" suggest? What relationship might there be between education and enlightenment? Why was a historical movement of 18th-century Europe called the "Enlightenment"?*

♦ Research the life of Denis Diderot. *How did he exemplify Enlightenment ideas? How have works like encyclopedias, dictionaries, and thesauruses been useful to you?*

Grades 7-8

♦ Write an appraisal of Immanuel Kant's "motto" of the Enlightenment, "Dare to Know! Have the courage to use your own intelligence!" *To what extent was the Enlightenment dependent on the Scientific Revolution?*

♦ Select two figures from the Enlightenment era and compare them in terms of how they exemplify Enlightenment thought and ideals. Consider such individuals as Montesquieu, Voltaire, Condorcet, Diderot, Rousseau, Malthus, Kant, Franklin, and Jefferson.

♦ Assume the role of an Enlightened philosopher and critique the laws and governmental system of an early 18th-century monarchy. Devise a plan to re-structure that system to put it in conformity with the Enlightenment.

♦ Investigate the social reforms advocated by the Italian philosopher Cessari Beccaria. *In what ways are his reform ideas about criminal justice taken for granted today?*

♦ Explain how Enlightenment thought promoted individualism. *How did the Enlightenment promote ideas of gaining freedom from ignorance, superstition, and rigid customs?*

♦ Analyze the Declaration of Independence as an expression of Enlightenment thought. *How did Jefferson make use of the concept of natural rights in the document?*

Grades 9-12

- Draw from excerpts of René Descartes's *Discourse on Method* to explain his approach to discovering truth. Assume the role of a scientist and a churchman and debate the apparent conflict between religion and science in the context of the 17th century.

- Research the Parisian salons and their influence in spreading Enlightenment thought. *What were the roles of aristocratic and bourgeois women in promoting the Enlightenment? What influence did the salons have on French political affairs? Why did some men criticize the salons as superficial and organize exclusively male salons?*

- Investigate how the Enlightenment changed political thought. How did the ideas of John Locke, Baron de Montesquieu, and Jean Jacques Rousseau threaten existing governments?

- Explain how the economic theories of François Quesnay and Adam Smith influenced the development of modern capitalism.

- Explain how episodes from Voltaire's *Candide* illustrate Enlightenment values. *How did Candide's experience in Portugal at the time of the great earthquake reflect superstitions prevalent in 18th-century Europe?*

- Research and cite specific examples of how Chinese humanist philosophy influenced the ideas of Voltaire, Leibniz, and Quesnay. *How did these European thinkers learn about Chinese philosophy? What rationale did Chinese philosophy offer these Enlightenment thinkers as a basis for human morality and ethics?*

- Construct a chart or diagram setting forth major Enlightenment ideas regarding education. *How are those ideals similar to or different from educational ideas and policies in the United States today? How did Rousseau think children should be educated?*

III. How large territorial empires dominated much of Eurasia between the 16th and 18th centuries.

A. The extent and limits of Chinese regional power under the Ming dynasty.

Grades 5-6

- Research the voyages of Zheng He in order to understand Chinese naval and commercial activities in the Indian Ocean in the early 15th century. *What do the fleets of Zheng He reveal about Chinese maritime technology? Why did the Ming emperor order the Chinese fleet to withdraw from the Indian Ocean? Where was the major military threat to China? What advantages and disadvantages might a Ming ruler have seen in continuing overseas trade?*

- Construct a journal for a minister of the Ming royal court during the late 15th or early 16th century. *How does the minister regard the emperor's absolute power? In what ways does he think China is prospering? How does he feel about overseas trade? What does he think of people who make their living as merchants?*

Grades 7-8

- Playing the role of a Chinese scholar-bureaucrat, explain why China is the "Middle Kingdom" in the world and why other countries have a tributary relationship to the celestial empire. *In what way are this gentleman's views an expression of ethnocentrism? Have other peoples seen themselves as inhabiting the "central" place in the world?*

◆ Assess the power of the Ming emperors at various stages of Ming rule. *Should Ming government be called despotic? To what extent was the ruler's control absolute? What aspects of Chinese society did the emperor control? What high offices did the Ming eliminate? What officials were responsible to the emperor?*

◆ Compare the services the state expected from the various groups in society. *What services were expected from the gentry? What were the roles of the military, merchant, and commoner classes? In what ways was a separation among the gentry, merchants, and peasants established and maintained in Ming society? What use did Ming leaders make of such things as jobs, clothes, taxation, and corvée?*

◆ Assess the military strategy of the Ming. *Did the Ming face major military threats? To what extent was defense their main concern?*

◆ Construct a diary for a farmer of 15th-century China. Depict his "ownership" of land, his attitudes toward government, his family's life, and his methods of farming.

Grades 9-12

◆ Explain methods the Ming used to bring cultural unity to China, particularly in eliminating Mongol influences and re-establishing Confucian and Daoist values. *How does this compare with efforts at tolerance and cultural pluralism in other empires at the time, such as the Mughal, Ottoman or Russian?*

◆ Drawing on selections from the satirical novel *The Scholars* or from *China's Examination Hell* by Conrad, assess the role of the imperial examination system. *What types of questions were included? How did the examination system foster neo-Confucian values and assure the appointment of bureaucrats of merit? How does the examination system compare with our civil service exams and SATs?*

◆ Evaluate the evidence that more than one-third of the silver mined in the Americas between 1527 and 1821 ended up in China. *Why did China receive so much silver? How did silver reach China? Why did Europeans want to export silver to China? What might the implications for Chinese society have been in moving from payment in kind to payments in silver?*

◆ List the various ways the central government of China controlled people's lives: for example, job allocation, service to the government including taxation and *corvée*, and where one lived. *What were the symbols of central authority that surrounded the ruler? What power did eunuchs have in the service of the court?*

◆ Construct a comparison of the royal court of China during the height of the Ming and that of Louis XIV of France. *How do the power of the two monarchs compare?*

B. How Southeast Europe and Southwest Asia became unified under the Ottoman Empire.

Grades 5-6

◆ Research the life of Suleiman the Magnificent. *Why is he given the title "the Magnificent"? Is there a leader living today that you would call "the magnificent"? Why?*

◆ Make overlay maps of the extent of the Byzantine and Ottoman empires at various periods, particularly focusing on the 14th and 15th centuries, to determine their relative strength. *How can you account for the changes in territory each empire controlled?*

◆ Taking the role of an investigative reporter, report on the battle for Constantinople in 1453 and write a report of the events from the perspectives of different people, such as a Christian resident of the city, an Ottoman soldier, or an official of the Vatican.

▶ Research and describe the various aspects of the Ottoman military and explain the importance of firearms in Ottoman conquests. *What motivated the troops? What made their enemies consider the janissaries such a formidable foe? Why did Christian Europeans regard the fall of the city as such a catastrophic event?*

Grades 7-8

▶ Describe and compare the military, political, and cultural achievements of Mehmed the Conqueror and Suleiman the Magnificent. *What contributed to their successes?*

▶ Construct a map of the main trade routes passing through the Ottoman Empire. *How important was international trade in the empire's economy? How did the development of the sea route around Africa affect trade in the empire?*

▶ Compare the *ghazi* warrior with both the European knight and the Japanese samurai as warriors and members of society.

▶ Make a model of one of the buildings designed by Sinan Pasha such as the Suleimaniye mosque in Constantinople. Compare this mosque in terms of ground plan, shape, purpose, and use of artistic elements other monuments, such as St. Peter's in Rome.

Grades 9-12

▶ Compare the emergence of the Ottomans as a world power between 1450 and 1650 with that of the Spanish during the same period. *How did both Ottoman Turks and Castilians come to dominate vast territories? How did they enlist the support of their subject peoples?*

▶ Analyze in what ways the Ottoman Empire was similar to the Byzantine Empire. *What administrative and legal practices were similar? What role did the Sultan's household play in ruling the state?*

▶ After reading excerpts from Ghislain de Busbecq's book describing the life of the Ottomans, write a letter from de Busbecq to the Austrian and Russian monarchs recommending changes they need to make in order to meet the threat from the Ottomans.

▶ On a map or map overlays, show the lands of the Ottoman Empire at different periods: the fall of Constantinople (1453); the defeat of the Safavids (1514); the second siege of Vienna (1683); and the rapid contraction of the empire at the end of the 17th century. Assess the difficulties in holding together such a vast empire.

▶ Research the lives of women in the Ottoman Empire. *What was the legal position of women in the empire? How did the legal status of women compare to that in Christian European states? What political and social roles did women of the imperial harem play in the Ottoman state? What rules applied to non-Muslim women within the Ottoman Empire?*

▶ Assess the state revenues of the Ottoman court under Suleiman. *What were the sources of revenue? How were they collected? On what did the Ottoman court spend its revenues? How important were building projects such as state-supported mosques, schools, and public baths? What role did pious charitable foundations play in establishing hospitals, schools, soup kitchens, and other public projects?*

▶ Make a map indicating the ethnic and religious diversity of peoples within the Ottoman Empire. Evaluate the effects of Ottoman governance on the various social, religious, and ethnic groups. *Why did many Jews expelled from Spain in 1492 settle under the Ottomans? How were Orthodox Christian populations such as those in Serbia and Bulgaria treated by the Ottoman Turks?*

C. The rise of the Safavid and Mughal empires.

Grades 5-6

▶ Write a newspaper article reporting on the policies and achievements of the Safavid ruler Shah Abbas. *In what ways did he support trade and commerce? Why did he encourage trade with European merchants?*

▶ Write a letter to a European court describing Isfahan during the reign of Shah Abbas I. Assemble illustrations of Safavid art and architecture to illustrate architectural style, paintings, ceramics, and carpets.

▶ Imagine you were a member of Babur's army as it conquered the armies of the Sultanate of Delhi. Report your impressions of the military campaign and of North India.

▶ *What spices did Vasco da Gama buy from local Indian merchants in 1498? What was included in the Indian mixture of spices that the early European traders called "curry"? How did the sale of the spices da Gama brought back to Europe set off a rush to India to deal in the spice trade?* Find recipes from American cooking today that use spices originating in India.

Grades 7-8

▶ On a map of southwestern Asia show the growth and extent of the Safavid Empire and create a timeline to show its expansion. *How did Shi'a Islam become dominant in Persia during the Safavid period? What other factors contributed to the success of Safavid rule?*

▶ Construct a map showing the locations from which the Safavid state began and indicate the movement of people into Iran and Afghanistan. Show the extension of the empire and the key cities of Tabriz and Isfahan.

▶ Describe Isfahan during the reign of Shah Abbas I, including such buildings as the Isfahan mosque. Compare Isfahan with Ottoman Istanbul, with Agra or Delhi under the Mughals, or with a European capital.

▶ Create a series of maps, charts, and timelines comparing the Ottoman, Safavid, and Mughal empires. Include geographic extension; penetration of other states; dates of their beginning, height, and demise; art and architecture; scholarship; degree of tolerance; and economic endeavors.

▶ Research Akbar's religious attitudes and his attempts to unite his culturally diverse empire. *How did he encourage religious tolerance? How do the policies he established for his religiously pluralistic empire compare with those of Elizabeth I of England?*

▶ Investigate Indian textiles that were popular among Europeans during the 16th and 17th centuries? *How did the large market for Indian cloth in Europe undermine the East India Company's goal of selling more British goods in India than it imported?*

Grades 9-12

▶ Assess the reasons Ismail was able to create the Safavid empire. *What was the basis of his legitimacy? What was his attitude toward Sufi, Shi'i, and Sunni forms of Islam?*

▶ Draft a statement to be sent throughout the Mughal empire listing Akbar's methods for creating harmony among the various groups he ruled. *How do his strategies compare with the way the Ottoman Empire treated minorities or the way Elizabeth I of England handled Protestant-Catholic tensions?*

▶ *How do the Agra Red Fort, the Taj Mahal, and the Audience Hall at Fatehpur Sikri suggest a synthesis of Muslim and Hindu architecture and artistic motifs?*

▶ Drawing upon visual and written sources, describe the monumental architecture or miniature art of the Mughal empire. *In what ways do these art forms reflect a blending of Persian, Islamic, and Hindu traditions?*

▶ Research the attitudes of Akhbar or Aurangzeb on an issue such as how to treat minorities, religious beliefs, military expansion, or architectural and literary accomplishments. Write an essay comparing their ideas and policies. *How can you account for the differences between these rulers?*

IV. *Economic, political, and cultural interrelations among peoples of Africa, Europe, and the Americas, 1500-1750.*

A. How states and peoples of European descent became dominant in the Americas between the 16th and 18th centuries.

Grades 5-6

▶ On a map of the Americas and India, locate areas of British and French influence. Explain why the British and French wanted to trade and control territory in these regions.

▶ Assume the role of an adviser to a European government and argue for or against the establishment of a policy of mercantilism. *How would this policy help the mother country? What advantages would it have for the colonists?*

▶ Using a chart compare and contrast the English, French, and Dutch colonial foundings and show how their early development differed.

▶ Locate on a world map military campaigns during the Seven Years War. *Why has this war sometimes been called a "world" war?*

Grades 7-8

▶ Create a chart showing the diversity of the government, economy, military, and organization of societies in different European colonies around the world. Analyze how colonization differed in trading-post colonies and settler colonies.

▶ Explain how the Dutch East India Company was chartered by the state to conduct diplomatic, economic, and military functions. *How did the Dutch East India Company get monopoly control over the world's supply of nutmeg and mace? What difference might that have made in the price of these spices?*

▶ Role-play a 16th-century Catholic missionary sent to the Americas to convert people. Write a letter home describing Amerindian beliefs and explaining how you might go about the conversion.

▶ 1763 has been called "the year of decision." Evaluate this statement with regard to the settling of the Seven Years War and the global competition between France and England.

▶ Analyze the role of Native Americans on both the British and French sides during the French and Indian (Seven Years) War.

Grades 9-12

▶ Compare and contrast examples of types of European activity and control: the Spanish empire of Peru, the French trading-post empire in the Great Lakes region, the slave plantation colony of Barbados, and the British settler colony of Massachusetts.

▶ Research daily life in the Spanish colonies in the Americas. Explain what occupations you and your friends might have if you lived there during the colonial period.

◗ Working with three other students, create lists of the duties of colonial administrators in the Spanish empire in Peru, a French trading-post empire in the Great Lakes region, a plantation colony of Barbados, and a British settler colony in Massachusetts. *What duties are the same? What duties are different?* Discuss the advantages and disadvantages of serving in the various areas.

◗ Define mercantilism and explain why colonial powers adopted this system. *In what ways was mercantilist theory and practice different in France, England, and the Netherlands? Would it be possible for this economic policy to be successful today?*

◗ Drawing on information contained in Alfred Crosby's books *The Columbian Exchange* and *Ecological Imperialism*, explain why Europeans founded large land empires and settler colonies in the Americas in the 16th and 17th centuries, but asserted these forms of control almost nowhere in Africa or Asia.

◗ Write an essay hypothesizing why Catholics were generally more successful than Protestants in converting non-Europeans between the 16th and 18th centuries.

B. Origins and consequences of the trans-Atlantic African slave trade.

Grades 5-6

◗ Draw a diagram of a slave ship to show how slaves were transported. *If slave merchants aimed to make a profit selling slaves in America, why did they transport them in harsh and unhealthy conditions?*

◗ Read primary sources recounting the capture and transporting of slaves to the New World. Write an account of a slave sale on the West African coast from the perspective of an enslaved man or woman, an African slave merchant, or a European slave ship captain.

◗ Study pictures of plantation life in the Americas and write captions for the illustrations from the point of view of a slave and plantation owner.

◗ Research the rising popularity of new consumer products such as coffee, tea, sugar and tobacco around the world in the 17th and 18th centuries. *Why did these products gain mass acceptance? What is the per capita consumption of these products in various nations today? How might government policy about teen-age tobacco consumption today differ from that in the 17th and 18th centuries?*

Grades 7-8

◗ Examine the working conditions on sugar plantations in the Caribbean. *Why did African slaves come to supply most of the labor needs for commercial plantations? Why not American Indian labor, European indentured servitude, or free wage labor?*

◗ Recount the efforts of the kingdoms of Kongo and Benin to resist the trans-Atlantic slave trade. *Why did some African governments oppose the trade and others participate in it?*

◗ Conduct a read-around using excerpts from the 18th-century autobiography, *The Interesting Narrative of the Life of Olaudah Equiano or Gustavus Vasa. How was Equiano enslaved? What happened to him before he was put on board a slave ship? How does he describe the Middle Passage? How might slaves have put up resistance during the Middle Passage??*

◗ Discuss and compare different forms of slave resistance and protest, including cultural defiance, sabotage, rebellion, and the founding of Maroon societies.

◗ Recount the history of the African kingdom of Palmares in Brazil. *Why did the kingdom eventually disappear?*

▶ Explain the encomienda system and assess its effects on Indians. *What was the intent of the encomienda when it was established? How was the encomienda used by Spanish colonists? Is the encomienda comparable to slavery?*

Grades 9-12

▶ Drawing on Philip Curtin's book *The Atlantic Slave Trade*, graphically represent the origins and destinations for slaves taken from Africa to the Americas on a large world map.

▶ Explain the *Leyenda Negra*. *How did other countries use the "Black Legend" to build opposition to Spain? How did the dealings of other European states with native populations differ from those of Spain?*

▶ Analyze primary and secondary source material, including illustrations of laborers in silver mines and on plantations, to assess the variety of ways in which Europeans exploited American Indian labor.

▶ Construct a comparative chart illustrating the ways in which ancient, medieval, and early modern societies instituted various forms of social bondage prior to the Atlantic slave trade. Compare and contrast ways in which bondage was practiced in the Islamic lands, Christian Europe, and West Africa. *How did the Atlantic slave trade differ from previous historical examples of slavery?*

▶ Research the institutions, practices, and beliefs of slaves working on plantations in the Western Hemisphere. List ways in which they preserved their African heritage.

▶ Assume the role of a slave on a plantation in the Caribbean, Brazil, or British North America and explain ways in which you resist the institution of slavery. Examine historical records to determine where slaves organized resistance movements. *What were the dangers involved in open rebellion against slavery? What other means of resistance were used?*

▶ Assume the perspective of a person sold into bondage in the Caribbean and describe conditions you endured in the middle passage and daily life on a Caribbean sugar plantation. *How was the life of a slave similar and different on a Brazilian plantation? On a plantation in British North America?*

C. Patterns of change in Africa in the era of the slave trade.

Grades 5-6

▶ Use books such as Scott O'Dell's *My Name is Not Angelica* and Paula Fox's *Slave Dancer* to describe the experience of Africans sold into slavery.

▶ After listening to a reading of the capture scene in the book *Roots* by Alex Haley, describe the visual imagery and express your personal reactions. *What do historians say in general about Europeans taking part in capturing slaves on the African mainland?*

▶ Drawing on E. W. Bovill's *The Golden Trade of the Moors*, recount the Moroccan adventure to send a military expedition across the Sahara Desert to conquer Songhay in 1590. *Why did the Sultan of Morocco want to conquer Songhay? What were the results of the expedition?*

Grades 7-8

▶ Examine the influence of international trade on such African states as Ashanti, Dahomey, and Oyo. *With whom did the West African states trade? What commodities were traded? How important was trade to West African kingdoms?*

▶ Explain the meaning of the Ashanti belief that the king was "first among equals." *How does this belief compare with European concepts of the "divine right of kings?"*

- Map the terrain of West Africa. On an overlay, indicate the extent of the states of Ashanti, Oyo, Dahomey, and Songhay. *What role did geography play in the development of these states? What items were traded and with whom?*

- Research how the slave trade affected family life and gender roles in West and Central Africa.

Grades 9-12

- Drawing on Philip D. Curtin's book, *The Atlantic Slave Trade*, research statistical studies related to the numbers of slaves involved in the Atlantic trade. Design a bar graph to illustrate the different statistics. *How are the different statistics determined? Can we determine the correct number of people taken forcibly from Africa? Why or why not?*

- Describe the political structure of the empire of Songhay. *What was the extent of the empire? In what ways were trans-Saharan trade important to its economy? Why did Songhay collapse so quickly?*

- Read Leo Africanus's account of his travels in the Songhay empire. *Why was Timbuktu an important city in the 15th and 16th century? What does Leo Africanus tell us about the importance of the book trade in Songhay?*

- Write an essay on the following question: "As in North America, Europeans planted a settler colony in South Africa in the 17th century." *In what ways and why did this colony develop differently from the British Thirteen Colonies in North America?*

V. Transformations in Asian societies in the era of European expansion.

A. The development of European maritime power in Asia.

Grades 5-6

- On a map of East Asia, locate Portuguese, Dutch, English, and French trading centers and identify the products that were traded.

- Assume the role of a British merchant of the 17th century and prepare a presentation to the Cabinet regarding the importance of the Asia trade. *What arguments would you present? What policies would you propose?*

- Make a map of Southeast Asia showing the locations of the various spices that the Europeans wanted to trade. Then identify how many of these sites of this spice trade were controlled by the Dutch as of 1770.

Grades 7-8

- Make a political map of China showing the major port cities and trade routes used by European merchants. *Why do you think Guangzhou (Canton) was a good choice of the Chinese government to center trade with Europeans? How did Chinese authorities control European merchants' activities there?*

- Research the growth of British, Dutch, and French naval power in the Indian Ocean from 1600-1700. Assume the role of an English, Dutch, or French admiral and develop a set of arguments on what the other two nations are doing to create a strong navy. *What should your own country should do to compete with your rivals?*

- Research how the Dutch developed a system of forced labor as a basis for their prosperity in Indonesia. Compare this system with the slave economy of sugar production in the Caribbean.

♦ Read the correspondence between the Chinese emperors and the British government regarding trading privileges during the period 1700-1770. Write a short dramatic presentation involving a Chinese and a British diplomat debating the issue of increased trading privileges for the British merchants.

Grades 9-12

♦ Research how Joseph François Dupleix developed the French policy of "divide and rule" in South India. *What impact did Dupleix's concept have on Robert Clive and the British East India Company's policy and on life for Indian peasants?*

♦ Research how the Mughal emperors such as Akbar, Jahangir, and Aurangzeb tried to limit and control the influence of European trading centers in India. Assess their relative success of these rulers in this effort and compare it to Chinese and Japanese attempts to regulate foreign trade and outside influences.

♦ Research why the Chinese emperors wanted to limit the amount of foreign trade. Assume that you are an envoy of the British government sent to Guangzhou in 1770 to find out the reasons for Chinese limitation on trade and the Chinese might be persuaded to open their country to more foreign trade. Write a memorandum to parliament summarizing your findings and suggestions.

♦ Research and compare various attempts by the Dutch, British, and French to redress the unfavorable trade balances that each suffered in Asia from 1500 to 1800.

♦ Research the spread of Christianity into predominantly Hindu, Buddhist, and Muslim areas after 1500. Write a dialogue between a Muslim and a Hindu on what they see as the reasons for the spread of Christian missions, what the impact might be on their faiths, and how best to resist the appeals of Christian missionaries.

♦ Assume that you are chief military adviser to the emperor Aurangzeb in 1700. Develop a list of arguments on the best way to defend his empire against the rising maritime power of France and England. *Would you stress building a larger army?*

B. Transformations in India, China, and Japan in an era of expanding European commercial power.

Grades 5-6

♦ Construct a map of the islands of Japan and the opposite coast of mainland East Asia. Locate on the map the peninsula of Korea, the Ming boundaries, the major warrior states on the island of Honshu, and the major cities predating the Tokugawa shogunate.

♦ Read sections of *Chushingura* (The Tale of the Forty-seven Ronin) and discuss the samurai ideals expressed there.

♦ Drawing on books such as Erik Haugaard's *The Samurai's Tale* and Robert D. San Souci's *The Samurai Daughter*, describe Japanese society between the 16th and 18th centuries. *Who is left out of the stories about samurai? Why?*

♦ Construct a map of the Ming dynasty and prepare an overlay showing the extent of the Qing dynasty in the 18th century. Label areas where ethnic minorities lived. *How do you think the incorporation of new territories and peoples affected the lives of Han Chinese?*

Grades 7-8

♦ As a reporter for a western newspaper develop a series of "investigative" articles describing the political and economic positions of Ming China at the beginning of the 17th century, and assess its stability and potential for survival.

♦ Assuming the role of a Jesuit missionary in China during the reign of the Kangxi emperor, prepare an appeal to the pope to recognize traditional Confucian values in your efforts to spread Christianity.

♦ As a Manchu (Qing) emperor, decide how to handle problems stemming from increasing population growth, agricultural output, commerce, and the incursion of European trading networks.

♦ Use an evaluation form to rate the treatment and opportunities open to women in 17th- and 18th-century China. Rate such items as footbinding, female subordination, patriarchy, a flourishing women's culture, and literature. Develop an oral or written report on one of these topics.

♦ Assume the role of a Korean before 1800 and explain why Korea was called the "Hermit Kingdom." Write a newspaper or magazine article defending or rejecting that title.

♦ Read the "Great Learning for Women" and assess the role and status of women in Tokugawa Japan.

♦ Define "feudalism" in 17th- and 18th-century Japan, and compare it to European feudalism of two or three hundred years earlier.

Grades 9-12

♦ Research how the demise of centralized control by the imperial Mughals contributed to the rise of Maratha and Sikh power in India. Write an essay comparing the fall of Mughal rule with the fall of Ming rule.

♦ Analyze how importation of American silver affected the economies of China and Japan between the 16th and 18th centuries.

♦ Prepare a list of Chinese goods desired by Europeans. From the perspective of a European country, devise a commercial treaty with China. *How did trading policies under the Manchus differ from those of the Ming dynasty? What factors contributed to the change?*

♦ Investigate the role of the European Catholic missionaries in India, China, and Japan. From this evaluate the impact of this effort on the political and economic structures of these lands.

♦ Discuss the family and its role in Chinese society, including business activity, property rights, individual vs. group identity, popular religion and life-cycle events. Draw on excerpts from *The Dream of the Red Chamber (The Story of the Stone)*.

♦ Evaluate the different positions of a neo-Confucian scholar, a nativist thinker, and a student of Dutch learning in 18th-century Japan.

♦ Compare and contrast the unification of Tokugawa Japan to the rise of nation states in early modern Europe. *How did the Tokugawa rulers centralize feudalism in Japan?*

♦ Compare Japanese attitudes regarding foreign trade with those of the Chinese. *What role did the Portuguese and the Dutch have in Japanese trade? Why did the Japanese decide to limit contacts? How successful was Japan in isolating itself from Europe? Why was Japan closed to the West but not to Asia?*

C. Major cultural trends in Asia between the 16th and 18th centuries.

Grades 5-6

♦ On a current map of East Asia indicate the dominant religion or religions of each nation. Research how these religions spread into these societies.

♦ Research what groups of people in India were most likely to have converted to Islam. *What was the appeal of Islam to these groups and what was the major vehicle for conversion?*

♦ Select one of the three regions—China, India, or Japan. Describe the major art forms being developed in this region between the 16th and 18th centuries.

♦ Compare Japanese and Chinese brush paintings. *What is their relationship to nature?*

Grades 7-8

♦ Read excerpts from *Monkey* translated by Arthur Waley. Act out a scene such as when "Monkey" steals the nectar of immortality from the celestial court. *In what ways is this novel a playful critique of Confucianism, Taoism, and Buddhism in China? In what ways does it affirm the synthesis of these three faiths in China?*

♦ Read the Tulasidas version of the *Ramayana*. *How does the author change the identity of Rama offered in earlier versions of the epic?*

♦ Compare the role played by Confucianism in China, Korea, Japan, and Vietnam. *How did differences in government and society affect the practice of Confucianism?*

♦ Research how the new religion of Sikhism represented a synthesis between Hinduism and Islam. *Which major features of the religion are more Hindu and which more Islamic?*

Grades 9-12

♦ Examine the art, architecture, and literature of Korea and Vietnam in the 17th and 18th centuries. *How do they reflect Chinese influence, and how do they express separate identities?*

♦ Compare the major world religions as of the mid-18th century in terms of numbers of adherents worldwide and relative degree of success at winning new converts.

♦ Research the life and writings of Mirabai (c. 1500-1550). *What does her life say about the role of women in Bhakti movements of the period? What metaphors of love infuse her poetry?*

♦ Read selections from the poet Kabir (c. 1440-1518) in Embree's *Sources of the Hindu Tradition* (pp. 263-265). Debate if his poetry is more Islamic or Hindu.

♦ Compare Nikko and Katsuru rikyu, the screens of Sotabu, the brush painting of literati, and the paintings of Shiba Kokan. *To what extent did the Japanese adapt techniques and designs from other parts of the world? What were the recurring themes used in Japanese art? How did art reflect Japanese society?*

VI. *Major global trends from 1450 to 1770.*

Major global trends from 1450 to 1770.

Grades 5-6

♦ Find data to create population density maps of each continent in 1450 and in 1750. *Why did the number and distribution of people throughout the world change so much during this period?*

♦ Compare a map of the Western Hemisphere at the time of first European contacts around 1500 with a map of the area in 1750. *Why did the boundaries change in such a drastic way during this period?*

♦ Create a set of maps showing the major urban and commercial centers of the late 15th century, those of approximately 1600, and those of 1750. *How might you account for some of the changes?*

◗ Research the origins of the major aids to navigation used by the European powers during the age of western European expansion. Develop a chart showing the first use of such essential tools and knowledge as: the mariner's compass, the astrolabe, knowledge of ocean currents, lateen sails, and mounting of cannons on ships.

Grades 7-8

◗ Using *3000 Years of Urban Growth* by Tertius Chandler, make a list rank-ordering the twenty major cities of the world in 1450 and compare it with a second list as of 1750. Locate the cities on a world map. *What might account for the changes in the ranking of the cities during this period?*

◗ Prepare a chart showing the number of adherents that Islam, Buddhism, and Christianity had in 1450. Make a similar chart for 1750. On two maps, show the areas where followers of these religions lived in these two periods. Compare the charts and maps and account for the changes in both numbers and area over the two-century period.

◗ Make a list of the ten most important technical discoveries and inventions during the period 1500-1770. *Which of these do we regularly use now? How would your life be different now if these things had not been created?*

◗ Make a chart of the major breakthroughs in military technology and tactics during the period 1500-1770. *What countries benefited the most from the new military innovations? Which countries suffered most as a result of them?* Write an essay describing how the life of an average soldier changed during this period as a result of the new technology.

◗ Analyze a major military event of this era. Using maps and narrative explain how the event transpired and show what impact technology had on it and the subsequent history of the region where the military event took place.

Grades 9-12

◗ Research the major reasons why the center of economic power moved from the Mediterranean Basin to northern Europe during the 16th century. *What factors help explain this dramatic shift in world power?*

◗ How did the expanding capitalist system affect the textile industry in India after 1700? *What groups of people in India joined the new expanding middle class and what occupations did they take up?*

◗ *What factors were present in England, France, and the Netherlands that might help explain the rapid development of capitalism in these states?*

◗ Research the core and periphery thesis of Immanuel Wallerstein. *How does he explain the rise of Western European capitalism? What were its effects on the rest of the world? What, according to Wallerstein, is a "world-system"?*

◗ Research the Confucian and Puritan attitudes toward investing in order to make a profit. Write an essay comparing the attitudes of the Chinese and the first generations of Puritans in Massachusetts toward the practice of buying and selling goods in order to get rich. *How did attitudes toward enterprise differ?*

◗ Create a series of overlay transparencies showing the political boundaries of Europe, Africa, Asia, and the Western Hemisphere. Make a map for every fifty years beginning in 1500 and ending in 1800. *How would you account for these changing boundaries? What generalizations could you make about the changing balance of world power during this period?*

ERA 7

An Age of Revolutions, 1750-1914

Giving Shape to World History

The invention of the railway locomotive, the steamship, and, later, the telegraph and telephone transformed global communications in this era. The time it took and the money it cost to move goods, messages, or armies across oceans and continents were drastically cut. People moved, or were forced to move, from one part of the world to another in record numbers. In the early part of the era African slaves continued to be transported across the Atlantic in large numbers; European migrants created new frontiers of colonial settlement in both the Northern and Southern Hemispheres; and Chinese, Indian, and other Asians migrated to Southeast Asia and the Americas. International commerce mushroomed, and virtually no society anywhere in the world stayed clear of the global market. Underlying these surges in communication, migration, and trade was the growth of the world population, forcing men and women almost everywhere to experiment with new ways of organizing collective life.

This was an era of bewildering change in a thousand different arenas. One way to make sense of the whole is to focus on three world-encompassing and interrelated developments: the democratic revolution, the industrial revolution, and the establishment of European dominance over most of the world.

Political Revolutions and New Ideologies: The American and French revolutions offered to the world the potent ideas of popular sovereignty, inalienable rights, and nationalism. The translating of these ideas into political movements had the effect of mobilizing unprecedented numbers of ordinary people to participate in public life and to believe in a better future for all. Liberal, constitutional, and nationalist ideals inspired independence movements in Haiti and Latin America in the early 19th century, and they continued to animate reform and revolution in Europe throughout the era. At the same time political and social counterforces acted to limit or undermine the effectiveness of democratic governments. Democracy and nationalism contributed immensely to the social power of European states and therefore to Europe's rising dominance in world affairs in the 19th century. Under growing pressures from both European military power and the changing world economy, ruling or elite groups in Asian and African states organized reform movements that embraced at least some of the ideas and programs of democratic revolution.

The Industrial Revolution: The industrial revolution applied mechanical power to the production and distribution of goods on a massive scale. It also involved mobilizing unprecedented numbers of laborers and moving them from village to city and from one country to another. Industrialization was a consequence of centuries of expanding economic activity around the world. England played a crucial role in the onset of this revolution, but the process involved complex economic and financial linkages among societies. Together, the industrial and democratic revolutions thoroughly transformed European society. Asian, African, and Latin American peoples dealt with the new demands of the world market and Europe's economic might in a variety of ways. Some groups argued for reform through technical and industrial modernization. Others called for reassertion of established policies and values that had always served them well in times of crisis. Japan and the United States both subscribed to the industrial revolution with rapid success and became important players on the world scene.

The Age of European Dominance: In 1800 Europeans controlled about 35 percent of the world's land surface. By 1914 they dominated over 84 percent. In the long span of human history European world hegemony lasted a short time, but its consequences were profound and continue to be played out today. Western expansion took three principal forms: (1) Peoples of

European descent, including Russians and North Americans, created colonial settlements, or "neo-Europes," in various temperate regions of the world, displacing or assimilating indigenous peoples; (2) European states and commercial firms established considerable economic domination in certain places, notably Latin America and China, while Japan and the United States also participated in this economic expansionism; (3) in the later 19th century European states embarked on the "new imperialism," the competitive race to establish political as well as economic control over previously uncolonized regions of Africa and Asia. Mass production of new weaponry, coupled with the revolution of transport and communication, permitted this surge of power. The active responses of the peoples of Africa, Asia, and Latin America to the crisis of European hegemony are an important part of the developments of this era: armed resistance against invaders, collaboration or alliance with colonizers, economic reform or entrepreneurship, and movements for cultural reform. As World War I approached, accelerating social change and new efforts at resistance and renewal characterized colonial societies far more than consolidation and stability.

Why Study This Era?

▶ The global forces unleashed in the second half of the 18th century continue to play themselves out at the end of the 20th century. Students will understand the "isms" that have absorbed contemporary society—industrialism, capitalism, nationalism, liberalism, socialism, communism, imperialism, colonialism and so on—by investigating them within the historical context of the 18th and 19th centuries.

▶ At the beginning of the 20th century, Western nations enjoyed a dominance in world affairs that they no longer possess. By studying this era students may address some of the fundamental questions of the modern age: How did a relatively few states achieve such hegemony over most of the world? In what ways was Western domination limited or inconsequential? Why was it not to endure?

▶ The history of the United States, in this era, was not self-contained but fully embedded in the context of global change. To understand the role of the United States on the global scene, students must be able to relate it to world history.

Cartoon image of Cecil Rhodes showing British influence from "Cape to Cairo." Punch, 1892

Essay

Democracy's Place in World History*
by Steven Muhlberger and Phil Paine

Are democratic institutions unique to the Western tradition? The following essay examines democratic traditions found in China, India, Africa, and among American Indian societies. The authors challenge readers to rethink the often repeated assertion that "the democratic idea is fundamentally alien to most human cultures." They contend that this belief results in the misconception that "Europeans have a special fitness for democracy." This notion leads students to dismiss or ignore identical experiences outside of Europe and its colonies. Muhlberger and Paine have a faith in democratic ideas and argue that "most people in the world can call on some local tradition on which to build a modern democracy."

Steven Muhlberger teaches history at Nipissing University in North Bay, Ontario. He writes on the history of democracy and on ancient and medieval historiography. Phil Paine is a historian and writer who lives in Toronto.

In the recent past, demands for democracy have come from all over the world. Almost no one expected this. It is an interesting and important reflection on those events that historical scholarship has little to say about democracy that contributes, intellectually or practically, to an understanding of them.

Democracy once had a prominent place in historical thought. Dramatic changes in nineteenth-century European and North American society produced a liberal historiography to put those changes into context by identifying the history of Europe with that of personal liberty. It held that Europe had evolved a unique notion of liberty out of a combination of classical and Christian ideas. This ideal had driven the political development of Europe and its more advanced colonies and set them apart from the rest of the world. It was taken for granted that the history of government (once any society had emerged from the historyless "state of nature") began with monarchy, and that non-European peoples, lacking the invigorating spark of European liberalism, had always obeyed either kings by divine right or primitive chiefs. The liberal historians were not champions of democracy, which they viewed with suspicion; still, demands for and experiments with democracy in their own time informed their entire view of human history.

When the liberal belief in progress sustained grievous wounds in World War I, the history of liberty went slowly out of fashion, to be replaced by conceptions of human history in which both personal liberty and democracy were reduced to the status of epiphenomena. In the twentieth century, the most prominent theoretical framework for approaching the big questions of human history has been the Marxist scheme. In it, democracy was a passing phase, a mere by-product of the capitalist relations of production in a certain period of world history, one that would eventually disappear with the advent of socialism. An alternative interpretive scheme has been called, among other things, "total history." Although its proponents are not all Marxists, they too emphasize the primacy of economic factors. Political events, when not ignored, are treated as depending on changes in relative economic power between different classes, peoples, or regions of the world. Democracy has little place in total history. With total history, we have a new twist on a traditional interpretation of the human experience, as the story of the "pursuit of power."

The millions of people who have risked life and limb to secure democratic reforms have demonstrated that historians have been too quick to dismiss democracy. Despite the best

*Reprinted from *Journal of World History*, Vol. 4, No. 1 (Spring 1993), pp. 23-45.

efforts of one-party governments to convince them otherwise, people in China, Poland, Benin, Burma, Chile, Albania, and the Philippines have insisted in the most direct fashion on the relevance of electoral democracy. They want not only prosperity, not only national sovereignty, but also elections by universal suffrage, among competing parties, under conditions that allow voters an informed and free choice. Calls for effective guarantees for human rights have been equally widespread. It is obvious, in the light of these movements, that historians will have to reformulate their ideas of world political development.

At the end of a century when antidemocratic theories have dominated theoretical discussion of history and politics, attempts to understand the development of democracy will have to overcome several stumbling blocks. In this article, we address one of them.

It is commonly thought that most people in the world have no democratic experience, and that the democratic idea is fundamentally alien to most human cultures. This is what lies behind the catchphrase, "the western concept of democracy." On this basis, many scholars have concluded that efforts to establish democratic institutions outside of a few favored regions are doomed to failure. The belief is found almost equally among friends and enemies of the democratic idea. Aristocratic and authoritarian thinkers have argued that democratic ideas are merely a local quirk of western European tradition; those sympathetic to democracy have feared that they were right. Both groups, as they consider the non-European world, have seen only a mass of churlish and intractable peasants, too dumb to understand voting or the principle of human equality, now or ever.

Recent events have put the lie to this, or should have. Room for confusion remains. The inevitable setbacks of new democratic regimes will soon be seized upon by unsympathetic or hyper-critical commentators as proof that this people or that are not yet ready for democracy, and probably never will be. Now is the time to point out that doubts about the viability of democracy in various non-European cultures are an outdated relic of nineteenth century liberal theories.

In the past, historians have supported the idea that Europeans have a special fitness for democracy (one more aspect of European uniqueness) by emphasizing every quasi-democratic institution or movement in European history while dismissing or ignoring identical experiences outside of Europe and its white colonies. We argue instead that most people in the world can call on some local tradition on which to build a modern democracy. We believe that democratic ideas are so simple and straightforward that people of any culture can grasp them, given half a chance. And we believe the historical record supports us. Quasidemocratic methods of government (that is, methods imperfectly democratic by twentieth-century standards, but using identifiable democratic techniques, as outlined below) are far more common than most historians realize.

In this article we have assembled examples of quasi-democratic institutions in the non-European world. They are all perfectly familiar to the specialists who deal with each of the specific regions. Usually they are considered in isolation. We have brought them together to challenge the half-unconscious assumption that democratic ideas are unique to Europe, and that examples of democratic thinking or action found elsewhere are somehow irrelevant exceptions, or at best evidence of European influence. Once this assumption is discredited, we hope that scholars will move on to a truer appreciation of humanity's democratic heritage.

Two factors have allowed historians, political theorists, and others to represent democratic theory or practice as uniquely western phenomena: ignorance, and the concentration of historical research on the largest and best recorded institutions. That many historians know little about history outside of Europe and North America needs no demonstration. It should be equally obvious that historians have traditionally been trained to see history as a parade of kingdoms and empires, and that most still do. This makes it easy to dismiss whole swaths of the map as lacking democratic experience. If historians concentrate on empires, on those who command armies, collect taxes, and engrave vainglorious inscriptions on cliff-faces, they will continue to believe that politics has almost always been a matter of despotism and bureaucracy, varied only by lapses into anarchy.

Yet the vast majority of all political events are local. It is on the local level that most collective action is taken, most of the constructive work of the world has been and still is done, and most conflicts of interest take place. By adjusting one's perspective to that local level, studied more often by anthropologists than historians, one often finds a style of decision making quite different from lordship or bureaucratic autocracy. Most human government has been a matter of councils and assemblies, which often incorporate a large proportion of the community and use a surprising degree of democratic procedure. In other words, humanity possesses a long history of government by discussion, in which groups of people sharing common interests make decisions that affect their lives through debate and consultation, and often enough by voting. By broadening the view of politics to include not simply geographic communities but also religious and voluntary self-help organizations—as De Tocqueville did when evaluating democracy in the early American republic—one finds a world full of quasi-democratic institutions.

Few if any of these groups could meet twentieth-century standards of democratic practice. Most have excluded all women and many men. Their decision-making procedures have often been loose and susceptible to manipulation by an inner circle of the elders or the wealthy. We argue that the existence and practices of such groups are nonetheless relevant to the story of democracy. Any group willing to submit to decisions arrived at by discussion and voting (formal or informal), or to abide by the judgment of elected representatives, is in some sense democratic, for it has devised methods to share political authority among its members. Who those members should be is a separate question, although a very important one. If one insists on perfect democracy in a community before conceding its relevance to the history of democracy, then democracy has no history and never will. The case is quite different if institutions and habits that promote political inclusivity are studied. And this is the common-sense position. In discussing the United States, one does not dismiss its political history before 1920 or 1965 as being irrelevant to the history of democracy. Similarly, historians with global interests should not ignore the imperfectly democratic practices of myriad small, and sometimes not so small, communities. The evidence is clear that both the idea and the practice of democracy are foreign to no part of the world; in fact, it is commonplace for people to make important political decisions in cooperation with their equals.

China provides a perfect example. Since that region has experienced long periods of rule by a vast bureaucratic empire, it is often assumed that the Chinese people have had no democratic experience, and that current democratic aspirations are a product of "westernization" or "modernization." A more detailed look reveals a different picture. Only during brief totalitarian frenzies has imperial power been able to reach into everyone's home. Under most emperors, the ordinary people of China have had a firm network of local institutions that administered local affairs and protected them from the worst predations of the central authorities. Some of these local institutions embodied a considerable degree of democratic practice.

Every study of the traditional Chinese village has shown that it enjoyed a great deal of autonomy. The magistrates and their clerks were based far away, in the district capitals. Of course they, like the land-owning gentry, could intervene in force in any given village if they chose, and they often imposed severe burdens on the inhabitants. Normally, however, village administration and even local law enforcement was left in the hands of the villagers themselves." Two institutions carried out all the functions of local government: village temples and ancestral halls. The latter were the organizational expression of the extensive and often powerful clans, which acted as a social support system for their member families. The property accumulated by the halls paid not only for the ritual veneration of the clan founders but also for such benefits as regular food distribution to the member families and, if a clan was prosperous enough, the education of its children. The halls varied in political structure but commonly had an executive council of twelve officers, elected annually from among and by all adult males. Liang Yu-Kao's account, written in 1915, does not suggest a passive electorate: "clan politics causes great commotion in the village."

Because the benefits provided by the ancestral hall were restricted to a certain group, the village temple exercised many important functions on behalf of the entire community: policing; the maintenance of roads, canals, and landing-places; schooling, if the clans were not providing this service; public relief work; and the provision of an annual festival, including theatrical or operatic performances. These functions, and the property that provided temple income, were administered by selectmen chosen annually by rotation from male householders, who acted on the advice of an informally chosen body of respected elders and educated men.

In parts of China where clan and temple organization was weak, other cooperative organizations filled the gap. The villages of Shandong in the late nineteenth and early twentieth centuries are better documented than most. Here important local business, such as watching the crops, enforcing internal law and order, defending the village from bandits, and running the local school, was done through village councils and other collective, and often purely voluntary, bodies. Decision making was very informal; indeed, the least impressive evidence of democracy is the sole local election, in which the *zhuangzhang,* or village headman, was chosen. In Daidou, according to Martin C. Yang, a native of the place, there was never any competition for the position, which always went to a rather insignificant person. That was because the *zhuangzhang* was seen by the villagers more as a government functionary, carrying out orders from above, than as a local leader. The real local leaders were men who, rather than being elected or appointed, were respected for their talents, character, and importance in local society. The *zhuangzhang* had to negotiate with them if he hoped to get government orders implemented. These "lay leaders," to use Yang's term, had no coercive power; their private leadership derived from their ability to influence others through public or private discussions, or from their acknowledged role as heads of families.

In addition to these more obvious types of village government, the Chinese people have engaged for millennia in a maze of guilds, surname clubs, societies for unmarried women, savings associations, tontines, Buddhist *sanghas,* scripture-reading clubs, and secret societies, many of which have employed conciliar, representative, and quasi-democratic techniques. Most of these would no doubt fail a test of ideal democracy. The influence of the elders and the well-educated could be suffocating. Martin Yang condemned the organization of his own Daidou as undemocratic because "local affairs had always been dominated by the village aristocracy" (using the term in a very loose way), and most individuals took no role in initiating or discussing plans. His chief criticism, however, was that the governance of Daidou was unprogressive, indeed obstructively conservative, and had no aim to improve life, being content merely to stave off disaster. Yet his account and those of others show that quasi-democratic cooperation—what an earlier observer called "the genius of the Chinese for combination"—was the key to accomplishing any task relating to the common good. The concrete, local experience of self-government by the Chinese people can be compared to that of Europeans over the centuries. There is nothing exceptional in the village self-government of traditional China. The great majority of all the human beings who have ever lived have been citizens of small agricultural villages. They have focused their loyalties on those villages and have experienced government in that context. Most of these millions of agricultural communities, past and present, have employed some democratic techniques of government: decisions made and leaders chosen by unanimous consent or majority vote, after extensive discussions in a public assembly. Almost all villages, everywhere, have had a village council. These have many names: the ancient *sings* of Scandinavia, the *kampong* assemblies of Malaysia, the famous council fires of the Amerindian confederacies, the communes of the vill of medieval England, the *gumlao* of the Kachin in Burma, the *Landesgemeinde* of central Europe, the Maori *hapus*, the *kokwet* of the east African Sebei, the *panchavats* of India, and countless others. Voluntary self-help groups have also been commonplace, and decision making within them has necessarily been by discussion and general agreement.

Africa is often portrayed as a continent dominated by kingship and authoritarian rule. Although specialists know better, the presence of kings in precolonial times is often cited as an explanation of the postcolonial plague of dictatorships. Nobody applies the same reasoning to Europe, although it has had no shortage of kings and emperors. The existence of kings in the past does not make for a destiny of kings.

Africa, in fact, has not been particularly fertile ground for kingship in past ages. Its monarchies and empires have been ephemeral by European standards. At least half of the "traditional" monarchies of the present were installed by the colonial powers a hundred years ago. Other precolonial kings were no more than oligarchs and war chiefs of limited power. Precolonial Africa was a latticework of decentralized farming villages and autonomous towns only occasionally subjected to genuine monarchical states. The chiefs that existed varied greatly in power, but most would fit Albert Doutreloux's description of Yombe chiefdom, as summarized by Wayne MacGaffrey: "Whatever the extent of a chief's power, chiefship is inevitably associated with a collection of people who surround the chief at least as much to control him as to assist him."

Quite often, the village councils were left to run things without an overlord to help or hinder them. Among the Sebei of Uganda, all villagers could attend the governing *koLwet,* and all circumcised males could speak there. Opinion was most easily swayed by *kirwokik* (judges), men with a reputation for eloquence, irrespective of wealth or station. "Judgeship," says a Sebei proverb, "is bought by the ear, not with cattle." Similar assemblies have been described for dozens of other peoples. Commonly village polities have combined in alliances—alliances organized through a series of nesting councils and assemblies. For instance, the Aguinyi "clan" among the Ibo of Nigeria is an acephalous confederation of seven autonomous towns. Although the confederation has no institutional expression, each of the towns is run by a council of delegates elected from the villages that make up the towns. Each village has an assembly in which everyone may speak, and which is responsible for roads, scholarship schemes, revolving loan funds, and (even in modern conditions) basic law and order. Below the village level, both wards and extended families deal with common business on much the same basis as the villages themselves. Life among the Aguinyi thus embraces a variety of democratic experience.

The Aguinyi and other Ibo peoples also provide an example of an individualist democratic ethic that appears to have grown entirely from indigenous roots. The Aguinyi often speak of the virtues of common effort and unanimity, but they also acknowledge the power of *chit Chi* originally meant a pagan deity or personal god and now stands for an individual's fate or destiny, as well as the combination of characteristics that makes someone "personally responsible and calculative in his life and actions." *Chi* is the strength that enables individuals to stand up for their own views when they disagree with the rest of the community. Obstructionism is not popular among the Aguinyi, yet the concept of *chi*, which makes the "individual . . . the last irreducible unit of responsibility who must [guard] against all undue imitation and blind compliance," gives the dissident the courage of his convictions and grants his opponents a basis to respect them. At the same time, *chi* enables a person defeated in politics to accept the defeat without bitterness, on the rationale that another *chi* has proved stronger than his own.

The large states that existed in Africa in the distant past did their best to subvert local councils by installing paramount chiefs and centrally directed headmen. The colonial empires did exactly the same thing. Contemporary dictators continue the effort. But village assemblies in Africa, as in the rest of the world, are resilient. At any period, local autonomy has been more common than central control, and autonomy has often been expressed through quasi-democratic arrangements of one sort or another.

India too, despite its now outdated reputation as the home of "oriental despotism" par excellence, has played a dramatic role in the history of democracy. During the sixth and fifth centuries B.C.E. northern India, then undergoing explosive economic growth, was primarily organized on the basis of city-states and regional federations. Indian republics, though little known except to specialists, were comparable to the contemporary polls communities of Greece, though the former were more numerous and more populous. In India, as in Greece, democracy—in the ancient sense—was commonplace. The democratic thought produced by an environment characterized by democratic practice is still accessible through the ancient literature of the subcontinent.

Before the sixth century B.C.E., Indian society is documented only through the religious writings known as the Vedas and Brahmanas. They depict an entirely rural society where kingship was the sole respectable form of government, and where religious functions, including teaching, were the monopoly of the Brahman class—at least, in the view of the Brahmans who composed and preserved the scriptures. Ideally, early Indian society was divided into four castes *(varnas)*, which were divinely destined to fulfill set social functions.

It is doubtful that Indian society was ever so neatly hierarchical. Even the Vedas show traces of what J. P. Sharma has characterized as republican government. Certainly with the revival of long-distance commerce and urban life about 600 B.C.E., the old model broke down. In a mobile society experiencing new prosperity and new strains, diversity was the order of the day. Communities both small and large organized themselves as gatherings of equals, taking collective actions through unanimous decision, voting, or both. Such organizations were called *sanghas* or *ganas*.

In many of these polities, it must be granted, the group of equals was relatively small, as in Greek oligarchies. It was common for the franchise to be restricted to the warrior caste *(ksatriyas)*, or even to a single clan among the warriors. But the number of warriors in a thriving city-state could be large, and despite the theologians there were often no hard and fast barriers to prevent new men from climbing into the caste. Furthermore, there were polities where artisans, traders, and agriculturalists shared in power. A final point is that it was relatively easy for those who did not like the distribution of power in the polity to assert the right of their own subgroup—a guild, a corporation, a warrior band, or an agricultural village—to self-government.

Decision making in such communities was either oligarchic or democratic in ways recognizable to Greek visitors. The members of a *gana* or *sangha,* who were usually numerous, interacted as members of an assembly. The terminology of corporate decision making by voting is preserved by the systematic Sanskrit grammarian Panini (fifth century B.C.E.), as are terms that reveal the division of assemblies into political parties and the use of committees or executive councils for certain purposes. The most detailed information about democratic practice in India comes, however, from the early Pali scriptures of Buddhism—a sixth-century religious movement that was itself a product of the diversification of Indian society and perhaps the most dramatic manifestation of a spirit of egalitarianism.

The Buddha was a wandering preacher, one of many who disputed the claims of Brahmans to a monopoly on spiritual instruction. He, like others of the type, resisted the hierarchical assumptions of Brahmanism and taught instead that all men were in important respects equal. It is clear that Buddhist egalitarianism, though primarily spiritual, was a product of an important strand of social and political thought in the India of the day. The *Mahaparanibbana-sutta,* which preserves the teachings of the Buddha just before his death, contains a passage in which the virtues of the ideal republic and of the order of Buddhist monks, itself called a *sangha,* are directly compared and said to be much the same. Foremost among those virtues is the holding of "full and frequent assemblies." This idea was supported by Buddhist practice. How ancient Buddhist monastic communities were run is well known from the Pali scriptures. The *sanghas* were expected to be punctilious about gathering all the monks together for every important occasion of community life, to make all decisions unanimously insofar as possible, and to resort to majority rule when unanimity broke down.

From the time of the Buddha until the invasion of Alexander the Great (327-25 B.C.E.), republics of various size, including large federal republics, dominated Indian political life. Alexander's destructive passage and active encouragement of monarchy tipped the balance. Soon after Alexander, the Mauryan empire, built by Chandragupta Maurya, engulfed most of the subcontinent. Nevertheless, republicanism survived in one form or another until the fourth century C.E. The predominance of such men as Asoka was fleeting and superficial enough that once an empire's grasp weakened, old *ganas* and federations sprang back to life.

The defeat of the democratic tendency in ancient Indian life was a complicated process, not simply the result of the greater military power available to a successful warlord. There was a revival of hierarchical thinking, and a willingness of the enfranchised members of *ganas* to accept it. The most obvious manifestations of the former can be found in the orthodox Brahmanic (Hindu) literature in the period between 200 B.C.E. and 200 C.E. Many of the most important treatises on caste ideology and the divine nature of monarchy were composed in this period, precisely because alternative ideas were well known and widely accepted. Yet both caste ideology and monarchy had something to offer the members of *ganas.* The first offered them a cosmic guarantee of whatever privileges they had won, if they recognized that these derived from the group's position in a cosmic hierarchy. Monarchy offered a down-to-earth guarantee of the same thing. According to Kautilya, a political theorist committed to the Brahmanic model of society, a king who was recognized as "the only monarch [that is, the *raja,* or chief executive] of all the corporations" would be in a position to preserve the legitimate privileges of each, and even to protect the lesser members of each *gana* from the abuses of their own leaders.' Eventually, willingly or under coercion, all *ganas* and *sanghas* accepted the offer—even the Buddhist *sangha*. This led eventually to the utter defeat of Buddhism in India by its Brahmanic rivals. The idea that a small republican community could maintain its independence was abandoned, and Indians apparently despaired of constructing a large-scale society on egalitarian or inclusive lines.

It would be wrong, however, to think that democratic practice has ever been completely suppressed on the Indian subcontinent. Despite the best efforts of various imperial authorities and all internal oligarchic tendencies, a surprising amount of quasi-democratic procedure always survived in the villages and subcastes of India. In the nineteenth century, grass-roots democracy intrigued British observers and inspired Indian seekers after self-government. During the twentieth century, attempts to revitalize the village *partchayat* have become the basis of efforts thoroughly to democratize Indian society.

The most important legacy of ancient Indian republicanism is undoubtedly Buddhism. Buddhism cannot be presented unambiguously as a force for egalitarianism or democracy. It has often enough served as an ideological prop for aristocratic or royal regimes. Buddhist (individual monasteries or specific orders) have themselves been run as aristocratic households. Yet the original egalitarianism of Buddhist thought and the continuing practical democracy of Buddhist religious communities have been very important in some political contexts. In southeast Asia, the village monastery-temple, administered by a committee of lay men, has long served to promote the welfare of the village as a whole, acting as a repository for community property and the means of educating village youth. Out of this tradition has often come a concern with fair government, not least in recent years.

The existence of quasi-democratic institutions among the aboriginal peoples of North America has been so much discussed by anthropologists and social scientists that it has become a cliche. Amerindian societies covered a great range of productive modes, kinship systems, and political forms, but almost all employed councils.

Nonagrarian societies, such as the western Apache, usually made all decisions outside the nuclear family by unanimous consent in council. Failure to reach agreement led only to inaction or to withdrawal of the dissatisfied. In such a political world view, the ultimate authority rested with the household, with each successive level of collective decision making—groups of neighbors and business partners, clans, tribes, and confederacies—commanding less loyalty. Such autonomy is easy where families can fend for themselves and choose their coworkers without risking economic failure. In more sedentary cultures, such as those of the eastern Woodlands, the problems posed by a need for more intense and consistent cooperation tended to be solved by elaborating the councils and loading them with more ceremony and mystique, but without sacrificing their democratic component. Elaborated conciliary systems existed among the Muskogean tribes of the southeast and the Iroquoians farther north.

The influence of the democratic aspects of Amerindian on the subsequent growth of Canadian and American political systems is hard to measure but widely acknowledged. In the supercharged atmosphere of the Enlightenment and the age of revolutions, exposure to Amerindian politics often provided inspiration. James Adair, an adventurer who lived among the Chickasaw in the 1770s, became an enraptured ideological convert. Undoubtedly primed by Rousseau, Montesquieu, and the Scottish philosophers, he clearly felt the excitement of one who at least thought he had leaped from theory to reality. A century and a half later, Gene

Weltfish, a young woman who lived among the Pawnee, was in the same way overwhelmed by the individualistic and democratic qualities she saw in their society.

This kind of discovery could work both ways. The Cherokee, setting up their independent republican the early nineteenth century, were thoroughly conversant with contemporary constitutional theory and adopted many of its conventions in an effort to preserve their traditional individual liberty.

Examples of quasi-democratic communities—some shadowy, some well recorded; some quite limited in their democratic development, some as impressive as the self-governing towns of early New England—could be multiplied almost indefinitely. But two questions would not be settled simply by bulk of documentation. They must be confronted directly.

First, is the degree of democracy seen in such communities, compared to undoubted inequalities in them, important enough for the communities to be worth studying as examples of democracy? Our answer is yes—if democracy is worth studying at all. Just as the history of monarchy is not simply a search for the perfect example of absolute one-person rule, the study of democracy must be more than the vain search for an egalitarian utopia. We argue that something reasonably called democracy exists in the present, and that a suitably comprehensive view of its history should include the quasi-democratic practices of many self-governing or partially self-governing communities that have existed around the world in all periods of history. An awareness of these phenomena is especially important for those interested in global history, since an appreciation of the universality of government by councils and through discussion among equals is more useful and appropriate than seeing all democratic development in the present as a result of modernization.

Second, given that nondemocratic institutions have predominated on the larger scale, do the grass-roots quasi-democracies discussed here have much significance? Both historians and political theorists have traditionally answered no. Karl Wittfogel devoted a section of his influential *Oriental Despotism* to a discussion of what he called "the Beggars' Democracy." Wittfogel, in writing an exhaustive analysis of traditional despotic government, here dealt with claims that there was room in despotic societies for autonomy and even "genuine democratic institutions" at the local level. Wittfogel was well aware that some "genuine elements of freedom" existed in such societies, and he conceded that although village politics lacked a "formal democratic pattern," it had a "democratic flavor." Yet he concluded that the freedoms of subjects under oriental despotism were "politically irrelevant freedoms" that in no way threatened the existence of despotic power, This is similar to the position of some Chinese historians who maintain that if the democracy of the village was not perfect and complete, it was not democracy at all, and was of no scholarly interest. It is equally valid—and perhaps more productive—for historians to reflect upon the fact that even under the most unpromising circumstances, "genuine elements of freedom" can exist, and that even "beggars" can exhibit behavior with a "democratic flavor." Whether or not such "beggars" are strong enough to throw off their oppressors at any given time or place, their political behavior is worthy of notice for those interested in human history as a whole.

Few other theorists have given as much consideration to this question as did Wittfogel, the passionate enemy of totalitarianism. Historians have usually accorded unique importance to the state as the most advanced type of political institution. The state (characterized by specialized, hierarchical structures of command and a relative monopoly of "legitimate" force) has attracted this attention not only because of its undoubted influence on the course of history, but also because historians have thought it to be a superior form of human organization. It is often said that the state has created peace and "integrated" activity over large areas, across barriers that in the past divided humankind into tribal societies and condemned them to live in a state of constant war.

This highly positive evaluation of the state rests on two assumptions, neither of which has ever been proved. The first is that states do create peace better than tribal society. The second is that states "integrate" human effort more efficiently than do other forms of collective activity. The history of Europe over the past century, when it has been dominated by states of unprecedented power, would hardly seem to give much comfort to either assumption, if examined from the point of view of an individual seeking to survive a normal life-span without being murdered, plundered, or uprooted. The twentieth-century experience of the people of Silesia, to take but one example, should be enough to make people pause in their praise of the state as an instrument of peace and prosperity.

There is no doubt that state institutions have often promoted economic specialization and have sometimes created spheres of peace. But equally there is no doubt that states, in their real historical origins and behavior, are raw manifestations of "the pursuit of power," and that their institutions were designed to create and enforce political and economic inequality. That is what states do best even today. Insofar as state institutions ever promote the general welfare, it is because they have been reined in by people concerned not so much with the "pursuit of power" as with "the pursuit of fairness."

How common the latter pursuit is compared to the former as a human motivation may be a matter for debate. But surely a concern with fairness is not restricted to any one time or place, and a concern with fairness, if taken very far, leads toward democratic institutions. The best way to assure that every individual's interests are considered when common business is done is to allow everyone access to the public forum where common decisions are made. That is why quasi-democratic procedures are so common in local communities around the world and why attempts to extend them through regional federation are not rare.

Historians should take the pursuit of fairness and its democratic manifestations seriously as global historical phenomena. The historical record demonstrates that a desire for fairness, as well as the institutions and customs that produce decisions fair to all concerned, is a survival trait. No one disputes that the huntergatherer bands in which humans have lived for most of their existence were egalitarian. They could not afford to be otherwise, because human cooperation was their key resource. That agricultural villages all over the world preserve a large degree of the egalitarian ethic and commonly act collectively through democratic or quasi-democratic institutions results from their need for fairness. That the most creative phases of urban history in many regions, such as the Mediterranean, northern India, and Europe, have been characterized by democratic tendencies is again symptomatic of the need for fairness, for democracy, if a society is to achieve constructive goals.

The same point can be made with reference to the present. The terrible record of undemocratic regimes in the handling of pollution and environmental problems shows as well as anything the destructive results for a modern society when democracy is suppressed and the state has its way unrestrained by considerations of fairness. It is not an accident that environmental degradation has been a central issue in democratic movements from Czechoslovakia to Siberia. Similarly, the disastrous economic condition of various undemocratic regimes, not least that of the former Soviet Union, is no accident: It is one unavoidable concomitant of the systematic crushing of both individual initiative and all manifestations of democratic decision making, whether on the local or higher levels.

The most interesting treatments of the "pursuit of power" have been useful because they looked on that pursuit as an aspect of human social adaptation—the adaptation of human beings to the presence of large numbers of their fellows, who long ago became their most important competitors in the struggle for survival. Perhaps it is time to realize that social survival is not only, or even primarily, a matter of competition in a zero-sum game. Such a realization, we believe, will lead to a renewal of interest, long overdue, in the history of democracy.

Father Miguel Hidalgo, Mexican patriot. Organization of American States

Sample Student Activities

I.   *The causes and consequences of political revolutions in the late 18th and early 19th centuries.*

A.   How the French Revolution contributed to transformations in Europe and the world.

Grades 5-6

▸ Design a banner for the beginning of the French Revolution proclaiming "Liberty, Equality and Fraternity." *Which people in France would have been most likely to follow your banner? Which would not? Why?*

▸ Create a timeline using pictures or headline statements to label the main political events in the Americas and France from 1770 to 1815. *Which events were the most important? Why? How were events in Europe and the Americas related?*

▸ Read the "Declaration of the Rights of Man and Citizen" and the U. S. "Declaration of Independence." Draw a chart comparing those rights and obligations that Americans considered important versus those the French emphasized.

▸ Draw a chart comparing French and American visions of nationalism as represented by their national anthems.

▸ Make a pictorial biography of Napoleon using art reproductions and original sketches.

Grades 7-8

▸ Construct a series of maps or map overlays showing France during the revolution, Napoleon's Consulate, the empire, and Europe after the settlement of the Congress of Vienna. *What explains the differences in the maps? How did each reflect the power of France relative to other countries?*

▸ Construct a timeline listing major events of the French Revolution. Assume the role of a noble, cleric, bourgeois, peasant, or sans-culotte and, from your perspective, record short entries in a journal about each of these major events.

▸ Recreate the meeting of the Estates-General by assigning representatives of the First, Second, and Third Estates. Write a position paper for each estate, stating which classes it represents, the rights and privileges of each, and what it expects to achieve at the meeting. Conduct a debate on the proposition: *"All delegates shall sit in one room and vote by head."*

▸ Read sections of the "Declaration of the Rights of Man and Citizen" and create "publication committees" to design illustrations and write short tracts defending the principles contained in the declaration. *What sections show possible influence of Enlightenment ideas and the American Declaration of Independence?*

▸ After studying paintings and drawings of events in the French Revolution, including such works as "The Fall of the Bastille," and David's "Oath of the Tennis Court" and "The March of the Women of Paris on Versailles," write accounts of each event as if you were there.

▸ Construct a classroom newspaper covering the Congress of Vienna from differing perspectives. Include character sketches of leading figures, editorials, and cartoons dealing with issues discussed at the conference.

▶ Write a journalistic account of the Haitian revolution and the role played by Toussaint L'Ouverture. Include background information on the social and economic conditions under French rule. *How important was sugar? Slave labor? How did events in France and the rise of Napoleon affect the Haitian revolution?*

Grades 9-12

▶ Create a political spectrum chart showing the ideological positions of radicals, liberals, moderates, conservatives, and reactionaries during the French Revolution. Give an example of the actions of an individual or an event that is characteristic of each position.

▶ Compare Olympe de Gouges's "Declaration of the Rights of Women and the Female Citizen" to the French Revolution's "Declaration of the Rights of Man and the Citizen."

▶ Using books such as *The Scarlet Pimpernel* and *A Tale of Two Cities*, assess the accuracy of such literary accounts in describing the French Revolution.

▶ Examine the "Code Napoleon" from the point of view of an early 19th-century reformer. *How would property owners, workers, women, and Catholic and Protestant clerics respond to the Civil Code?*

▶ Write an essay in response to the question: "To what extent can Napoleon be considered a legitimate heir to the ideals of the French Revolution?"

▶ Assume the role of different groups in Haiti such as plantation owners, free blacks, and slaves. From that perspective, construct an account of the fears, demands, and actions of each group in the Haitian Revolution.

B. How Latin American countries achieved independence in the early 19th century.

Grades 5-6

▶ Compare maps of Latin America in 1790 with maps in 1828. Identify and label the key colonial powers of 1790 and the new independent countries. *Why did some countries become independent and others did not?*

▶ Make relief maps of the territories liberated by Simón Bolívar and those liberated by José de San Martín. *What role did geography play in Latin American independence?*

Grades 7-8

▶ Research the role of Father Miguel Hidalgo in the Mexican Revolution of 1810 and the role of Augustin de Iturbide in the revolt of 1821. *How was the 1810 movement led by Hidalgo different from the independence movements in South America? Which forces supported Hidalgo? What prompted the creole-dominated revolt of 1821?*

▶ Write a short chronological narrative based on the arrival of Napoleonic forces in Portugal and the departure of the Portuguese royal court to Brazil. Contrast the form of independent government set up in Brazil with those of other Latin American countries.

▶ Assume the role of a Latin American and explain how you would react to news that Napoleon had taken control of Spain. *Would you be willing to support Joseph Bonaparte as your king? Why or why not?*

▶ Create a timeline of events in France, Spain, and Portugal for the period 1770-1825. Construct a parallel timeline for the Caribbean, Latin American, and Mexican independence movements. *How did events in France and on the Iberian Peninsula affect the Haitian and Latin American revolutions?*

Grades 9-12

▶ Role-play a meeting of liberal leaders in New Granada and propose a plan for the establishment of an independent government. *What role should the Creole elite play in the new government? What should be the position of the Roman Catholic Church? To what extent should all persons be given the right to vote in the new nation?*

▶ Prepare a chart comparing a Spanish American independence movement with the American, French, and Haitian revolutions. *How were pre-independence social and political conditions the same? different? What regimes and policies did the movements oppose? How did revolutionaries justify their independence claims? To what extent did the revolutionaries represent particular classes?*

▶ Compare the legal status of women in Latin America before and after the independence movements. *How did independence change the status of women? Did this vary by region? by class?*

▶ In a panel representing the U.S., England, Spain, Mexico, and Argentina, discuss the provisions of the Monroe Doctrine from the Latin American point of view. *Do you approve of the U.S. role in carrying it out?*

▶ Construct a broadside or political cartoon using the American and French revolutions as models for an independence movement in Latin America.

▶ Write a declaration of independence for a Latin American state in the early 19th century. *What is the ideological basis for your declaration? What are your political objectives in declaring independence? How did Brazilian independence differ from that of the other Latin American countries?*

▶ Create a graphic to illustrate racial and social divisions, including the position of the creoles, mestizos, mulattoes, Indians, and blacks, in most Latin America countries following the independence movements. *What had changed? What were the attitudes of these groups toward the Catholic Church?*

▶ Recreate a tertulia, or social gathering, held by woman leaders such as María Josefa Ortiz in Mexico, Manuela Sanz de Santamaria in Colombia, or Manuela Canizares of Quito in the period before the wars of independence. *How did the gatherings serve as arenas for discussion of revolt? How were ideas and discussions of events in Spain and France transmitted through them? How influential were these gatherings in forming public opinion among men and women in various social classes?*

II. *The causes and consequences of the agricultural and industrial revolutions, 1700-1850.*

A. Early industrialization and the importance of developments in England.

Grades 5-6

▶ Research the inventions of Jethro Tull and Charles Townsend. Graphically show agricultural methods before their inventions and after. *How did changes in agriculture influence the industrial revolution?*

▶ From visual sources of the period, describe daily life in an English cottage industry before the industrial revolution. Depict spinning in a factory setting and compare daily life in the two workplaces. *What major changes took place?*

▶ On a map of Britain, illustrate the shifts in population caused by the industrial revolution. Write a diary account of what it would have been like to migrate from a rural area to an industrial center.

▶ Write an illustrated biography of an inventor such as John Kay, James Hargreaves, James Watt, Edmund Cartwright, or Richard Arkwright. *Why were the inventions of these people important? What are some important inventions of the late 20th century and why are they important?*

Grades 7-8

▶ Brainstorm the reasons why the industrial revolution began in Great Britain. Create a class chart to be displayed on the wall for easy reference.

▶ Using a chart of inventions relating to agriculture such as the seed drill, crop rotation, stock breeding, mechanical reaper, steel plow, barbed wire, and chemical fertilizers, assess the consequences and relative importance of each to the agricultural revolution.

▶ Construct a physical map of Britain that identifies the geographic features favorable to industrialization. Explain how physical geography and natural resources aided industrialization.

▶ On a world map label Britain's international commercial connections during the period of early industrialization. *How did these connections contribute to the industrial revolution?*

▶ Assume the role of an inventor such as John Kay, Richard Arkwright, or Edmund Cartwright and prepare a presentation to persuade business leaders that your invention will revolutionize the textile industry. Include a sketch or drawing of your invention. *What was the effect of new technologies on the textile industry? To what extent was the textile industry the "mother of the industrial revolution?"*

▶ Debate the benefits of interchangeable parts and mass production from the point of view of a craftsman, a factory worker, and entrepreneur, and a consumer.

Grades 9-12

▶ Explain the distinctions between mercantilist and free-market economies, and assess the influence of new economic theories on industrial policies and practices.

▶ Analyze the paintings of Constable and Turner for what they say about the beauties of the English countryside and villages. *Do the paintings romanticize the pre-industrial world? To what extent does their view reflect social or economic reality?*

▶ Using primary sources such as Edward Baines's *The History of the Cotton Manufacture in Great Britain*, explain the factors contributing to England's leadership in the Industrial Revolution. *Which was the most important factor in the development of England's industrialization? Why? How did England's location in Europe and the world affect its industrial development? What characteristics of English society and government contributed to industrialization?*

▶ Using Ralph Davis's *Aleppo and Devonshire Square* research the life of an English "factor" or trade agent for a textile company in Aleppo, Syria, in the late 18th century Write a letter home describing the goods he handles, his worries and concerns, the people he does business with, and his leisure-time activities.

▶ Compare the political, social, economic, and technological conditions in Great Britain and India in 1750. *What factors explain the more rapid development of industry in Great Britain after that time?*

▶ Compare an English cotton mill and a Caribbean slave plantation as systems of mass production and factory labor. *Can a sugar plantation producing for the world market be described as factory? What impact did commercial agriculture in the Americas using slave labor have on the Industrial Revolution?*

B. How industrial economies expanded and societies experienced transformations in Europe and the Atlantic basin.

Grades 5-6

- Read selections from *A Christmas Carol* and *Oliver Twist* and write a journal entry about the daily life of a working-class person in Britain during the industrial revolution.

- Create an illustrated timeline of technological advances in communication and transportation during the industrial revolution. *What effects did the railroad have on everyday life?*

- Study the beginning of labor unions and prepare posters identifying a conflict that might have occurred in 1900 between representatives of workers and big business.

- Design and label a bar graph showing the growth of population in Europe during the industrial revolution. Cover the period 1750 to 1900. Show statistics in 50-year increments. *What major patterns do you observe, and what causes would you hypothesize for those changes?*

Grades 7-8

- Study a bar graph of railway miles constructed in Great Britain from the 1840s to 1900. Research similar data for the same period in the United States and create a comparative graph. *What conclusions can you make about the pace and extent of the industrialization in both countries?*

- Research Robert Owen's New Lanark System. Assume the role of Robert Owen and prepare a speech to European industrialists explaining the benefits of your approach. *How did Robert Owen propose to deal with social problems caused by the industrial revolution? How did other industrialists respond to Owen? How successful was New Lanark?*

- Simulate a parliamentary debate of the Reform Bill of 1832. *How great was the "Great Reform" legislation? What problems connected with the industrial revolution did it address? Which did it leave untouched?*

- Create a statistical table showing percentage distribution of the world's manufacturing production for the following countries: Great Britain, United States, Germany, France, Russia, and Italy in the periods 1800, 1850, and 1900. *What new patterns in world manufacturing production can you detect?*

Grades 9-12

- Using selections from *The Wealth of Nations* by Adam Smith, identify the characteristics of capitalism and analyze Smith's view of its strengths. *How are free enterprise, the profit motive, and competition the building blocks of capitalism? How does Smith use the "pin" story? Why? How does the Invisible Hand work? What are the strengths and weaknesses of Smith's argument?*

- Using descriptions and pictures of "The Great Exhibition of the Works of Industry of All Nations" in London's "Crystal Palace," compare the development of industrialization on the continent with that of England. Explain why there were differences in development.

- Read excerpts from 19th-century literature such as Charles Dickens's *Hard Times* or Emile Zola's *Germinal*, describing working and living conditions in an industrialized nation. *What do they say about the new classes that emerged with industrialization and the quality of industrial work life? How confident can we be that these works are accurate witnesses to industrial life?*

◗ Research conditions of children employed in factories, trades, and mines in England in the early 19th century. From primary documents, summarize the debates over child labor and factory legislation. *What changes were brought about by the Factory Act of 1833? The legislation of 1842? The Ten Hours Act of 1847? What general changes took place in the lives of women and children, as well as the structure of the family, as a result of the industrial revolution?*

◗ Develop a typology for the types of organizations and activities devised by working people in England, Western Europe, and the United States in response to conditions of industrial labor.

◗ Stage a debate on the benefits of the industrial revolution. Write a summary position paper assessing the positive and/or negative aspects of industrialization.

◗ Examine reproductions of advertisements from 19th-century magazines and newspapers. *How do these reflect the rise of industrial economies? Changes in family life? The role of women?*

C. The causes and consequences of the abolition of the trans-Atlantic slave trade and slavery in the Americas.

Grades 5-6

◗ Assume the role of an abolitionist and write a small pamphlet describing the evils of slavery. *Why did the slave trade continue for many years after Britain and the United States outlawed it?*

◗ Research the life of William Wilberforce and his role as a leader in the British abolition movement. *What contributions did Wilberforce make to outlawing slave trade and slavery?*

◗ Analyze the depiction of slavery in the famous Wedgewood China piece showing a slave boy in chains. *What do you think was the purpose of the artist in designing this piece?*

Grades 7-8

◗ Draw on a map the places where slavery was permitted in 1800, 1830, and 1880. *How might the differences be tied to revolutionary ideology and economics?*

◗ After reviewing primary source readings, re-enact the debate on the abolition of slavery in the colonies as it took place in the National Assembly during the French Revolution. *Why would the National Convention have been the body most likely to pass such a declaration?*

◗ Make a chart listing the many strategies employed by different peoples in the Americas to resist slavery. Include some examples from the Caribbean and Brazil. In as many cases as possible, name the people associated with each strategy and evaluate its success or failure.

◗ Research the life and work of Olaudah Equiano (Gustavus Vasa). *What were Equiano's experiences during the "middle passage"? How was he involved in the anti-slavery movement?*

Grades 9-12

◗ Compare the African slave trade with the migration of Chinese workers to North and South America and Indian workers to the Caribbean or other parts of the world in the 19th century.

◗ Using selections from the writings of William Wilberforce, analyze evangelical factors in the anti-slavery movement. *To what extent was Britain's abolition of slavery the result of the Evangelical movement? The Enlightenment? Economic failures?*

◗ Using trading maps and primary sources, analyze the reason why Brazil was the last nation to abolish slavery and the slave trade.

▶ Drawing on Philip D. Curtin's book *The African Slave Trade: A Census*, create a chart listing the estimated slave imports to Brazil, Spanish America, the British West Indies, the French West Indies and British North America, and the United States for the years 1701-1810 and 1811-1870. *When was the largest influx of slaves to the Americas? Where? What might account for this?*

▶ Read selections from the writings of *philosophes*, such as Voltaire's "Essay on Morals and Custom" (1756), Rousseau's "The New Heloise" (1761), and Diderot's "Natural Liberty" from the *Encyclopedia* (1765). *On what grounds did these men argue against slavery and the slave trade in the French colonies? On what grounds had slavery been justified earlier?*

▶ Research the organization, participants, and proceedings of the World Antislavery Convention held in London in 1840. *Who were the main participants? Where did they come from? What were the main issues discussed?*

III. The transformation of Eurasian societies in an era of global trade and rising European power, 1750-1850.

A. How the Ottoman Empire attempted to meet the challenge of Western military, political, and economic power.

Grades 5-6

▶ Write an historically accurate story about one aspect of Ottoman life such as a day in the life of a janissary or life in the Palace School.

▶ Create a project illustrating the Western-style reforms made in the Ottoman Empire during the reign of Selim III.

▶ Write a eulogy for Muhammad Ali telling of his life, how he came to power, and what he attempted to do as ruler of Egypt. *How successful was he? Why was he called the "father of modern Egypt"?*

Grades 7-8

▶ Find evidence to support or refute the statement: By the late 19th century the Ottoman Empire might justifiably have been called "the sick man of Europe." Draw a political cartoon to illustrate this evidence and statement.

▶ Compare the training and equipment of the Janissary Corps with that of Japanese samurai, Mongol soldiers, European knights, and modern infantry.

▶ Draw a series of maps reflecting the major territorial changes in the Ottoman Empire during the first half of the 19th century. *Which new nations were created? Which were made autonomous within the Empire? Which were controlled by other foreign powers?*

▶ Write a script for and present a "You Are There" program covering the main events of the Crimean War. Include dialogue on the causes of the war, the major nations involved, and the form of fighting and technology used.

Grades 9-12

▶ Design a chart of the many religious communities and nationalities within the Ottoman Empire in 1800. Include Sunni and Shi'ite Muslims, Druses, Wahhabis, Jews, and Christians, as well as various nationalities. List the regions or major areas where each group resided. *What was the prevailing policy toward religions under Ottoman rule? What was the relationship between religion and political authority?*

◆ Create an illustrated biography of Selim III. Describe his education. Give some examples of his poetry, with illustrations, and discuss his accomplishments as a composer of Ottoman music. *What were his greatest successes? failures?*

◆ Conduct an interview with English, French, and Ottoman diplomats questioning the motives and strategies for the Crimean War. *What interests did each represent? What military technology, including naval capacity, did each possess? To what extent were each country's interests actually served after the war?*

◆ Create a grid listing the political, military, and economic problems of Selim III's rule, the reforms he instituted to deal with those problems, the actual consequences of the reform attempts, and whether they can be said to have succeeded or failed. Summarize the state of affairs in the Ottoman Empire at the death of Selim III. *What other reforms might he have tried to save the empire?*

B. Russian absolutism, reform, and imperial expansion in the late 18th and 19th centuries.

Grades 5-6

◆ Create a map showing the Russian expansion across Asia and into Alaska and along the California coast. What did California have to offer that Russia wanted/needed?

◆ Create an archaeologist's log of cultural and physical artifacts that could describe life in the Russian settlements at Sitka and Bodega Bay.

Grades 7-8

◆ On a map of eastern Europe and central Asia, show the territories conquered during the reign of Catherine the Great, including territories gained from the Ottoman Empire. Mark the three partitions of Poland with the years 1772, 1793, and 1795. *What port did Russia have on the White Sea? On the Baltic? On the Black Sea? Why was the Black Sea so important to Russia?*

◆ Read an appropriate biography of Catherine the Great and conduct a mock interview with her. *How did she come to rule Russia? What were her literary and intellectual interests? What was palace life like in the Russian court? What problems did she encounter in trying to be an "enlightened" ruler?*

◆ Make a chart describing the general political, social, and economic structure of Russia in the 1800s. *What is autocratic rule? How would you characterize relations between landowners and peasants?*

◆ From the point of view of a Western European journalist, review the events of the Pugachev Rebellion of 1773 and write a story summarizing Catherine the Great's subsequent policies toward the peasantry, serfdom, and the nobility. *What do these policies this reveal about the character of absolutism in Russia?*

◆ Research the reign of Csar Alexander I. *What reforms did he plan? In what ways did they reflect Enlightenment influences? How successful was he in putting them into practice? Why did he turn away from reform later in his reign?*

Grades 9-12

◆ Construct leaflets, one for distribution to uneducated peasants, the other to army officers, advocating social reforms in Russia in the 1820s.

◆ Examine the causes of the Crimean War. *What consequences did it have for Russia, the Ottoman Empire, Britain, and France?*

◗ Issue a series of policy statements from Csar Nicholas I on such issues as a constitution, freedom of the press, the Decembrist uprising, the Polish rebellion, and Russification.

◗ Map Russian expansion eastward across Siberia and southward beyond the Caspian Sea. *Why did Russia invade Ottoman territories in the early 1850s? What was the significance of the Crimean War for Russian expansion? What did it show about Russian strength?*

◗ Create a poster, banner, or flag depicting Pan-Slavism and how it affected Russian foreign policy in the late 19th century. *Which groups, both within and outside Russia, supported or opposed this? On what grounds?*

◗ Refer to a map of Russian territory and expansion, including diagrams of the Trans-Siberian Railroad and other railroad routes for the period 1801-1914. *Which cities had the most rail service? What would you predict about Russian development from a railway map?*

◗ Write an essay in response to this statement: "Despite all his efforts, Alexander II failed in his goal to strengthen Russia by reform."

C. The consequences of political and military encounters between Europeans and peoples of South and Southeast Asia.

Grades 5-6

◗ On a world map, draw the main trade route linking India with China and Europe about 1800. *What goods were traded at each port? With which groups of people would trade be carried on? What was the impact of world trade on Indian agriculture and industry?*

◗ Construct an exchange of letters between a representative of the East India Company and an Indian ruler in the 18th century on the subject of trade.

◗ Construct a series of map overlays to illustrate the religious and linguistic diversity of India in the early 18th century.

Grades 7-8

◗ Debate the competitive policies of the British and the French in India. *How was the British East India Company able to prevail over the French?*

◗ Compare a map of Dutch territories in Asia in 1815 with Dutch-ruled territories in 1850. *What factors led to this change?*

◗ View a series of political maps of India from 1798 to 1850. Write a report of your observations about changes in political boundaries, region by region. *What different political forces were present in 1798? How was India organized politically in 1850?*

◗ Give an oral report on either the history of the British or French East India Company. *How did they receive charters? What did the charters enable them to do? What role did the home country expect these companies to play in India?*

◗ Show on a world map, the trade routes linking India with both China and Europe in the 19th century. Include the Suez Canal in the route. *What products were traded at each station? What goods were imported to India? exported from India? How would hand-manufactured goods compete with machine-produced products?*

◗ Construct a timeline of the stages of British penetration of India from 1750 to 1858. Include the grant of *diwani* to the East India Company, the battle of Plassey with the French, the defeat of Tipu Sultan of Mysore, the taking of Delhi, the defeat of the Marathas, the First Afghan War, the conquest of the Punjab, the uprising of 1857, and finally the official transfer of power from the East India Company to the British Crown. *What place did Indians have in the Indian Civil Service that was created by the British to govern India?*

♦ Write a travel diary of a Dutch merchant traveling through the East Indies. *What products would he find? How did the Dutch rule their colonies? What languages would people speak?*

Grades 9-12

♦ Write a diary entry for a member of the Indian elite and for an average peasant describing your relationship to Europeans and its effect on your life. *In what ways did Western culture influence the lives of elite groups in India or Indonesia? How were Europeans living in those colonies influenced by local cultural styles and practices?*

♦ Role-play a discussion between an upper-class Hindu and a Muslim about their reaction to the British presence in India in the late 19th century.

♦ Read original speeches and writings on the life of Ram Mohan Roy. *What was his attitude toward Western science, technology, and culture? Toward the use of English in India? What did he hope to achieve for India in the mid-19th century? How did these attitudes changes?*

♦ Research the "modernizing" administration of Lord Dalhousie (1848-1856) and British policies in India. Evaluate the social and political impact of the railroad on Indian life. *Which people might have benefited most? least? How did the railroad help or hinder the unity of India?*

♦ Create a chart comparing and contrasting the colonial policies of the British in India with Dutch policies in the East Indies. *Where were the areas of greatest similarity? of greatest difference?*

D. How China's Qing dynasty responded to economic and political crises in the late 18th and the 19th centuries.

Grades 5-6

♦ Write a Letter to the Editor assuming either the role of a Chinese or a European stating your reasons for supporting your trade policy. *Why did the Chinese want to keep foreigners out?*

♦ Based on historical evidence, role-play a meeting between a Chinese who emigrated to the U.S., one who emigrated to Southeast Asia, and one who remained home, discussing their reasons for leaving or staying.

Grades 7-8

♦ Write an article that might have appeared in a Chinese newspaper of the time about the events of the Opium War or the Boxer Rebellion. Graphically illustrate the main points of your article.

♦ Create a timeline which focuses on Chinese-European contacts between 1839-1914. *What alternative responses did Chinese statesmen and intellectuals propose to deal with European influences?*

♦ Read Lin Zexu's letter to Queen Victoria (1839). Analyze Lin's argument for his position on the British sale of opium in China. Debate his position with an English merchant or statesman.

Grades 9-12

♦ Draw evidence from the Qianlong Emperor's correspondence (1793) with King George III of England to determine how the Chinese emperor viewed the world. *What reasons does the emperor give for denying English trading rights in China? In the emperor's view how does his Celestial Dynasty compare with other monarchies?*

♦ Read excerpts from the documents of the Taiping rebels, such as the "Land Regulations of the Taiping Heavenly Kingdom." Discuss the influence of Christianity, rural class relations and problems of rural poverty on the impending century of revolution.

◆ Read Wei Yuan's statement on maritime defense (1842) and selections from Lord Palmerston in parliament on the necessity of going to war with China. *What was Wei Yuan's perception of the West and of imperialism in China?*

◆ Discuss the terms of the Treaty of Nanjing (1842) following the Opium War and those of the Treaty of Shimonoseki (1895) following the Sino-Japanese War. Analyze the development of European or Japanese imperial interests in China in the latter half of the 19th century.

◆ Based on historical information, construct interviews with an English merchant, a Chinese merchant, a Confucian scholar, a Catholic missionary, a Chinese official, and a British member of Parliament concerning their stand on the opium trade.

E. How Japan was transformed from feudal shogunate to modern nation-state in the 19th century.

Grades 5-6

◆ Make a drawing, using woodblock prints, of the "black ships" and assess their meaning for Japan in the 1850s and 1860s.

◆ Read *Commodore Perry in the Land of the Shogun* by Rhoda Blumberg. Write a biographical sketch or poem about Commodore Perry.

◆ Rewrite the Charter Oath in your own words. Defend this statement: The Charter Oath marked a momentous change in Japan's attitude toward itself and the outside world.

Grades 7-8

◆ Debate the proposition "modernization equals Westernization" in terms of the Japanese experience. *What knowledge did Japanese have about the West before the arrival of Commodore Perry? What advantages did Japan gain from their "window on the West"?*

◆ Read Sakamoto Ryoma's letters and assume the role of a "samurai man of spirit" (*shishi*) in the events leading up to the Meiji Restoration. *As a samurai, what is your view of the reforms?*

◆ Draw charts of the feudal Japanese social structure and the social structure that emerged during the Meiji era.

Grades 9-12

◆ Read the Charter Oath and analyze the goals of the new imperial government in 1868. *Which of the goals was achieved and when?*

◆ Read songs and diaries from Tsurumi's *Factory Girls*, and write an autobiography of a factory girl in Meiji Japan.

◆ Compare the Meiji Restoration to the French and American revolutions. *Which movement made the profoundest changes in society?* Compare and contrast their causes and leadership.

◆ Analyze reasons for Japan's rapid industrialization, and compare Japan and China in their response to Western commerce and power in the 19th century.

◆ Read excerpts from writings about visits of 19th-century Japanese travelers to the West (Masao Miyoshi's *As We Saw Them*). Hypothesize those features of Western culture and society the Japanese were most likely to find attractive.

◆ Discuss the meaning of three Meiji slogans: "Civilization and Enlightenment;" "Rich Nation, Strong Army;" and "Increase Production and Promote Industry."

◆ Using stories in Hane's *Peasants, Rebels, and Outcasts*, make a social map showing the people who benefited and those who suffered in the first decades of industrialization and nation-building.

IV. Patterns of nationalism, state-building, and social reform in Europe and the Americas, 1830-1914.

A. How modern nationalism affected European politics and society.

Grades 5-6

▶ Role-play a young Italian who has joined Garibaldi's redshirts and write a letter home explaining what your leader is having you do and why.

▶ Research major leaders of Italian and German unification and write a nationalist speech for each. *How did the aims of some of these leaders differ?*

Grades 7-8

▶ Review cartoons and drawings of German and Italian unification and create captions or titles for each.

▶ Construct a timeline listing the Revolutions of 1848 and, on a map of Europe, locate the areas where the revolts occurred. *To what extent were the Revolutions of 1848 a chain reaction? What was the moving spirit behind each revolution? What were the goals of the revolutions?*

▶ Use a television interview format to conduct a panel discussion of leading figures in the revolutionary era such as: Louis Philippe, Louis Napoleon, Louis Kossuth, Pope Pius IX, George Sand, Giuseppe Mazzini, Klemens von Metternich, Nicholas I, George Sand, and Frédéric Chopin.

▶ Construct a timeline showing each of the events you consider to have been important in the unification of Italy and Germany, and give your reasons for including each event.

▶ Write a speech supporting liberal political reforms from the point of view of a Pole, Hungarian, Austrian, German, Italian, or Spaniard. *What reforms are you supporting? What appeals would you make to arouse nationalist feelings?*

▶ Construct a visual display to accompany a dramatic reading of Bismarck's "Blood and Iron" speech. *What were the previous attempts at unification to which Bismarck referred?*

▶ Construct a poster, patriotic speech, poem, or song to help recruit for the "Red Shirts." *To what extent did Garibaldi reflect 19th-century Romanticism?*

Grades 9-12

▶ Give an account of the Franco-Prussian war as it might have appeared in a retrospective written, first, in a French, Prussian, Bavarian or British newspaper.

▶ Define *realpolitik*. Write comparative biographical sketches of Cavour and Bismarck. *To what extent did Cavour and Bismarck exemplify the use of realpolitik? Who would you rank as a master of realpolitik today? Discuss the pros and cons of realpolitik as a type of policy.*

▶ Draw evidence from the original and edited Ems Telegram and role-play Bismarck's editing of the dispatch. *How did Bismarck's understanding of history enter into this editing? What effect did the edited version of the dispatch have on the French?*

▶ Compile a sketchbook of caricatures and cartoons of nationalist movements in Italy and Germany. Explain the meaning of the illustrations.

B. The impact of new social movements and ideologies on 19th-century Europe.

Grades 5-6

▶ Create and analyze a rural/urban population graph for France or Germany at different points in the 19th century. *What changes do you observe, and how might these changes be explained?*

▶ Identify a person from the woman's suffrage movement and cite important contributions that person made to women's rights.

▶ Write a slogan for the woman's suffrage movement and create a poster expressing the changes women wanted.

▶ Make a line graph of the population of Europe from 1650-1950. Use increments of 50 years. *Which years mark the highest rate of growth?*

Grades 7-8

▶ On a map of Europe show rural-to-urban migration in the 19th century. Investigate the causes for each of the major demographic changes.

▶ Trace the development of the women's suffrage movement in Britain. *Who were the leaders in the movement? What was accomplished by the end of the 19th century?*

▶ Construct maps or charts to illustrate and explain large-scale population movements within and beyond Europe in the 19th century.

▶ Write a slogan for the European factory workers who wanted to set up trade unions. Create posters using this slogan and listing their demands.

▶ Make charts of major political, social, and economic reforms in Britain between 1815 and 1914. Write an essay using the information in the charts which responds to the statement: "From 1815 to 1914, Britain evolved into a more democratic society."

Grades 9-12

▶ As a member of the English Workingmen's Association, prepare a speech explaining the need for political reform. *How radical were the six major demands of the Chartist movement? How did the ruling classes react to the Chartists? What effect did the continental revolutions of 1848 have on the Chartist movement?*

▶ Construct two 19th-century newspaper editorials, one that supports the agitation for women's suffrage at the time and one that opposes it.

▶ In the context of the political, economic, and social conditions of the mid-19th century, debate the "10 point program" Marx outlined in the *Communist Manifesto*. *To what extent were these points radical in the context of the late 19th century?*

▶ Draw evidence from Mary Wollstonecraft's *Vindication of the Rights of Woman* to list the goals of the women's movement in the 19th century. Debate various ways that these goals might be achieved.

▶ Using diverse visual, literary, political, and scientific documents as evidence, debate the benefits and problems of the industrial revolution in at least one European country.

▶ Reading such sources as *J'Accuse*, Emile Zola's indictment of the handling of the Dreyfus Affair, analyze why the French political and military establishment was so resistant to pardoning Dreyfus in spite of growing evidence of his innocence. *To what extent was the Dreyfus Affair a political conflict between conservatives and progressives?*

C. Cultural, intellectual, and educational trends in 19th-century Europe.

Grades 5-6

▶ Marshal evidence from primary, literary, and pictorial sources to devise a schedule for an average school day for a male and female student during this period.

▶ Write "A Day in the Life of...." a child from an upper, a middle, or a working class family in a 19th-century European country.

▶ Assume the role of a child of twelve who has never gone to school and probably never will. List things you will never be able to do because of your lack of education. Compare your list with other pairs. *How did the lives of people in 19th-century Europe change when they were able to attend school?*

▶ Create a mural-sized, illustrated, and annotated timeline of inventors and inventions of 19th-century Europe and America.

Grades 7-8

▶ Construct a comparison chart illustrating changes in the standard of living in Europe from the beginning to the end of the 19th century. *What factors account for the changes? Did everyone benefit from the changes?*

▶ Compose a sports and entertainment section for a metropolitan newspaper of about 1890. Trace changes in leisure activity and popular culture through the century. *What factors contributed to the changes? What were the activities most associated with "high culture"? What types of entertainment were open to the middle and working classes?*

▶ Assemble a collection of illustrations to demonstrate the major movements in the arts (literature, painting, music, architecture) during the 19th century. *How did these works reflect or express changing attitudes in society?*

▶ Analyze various artistic depictions of the railroad. *What do they say about the source's attitudes toward changes the railway brought?*

▶ Role-play a discussion between parents of peasant, middle-class, and urban factory worker backgrounds about the advantages and drawbacks of their children's attending school.

Grades 9-12

▶ On a map, identify the countries of the world that had compulsory education and graphically portray the numbers of people who attended school before and during the industrial age.

▶ Bring to class books showing illustrations of Romantic, Realist, and Impressionist art, explaining what features of your examples make them characteristic of the style they illustrate.

▶ Construct a series of diary entries and illustrate the life experiences of 19th-century middle- and working-class women and men. The diaries may be patterned on models such as are available in John Burnett's *The Annals of Labour*; and E. O. Hellerstein's *Victorian Women*.

D. Political, economic, and social transformations in the Americas in the 19th century.

Grades 5-6

▶ Using a physical map of Latin America, list ways geography might have influenced nation-building in Latin America.

▶ Construct a diagram of class systems in Latin American countries. *What part did race play in such systems? Who were Creoles?*

Grades 7-8

▶ Create a visual depiction of caudillo rulers such as Portales and Rosas in Latin America. *What was a caudillo? Which forces backed his rule? How did he maintain himself in power?*

▶ Using a provincial map of Canada, draw the routes of the Canadian Pacific Railway to show how the new Dominion of Canada was linked together.

▶ On a world map, represent the stream of immigrants into Latin America between 1750 and 1914. *When did various groups come? What kinds of work did they do? To what extent did they become integrated into their new societies?*

Grades 9-12

▶ Assume the role of a caudillo, a military official, landowner, member of the urban bourgeoisie, or church official in postindependence Latin America. Propose and defend a program of development for your country.

▶ Examine the leadership of Benito Juárez within the framework of the Liberal/Conservative civil wars and the French intervention.

▶ Using the economic policies and consequences of the rule of General Porfirio Díaz as an example, write a position paper on the benefits and problems of 19th-century foreign investments.

▶ Using excerpts from such sources as the writings of José Martí of Cuba (1870s), describe Latin American attitudes toward nationalism and cultural identity.

▶ Create a graphic showing the governmental structure of the new Dominion of Canada created in 1867. *What was "dominion status" or the Canadian idea?*

V. *Patterns of global change in the era of Western military and economy domination, 1800-1914.*

A. Connections between major developments in science and technology and the growth of industrial economy and society.

Grades 5-6

▶ Describe how you would send a message from London to Hong Kong in 1800. In 1850 and 1900. *How long would it take in each case?*

▶ Make a collage illustrating how new inventions affected transportation in the early 19th century. Explain how new transportation systems changed peoples' lives. *How have these methods of transportation changed in the 20th century? What will transportation be like in the 21st century?*

▶ Read a biography of Louis Pasteur. Explain the significance of his contributions to bacteriology.

Grades 7-8

▶ Create a photo album entitled "Scenes From Urban Life: 1800-1900." *What does it suggest about changes in lifestyles and demography? What accounts for the changes?*

▶ Research the development of the "Yellow Press." *What technological advances allowed for its growth? What kinds of features and stories did it stress? How did political leaders use the press to influence the masses? How did the press influence political leaders?*

▶ Make a collage on the theme "1870-1914: The Second Industrial Revolution." *What would be different from a collage on the first industrial revolution?*

- Research the new scientific thinkers of the 19th century. *How did they build on or reject each other's theories?*

- Develop a classroom newspaper profiling the leading scientists of the 19th century and explain how advances in science affected society. *What were the obstacles scientists faced? How did new scientific discoveries improve the health of children and adults?*

Grades 9-12

- Design a World's Fair exhibit of 19th-century technological developments in transportation and communication. Explain why you chose the items in your exhibit.

- Research the development of eugenics. *What were its purposes? In what ways was it related to Darwinian theories of evolution? What distinguished it from genetics? In what ways was it linked with political and social theories and policies?*

- Develop a case study of the development of weapons technology in England or Germany between 1870 and 1914. *What role did government play in stimulating research? How did weapons development affect research in related fields?*

- Construct a chart tracing changes in food production in England, the U.S., Egypt, Russia, and Japan between 1800 and 1900. Assess the relative importance of technological, political, and social factors to explain the data.

- Design a world tour in 1800 and another in 1900. Map your itinerary. Describe your modes of transportation and estimate your travel times. *What obstacles would you face on the earlier trip that might be lessened by 1900?*

- Research the debates over Darwin's theories that developed within the scientific community. *What issues did scientists dispute? How were their positions related to the "Nature-Nurture" controversy?*

B. The causes and consequences of European settler colonization in the 19th century.

Grades 5-6

- Make a horizontal bar graph of migrations of Europeans between 1840 and 1940. Label the columns "millions of people," and assign intervals of 5 million, 0 to 60. Label rows "Emigrants to:" the United States, Argentina, Siberia, Canada, Brazil, Australia, South Africa, Uruguay, and New Zealand. Put in the correct information and summarize the information expressed in the graph. *What other visual means could you create to convey this data?*

- Write a series of letters between a European who is considering emigration and an established European in Canada. *What was Canada like around 1870? Which cities were being settled? What things might entice a new settler to Canada?*

Grades 7-8

- Make a double chart of (a) migrations from European countries, 1846-1932 and (b) immigration into other countries from Europe, citing numbers of people involved. *What inferences about new European settlements can you make?*

- Make a line graph of the population of Europe from 1650-1950. Use increments of 50 years. *What is the general trend or pattern of population growth in Europe? Using factors such as birth, death, and infant mortality rates, what accounts for the highest rise in European population? What accounts for the leveling off or stabilizing of the population?*

- Develop a typology of why people left Europe. Use such factors as overpopulation, political persecution, religious persecution, and improvement of living standards. *Which European countries or peoples would fit some of these categories?*

♦ Design a poster promoting ways that new technologies, such as the steamship or the railroad, can make your emigrant voyage safer and more secure.

♦ Recount the rise of the Zulu empire in South Africa. *Did this event have a historical connection to European settlement in the Cape region of South Africa? What were the characteristics of relations between migrating European and African peoples in South Africa in the 19th century? In what ways did these relations lay the foundations of the apartheid system of the 20th century?*

Grades 9-12

♦ Drawing on historical evidence, explain the settlement of the western part of North America by peoples of European descent. *How was this westward movement part of a larger pattern of European overseas settlement that included such regions as Argentina, South Africa, and Siberia? Were the consequences of this settlement for indigenous peoples similar in these different regions?* Compare this settlement to other eras of migration in such categories as: reasons, extent, and effects on indigenous peoples.

♦ Select one area of new European settlement and research the foods and raw materials produced by the settlers. *How did settlement and increasing economic ties with Europe change the region?*

♦ Research and develop a case study of one emigrant European group, for example, Italians who went to Argentina. Find out the main factors that led them to leave Italy and the main reasons they chose Argentina. *What backgrounds did they come from? How similar were their new surroundings to the ones they left? What was different?*

♦ Using the case of Australia, research the environmental impact of the new immigrant populations on the land. *Where else might we find a similar case?* Describe relations between European settlers and indigenous people.

♦ Map the overall settlement of "European communities" throughout the world. *How might these migrations have affected the political and economic lives of the local regions in which they settled?*

C. The causes of European, American, and Japanese imperial expansion.

Grades 5-6

♦ Write a mini-biography of an important European figure of the period of the New Imperialism. Choose from the following: Pierre de Brazza, Charles "Chinese" Gordon, King Leopold II, David Livingstone, Carl Peters, Cecil Rhodes, or Henry Morton Stanley. *How did the individual you have chosen advance the imperial interests of his country? How did the people of his country regard him?*

♦ On a map or bulletin board graphically depict the motives for European expansion in Africa, Southeast Asia, and China. *How did motives differ depending on the region where expansion was taking place?*

Grades 7-8

♦ Read and report on a biography of Cecil Rhodes. *What were his motives and goals in the "scramble for Africa"? How did the railroad contribute to imperial expansion?*

♦ Read the provisions of the Treaty of Nanking (1842) following the Opium War. Discuss what interests the Western powers had in China and what imperialism meant to the Chinese.

♦ Playing the part of a European journalist reporting on the Russo-Japanese War, draw on historical evidence to explain to your readers why that war was fought and how the Japanese won it.

▸ Write a series of letters to the editor of an American or European newspaper arguing for and against colonial expansion into Africa.

Grades 9-12

▸ Write an essay on the chain of developments in both Europe and Africa that precipitated the so-called "scramble" for African territory. *Is it possible to identify a single precipitating event? In what ways did particular African governments or peoples play a part in shaping the way the European partition of Africa took place?*

▸ Construct a balance sheet listing the positive and negative features of imperialism. *What were the chief benefits of the introduction of new political institutions and advances in communication, technology, and medicine? What were the costs of the introduction of European institutions and new technology?*

▸ Using multiple sources summarize the intellectual justifications for British imperialism or French *mission civilisatrice* as part of European imperialism.

▸ Read Chinua Achebe's *Things Fall Apart* or Markandaya's *Nectar in a Sieve* to assess the impact of European expansion on village life, including legal, familial, and gender relations in Africa or India.

▸ Develop case studies from Daniel Headrick's *Tools of Empire* to illustrate the role of medical advances, steam power, and military technology in European imperialism.

▸ Prepare a map of Africa and Eurasia showing major national and international railroad lines constructed during the late 19th- and early 20th-century. Gather information about the history of their construction and funding. Write a report assessing the importance of these routes and analyzing the potential benefits to imperial powers and indigenous economies.

▸ Argue Japan's case for its imperial expansion in East Asia, taking either of the following two positions: (1) Japan should "Escape from Asia," treating Asia as the West does, or (2) Japan should be "Leader of Asia," protecting Asia from Western imperialism.

D. Transformations in South, Southeast, and East Asia in the era of the "new imperialism."

Grades 5-6

▸ Write accounts of the Boxer Rebellion from the Chinese and European perspectives. *How do these accounts differ?*

▸ Write an article that might have appeared in a Japanese newspaper after the death of the Meiji Emperor in 1912. *What were the main achievements of Meiji Japan?*

Grades 7-8

▸ Map the European presence in South, Southeast, and East Asia in the late 19th century. *How did Thailand avoid direct European contact? To what extent was the land influenced by European culture?*

▸ Construct a graphic display of the Uprising of 1857 in India and British reaction to it.

▸ Draw from historical evidence to construct a speech encouraging a sepoy to rebel against British authority. Write a second speech calling upon loyal soldiers in the British Army to resist the rebels. *What values does each speech express?*

▸ Hold a dialogue, based on historical information, between the Empress Dowager Cixi and a leader of the Righteous Harmonious Fists (Boxers) secret society about the presence and activities of foreigners in China in the late 1890s.

Grades 9-12

▶ Write a series of newspaper accounts of the Indian uprising of 1857. *Why did the army revolt? What religious policies were they rebelling against?* Describe the march on Delhi and the other forces that joined the soldiers there. *Why did the rebellion spread so quickly? What demands did Muslim rebels make? What was the reaction of the princes and maharajahs who had made alliances with the East India Company? Would you label the uprising a mutiny, rebellion, or failed revolution?*

▶ Trace the life of Sun Yatsen and describe the role of overseas Chinese in the 1911 revolution.

▶ Construct a timeline showing the chronology of the introduction of major social, economic, political, and technological changes derived from the West into 19th-century Japan. *Why was Japan able to reform so quickly?* Compare the Japanese and Chinese governments' response to western influences.

▶ Analyze the role of the Emperor in Meiji Japan. Compare his political and symbolic roles with those of the British or other Western monarchs of the time.

E. Varying responses of African peoples to world economic developments and European imperialism.

Grades 5-6

▶ After viewing video clips of the discovery of diamonds and gold in South Africa in Basil Davidson's *The Africans*, explain how these developments might have changed economic life and race relations.

▶ Make a map and an overlay showing how political boundaries changed on the continent of Africa between 1850 and 1900. Include on the first map major African states of the mid-19th century. *Why did the map change so drastically by 1900?*

Grades 7-8

▶ Write a description of one of the following resistance leaders or movements: Abd al-Qadir in Algeria, Samori Ture in West Africa, the Mahdist state in the Sudan, Memelik II in Ethiopia, the Zulus in South Africa. Attach your description to a map of Africa.

▶ Construct a map of the Eastern Hemisphere, labeling the Suez Canal. *How did the Suez Canal affect world trade? World political alliances? What part did the Egyptian government have in its building?*

▶ Recount the career of the East African empire-builder Tippu Tip. *How did 19th-century trade in clover, ivory, and slaves stimulate empire-building in East Africa? Was Tippu Tip a leader of resistance against European imperialism?*

▶ Create a transparency map of the political divisions of Africa before 1870. Produce an overlay of the political division of Africa in 1914. *What political conflicts between Africans and Europeans might you anticipate?*

Grades 9-12

▶ Research evidence that slavery and slave trade became more widespread in both West and East Africa in the 19th century, even as the trans-Atlantic slave trade came to an end. *How did world demand for West African products contribute to increased enslavement of people in that region? How was slave labor used in 19th-century West Africa? How did the development of clove plantations on the East African coast, as well as international ivory trade, contribute to an increase in long-distance slave trading in that region? What connections were there between slave and ivory trading in East Africa and the emergence of new empires in the interior?*

◗ Drawing on historical evidence, chart reasons for both the successes and the failures of resistance movements in Africa such as those led by Abd al-Qadir in Algeria, Samori Ture in West Africa, Menelik II in Ethiopia, and the Zulus in South Africa. *What conditions or events favored success or failure?*

◗ Assess the relative strength of Islam and Christianity in Africa at the beginning of the 20th century. *What attracted people to either of these faiths? What forms did rivalries take among Christian denominations in proselytizing Africans? In what ways were both Islam and Christianity linked to the interests of governments?*

◗ Research the role of Mahdi Mohammad Ahmed in opposing the British in the Sudan. *How effective was the Mahdi uprising? What did it illustrate regarding popular opposition to British imperialism in the Anglo-Egyptian Sudan?*

◗ Research how the Fulbe (Fulani) people were important as religious and political reformers in 19th-century West Africa. *How did Muslim reform movements change the political and religious map of West Africa? Who was Usuman dan Fodio, and what contributions did he make as a scholar and reformer?*

VI. *Major global trends from 1750 to 1914.*

Major global trends from 1750 to 1914.

Grades 5-6

◗ View visual sources of North and South American immigrants in the 19th century. Choose one photograph and do a "quickwrite" about what she or he might have thought about migrating to a new land.

◗ Map Asian or African migrations from 1750-1900. *Where did people go? Why?*

◗ Report on the history, layout, and size of one of the following cities during this era: Guangzhou (Canton), Cairo, Sydney, Tokyo, Buenos Aires, Bombay, Moscow, San Francisco, or London. *How did these cities change?*

Grades 7-8

◗ Using information from a computer data source, create a graph of world population figures by century from 1500-1900. *When did the greatest increases occur? Where? What factors might account for this?*

◗ Construct a bar graph of major world religion statistics for 1750 and 1900. Research the regions where both Christianity and Islam expanded.

◗ Using various visual, literary, and documentary resources from one country, list the ways a rural family unit might have been affected by the industrial revolution. Create a visual representation of the findings. *How might the lives of rural women have been affected? How did child-raising change?*

◗ Write a pamphlet or series of newspaper articles describing the daily life of an industrial working man or woman. *How were they similar? Different?*

◗ Draw a world map for 1750 and another for 1914. Draw the size of countries to represent political, economic, and military power rather than actual physical size. *What accounts for the differences in the two maps?*

Grades 9-12

♦ Make two maps showing the location of major cities of the world, one dated about 1750, the other about 1900. *Where did new large cities appear? Why did more large cities appear in Europe? In Latin America? In what regions was migration likely to have contributed to the growth of cities? Where would trade or industrialization most likely have been important? In what regions was urbanization linked to European colonialism?*

♦ Research and report on two major religious reform movements in Buddhism, Christianity, Hinduism, Islam, or Judaism in the 19th century. *What reforms were undertaken? What problems did they address? How successful were they?*

♦ Create a series of political slogans or cartoons for the liberal and/or socialist interests of a 19th-century nation-state. *How were these connected to new- or old-class interests? What specific demands were being made?*

♦ Using excerpts from novels such as Chinua Achebe's *Things Fall Apart* or Kamala Markandaya's *Nectar in a Sieve* describe people's struggles to maintain cultural values and traditions in the changing world of the late 19th and early 20th centuries.

♦ Research the lives and explore writings of Jamal al-Din al-Afghani, Rashid Rida, and Muhammad Abduh. *What was their vision of progress, and how did they differ in blending Western ideas and values with Muslim values?*

♦ Research educational reform in various Muslim regions during the 19th century. Make a chart describing and arranging these efforts on a continuum of traditionalist rejection of Western ideas, wholesale embrace of Western forms and ideas, and synthesis of Western and indigenous ideas. *What new institutions were established, and how did older ones change? How did educational reforms affect women?*

Ethiopians battle Italians at Adowa, 1896. American Museum of Natural History

ERA 8

A Half-Century of Crisis and Achievement, 1900-1945

Giving Shape to World History

On a winter's day in 1903 the "Kitty Hawk," Orville and Wilbur Wright's experimental flying machine, lifted off the ground for twelve seconds. In the decades that followed air travel was perfected, and all the physical barriers that had obstructed long-distance communication among human groups virtually disappeared. Oceans, deserts, and mountain ranges no longer mattered much when people living thousands of miles apart were determined to meet, talk, negotiate, or do business. For the first time in history the north polar region became a crossroads of international travel as air pilots sought the shortest routes between countries of the Northern Hemisphere. Radio and, at mid-century, television revolutionized communication in another way. Long-distance messages no longer had to be transported from one point to another by boat or train or even transmitted along wires or cables. Now messages, whether designed to inform, entertain, persuade, or deceive, could be broadcast from a single point to millions of listeners or watchers simultaneously.

These and other technological wonders both expressed and contributed to the growing complexity and unpredictability of human affairs. In some ways peoples of the world became more tightly knit than ever before. Global economic integration moved ahead. Literacy spread more widely. Research and knowledge networks reached round the world. However, in other respects division and conflict multiplied. Economic and territorial rivalries among nations became harsher. Laboratories and factories turned out more lethal weapons and in greater quantities than ever before. People rose up against autocratic governments on every continent. Among the turbulent trends of the era, two developments seem most prominent.

▶ **The 20th Century's Thirty Years War:** The powers of destruction that centuries of accumulated technical and scientific skill gave to human beings became horrifyingly apparent in the two global wars of the 20th century. In the Thirty Years War of the 1600s, one of Europe's most destructive contests, more than 4 million people may have died. The wars of 1914-1945, by contrast, took 45 million lives. Since World War I sowed copious seeds of the second conflict, the complex links of cause and effect over the entire period make a compelling subject for the world history student. Though both wars engulfed Europe, the globe is in the proper context for understanding them. Air power, especially in World War II, meant that no country's borders were safe, whatever the distances involved. Campaigns were fought from the mid-Pacific to West Africa and from Siberia to the North Atlantic. Combatants came from many lands, including thousands from European colonial possessions. The century's first five decades were not, however, all violence and gloom. In the midst of war and world depression heroism and ingenuity abounded. Age-old diseases were conquered or brought under control. Democracy endured in many states despite recurrent crises, and governments responded with remarkable efficiency to the demands of war-time management and welfare.

▶ **Revolution and Protest:** Human aspirations toward democratic government, national independence, and social justice were first expressed on a large scale in human affairs in the 1750-1914 era. These aspirations continued to inspire revolutions throughout the first half of the 20th century. The most dramatic political changes occurred in Russia, China, Mexico, and Turkey. In all these places jarring shifts and disturbances in economic life, both local and international, were at the root of the political crises. In all of them, moreover, contests quickly developed between the advocates of liberal, parliamentary democracy and those who championed an authoritarian state as the most efficient instrument of political and economic transformation. Apart from revolutions, relatively peaceful movements of protest and dissent forced a broadening of the democratic base, including voting rights for women, in a number of countries. The European colonial empires saw few violent rising between 1900 and 1945. There was, however, no colonial "golden age." Resistance, protest, and calls for reform, drawing heavily on the liberal and nationalist ideals that the Western powers proclaimed, dogged imperial regimes all across Africa and Asia.

Why Study This Era?

▶ Exploration of the first half of the 20th century is of special importance if students are to understand the responsibilities they face at the close of the millennium. The two world wars were destructive beyond anything human society had every experienced. If students are to grasp both the toll of such violence and the price that has sometimes been paid in the quest for peace, they must understand the causes and costs of these world-altering struggles.

▶ In this era the ideologies of communism and fascism, both rooted in the 19th century, were put into practice on a large scale in Germany, Italy, and Russia. Both movements challenged liberal democratic traditions and involved elaborate forms of authoritarian repression. The fascist cause was discredited in 1945 and communism by the early 1990s. Even so, assessing the progress of our own democratic values and institutions in this century requires parallel study of these two alternative political visions. What did they promise? How did they work as social and economic experiments? In what conditions might they find new adherents in the future?

▶ Active citizens must continually re-examine the role of the United States in contemporary world affairs. Between 1900 and 1945 this country rose to international leadership; at the end of the period it stood astride the globe. How did we attain such a position? How has it changed since mid-century? What of our tradition as global peacemaker? Any informed judgement of our foreign policies and programs requires an understanding of our place among nations since the beginning of the century.

▶ In both scientific and cultural life this era ushered in the "modern." The scientific theories as well as aesthetic and literary movements that humanity found so exhilarating and disturbing in the first half of the century continue to have a huge impact on how we see the world around us.

U.S. Army forces in World War I, 1918.
National Archives

Essay

Russia in World History*
by Marilynn Hitchens

While many textbooks relegate Russia to the fringes of historical study, Marilynn Hitchens states the case for developing a course of study that moves Russia from "its peripheral connection with Europe" to an integral place in a comprehensive world history program. Hitchens recommends employing comparative analysis and exploring how Russian history reflects world trends.

Marilynn Hitchens taught history for many years at Wheat Ridge High School in Colorado. She is past-president of the World History Association.

It comes as a surprise to many of us who have labored for years in the history of a particular part of the globe, that "our history" is not a very important one in the scheme of world history. Such was my shock when I reviewed Roy Willis's *World Civilizations* textbook some years ago and found that out of 1,485 pages, there were a scant six pages on Russia and another eight pages on the Bolshevik Revolution. Many other references were only in passing. His later retort to my chiding on this matter was that Russia had been a relatively unimportant part of the "civilizational" history of the world. Of course, he was right. Equally distressing is the fact that Russia is likewise unimportant in the axial world history approach where trade, links and cultural diffusions are the major conceptual patterns. Russia has been a cultural importer, not a diffuser, and trade routes run thin in Russian history. Even the Mongols are given more play than Russia when it comes to this story. Philip Curtin's approach of identifying "relevant aggregates" of human relationships that define space-time boundaries of a historical problem *(American Historical Review, 1984)* may be the most appropriate way of fitting Russia into world history. This is because a major Russian story has been the fanning out of the Russian nationality from its central nexus in the Moscow area to envelop the north Asian land mass, thus bringing it into the scope of world history much as the Atlantic basin brought, three continents together. Still, there is the lingering thought that Russia in world history is limited to its peripheral connections with Europe and its imperial relationships with a small ring of nationalities on its borders, neither of which are "major" stories. Even the communist era has its roots in Europe and its participation in World War era politics. And contemporary events in the former Soviet Union, decolonization and democratization, are peripheral reflections of world trends impacting Russia.

How is one to integrate Russia into world history then? At the macro level, Russia can be used as illustration of world trends. For example, by 3000 B.C. agriculture had spread to the southern part of Russia from the Middle East. By 1000 B.C. Indo-European invasions brought iron and caused the Slavic migrations splitting the slays into three branches, Eastern (Russian, White Russian and Ukrainian), Southern (Yugoslav) and Eastern (Poles, Slovaks). This defined the major territorial and linguistic divisions of the slavic world for the future. From the seventh to third centuries B.C. Scythian and Sarmatian nomadic warriors ruled the area of south Russia, and their trade links with the Greek and Persian world brought cultural and artistic influences which Russian historian Rostovtzeff identifies as the beginning of Russian civilizational history. During the Roman Empire, Germanic tribal movements influenced the development of regional kingdoms in the area. The movement of the Turkic peoples of the late Roman Empire including the Huns and Avars overcame Russia too and threatened Byzantium. The Khazar

*Reprinted from *World History Bulletin*, Vol. 9 (Fall/Winter 1992-93), pp. 19-20.

state of the seventh century A.D. in the lower Volga played a major role in bulwarking Russia from the spread of Islam and in founding the seminal trade towns which became part of the Kievan trade complex. The classic story of the founding of Kiev by Rurik A.D. 862 is connected with the migrations of the Norse and the later Kievan state became a supreme reflection of the spread of Byzantine Orthodoxy and its culture.

Russia, of course, becomes a major part of the Mongol invasions of the thirteenth century A.D. with establishment of the Golden Horde and Russia's 200-year subjugation under the "Mongol Yoke." With liberation from the Mongols and the establishment of the Russian state in the seventeenth century A.D., Russia like the European world became engaged in exploration and development of Russia's New World to the East—the Volga Basin, Siberia, and finally the American west coast. Westernization and imperialism of eighteenth and nineteenth century Europe is reflected in Russian history as well, especially during the reigns of Peter, Catherine, and Alexander I. The origins of World War I involve Russia directly, and the story of twentieth century communism with its roots in German industrialization and Russian backwardness, its export to other countries, and its pivotal role in World War II bring Russia to its most important chapter in world history. In contemporary world history, Russia can be attached to many stories, among them the Wallersteinian paradigm in which Russia is a world hinterland, the modernization approach of Cyril Black in which Russia becomes a major illustration of other routes to industrialization, in the world politics of the Cold War, in the decolonization story in which new nationalisms emerge on the heels of empire, in the emerging story of industrial ecological wastelands, and in the ongoing spread of democratic secularism.

Until the twentieth century, at most connecting points with world history, Russia is at the fringes, like Africa. It becomes a question of the influence of worldwide trends on Russia and their particularization to a given Russian situation. Even in the twentieth century, while Russia is a central player, it is probably still not a contributor in the big picture. In fact, the Russian soul finds its uniqueness in this particular historical situation—a soul characterized by xenophobia, isolation, and exceptionalism. More than one Russian thinker has pondered the peculiarities of Russian history, and many have found their explanations in geography. An enormous land mass, but beyond the hospitable climate zone, blessed with resources but beyond extraction capabilities, size which breeds unfulfilled dreams of greatness and encourages bureaucracy, Russia is neither East nor West according to these writers, a land in search of a place in the world. So it remains in world history at the macro level.

Besides the macro level, that is noting how world trends are played out in Russian history, it is possible also to approach Russia in world history from the micro level. That is, it is possible to think about how internal Russian history reflects world trends. In this respect, the conversion to Christianity by Vladimir can illustrate larger world trends connected with the spread of Christianity, the politics and trade of the Byzantine Empire, and the pressures of Islam on the Christian world. The tartarization of Russia during the Mongol yoke can illustrate how the internal politics of a country can be altered by conquest and destruction, creating a national liberation myth strong enough to justify autocracy. Westernization by Peter and Catherine can reflect how secular patterns in the West were incorporated into a system of state rather than pluralistic economic, political, and social control. Modernization by means of emancipation during the reign of Alexander II can tell a worldwide story of the leap from agrarian societies into industrial societies, with its consequential stillborn merchant phase. The application and interpretation of socialism in Russia by Lenin can reflect both the peculiarities of the Russian situation and the similarities with other twentieth century societies which have also adopted and adapted socialism to their situation. Finally, industrialization Russian style, whereby capital formation is made by collectivization, can serve as an interpretive model for other developing countries of the twentieth century world.

Besides integrating Russian history by means of the macro or micro approach, that is, by taking world trends and mirroring them in Russia, or alternately taking Russian trends and mirroring them in the world, there are other ways to do this. A fertile approach might be comparative. Some topics which might prove extremely beneficial to world history in general are: comparisons of slavery and serfdom and the path to emancipation and its consequences, exploration and discovery in its comparative context including motivation and consequences, comparative paths to modernization, comparative communism, comparative nationalism and rule of multinational states, comparative agrarian and imperial systems, comparative religiously legitimized states and so on. Finally, it is possible to think in terms of topics and themes important to twenty-first century world history like the Green Revolution which could be told in terms of the Virgin Lands project, ecology and environment which could be related to the desiccation of the Aral Sea and pollution in Lake Baikal, LDC (less developed country) and NIC (newly industrializing country) themes to which Russia relates in its retarded market system and infrastructure, regional trade networks now being developed within a republican political structure, world youth culture to which Russia is linked by music, video and clothes, telecommunications and space, and so on.

The methods and habits of thought pertinent to integrating Russia into world history can be useful generally in world history. Various particular histories can be used as illustration of world trends, as histories reflective of world trends, as comparative studies and as launch pads for future areas of research and study in world history. Particular histories remain important in world history as fundamental parts of the story, but as the world moves in its form from a nation-state world to a more global one, questions asked by national histories must become broader and research must no longer be tied to the boundaries of nation-states.

Vladimir Ilich Ulyanov
(Lenin).
Library of Congress

236

Sample Student Activities

> **I.** *Reform, revolution, and social change in the world economy of the early century.*

A. The world industrial economy emerging in the early 20th century.

Grades 5-6

▶ List the major industrial nations of the world at the turn of the century. Draw evidence from art works, photographs, and documentary films to examine the ways of life of people in these industrialized countries.

▶ List commodities of trade such as rubber, tin, sugar, wheat, palm oil, ivory, coal, iron ore, gold, and diamonds. Locate on a map major regions of the world where these commodities were produced or extracted in the early 20th century. *What was the importance of international trade at that time?*

▶ Recount the main events of the Russo-Japanese War. *What effect did the war have on Russia? On Japan? What role did President Theodore Roosevelt play in ending the conflict? How did the war change the European and American view of Japan?*

Grades 7-8

▶ Identify industrial outputs of Britain, France, Germany, the United States, and Japan in the early 20th century and examine the importance of industrialization in these northern hemisphere nations. Write an essay examining the importance of industrial development in the modern world.

▶ Research the life of a leading European conservative, liberal, or socialist at the beginning of the century such as Stanley Baldwin, Ramsay MacDonald, Emmeline Pankhurst, Jean Jaures, Raymond Poincaré, Peter Stolypin, Alfred Krupp, or Rosa Luxemburg. *How did the selected individual influence political or social policy in pre-war Europe?*

▶ Examine the impact of Japan's victories in the Sino-Japanese and Russo-Japanese wars on industrialization and economic development of Japan. *How did the annexation of Taiwan and a sphere of influence in Korea affect Japan's economy?*

▶ Define the "welfare state" in terms of liberal ideals of the early 20th century. *What programs were promoted by early 20th-century liberals? How did these programs differ from those of "classical" liberalism?*

▶ Prepare a chart illustrating the agricultural products and raw materials of Latin American states. *On what were the economies of Latin American states based? What countries had large investments in Latin America? Why did Latin American nations fail to develop industrial economies at the turn of the century?*

Grades 9-12

▶ Examine the role of government in the industrial nations of the Northern Hemisphere in promoting social legislation. Debate the efficacy of Social Security, minimum wage laws, compulsory free public education, and state-financed public works from the point of view of a liberal and a conservative in the early 20th century.

▶ Research the impact of new technology on labor, capital investment, and industrial production. *What social changes resulted from technological developments in manufacturing? How did these changes affect the standard of living?*

◗ Examine how changes regarding land ownership and government promotion of new technology in Japan in the late 19th century encouraged industrial development. *What impact did government subsidies have in promoting Japanese industry? How did Japan's industrial leaders influence government policy? In what ways was the industrial development of Japan similar to mid- and late-19th century industrialization in Western Europe and the United States?*

◗ Examine the policy of a European country toward industrial development of its colonial possessions. Prepare a position paper assessing policies that promoted or retarded industrial development from the perspective of a member of the colonial office or a prominent citizen in the colonized nation. *Did the policy promote or retard the development of an industrial economy? To what extent was the colonial policy similar to or different from those of the British during the pre-American Revolutionary era?*

B. The causes and consequences of important resistance and revolutionary movements of the early 20th century.

Grades 5-6

◗ Assume the role of a Russian worker in 1905 and describe the events of that year. *Would you have supported the Revolution of 1905?*

◗ Research the lives of Francisco Madero, Emiliano Zapata, and Francisco Villa and write accounts of the role each played in the Mexican Revolution.

◗ Write a biography of Dr. Sun Yatsen. *Why is he called the "Father of Modern China"?*

◗ Study the murals and paintings of Diego Rivera and José Clemente Orozco. *Did this work celebrate the Mexican Revolution and the Mexican nation? How? How might such works of art create support for the revolution among the peasants?*

Grades 7-8

◗ Construct posters and banners representing the issues raised by Russian workers in 1905 and describe the events of "Bloody Sunday." *As a Russian worker, how would you have reacted to the events of "Bloody Sunday"? What were the consequences of the "Revolution of 1905"?*

◗ Research the life of Csar Nicholas II. *What beliefs or principles motivated his actions? How did he react to the revolution of 1905? What personal steps did he take? What political actions did he take?*

◗ Compare motivations of the peasants and the middle class in the Mexican Revolution. *How did peasants play a prominent role? What became the goals of the Mexican Revolution?*

◗ Investigate the New Culture movement in China. *Who were the leaders of the movement? What were its goals? Why did it fail to win support in rural areas?*

◗ Assume the role of a peasant supporting the Mexican or Chinese revolution and create a protest poster or banner that express the reforms you are demanding. *Is there a common theme among the peasants' demands?*

◗ Research the rise of the Young Turk movement and its attempts to restore constitutional government in Turkey. *To what segments of the population did the Young Turks appeal? Who were the leaders of the movement? How effective were the Young Turks in using nationalism as a means of promoting their cause?*

◆ Assume the role of a member of the British Foreign Office and defend a proposal for the measures British troops should take to respond to the guerrilla tactics employed by the Boers in South Africa. *What were the major causes of the war? What role did Africans play in the war? Why might this conflict be considered a "total war"?*

Grades 9-12

◆ Draw evidence from a variety of primary sources, and visual images from movies such as *Nicholas and Alexandra* and *Dr. Zhivago* to examine the Revolution of 1905. *What impact did the Russo-Japanese War have on discontent in Russia? What were the issues that led to "Bloody Sunday"? What groups of people supported political reform? What groups called for radical changes in Russia? How effective was the October Manifesto in meeting the demands of various groups of revolutionaries?*

◆ Examine illustrations of the murals depicting the Mexican Revolution by José Clemente Orozco, David Siqueros, and Diego Rivera, and explain how they were an expression of nationalism. *How do the muralists portray the revolution? Was the revolution a class struggle?*

◆ Write an essay analyzing the social and cultural ferment in China that culminated in the New Culture or May Fourth movement. *What were the consequences of the movement?*

◆ Use a variety of primary sources and excerpts from films such as *Breaker Morant* to examine British attitudes toward non-British people and the use of colonial troops in the Anglo-Boer War. *What were the consequences of the war for the Boers, the British, and the African populations?*

◆ Trace the roots of the Young Turk movement in Turkey. *What accounts for the success of the movement? What reforms did the Young Turks advocate? How effective were these reforms?*

◆ Draw evidence from Sun Yatsen's *Manifesto* for the Tong Meng Hui (Revolutionary Alliance) to examine the issues raised by the Chinese Revolution of 1911. *What four points were presented in the* Manifesto? *To whom did the revolutionary goals appeal? What were the "Three People's Principles"?*

II. *The causes and global consequences of World War I.*

A. The causes of World War I.

Grades 5-6

◆ Role-play situations when members of an alliance must come to the aid of one of its members. Discuss how the alliances worked or did not work. Locate on a map the two European alliances of World War I. *What are the advantages and disadvantages of an alliance? What geographic advantage did each alliance have? What countries made up the Allied Powers? The Central Powers?*

◆ Using a pyramid model, show how the assassination of Archduke Ferdinand of Austria led to world War I. Put the Archduke at the apex of the pyramid and include the countries of the two European alliances.

◆ On a map of Europe and Southwest Asia, locate the major areas of combat in World War I. *Why did a stalemate occur? What plans would you propose to break the stalemate?*

Grades 7-8

▸ Write a nationalist song expressing loyalty to your country. *How might the ideas or feelings you include in it affect your attitude toward other nations?*

▸ Construct a graphic organizer examining the long-range causes of World War I. Assuming the role of a nationalist leader of one of the major powers, write a speech defending your country's position on the eve of war.

▸ Examine the system of alliances through which nations in Europe sought to protect their interests, and explain how nationalism and militarism contributed to the outbreak of war. *What measure might have been taken to avert war? How did the war expand beyond European boundaries to become a world war?*

▸ Draw a map of the Austrian-Hungarian empire and its neighbors in 1914. Identify the ethnic groups living in this region. *How did neighboring ethnic groups tend to regard one another? What was the empire's policy towards its minorities? What did neighboring countries consider to be their legitimate national interests regarding these minorities?*

▸ On a world map identify conflicts and areas of competition between the major powers between 1900 and 1914. *How were crises resolved? Did they contribute to the outbreak of World War I?*

▸ Write a position paper from the perspective of one of the Allied or Central Powers in August 1914 explaining the immediate causes for your nation's entry into war.

Grades 9-12

▸ Assume the role of a political leader in either France, Germany, Britain, Austria-Hungary, or Russia and defend the recommendation that your government should press an active foreign policy in order to "smother internal problems." *How did ethnic conflicts in European states, particularly Austria-Hungary and Russia, contribute to the outbreak of war? How valid is the argument that the desire to suppress internal disorder encouraged some European political leaders to advocate war?*

▸ Debate the position that France should take regarding the war from the perspective of socialist leader Jean Juarès, French President Raymond Poincaré, or members of the rightist Action Française.

▸ Write an essay from the perspective of an idealist in early 1914 examining how the quality of life and advances in science and technology would preclude Europe from engaging in a major war. *To what extent did Europeans persuade themselves that a massive war was inconceivable?*

▸ Construct a timeline of major events that occurred and decisions made in Europe between June 28, 1914 and August 4, 1914. *Was the outbreak of war inevitable? Can you assign responsibility for the outbreak of war? How did the events and decisions of the summer of 1914 reflect long-term trends in European diplomatic history?*

▸ Examine the Schlieffen Plan. *Did the Schlieffen Plan contribute to the war's stalemate? Explain.*

▸ Debate the proposition that World War I was inevitable considering the nationalism, militarism, and imperialism of the day. *Did decision-makers in various European countries believe war was unavoidable? What were the miscalculations that ultimately led to the "war"?*

B. **The global scope, outcome, and human costs of the war.**

Grades 5-6

▶ On a world map locate the areas in which fighting occurred during World War I and identify the countries that fought in each of these regions.

▶ Assume the persona of one of the people in a photograph depicting trench warfare. Write a letter to a friend describing life in the trenches and your feelings regarding the war. *What might you see, taste, smell, and feel as you are writing this letter? What would you say to your family or friends in a letter that might be your last?*

▶ Draw evidence from photographs and paintings of the war's devastation to determine the cost of the war in terms of environmental damage.

▶ Create a visual timeline of the events of the war. *What do you think might have happened if the United States had not entered the war?*

Grades 7-8

▶ Design a propaganda poster that might have been used to mobilize civilians to support the war. *Why are they called "propaganda posters"?*

▶ Graphically show on a map of the world the principal theaters of the conflict, including Europe, the Middle East, Sub-Saharan Africa, and East Asia. *What were the major turning points of the war? How did the physical geography of a region affect the war?*

▶ Draw evidence from literature, recruiting posters, popular graphics, and songs to examine changing attitudes toward the war in Europe or the United States. *Why were men so eager to enlist at the beginning of the war? What caused a change in their attitudes as the war progressed?*

▶ Examine primary sources, including excerpts from Woodrow Wilson's war message, to determine the reasons why the United States entered the war.

▶ List the new and improved weapons of warfare and explain how technological advances made World War I an unusually brutal war. *How did weapons like "Big Bertha," poison gas, tanks, machine guns, airplanes, and submarines change warfare? How effective were these weapons of war?*

▶ Analyze photographs and paintings of battle scenes in order to explain the nature of the war in Europe. Investigate how technological developments employed in the "Great War" contributed to its brutality.

Grades 9-12

▶ Construct a flow chart comparing strategies of the Allies and Central Powers at the beginning of the war and identify at which point those strategies changed and why.

▶ Research military units made up of colonial subjects who fought with the Allies during World War I. *Why did the Allies call upon people living in their colonial empires to fight? Were the colonial units integrated with European units? As a person living under colonial rule, how would you have responded to an appeal to fight? What would you have expected as a result of helping the colonial power in the conflict?*

▶ Compare casualty figures from World War I with those of other wars. *Why was there such a heavy death toll in World War I?*

▶ Draw upon books such as Erich Maria Remarque's *All Quiet on the Western Front* to describe the physical and mental effects of trench warfare.

▶ Infer from a study of posters and cartoons in what ways and to what extent women's social status and occupations changed during the war. Evaluate the reliability of conclusions based on this evidence.

▶ Comparing newspaper editorials, poster art, and cartoons from the perspective of the Allies and Central Powers, discuss divergent views on how the Russian Revolution affected the war.

C. The causes and consequences of the Russian Revolution of 1917.

Grades 5-6

▶ Compile a list of the causes of the Communist Revolution. *If you had been a member of the republican government following the February Revolution of 1917, what action would you have proposed to address these issues?*

▶ Research the lives of Russian leaders such as Csar Nicholas II, Rasputin, and Lenin, and create biographical sketches or poems examining their importance in Russian history.

▶ Explain how Joseph Stalin rose to power in the Soviet Union. *What policies and actions did he undertake to maintain power?*

▶ Draw evidence from stories about life in the Soviet Union under Stalin. Assume the role of a Russian student in the 1930s and write a secret letter to a friend in another country telling about life in the USSR.

Grades 7-8

▶ Using biographies, examine Rasputin's role in determining Russian policy. *What influence did Rasputin have in the imperial court? How did Rasputin represent Russian mysticism?*

▶ Create epitaphs for the family of Csar Nicholas II. *What is the mystery surrounding one of his daughters, Anastasia? What historical evidence, if any, supports the belief that Anastasia survived?*

▶ Draw from books such as Felice Holman's *The Wild Children* to describe how Russian life changed after the Bolshevik Revolution.

▶ Use excerpts from George Orwell's *Animal Farm* to investigate the discontent in Russia at the time of the revolution. *How do the farm animals represent characters in the Russian Revolution?*

▶ Explain Lenin's New Economic Policy. Using a Venn diagram or T-Chart, compare and contrast the New Economic Policy with Stalin's Five-Year Plan.

▶ Research Stalin's policy of collectivization. *How did Stalin change Lenin's policy? How did the Kulaks resist collectivization? What were the consequences of their resistance?*

Grades 9-12

▶ Compare and contrast the promises and platforms of Kerensky and Lenin in 1917. *What impact did the war have on Kerensky's program? How important was Lenin's promise of "land, bread, peace"?*

▶ Based on historical evidence, role-play a dialogue focusing on attitudes toward the Russian Revolution among a Red, a White, and a British, French, or Japanese soldier sent to intervene in the Russian civil war.

▶ Examine Lenin's program following the October Revolution and compare it with Marxist doctrines. *What accounts for the differences in Lenin's communist program? Why did Lenin fail to follow a doctrinaire Marxist economic policy?*

▶ Compare Lenin's statements concerning women's equality with statistics on women in the labor force and in education in the Soviet Union.

▶ Assess the degree to which Stalin succeeded in his objective of bringing the USSR to industrial parity with the West. Compare Soviet industrialization to that of other nations. *How was the Soviet model different? What methods of coercion did Stalin use to industrialize?*

◗ Drawing evidence from recently released documents, assess the human cost of Stalinist totalitarianism in the Soviet Union in the 1920s and 1930s. *How has our knowledge of Stalin's regime changed with the de-Stalinizations programs initiated by Khrushchev? How have documents released in the 1990s furthered our understanding of the Stalinist era?*

◗ Research statements by Americans who visited the Soviet Union in the 1920s. *What reactions did they have to developments there? How did reactions differ?*

III.   The search for peace and stability in the 1920s and 1930s.

A.   Postwar efforts to achieve lasting peace and social and economic recovery.

Grades 5-6

◗ On a map draw the boundaries of European nations after the peace treaties ending World War I. Compare this map with a prewar map of Europe. *Which countries were winners? Which were losers?*

◗ Assuming the role of a representative of Britain, France, Japan, Italy, or the United States at Versailles, write an editorial expressing the hope your nation has for peace.

◗ Explain the goals of the League of Nations. Write a letter defending or opposing the League of Nations. *What countries became charter members of the League? What major countries were not members of the League? Why did they not join?*

◗ Write a poem or biographical sketch about one of the women who was active in the women's suffrage movement around the world. *What were her hopes and dreams? How did she work to achieve her goals?*

Grades 7-8

◗ Role-play discussions at the Versailles conference regarding reparation payments and Woodrow Wilson's Fourteen Points. *How did the representatives of the "Big Five Powers" stand on these issues? Why did China object to the settlement? What was Germany's response?*

◗ Write a protest ballad that captures the feeling of the women's suffrage movement. *Why is music such a strong medium for expressing political issues?*

◗ Investigate United States foreign policy following the war. Stage a debate on the topic, "Should the United States isolate itself from European affairs?" *Why did the U.S. adopt an isolationist policy in the postwar era? How different was this policy from that of the prewar era?*

Grades 9-12

◗ Contrast the treaties ending World War I with Woodrow Wilson's Fourteen Points. *Why did France and Britain insist on reparations for all direct and indirect costs of the war? Why did Turkey refuse to accept the Treaty of Sevres? Why was Italy dissatisfied with the provisions of the peace settlements? How did peoples in the colonial empires react to the failure of the settlements to address their concerns?*

◗ Identify major refugee populations created as a result of World War I and trace their movements and dispersion.

▶ Compare maps of southern Europe and the Middle East before and after World War I. *How closely did the new borders reflect the European powers' "spheres of interest" before the war? What long- and short-term interest influenced the decision-making process? To what extent did inhabitants of the region bring influence to bear upon the major powers?*

▶ Discuss the goals and assess the successes of the "racial equality clause" in the preamble to the Covenant of the League of Nations.

▶ Investigate reactions in China to the provisions of the Versailles Peace Treaty. *Why were the demonstrations that followed the treaty regarded as the first expression of nationalism in China? What attracted Chinese intellectuals to Marxist-Leninist theory?*

▶ Investigate the effects of industrial conversion from war to peace in Britain, France, Italy, and Germany and how the war affected the international economy. *What effect did German inflation have on the Weimar Republic? How did the U. S. help to improve the economic situation in Europe? How strong was the economic recovery between 1924 and 1929? Did all European powers share in the relative prosperity of the era?*

B. Economic, social, and political transformations in Africa, Asia, and Latin America in the 1920s and 1930s.

Grades 5-6

▶ Compare political maps of Africa before and after World War I. *What changes occurred? How did these changes affect peoples living in East and West Africa?*

▶ Explain what is meant by the term "mandate" and by the League of Nations mandate system in the Middle East. *What areas became French mandates? British mandates? What countries became independent?*

Grades 7-8

▶ Write an editorial either urging your government either to establish or not establish colonies. Include reasons for your views as well as the benefits and drawbacks of the recommended course of action. *How would you justify your government ruling other peoples?*

▶ Prepare a timeline showing important events in the growth of the Chinese Communist Party from 1927 to 1949. Map the areas controlled by the Kuomintang and Chinese Communist Party after the Long March in 1934, and infer what social classes were the major supporters of each.

▶ Assume the role of either Jiang Jieshi or Mao Zedong and write an appeal either to Washington or Moscow for support.

▶ Research the career of Abd al-Krim, the Moroccan resistance leader of the 1920s. *Why did he challenge Spanish rule in northern Morocco? What tactic did his fighting forces use? Why was he finally defeated? Was he a nationalist leader?*

▶ Construct a map of the Caribbean and indicate areas in which the United States intervened in the first two decades of the 20th century. *What factors led to intervention? What were the short-term and long-range consequences of the intervention?*

Grades 9-12

▶ Based on historical evidence, debate the following proposition: Japan's democracy fell victim to the country's imperialist foreign policy.

▶ Debate issues from the perspective of the Kuomintang and Chinese Communist Party before groups reflecting the interests of Chinese landlords, peasants, urban workers, and entrepreneurs, and attempt to persuade them to support your cause. *To whom did the Kuomintang and Chinese Communist Party appeal? To what extent did the Japanese invasion of China in the 1930s change viewpoints regarding the two conflicting ideologies?*

- Read excerpts from Mao Zedong's *Report on an Investigation of the Peasant Movement in Hunan* (1927). Discuss Mao's understanding of the peasants as a revolutionary force. Compare Mao's analysis of the potential of the peasantry with classic Marxist theory. Discuss how his adaptation of Marxism fits the Chinese situation. Analyze his emergence as a major force in the Communist movement.

- Compare and contrast the Republican Revolution of 1911-12, the Nationalist Revolution of 1925-1928, and the Communist Revolution of 1949 in terms of who was involved, what were the goals, and to what extent the goals were achieved.

- Compare maps of southern Europe and the Middle East before and after World War I. *How closely do the new borders reflect the Great Powers' "spheres of interest" before the war? What long- and short-term interests influenced the decision-making process? How did inhabitants of the region influence the major European actors?*

- Develop a case study of a Latin American nation in the first quarter of the 20th century. Examine its political system, economic development, and class divisions. *How did foreign relations with the United States change during this period?*

- Compare the Hussein-McMahon correspondence and the Sykes-Picot agreement and contrast these with the settlements reached in the treaties of Versailles and San Remo with regard to the Middle East. *What purposes did these diplomatic efforts serve each party to the negotiations?*

- Prepare a report on the methods and successes of Ataturk's program of modernization in Turkey. Write an interview with a "person on the street," assessing reaction to his policies. *What effects did the appearance of the nation-state of Turkey have on international relations?*

C. The interplay between scientific or technological innovations and new patterns of social and cultural life between 1900 and 1940.

Grades 5-6

- Identify the new technologies of the early 20th century and explain how they altered lifestyles. *To what extent did technology bring people closer together? What impact did the automobile have?*

- Construct a chart listing the major scientific and technological advances at the turn of the century. *How did these innovations in science, medicine, and industry affect peoples' lives? What would our life be like today without these innovations?*

- Investigate the life of a scientist or inventor such as Thomas Edison, Marie Curie, Albert Einstein, or Guglielmo Marconi. *How did the work of the person you selected change society?*

Grades 7-8

- Write a series of biographical sketches entitled "Great Scientists of the Early 20th Century." Aim your writing to an audience of third graders. *What did each scientist contribute to our knowledge? What earlier theory did each challenge?*

- Construct a timeline of major discoveries in science and medicine in the first half of the 20th century. *Which were the most significant? Why? How did these discoveries affect the quality of life?*

- Make a chart identifying major medical advances of the period 1900-1940. *Which diseases were eliminated? Which were not? To what extent were these developments the work of large-scale research laboratories rather than of individuals?*

▶ Write a series of journal entries for people who migrated within and between different parts of the world between 1900-1940. *What different kinds of motives did they have? What role did technology have in their decisions and experiences?*

▶ Research the propaganda techniques (such as the "Big Lie") used by the Nazis. *How did they apply them at rallies? On the radio? In movies? What images were used in movies to broadcast their message? How was Nazi propaganda similar to or different from Soviet propaganda under Stalin?*

Grades 9-12

▶ After viewing Lawrence Olivier's "Hamlet," discuss the film as a Freudian interpretation of Shakespeare.

▶ Create a "World Airline Atlas" identifying the development of airline routes in the years 1920, 1930, and 1940. Compare the relative significance of airplanes, trains, and ships in the transporting of goods and people in each year.

▶ Produce a mail order catalogue for the year 1928 to be distributed to middle class families in England. *To what extent do the items advertised diminish differences between rural and urban people? What evidence is there that a global economy was developing?*

▶ Research the theory and practice of Social Realism in Soviet art. *Why did Stalin support this style? How did this art form serve as political propaganda?*

▶ Read a series of Franklin Roosevelt fireside chats with the American public and Hitler's speeches broadcast on German radio. *How does each try to persuade his audience?*

▶ Analyze excerpts from such texts as Civilization and Its Discontents by Sigmund Freud. *How did Freud's development of psychoanalytic method and his theories of the unconscious change prevailing views of human motives and human nature?*

D. The interplay of new artistic and literary movements with changes in social and cultural life in various parts of the world in the post-war decade.

Grades 5-6

▶ View and discuss the art of Henri Matisse and Pablo Picasso. *How are their techniques different from previous artists? What are some of these techniques?* Using one of their techniques create a picture that represents a cultural theme of today.

▶ Investigate how people spent their leisure time in the first half of the 20th century. *How did radio and motion pictures affect the way people spent their time? Did most people participate in sports or were they spectators? What were the popular sports of the period? How similar were leisure activities in the first half of the century from those today?*

▶ Draw evidence from documentary photographs to examine changes in clothing and styles in the first half of the 20th century. Imagine you were in a "Rip Van Winkle sleep" for nearly a half century. Awakened in 1940, describe the changes you observe. *How drastic were the changes in men and women's styles? What do these changes reveal about attitudes and values of the period?*

Grades 7-8

▶ Research one of the popular media of the interwar period: newspapers, magazines, commercial advertising, film, and radio. Develop a report on how it contributed to the rise of mass culture around the world. Use the same format for your report as the chosen media.

▶ Write parallel biographies or create a multi-media program of two artists, architects, musicians, or writers of the early 1900s and compare their styles and the impact of their works.

▶ Assemble a collection of examples of early 20th-century art from different parts of the world. Explain how the art styles and media of expressions were similar or different. *What art forms were used to convey support for a social, political, or economic philosophy?*

Grades 9-12

▶ Explain the expression "Lost Generation" in the post-World War I era. *What were the themes of "Lost Generation" writers? How did post-war society influence their works? What impact did their works have?*

▶ Select excerpts from the works of such writers as Bertolt Brecht, e.e. cummings, Robert Graves, Ernest Hemingway, or Erich Maria Remarque, and analyze how their works express post-war social and cultural attitudes.

▶ Research the Dada or surrealist movements and establish their connections with the war.

▶ Research a leading musician and one or more of his or her works that were popular in the first half of the 20th century. *How did their music reflect cultural trends? What impact did the musical work have in different parts of the world?*

▶ Compile a list of major directors and performers in Hollywood in the 1920s and 1930s. *Which ones arrived there from other countries? What techniques, styles, and themes did they develop in cinema? Were American films seen widely in other countries?*

E. The causes and global consequences of the Great Depression.

Grades 5-6

▶ Create a wall newspaper reflecting the worldwide economic crisis of the Great Depression. *How did the depression affect different countries in the world?*

▶ Assemble a collage of pictures showing human suffering and courage during the worldwide economic depression.

Grades 7-8

▶ Examine art works and photographs depicting hunger and poverty, such as those by German artist Käthe Kollwitz, Mexican muralist José Clemente Orozco, and American photographer Dorothea Lange. *How do you think individuals and families coped with the hardships of the depression?*

▶ Create a model to explore the chain-reaction of a depression in a highly industrialized economy and how it affected countries that relied on trade of commodities such as rubber, coffee, and sugar. *How were countries that depended on foreign markets and foreign capital investment affected by the depression?*

▶ Compare graphs of changes in industrial production in different countries between 1920 and 1940. *What conclusions could be drawn from the statistical information?*

▶ Draw evidence from poster art to illustrate how economic depression contributed to the growth of fascist and communist movements in different parts of the world.

▶ Appraise the following quotation attributed to Hermann Göring: "Ore has always made an empire strong. Butter and lard have made people fat at best." *What is the meaning of the quotation? How would you respond to Göring?*

Grades 9-12

▶ Using audio or video tape, interview a family member or neighbor who lived through the depression. *How did economic conditions affect this person's employment or family life? How did the person's family cope with hard times? How did a church or other group provide support during the depression?*

▶ Prepare a table showing ways in which the world depression affected the United States, Germany, and Japan. Show both the effects of the depression and how each country responded to them.

▶ Develop a case study comparing the effects of the Great Depression on an industrial and an agrarian nation. *How severe was its impact in each of the selected countries? Did it have the same impact worldwide? Why or why not?*

▶ Research the impact of the depression on international trade. *What was the effect of the United States' enactment of the Smoot-Hawley Tariff? How did other nations respond to the U.S. tariff? What effect did the tariff have on international trade? On economic recovery?*

▶ Examine statistics reflecting military production in the 1930s in nations such as Britain, Germany, Japan, the Soviet Union, and the United States. *To what extent was the military-industrial complex created as a means of stimulating recovery from the Great Depression?*

IV. Causes and global consequences of World War II.

A. The causes of World War II.

Grades 5-6

▶ Explain major characteristics of different forms of government such as communism, democracy, fascism, and socialism. Create a poster of one of these ideologies.

▶ Describe Mussolini, Hitler, and Franco's rise to power in their respective countries. *How did Mussolini and Hitler come to control their governments? How was Franco's rise to power different?*

▶ Draw on excerpts from such books as Judith Kerr's *When Hitler Stole Pink Rabbit* to describe Nazi oppression in Germany.

Grades 7-8

▶ Compare and contrast the steps that led to the ascendance of Mussolini and Hitler, and explain the statement, "Hitler's success grew out of the German people's despair." *What other factors help explain Hitler's rise to power?*

▶ On a map of the post-World War I world indicate the territorial ambitions of Italy, Germany, and Japan. *How would the German concept of* lebensraum *affect Eastern Europe? Why would attempts to extend influence or annex new territories cause international problems? How did other major powers react to seizure of land by Italy, Japan, and Germany?*

▶ Examine the reaction of Britain, France, the United States, and the Soviet Union to fascist aggression. Write a position paper from one of the major powers explaining policies that should be taken to stop aggression. *Why did the major powers fail to stop aggression?*

▶ Construct a timeline of international events from the Japanese seizure of Manchuria in 1931 to the Nazi-Soviet Non-Aggression Pact of August 1939. Analyze how each of these events may have contributed to the outbreak of World War II.

▶ On a world map illustrate the German, Italian, and Japanese advances between the invasion of Poland in 1939 and the fall of Singapore in 1942. *What accounts for Axis victories in the early years of the war?*

Grades 9-12

‣ Using historical evidence such as excerpts from *Mein Kampf* and Nazi Party platforms, identify elements of Nazi ideology. Explain the use of terror as a technique for gaining and keeping power.

‣ Using excerpts from Leni Reifenstahl's films, identify what propaganda techniques were used to promote Nazi ideas.

‣ Draw evidence from speeches and writings from Italy or Germany in the 1920s and 1930s to examine the debates among political factions over the fate of the nation. *What role did nationalism play in the fascist drive for power? How did the economic situation in either Italy or Germany affect the political debate? What parties stood in opposition to Mussolini and Hitler? What strategies did they employ to stop the fascists? Why did they fail?*

‣ Draw evidence from a variety of sources including George Orwell's *Homage to Catalonia* and novels or short stories by Ernest Hemingway to examine the human costs of the Spanish Civil War. *To what extent did foreign intervention affect the outcome of the war?*

‣ Debate the *Diktat* thesis that the harshness of the Versailles agreement made revolt against its provisions inevitable.

‣ Present arguments to support or reject Japan's Greater East Asia Co-prosperity Sphere." *As an individual in a European colony in East Asia, how would you react to the Japanese initiative? Might you feel differently in 1942 than in 1937?*

‣ Examine newspaper and magazine reports on international issues from the Munich Conference to the declaration of war in September 1939. *What were the consequences of the Munich Agreement? What was Stalin's perception of the Munich Agreement? To what extent did this lead to the Non-Aggression Pact of August 1939?*

‣ Debate the following proposition as if you were English or French in 1938: "Resolved: the best way to ensure peace is to negotiate with the Axis to relieve their legitimate grievances."

B. Global scope, outcome, and human costs of the war.

Grades 5-6

‣ On a world map locate the turning points for the allied forces during World War II. *How important were these events in changing the course of the war?*

‣ Review the treatment of children during the Holocaust and share poems from the book *I Never Saw Another Butterfly*. Illustrate one of the poems.

‣ As part of a group draw up a Declaration of Human Rights for Children. Discuss: *Would it be possible for the world to honor such a document? Is there such a document in existence today? Would there ever be situations when human rights should not be honored?*

‣ Use books such as Monika Kotowska's *The Bridge to the Other Side* to discuss the human costs of war and the resulting social problems.

‣ Investigate the career of a World War II leader such as Winston Churchill, Charles DeGaulle, Franklin Roosevelt, Harry Truman, or Dwight Eisenhower. *How did the individual's leadership affect the course of the war?*

Grades 7-8

‣ Drawing from books such *Cigarette Sellers of Three Crosses Square* by Joseph Ziemian and *Children of the Resistance* by Lore Cowan, describe the ways in which Jews and other Europeans resisted the Nazis and their policies.

‣ Use books such as Grigory Baklanov's *Forever Nineteen* to discuss the experiences of soldiers fighting in World War II.

▶ Compare Nazi public announcements concerning Jews during 1941-44 with Holocaust survivors' accounts of their experiences during this period.

▶ Conduct research on the impact of World War II on science, technology, transportation, communication, or medicine. Create class projects illustrating research findings.

▶ Use *The Diary of a Young Girl* by Anne Frank to assess the personal impact of Nazi occupation of Europe. *How did Anne Frank's experiences differ from those of Jews living in other occupied countries of Europe?*

▶ Read the Potsdam Declaration and assess its importance in the Japanese decision to surrender.

Grades 9-12

▶ Develop an annotated timeline of the history of the Nazi's "war on the Jews." Construct a map depicting the location and scale of Jewish deaths resulting from the implementation of Nazi policy.

▶ Use books such as Thomas Keneally's *Schindler's List* to describe why some people were motivated to defy Nazi orders while other complied or failed to object to Hitler's "final solution."

▶ Drawing upon books such as Alexander Ramati's *And the Violins Stopped Playing: A Story of the Gypsy Holocaust* and Elie Wiesel's *Night*, examine the personal stories of Holocaust victims and the brutality of Nazi genocide.

▶ Identify the battles you consider turning points in both the Atlantic and Pacific theaters of the war, and explain your choices.

▶ Debate the moral implications of the use of military technologies in World War II such as the bombing of civilian populations in order to shorten the war.

▶ Construct a map showing the direction and scale of population displacements resulting from World War II.

▶ Debate the following issue: The United States was right to use the atomic bomb to end the war with Japan.

▶ Research the experiences of prisoners of war held in Britain, Germany, Japan, the Soviet Union, and the United States. *How were prisoners of war treated differently in these countries? How might these differences be explained?*

V.   *Major global trends from 1900 to the end of World War II.*

Major global trends from 1900 to the end of World War II.

Grades 5-6

▶ Examine political maps of the world in 1900, 1920, and 1945. *What new countries appeared? What countries disappeared? Why did these changes occur? Which of the three maps most closely resembles the world today?*

▶ Construct posters to represent the major new technologies and scientific discoveries of the first half of the 20th century. *Was the new technology used to benefit society? Did inventions involving weapons of destruction sometimes have other uses? How have men and women today used these scientific advances to benefit society?*

Grades 7-8

♦ On a bar graph, represent industrial and agricultural production in various parts of the world in 1900 and in 1945. *What changes do you observed in the leading centers of economic power?*

♦ Conduct a debate on the following proposition: "Resolved: Scientific developments in the first half of the 20th century have made the world a better place to live."

♦ Research an independence movement in East, Southeast, South or the Middle East. Study such topics as leadership, organization, symbols, slogans, ideology, and methods. Draw a poster which uses this information to arouse support for independence. *To what extent did independence movements grow out of local values and traditions? To what extent were they influenced by European ideas?*

♦ Write a series of diary entries for a worker or farmer who was born in 1900 and lived through World War I, the Great Depression, and World War II. Select a country where your worker or farmer lived, such as the United States, Canada, Britain, France, Germany, Japan, India, Turkey, Nigeria, South Africa, Mexico, or Brazil. *To what values or institutions did your person turn for support during bad times?*

♦ Make an inventory of the items found in the house of a prosperous merchant in Mexico City, Berlin, Istanbul, Calcutta, and Singapore in 1900. Update the list for 1940. *What accounts for the similarities and differences between cities and times?*

♦ Make a timeline from 1900-1940 of international conferences and agreements intended to maintain world peace. Make another timeline of actions and events that led to war. *What factors underlay the efforts represented by each timeline?*

Grades 9-12

♦ Write an essay in response to this question: Which ruler exercised the most complete power within his state, Napoleon or Hitler? Explain.

♦ On world maps, represent the relative industrial and military strengths of the major powers and alliance systems in 1900 and 1945. *What factors are included in your assessment of relative strength? What explains the differences on the maps?*

♦ Conduct a roundtable discussion on the theme: "What human progress means to me." Participants might include Karl Barth, Mussolini, Trotsky, Mao Zedong, Ataturk, Pope Leo XIII, John Maynard Keynes, and Franklin Roosevelt.

♦ In the role of a 20th-century revolutionary leader, engage in a dialogue with Thomas Jefferson or Robespierre on your goals for creating a more just society. *On what positions do you agree? In what ways are your disagreements the result of differing circumstances?*

♦ Read the 14 Points and the Atlantic Charter. *In what ways are their principles comparable? To what extent did the agreements ending each war implement those principles? Were those principles compatible with the actual distribution of wealth and power in the world?*

♦ Compare and contrast the development of Communist parties in Russia, Germany, Vietnam, and China between 1900 and 1945. *To whom did each appeal? How effectively were they resisted? What programs did they sponsor? How were they structured? How did they accommodate the ideal of nationalism into their programs?*

ERA 9

The 20th Century Since 1945: Promises and Paradoxes

Giving Shape to World History

The closer we get to the present the more difficult it becomes to distinguish between the large forces of change and the small. Surveying the long sweep of history from early hominid times to the end of World War II, we might reach at least partial consensus about what is important to the development of the whole human community and what is not. The multifarious trends of the past half-century, however, are for the most part still working themselves out. Therefore, we cannot know what history students one or two hundred years from now will think was worth remembering about the decade after World War II. Clearly, the era has been one of tensions, paradoxes, and contradictory trends. Some of these countercurrents provide students with a framework for investigation and analysis.

▶ **Democracy and Tyranny:** In the three decades following World War II a multitude of new sovereign states appeared around the world. The breakup of the Soviet Union that began in 1990 introduced fifteen more. Triumphant nationalism, in short, has radically transformed the globe's political landscape. Even so, peoples on every continent have had to struggle persistently for democracy and justice against the powerful counterforces of authoritarianism, neo-colonialism, and stolid bureaucracy. Many of the newer independent states have also faced daunting challenges in raising their peoples' standard of living while at the same time participating in a global economic system where industrialized countries have had a distinct advantage. The political, and in some places economic, reform movements that bloomed in Africa, Eurasia, and Latin America in the 1980s are evidence of the vitality of civic aspirations that originated more than two centuries ago.

▶ **War and Peace:** World War II ended amid anxious hopes for genuine world peace. In 1945, however, the Cold War was already underway. For forty years recurrent international crises and the doubtful consolations of mutually assured destruction dominated world affairs. The European colonial empires were dismantled and power transferred to new nationalist leaders with less violence or acrimony than anyone might have expected—with some exceptions. Nationalists waged protracted anti-colonial wars in Vietnam, Algeria, Angola, and Mozambique. When the Soviet Union collapsed, the threat catastrophe receded and the world sighed in relief. On the other hand, local wars and terrorist assaults multiplied as ancient enemies settled old scores and ethnic or nationalist feelings rose to the surface. Amid the ruthless confrontations of the second half of the century, people of good will have continued to seek peace. The achievements and limitations of the post-World War II settlements, the United Nations, the European Economic Community, Middle East negotiations, and numerous other forms of international cooperation are all worthy of serious study for the lessons they may offer the coming generation.

▶ **Global Links and Communal Identity:** The transformations that the world experience in the previous three eras appear modest in comparison with the bewildering pace and complexity of change in the late 20th century. The revolution of global communication has potentially put everyone in touch with everyone else. Business travelers, scientists, labor migrants, and refugees move incessantly from country to country. Currency transfers ricochet from bank to bank. The young men and women of Bangkok, Moscow, and Wichita Falls watch the same movies and sport the same brand of jeans. In economy, politics, and culture the human community is in a continuous process of restructuring itself. Global interdependence, however, has a flip side. As the gales of change blow, people seek communal bonds and identities more urgently than ever. Communalism has frequently led to fear and suspicion of the "other." Even so, the institutions and values that communities share also protect them in some measure from the shocks of the new and unforeseen. The social and cultural bonds of family, village, ethnic community, religion, and nation provide a framework for estimating how others will think and behave and for calculating with some confidence the pattern of affairs from day to day.

▶ **Countercurrents in the Quality of Life:** The early 20th century promised, at least in the industrialized countries, a new age of progress through science, technology, and rational policy-making. Fifty years and two world wars later, humanity was less optimistic about its future. Art and literature after 1945 starkly reported the era's skepticism and angst. Science, medicine, and techniques of human organization continued to benefit society in wondrous ways. A truly global middle class emerged, and it enjoyed rising prosperity for several decades. Several countries, notably along the eastern Pacific rim, became economic powers to be reckoned with. On the other hand, the world population explosion, persistent poverty, environmental degradation, and epidemic disease have defied the best efforts of statesmanship, civic action, and scientific imagination. Amid the distresses and dangers of the era, people have sought not only communal ties but also moral and metaphysical certainties. Spiritual quests and ethical questionings have been a vital part of the cultural history of the past half-century.

Why Study This Era?

▶ The economic and social forces moving in our contemporary world will make sense to students only in relation to the rush of events since 1945. Historical perspectives on the Cold War, the breakup of empires, the population explosion, the rise of the Pacific rim," and the other sweeping developments of the era are indispensable for unraveling the causes and perhaps even discerning the likely consequences of events now unfolding. Students in school today are going to be responsible for addressing the promises and paradoxes of the age. They will not be able to do this by reading headlines or picking bits of "background" from the past. They must gain some sense of the whole flow of developments and build a mental architecture for understanding the history of the world.

Essay

"The New English Empire"*
The Economist, December 10, 1986

The growth of English as a world language exemplifies the development of a global culture in the 20th century. The official language of more than 40 countries, English is spoken by 330 million people. It is one of the two official languages of the United Nations, the language of the European Free Trade Association, and the language of modern science and international youth culture. This article explores factors that have propelled English as a universal language. It is suggested, partly in jest, that "English...is easy to speak badly," a requirement for a world language!

The worldwide spread of English is remarkable. There has been nothing like it in history. Spanish and French, Arabic and Turkish, Latin and Greek have served their turn as international languages, in the wake of the mission station, the trading post or the garrison. But none has come near to rivalling English

Four hundred years ago, English was the mother tongue of 7m speakers tucked away on a foggy island in Western Europe. Today, about 330m people throughout the world speak it as a mother tongue. That leaves it a distant second to Guoyo (Mandarin Chinese), which is estimated to have 750m speakers. But in international diffusion and acceptance, English is in a class of its own. Add to its 330m mother-tongue speakers the same number using English as a second language (ESL) and the same number again with reasonable competence in English as a foreign language (EFL), and you approach 1 billion English speakers.

As an official language, English serves more than 40 countries; French serves 27, Arabic 21 and Spanish 20. English is the language of international shipping and air travel. It is one of the two working languages of the United Nations (French is the other). And it has become the language of both international youth culture and science (two-thirds of all scientific papers are published in English).

Its appeal is irresistible: advancement in the civil or diplomatic service almost anywhere will be aided by a good grasp of English; preliminary trade negotiations between a Hungarian and a Kuwaiti will probably be conducted in English; half of all foreign-language courses in the Soviet Union are English courses; and a quarter of China's 1 billion people is engaged in studying English, in one way or other.

English, then, is a world language. What befits it for that role? It is chiefly, of course, thanks to the power of Britain in the nineteenth century and America in the twentieth. But English has spread far beyond its spheres of political influence in a way that French and Spanish have not. Luckily, English fits its role well, thanks to the structure of the language.

English is relatively easy to pronounce: it has few of the tongue-knotting consonant-clusters of Russian or the subtle tone-shiftings of Chinese. The basic syntax is fairly straightforward, too. Words can be readily isolated (Turkish words cannot), and they are relatively "stable" (having few of the inflections of Russian). English dispensed long ago with informal vocatives (*du, tu*) and with the gender-system (*der, die, das; le, la*) that most other European languages rejoice in and most students of them despair at.

---

*Reprinted by permission of the *New York Times* Syndicated Sales Service from *The Economist*, December 20, 1986, pp. 127-131.

The Roman alphabet is supple and economical (more efficient than the Arabic alphabet; easier to learn than the ideography of Chinese). The problem is spelling, which, for historical reasons, is out of kilter with pronunciation. *Ough* can be pronounced in at least seven different ways (*though, rough, thought, cough, hiccough, plough, through*).

The huge vocabulary, on the other hand, is no drawback to its use as a world language, though many people have sought to disqualify it on that ground. No one needs Shakespeare's command of the language for everyday communication. The more adept speaker can always adjust his register to suit the less adept.

English, in short, is easy to speak badly—and that is all that is required of a world language, if what you mean by a world language is an attenuated code, a means of transmitting and receiving simple information. English is the official language of the European Free Trade Association, composed of six countries none of which has English as a mother tongue. Its secretary-general says: "using English means we don't talk too much, since none of us knows the nuances."

As a means of more complex social exchange, however, English is, on the face of it, less well suited to being a true world language. Here, its vast vocabulary does begin to prove a formidable obstacle. Idioms—as in all languages—confront the learner with their opacity. English is particularly well endowed with idioms: *a dark horse, a horse of a different colour, hold your horses* and *from the horse's mouth*. And English has the added irritation of a plethora of phrasal and prepositional verbs. *Put someone down, put someone up, put up with someone, put someone up to something*: such "simple" phrases are much harder for students to grasp than the corresponding "advanced" vocabulary (*humiliate someone, accommodate someone, tolerate someone* and *incite someone to something*).

More recondite still is idiom itself—the deep, sometimes unanalysable determinants of natural construction and usage. Why is it acceptable to say "You'll succeed provided that you prepare sufficiently" but not "You'll fail provided that you prepare insufficiently"? Why do people say "a *very* affected lady"; "*much* affected by your kindness", and "*greatly* affected by a change in pressure"? Why should "I haven't got a clue" mean "I don't know" but "You haven't got a clue" mean "You're a fool"?

Whose English

Even in England, "standard English" has always been a will-o'-the-wisp. True, the language of south-eastern England began to acquire its prestige in Chaucer's time and, by the early days of the BBC, was so well established that the job of a radio announcer was closed to anyone whose accent was regional or not upper-middle class. But many linguists now reject the notion of a blanket uncountable noun "English," with its suggestion of a relatively homogenous language. They use instead the unlovely term "Englishes" which, in effect, challenges the very notion of an ideal English *tout court*.

Englishes are:

- **Pidgins and creoles.** Pidgins are makeshift. They started as elementary systems of communication between traders, explorers or soldier and suppliers, guides or slaves. The outsider's language—the "base" language—usually contributes 80% or more of the vocabulary, often in distorted form. *Pidgin* itself probably began life as a pidgin English word for *business*, hence the expression "That's not my pigeon." Syntax and pronunciation are often simplified by the constraints of the local vernacular.

A creole is a pidgin that has become a mother-tongue and developed into a sophisticated and well equipped language. The main fully-fledged English creoles are broad Creole in Jamaica, Krio in Sierra Leone and Tok Pisin in Papua New Guinea. English pidgins and creoles fall into two families: the Atlantic (in West Africa, the Caribbean, and parts of Nicaragua, Florida and Georgia); and the Pacific (spoken by Australian Aborigines, in Papua New Guinea and other Pacific islands, and formerly along the coast of China).

Educated creole speakers can shift back and forth along a kind of linguistic spectrum that stretches to standard English; their shift is mimicked by the communities as a whole. If the experience of black American English during the nineteenth century is anything to go by, all creole speakers may be drifting towards standard English (though, as if in rearguard action, a distinctive and energetic creole literature is emerging in both the Atlantic and Pacific families).

- **English as a foreign language.** EFL is big business. American universities offer PhDs in the teaching of it. In Britain, it earns dollops of foreign currency and goodwill. There is a quiet war going on between Britain and America over the international EFL market, with Australia increasing its share of EFL-teaching.

  The plum, China, has fallen to Britain: the BBC's "Follow Me" is probably the most widely followed teaching course in history. But the most lucrative market, Western Europe, seems to be changing from British English to American. The countries of Latin America keep faith with the American variety; even the partial-exception is swinging away from its traditional preference for British English; that odd-man-out is, or was, Argentina.

  It is impossible to be sure how many foreigners "know" English; 330m is a convenient speculation (though whatever number you choose, it is certainly rising rapidly every year). The reason is that the "linguistic spectrum" is wider in EFL than in any other kind of English. At one end lie the excited unintelligibilities of a souvenir-seller in Siena or Sao Paulo: at the other, the accented, but serene, fluency of a teacher from Tel Aviv or Tübingen.

- **English as a second language.** This is the English of the Commonwealth, the Philippines, Pakistan, and of American Hispanics, Pakistan, and of American Hispanics, Québecois, black South Africans, Afrikaners and so on. ESL is usually modelled on British English rather than American. The Philippines is the main exception; Liberia and Sierra Leone are partial exceptions.

  English acts as an instrument of national unity, a relatively neutral lingua franca. Tribal rivalries can be allayed more easily when neighbouring peoples—Hausas, Yorubas, and Ibos, for instance—can speak the same language. Understanding (comprehension) breeds understanding (tolerance).

  As the sun set on the British Empire, each newly independent country had to commit itself to an official language. English was usually entrenched as the language of education, the law and the civil service. Sometimes, it could be edged out—as in Tanzania by Swahili (a *lingua franca* anyway) and in Pakistan by Urdu (another *lingua franca*, though one spoken as a mother tongue by only 5m of the country's 90m inhabitants compared with 60m who use Punjabi as theirs). But such edging-out has not proved easy. Malaysia imposed Bahasa Malaysia (a standardised form of Malay) as a national language in the 1960s. Not only was this of doubtful fairness to the Chinese and Tamil minorities, it has also meant that young Malays, educated in Bahasa Malaysia to secondary school and beyond, are finding it hard to get places at English-speaking universities abroad.

India, with a dozen or more main indigenous languages, and more than 150 languages in all, resolved at independence to establish Hindi as its sole official national language by 1965. Hindi is the mother tongue of about a third of the population. But in 1965, the government conceded that English should, for the time being, remain an "associate official language." Professional advancement and social prestige among middle-class urban Indians still depend upon skill in English. In the southern states, where the indigenous languages are unrelated to Hindi, many people are reluctant to learn the northerners' tongue when it is more useful (and no harder) to learn English.

Indian English shows how one variety of the language can take on a life of its own while still remaining comprehensible to speakers of standard English (indeed, British English continues to coexist with the new indigenous form). Just as Australia, with its robust cultural self-confidence, has ceased looking over its linguistic shoulder at London, so India can now fairly lay claim to possessing a separate English (in a way that Nigeria, say, cannot yet do). Indian English occurs in writing, not just in speech, and might be adopted even by an author accustomed to writing standard British English.

The influence of Indian English is felt far beyond the Indian subcontinent. Foreign students studying at Indian colleges take it home with them. Thousands of Indian teachers elsewhere in Asia and in Africa spread it abroad. School and college textbooks are written in Indian English—they are even sometimes "translated" into Indian English from British and American English. This pleads eloquently on behalf of English's claim to be a true international language, not just a national language used internationally.

- **English as a mother tongue.** A Scot might say "Will I write a letter of complaint?" where an Englishman or North American would say "Should I write a letter of complaint?" Scots also, like South Africans, may say "Where do you stay?" when asking where you live. A Miami Beach realtor (estate agent), if she ever had occasion to refer to a hot-water bottle, might call it *a haat wáa-derr báa-dill*. A Cockney shop assistant (sales-clerk) call hers a *'o' wáw-uh bó-oo*. Cornishmen and Newfoundlanders speak of farmers as *varmers*.

The broadest divide in mother-tongue English lies between British English and American English. There are systematic differences of spelling (*colour/color, manoeuvre/maneuver*) and of pronunciation (*hostile* [Britons and Canadians distinguish it from *hostel*] and *ballet*). There are "morphological" differences: *aluminium/aluminum, zip/zipper, at a loose end/at loose ends*. Above all, there are lexical and idiomatic differences—*drawing pin/thumbtack, unit trust/mutual fund*.

These are straightforward enough. But the same word may have different meanings on different sides of the Atlantic. Or a word or phrase may have a common transAtlantic meaning, but have an additional sense in one variety that it lacks in the other. In British English, *majority* does service for a "relative majority" as well as for an "absolute majority." In American English, it means only an "absolute majority"; a "relative majority" is a *plurality*.

This asymmetry is best demonstrated by words or phrases that have suffered "semantic taint" on one side of the Atlantic but not on the other. A *rubber* refers to an eraser in British English; in American English, a condom. An American sociological study called "Women on the Job" had to be retitled when published in Britain.

Such differences take only a little application to identify and remember. But other subtleties are harder to master—even to define. Wilde's dictum about "two great countries divided by a common language" applies mostly to this twilight zone. Two examples must suffice, both tentative. First, the "register" of the word *toilet*: it seems to have a coarser ring to it in American English. Second, the size of a *pond*: in British English, any pool of water wider than about 40 yards would probably be called a *lake*; American English on the other hand, provides for much larger ponds.

Noah Webster and H. L. Mencken both thought that British and American English were diverging. That may have been true once, but is not longer. The changes can be traced by comparing the various vocabularies to do with communication. Before 1776, sailing terms were almost identical in both American and British English. In the nineteenth and early twentieth centuries, in a proud assertion of linguistic independence, American English chose to go its own way: hence the differences in *railway/railroad* vocabulary (*goods train/freight train, sleepers/cross-ties*) and in *motor car/automobile* terms (*boot/trunk, wing/fender*). But technical vocabularies are coming together again. Aerospace terminology has fewer transAtlantic variations than that of motor cars; computer terminology shows hardly any differences at all. America's *program* and *disk* have ousted Britain's traditional *programme* and *disc*.

The current "convergence" of British and American Englishes is mainly the result of British adoption of American usages. The American pronunciation of *suit, lute* and *absolute* has almost ousted the traditional standard British pronunciation with its y-sound after the *s* or *l*. (Curiously, *pursuit* remains resolutely *pur-syóot* in British English and *nuclear* shows no signs of going *nóo-clear*.)

In vocabulary and meaning, too, American English calls the shots. The American sense of *billion* has been widely adopted in Britain. Many American imports to Britain have been quietly absorbed: *teenager, babysitter, commuter; striptease, brainwash, streamline; lean over backwards, fly off the handle, call the shots*. Even *stiff upper lip* seems to be American in origin.

Although most transAtlantic lexical traffic runs eastward, *central heating* and *weekend* crossed the Atlantic from east to west before 1900. They have been followed by *miniskirt, opposite number, hovercraft, the Establishment, smog, brain drain* (appropriately) and, probably, *gay*, in the sense of homosexual.

The future of English

Mr Robert Burchfield, who recently retired as chief editor of the "Oxford English Dictionary," once suggested that the varieties of English (ESL as well as mother-tongue English) might one day become separate languages, just as Latin, after the fall of the Roman Empire, broke up into French, Italian, Spanish, and so on. Almost 100 years before Mr Burchfield, another language scholar, Henry Sweet, wrote:

> In another century...England, America and Australia will be speaking mutually unintelligible languages.

Such a divergence did not occur then because, though communications were slow in those days, language changed slowly, too. Such a divergence is not likely to take place in the next 100 years because, though language is changing faster today, so, are communications, and hence mutual linguistic influences.

True, a few new dialects might develop, joining the ranks of English creoles that are unintelligible to most mainstream English speakers. British and American English are never likely to become indistinguishable but they are never likely to become mutually unintelligible either. Indian English will remain widely comprehensible elsewhere. It is precisely because of its international intelligibility that English is so earnestly courted by governments and citizens alike.

This does not mean English is in the process of unbuilding the Tower of Babel, as the extreme proponents of a universal language want. Equivocation, likes and babble flourish as much in communities united by one language as they do in those divided by two. Nor is English replacing other languages, as opponents of its spread fear. For the most part, it is supplementing them, allowing strangers to talk to each other. A more temperate and useful role this—and one that English fulfils creditably and deservedly, in all its variety of varieties.

Nigerian government poster, 1967.

Sample Student Activities

I.   *How post-World War II reconstruction occurred, new international power relations took shape, and colonial empires broke up.*

A.   Major political and economic changes that accompanied post-war recovery.

Grades 5-6

- Explain the reasons for the founding of the United Nations. Make a list of the areas of the world in which the U.N. has played an active role. *How successful has the U.N. been as a peacekeeper?*

- Make posters depicting the work of UNICEF. *Why did the U.N. set up this body? What benefit has it had to the world?*

- Using documentary photos of the destruction of Europe, explain the importance of reconstruction after the war. *What was the Marshall Plan? How did it promote the rebuilding of Western Europe?*

- Create a map of the world that shows the pre- and post-World War II boundaries of England, Germany, France, the USSR, China, and Japan. Use colored pencils to show the differences in these boundaries.

Grades 7-8

- Debate the statement that the United States economy from 1945 to 1950 was stronger and better than that of the period 1918 to 1922.

- Define the terms "isolationism" and "internationalism" in terms of the post-World War I and World War II United States.

- Construct a chart of the United Nations' agencies and organizations in its original form (1945 to 1950). Define the task of each agency and organization in a sentence or two.

- On a world map locate the "hot spots" that the United Nations responded to in the period 1945-1970. Briefly explain the nature of the problem and the response.

- Construct a brief biographical sketch of George C. Marshall. Define his role during World War II and explain why he is called "the hero of European recovery."

- Compare the reasons for the United States' support of post-World War II Germany and Japan.

- In a newspaper article explain how the Marshall Plan came into being. Define the key elements of this plan for your readers. Adopt a pro- or anti-Marshall Plan stance in your article.

- Define the relationship between a "welfare state" and "socialism" as evidenced in at least one country adopting each model in post-World War II Europe or Asia.

- Evaluate the efforts of the European Economic Community to develop a "cooperative" economic system in Western Europe after World War II.

Grades 9-12

- Assess the differences in economic and social systems of Western Europe and the Soviet Eastern European block in the period 1945-1955.

- Select one "major" world crisis of the period 1945-1970 (Korean War, Congo Crisis, Cuban Missile Crisis or others) and evaluate the response of both the U.N. and individual nations involved.

- Prepare a position paper for the President in 1945, 1950, and 1955 evaluating the domestic and international rationale for helping Germany and Japan rebuild. Be sure to include the opposition to these programs in your paper.

- Research the demise of "fascism" as a political, social, and economic force at the end of World War II. Explain why it failed to remain a force, and how it may have stimulated the rise of democratic institutions in Germany, Italy, and Japan.

- Create a chart of new democracies in Germany, Greece, Spain, India, and Portugal showing those factors that led to the development of democracies in these states and how far they went in developing democratic institutions.

- Select and analyze characteristics that would qualify a country as a democracy. Draw two world maps, one for 1940 and one for 1975. Designate on both maps the countries of the world that could be called democracies. *How would you explain changes that occurred during these thirty-five years?*

B. Why global power shifts took place and the Cold War broke out in the aftermath of World War II.

Grades 5-6

- Draw a simple cartoon illustrating the term Cold War. On a world map indicate the Cold War alliances of the postwar period.

- Draw on books such as Margaret Rau's *Holding Up the Sky* to discuss social and political conflict in China.

- As an international reporter prepare an article for your home newspaper explaining the Berlin Blockade, the Hungarian Revolution, or the Polish worker's crisis. Present your article to the class.

- Research the causes of the Korean War, how the United Nations became involved, and the final results.

Grades 7-8

- Construct a map showing the new alliance systems that emerged as a part of the Cold War. On an accompanying chart, list the membership in each alliance and explain its purposes. *Why were these alliances formed after the war? Do they exist today?*

- Analyze the goals of the U.S. occupation of Japan. *How successful was the occupation in meeting them?*

- Research the Soviet Union's political influences on an Eastern European nation in the postwar era and compare it with the role of the U.S. occupation of Japan. *To what extent did the USSR interfere in popular elections in Eastern European countries? How did political development in Japan differ?*

- On a map of central Europe illustrate the division of Germany and Berlin. Assuming the role of an adviser to the British or French foreign office or the U.S. Department of State, write a position paper outlining problems that the partition may provoke. *What action would you have advised in the 1948 Berlin crisis?* Defend your position.

▶ Construct a timeline tracing the major events that led to the Communist takeover in China from the Long March to the establishment of the People's Republic in 1949. *How did Mao's programs change China? What led to the Great Leap Forward? How successful was it? What factors contributed to the Cultural Revolution? What was its result in terms of both economic development and human suffering?*

▶ Draw a map of the Korean Peninsula showing the divisions between North and South Korea, between China and Korea, the capitals of each, and the major battles of the Korea War.

▶ Define NATO, CENTO, SEATO, and the Warsaw Bloc. List the membership in each of these organizations and explain the major purpose of each in the period 1945-1970.

▶ Define the political and economic nature of communism as practiced in the USSR. *Why did the Soviets feel that they would ultimately triumph over the West and make the world communistic?*

Grades 9-12

▶ List the characteristics of the U.S. and USSR that made them "superpowers," and explain how they acquired these characteristics. Construct a historical analysis of the role of the space race in defining the competition between the superpowers.

▶ Develop a case study examining a major cold war conflict from the Berlin Blockade to the Soviet invasion of Afghanistan. Explain the developments that led to the conflict and the significance of the event in world affairs.

▶ Evaluate the strategic role of the Muslim countries in the Middle East during the Cold War. Compare the importance of geographic, economic, and political factors. *How has the role of the region changed since the breakup of the Soviet Union?*

▶ Debate the proposition: *Communist success in the Chinese civil war was the result of Jiang Jisei's failure as an effective leader rather than a victory for Mao Zedong.*

▶ Write an essay analyzing why China made an alliance with the Soviet Union. *Considering that both countries had Communist governments, why did strains develop in the alliance?*

▶ Analyze the relative strengths and weaknesses of the United States and USSR as superpowers in a position paper for the President of the United States.

C. How African, Asian, and Caribbean peoples achieved independence from European colonial rule.

Grades 5-6

▶ Construct a timeline showing the evolution of the state of Israel from its pre-World War II colonial status through 1973.

▶ Assess those factors that led to Britain and the United States advocating the founding of Israel as an independent nation.

▶ Write a mini-biography, including a map, on the life of one of the following nationalist leaders: Jomo Kenyatta, Kwame Nkrumah, Leopold Senghor, Mahatma Gandhi, Achmed Sukarno, Ho Chi Minh, or Muhammad Ali Jinnah.

Grades 7-8

▶ Explain the role India played in World War II and assess the significance of the war for the struggle for independence.

▶ Analyze Mohandas Gandhi's statement, "Through nonviolent means the Indian people could achieve independence from British rule." *Did the claim prove to be true?*

▶ Trace the rise of independent nations in Southeast Asia such as Burma, Malaysia, Singapore, Indonesia, Cambodia, Laos, or Vietnam.

▶ Construct a timeline of important events in the struggle between Israelis and Palestinians since 1948. Debate the question of rights to disputed land from an Israeli and Palestinian perspective.

▶ Use books such as Margaret Sacks's *Beyond Safe Boundaries* to discuss the moral, social, political, and economic implications of apartheid.

▶ Investigate the regime of Kwame Nkrumah in Ghana, Jomo Kenyatta in Kenya, or Idi Amin in Uganda. Decide under which regime you would have preferred to live and explain the reasons why.

▶ Evaluate the migration of Africans to South Africa from other regions in the post-World War II period. *What caused them to move to South Africa when they knew that that nation was ruled by a minority group of European descent?*

Grades 9-12

▶ Examine the dispute over Kashmir resulting from the partition of the Indian subcontinent. *What interests were at stake for the disputants? What role did the United Nations play in mediating the dispute?*

▶ Analyze the language of the Balfour Declaration and its relationship to the exercise of Britain's mandate in Palestine. Prepare a chart listing the goals of the Arab League and the Zionist Movement and report on how these goals conflicted with each other and were at odds with the mandate system.

▶ Prepare a map showing the distribution of Hindu and Muslim populations in South Asia and devise a plan for the division of the subcontinent into Muslim and Hindu states. Investigate the actual partition and account for similarities or differences from the political boundaries you prescribed. *What conclusions can you make about the withdrawal of the British and the role of religion in the formation of the two new nations?*

▶ View the film "The Battle of Algiers" and place the events it describes within the chronological context of the Algerian Revolution of 1954-62. *How did the presence of a large group of French settlers in Algeria affect the course of the war? What tactics did the French and Algerian revolutionaries use against one another to win the battle of Algiers? Were these tactics justified on either side?* Explain why the revolutionaries lost the battle of Algiers but nevertheless won the revolution. *To which side in the struggle does the filmmaker seem to be sympathetic? How does he show his view cinematically?*

▶ Construct case studies of independence movements in two African or Asian countries, one through an evolutionary process and the other through revolution. Select from countries such as Ghana, Kenya, Algeria, Zaire, Angola, Mozambique, the Philippines, Indonesia, Burma, or Vietnam.

▶ Draw on books such as Alan Paton's *Cry the Beloved Country* and Mark Mathabane's *Kaffir Boy* to discuss Africans' survival and resistance under apartheid.

▶ Prepare a map of the Caribbean Sea and Central America. Denote the national boundaries of emerging states, and clearly indicate the dates on which each became independent of colonial rule.

> ### II. *The search for community, stability, and peace in an interdependent world.*

A. How population explosion and environmental change have altered conditions of life around the world.

Grades 5-6

▶ Use photographs and posters to examine changes that took place when cities proliferated after World War II. *What was the impact of urbanization on family life and standards of living? How has industrialization contributed to changes in the environment?*

▶ Make a scrapbook of newspaper and magazine articles about the ongoing activities of groups trying to save the environment. *What can individuals do to help?* Organize a class project of recycling.

▶ Research United Nations programs to promote health and medical care and to improve the standard of living in developing nations. *How successful are these programs?*

Grades 7-8

▶ Research one of the following: population growth, urbanization, warfare, or the global market economy. Assess the ways it has contributed to altering or degrading the environment. Create a large symbol representing the selected topic and record your findings.

▶ Select readings from poems or articles about the environment from various countries around the world. Create a class Reader's Theater of significant passages.

▶ Debate the issues associated with the protection of the Brazilian rain forest from the perspectives of an environmentalist, a landless peasant farmer, and a cattle rancher. *Is this a national or international issue? What proposals might be offered to address the issues raised by different interest groups? In what areas of the world are there similar issues? What should be the role of industrialized nations in meeting these challenges?*

Grades 9-12

▶ Trace population changes in selected countries, such as India, Egypt, Nigeria, Brazil, the United States, and Italy. *What assumptions can you make about population changes in relation to scientific, medical, and technological breakthroughs?* Test these assumptions with research and prepare a report with a bar graph.

▶ View the video "World Population" by Zero Population Growth. *What is the frame of reference of the filmmaker? How does this film achieve a dramatic effect and stimulate discussion of population growth?*

▶ Examine the issues raised by the 1994 Cairo Conference on World Population. *How did these issues address patterns of population growth? What were the objections raised regarding proposals restricting population growth? How difficult is it to arrive at a consensus document on population growth?*

▶ Prepare a graph illustrating China's population growth from the 1700s through 1990. Analyze the effects of China's "one-child" policy of the 1990s. *Why did China's population growth rate increase dramatically? How has China's population growth affected economic development from the 1800s onward?*

▶ Research United Nations efforts to promote programs to improve health and welfare, and assess the effectiveness of these programs. *Which major U.N. programs promote scientific and technical assistance? Does the U.N. provide adequate programs to avert catastrophes? How expensive are these programs? Who bears the cost of implementation?*

B. How increasing economic interdependence has transformed human society.

Grades 5-6

▶ Construct an illustrated chart depicting major scientific, technological, or medical breakthroughs of the postwar decades. *What would your life be like without these advances?*

▶ On a map show major patterns of world migration since World War II. Assume the role of one of these migrants and write a letter explaining your reasons for moving. *What are the risks you are taking? What are your expectations?*

▶ Make a map centering on the Pacific Ocean that identifies the established and newly industrialized countries of the Pacific Rim. *What is the Pacific Rim economy?*

Grades 7-8

▶ Construct a case study of two developing countries. Compare and contrast development in the two countries. *What are some of the challenges to economic development? How can the countries address these challenges?*

▶ Assume the role of one of the following migrant workers: a Southeast Asian domestic worker in the Persian Gulf; an American oil executive in Saudi Arabia; a Moroccan factory worker in France; an Egyptian professor in the United States; or a Turkish Muslim religious teacher in Germany. Write a letter home. *What do you like and dislike about your new home? How difficult is it to adapt to a different society?*

▶ Construct a timeline or line graph of world oil price changes since 1950. Assess the reasons for these changes, both in the oil-producing and oil-consuming countries.

▶ Explain the formation of the European Economic Community (EEC). *What are the advantages of the EEC? What similar economic partnerships have been formed in other parts of the world? Would a United States of Europe be a good idea?*

Grades 9-12

▶ Assume the role of a representative to a world forum called to discuss the disparities between industrialized and developing countries. Examine statistical information regarding resources, production, capital investment, labor, and trade. *What accounts for the disparity? What measures should be taken by industrialized states to assist developing nations? What programs should developing nations undertake?*

▶ Assess the relationships between United States domestic energy policy and foreign policy in oil-producing regions since 1970.

▶ Research the development of multi-national corporations and explain in what ways they have had an impact on the world economy. *What are the benefits of multi-national corporations? Why are they moving production units into developing countries? How have multi-national corporations contributed to the migration of people?*

▶ Write a report explaining why the countries of East Asia have experienced comparatively rapid economic development in the late 20th century. *What factors may explain why the economies of some countries of Africa have not significantly advanced in the late 1980s and 1990s?*

▶ Construct a map showing the migration of workers from North Africa and Turkey to Europe since the 1970s. *Why have so many people from these regions sought work in Europe? What social problems have they encountered? How does this phenomenon compare with the migration of people from Mexico, Central America, or the Caribbean to the U.S.?*

C. How liberal democracy, market economies, and human rights movements have reshaped political and social life.

Grades 5-6

▶ Interview a female family member or friend who was a teenager or adult before World War II. *How do they think women's lives are different today in regard to social equality and economic opportunity?*

▶ Gather information from biographies and write character sketches of Nelson Mandella, F. W. de Klerk, and Bishop Desmond Tutu. *How have these three men contributed to the ending of apartheid in South Africa?*

▶ List the basic ideas contained in the United Nations Declaration of Human Rights. *How are these rights similar to and different from the provisions of the U.S. Bill of Rights? What other rights do you think should be added to the U.N. declaration? Why?*

Grades 7-8

▶ Create an illustrated timeline of the events leading up to the collapse of the Soviet Union. On a map of the Soviet Union draw and label the independent countries formed from its boundaries. *Would changing any of the events on the timeline have altered the collapse of the USSR? How were the borders of newly established states decided?*

▶ Research the U.N. Declaration on Human Rights of 1948. *Why was this document written?* Write an expository essay on the progress or lack of progress of human and civil rights around the world or in one country.

▶ Use newspaper articles to research and role-play an interview with the leader of a separatist movement in a country of your choice. *What moral issues are involved? What means are used by the separatist to achieve his or her goals? Why does he or she believe the struggle is necessary? What will be the effect on the people in that country?*

▶ Assemble a collection of documentary photographs or construct a collage to illustrate the system of apartheid in South Africa. Explain how the system was abolished. *What external pressures were placed on the South African government to end apartheid?*

▶ Explain how Mikhail Gorbachev's policies of *perestroika* and *glasnost* changed the U.S.S.R. and Soviet relations with Eastern European nations. *What impact did the United States military build-up have on Soviet willingness to negotiate with the West?*

Grades 9-12

▶ Use political and demographic maps showing the distribution of ethnic and religious groups in an African country to analyze the prevalence of ethnic and border conflicts since independence. Identify countries where several ethnic groups have come under one national roof as a result of decolonization. *What are the implications for state-building?*

▶ Analyze the development of nationalist movements in Eastern Europe from the pre-World War I to the post-Cold War period. *How does the map of Eastern Europe in 1920 compare with the maps in 1950 and 1995? Why was there a resurgence of nationalism and ethnic tension in the region in the 1990s?*

▶ Analyze the writings of male and female members of various religious groups. *How do they differ in their views of relations between men and women?*

▶ Compare and contrast the legal status and social roles of Muslim women in various countries. *What changes have taken place for women of various classes in the past century?*

▶ Evaluate the relationship between demands for democratic reform and the trend toward privatization and economic liberalization in developing countries and former communist states. Assess the influence of multinational corporations in supporting or challenging these trends.

D. Major sources of tension and conflict in the contemporary world and efforts that have been made to address them.

Grades 5-6

▶ Write a diary of a young person concerned about ethnic or religious dissension or conflict in his or her country. Choose a country such as Canada, Ireland, Bosnia, Iraq, or Ruanda.

▶ Examine photographs of student protest in Tiananmen Square in China in 1989. *What were the reasons for the protest? Why did student protesters demonstrate with miniature versions of the Statue of Liberty?*

Grades 7-8

▶ Develop criteria for defining a terrorist act. Analyze acts characterized as terrorism in news reports in terms of means, motivation, and victims. *What factors in modern society facilitate politically motivated terrorism? What methods can nations use to protect their citizens from terrorist acts? Is international cooperation necessary to stop terrorism?*

▶ Analyze the term "religious fundamentalism" and trace its origin. *How does the modern connotation of the term differ from its historical use? How appropriate is the term to certain religious movements in the late 20th century?*

▶ Research the opening of China and the impact of changes in the communist system in the post-Mao era. *How did world events help give rise to a reform movement in 1989? What actions did Deng Xiaoping take to crush the movement? How did world leaders react to the events in Tiananmen Square?*

▶ Compile a list of nations that have faced the breakdown of central authority in the last two decades of the 20th century. *What are the pressing problems facing these nations? Why have their respective governments been unable to cope with these problems? What has been the reaction of the international community?*

Grades 9-12

▶ Research the application of economic and arms embargoes sponsored by United Nations resolutions, including the cases of Iran, Iraq, the former Yugoslavia, and Haiti. Assess the enforcement and political consequences for sanctioned countries. Evaluate criteria for applying and lifting various types of embargoes and on the exclusion of humanitarian aid.

▶ Define the meaning of *jihad* in Islamic belief. *What Islamic principles are relevant to military activity? How does* jihad *incorporate the concept of "warfare with oneself"?*

▶ Debate the question: *"Does the nation-state have a future in the 21st century?"*

▶ Define the term "genocide" and analyze possible examples of genocide since World War II. Conduct a tribunal that judges whether or not the Pol Pot regime committed genocide in Cambodia.

E. Major worldwide scientific and technological trends of the second half of the 20th century.

Grades 5-6

▶ Chart the changes that have taken place in the 20th century in communication. *How have these changes affected life? To what extent have they helped bring people from different parts of the world together?*

▶ Research the development of the U.S. space program and explain how it has served the public. *How important are communications and weather satellites? How has the space program affected medical research? How has the space program improved our knowledge of the universe?*

♦ Conduct a hypothetical interview with Neil Armstrong, asking him about his experience landing on the moon and how he thinks the expeditions to the moon have changed the world.

♦ Assume the role of a 19th-century scientist who has traveled forward in time. *How would you describe the social and cultural implications of recent medical successes such as antibiotics and vaccines? What challenges do you see for medical research in the 21st century?*

Grades 7-8

♦ Trace the development of computer technology from World War II to the present. *How has the widespread use of computers affected the daily life at home and at work? To what extent has computer technology facilitated scientific research in other fields?*

♦ Research the "Green Revolution." *What agricultural techniques contributed to the growth in agricultural productivity? What new varieties of crops appeared? What were the benefits of these changes? How have scientists and governmental officials responded to unintended consequences of the "Green Revolution"?*

♦ Research important medical discoveries of the latter part of the 20th century and explain how these have enhanced the quality of life. *Have all nations shared in advanced medical research?*

Grades 9-12

♦ Respond to *Life* magazine publisher Henry Luce's 1941 declaration that the world had entered into "the American Century" where the United States was "the intellectual, scientific and artistic capital of the world." *What evidence can be given to support Luce's declaration? Why have increasing numbers of foreign students sought advanced degrees from American universities since the end of World War II? In what fields has American science dominated? What factors account for innovation in scientific research in the U.S.?*

♦ Debate the issue: "Resolved: Nuclear power is the most efficient and environmentally feasible energy source for the 21st century." *How have demands for energy increased in the last generation? How do the industrialized nations of the world compare with developing nations in energy consumption? How many nations in the world rely heavily on nuclear power as an energy source? How do the costs and risks of nuclear power compare with those posed by continuing use of fossil fuels?*

♦ Analyze the role governments and international corporations play in scientific research. *Should governments fund programs of scientific and medical research? Why or why not?*

♦ Investigate how World War II stimulated scientific research and technical innovations that advanced human well-being and standard of living. *What medical advances came out of World War II? What new consumer products?*

♦ Write a letter to the editor of a magazine which featured an article entitled "We Can No Longer Identify Science with Progress." Express your view either supporting or opposing this assertion.

F. Worldwide cultural trends of the second half of the 20th century.

Grades 5-6

♦ List major challenges confronting contemporary society and explain the ways in which different religions have sought to help solve these problems.

♦ List 10 consumer items that you consider important today. *Would people in other parts of the world select the same items? Why or why not?*

▶ Construct a bulletin board display showing examples of contemporary art and architecture from around the world. *In what way do styles reflect local culture? In what way do they show evidence of a "global culture"?*

▶ Using the Internet, compile information and images on a cultural or artistic movement such as Surrealism, Pop Art, musical comedy, animated film, or early rock and roll. *How have these movements affected society?*

Grades 7-8

▶ Create a large bulletin board picture and word collage of examples of "global culture." Include examples of global communications, information technology, and mass marketing. *How have these developments accelerated social change?*

▶ Research the global influence of CNN in the past ten years. *In how many countries of the world can CNN be viewed? What role did CNN play in the Gulf War?*

▶ Analyze books or articles on contemporary political, economic, and social issues published by Muslim, Christian, and Jewish religious groups. Compare and contrast their solutions to modern dilemmas.

▶ Debate the proposition that the late 20th century is a time of religious ferment and experimentation around the world.

▶ Construct a chart listing differences in ways of life in an industrial nation and a predominantly agrarian nation. *What consumer goods are valued in each society? How has modern communication affected demands for consumer goods in different parts of the world?*

Grades 9-12

▶ Debate the advantages and disadvantages of increased participation in the world economy for a country eager to preserve its traditional cultural identity. Use evidence from specific countries to support your argument.

▶ Define "liberation theology" and explain the ideological issues surrounding the philosophy.

▶ Assess the rationale behind the Soviet development of great art museums such as The Hermitage, the growth of the state opera and ballet programs, and reverence for Russian church architecture and music. *How did this relate to the Communist ideal of the workers' revolution and state?*

▶ Investigate why New York City became the world's "art capital" after World War II. *What art movements arose there, and why were they often controversial?* Collect images of paintings by leading Abstract Expressionists, and analyze how these works might express 20th-century values. *Which artists migrated to the U.S. from Europe?*

▶ Write a research paper on public controversies that arose in the U.S. in the 1980s and 1990s over the teaching or museum presentation of American history. *What were the major issues in these controversies? Why is the "collective memory" important to Americans?* Compare "history wars" in the U.S. with controversies or radical changes that have occurred in history teaching in recent years in Britain, Russia, or South Africa.

III. *Major global trends since World War II.*

Major global trends since World War II.

Grades 5-6

▸ Interview three people in your community who migrated to the United States from another country either as a child or an adult. Construct a classroom world map showing the place of origin and time of migration of each person interviewed by all students in the class. Make a chart of different motivations for migrating to the U.S. *What changing patterns can you observe in the origins of migrants?*

▸ Analyze the characteristics that make a country democratic, examining both form of government and attention to civil and human rights. Construct world maps for 1900, 1950, and 1995 designating countries that you consider to be democracies.

Grades 7-8

▸ Make a chart listing the independent nations of the world in 1900, 1920, 1950, 1975, and 1995. *What are the characteristics that make a country sovereign?* For each interval between dates explain why the number of independent countries in the world grew.

▸ Write in narrative form a chronicle of the Cold War, highlighting major events and turning points and explaining why they occurred. *Why did the Cold War begin? When did the most dangerous Cold War crises occur, and what threats did they present? In what ways might the United States and the Soviet Union have misunderstood each other's aims and interests? Why did the Cold War come to an end in the 1990s?*

▸ At the end of World War II the publisher Henry Luce predicted that the next hundred years would be the "American century." *Was Luce's prediction fulfilled during the first half of that century in regard to the United States' political, military, and economic role in the world? How did world power shift in that half-century from one of "superpower bipolarity" to one of "multipolarity"? What effects did both the Vietnam War and the collapse of the Soviet Union have on the prospects for an "American century"?*

Grades 9-12

▸ Analyze major characteristics of "post-industrial society" in the contemporary world. Identify such factors as the computer revolution, the knowledge explosion, women's movements, the growth of suburbs, and the pervasiveness of television. Assess how they have changed human society since World War II.

▸ Debate the issue: "The world has become simultaneously more culturally unified and more culturally divided since World War II." *What evidence exists of an emerging "global culture"? What evidence exists of a resurgence of nationalism and communalism based on cultural distinctions? How can these two trends exist simultaneously?*

▸ Drawing on library research, compare and contrast basic ideas of "modernization theory," which argues that Third World countries can achieve economic growth and development by following the political and economic model of the industrial democracies, with "dependence theory," which argues that sustained economic growth in the industrial countries depends on the continued underdevelopment of many other countries. *Which theory do you find more convincing and why?* Identify countries that seem to defy the assertions of one theory or the other.

▶ Research a religious movement that was founded in the 19th or 20th century and that has subsequently had world-wide scope. Consider such movements as Baha'i, Christian Science, the Church of Jesus Christ of Latter Day Saints, Hari Krishna, Jehovah's Witness, or the Salvation Army. *Where did the movement you have chosen originate? Was its founding associated with a particular leader? What are its basic teachings? What concerns of the modern world might this movement have wished to address? How might its success be measured as a world-wide movement?*

Women at a well, India. Photo by Don Johnson

World History Across the Eras

Not all of the events in world history that students should address can be bracketed within one of the nine eras presented in this book. The complexities of today's world are in part a consequence of changes that have been in the making for centuries, even millennia. Important historical continuities can be discerned that link one period with another. And even though history may not repeat itself in any precise way, certain historical patterns do recur. Studying one development in world history in the light of an earlier, similar development can sharpen our understanding of both.

This final essay and set of activities invite teachers and students to give attention to long-term changes and recurring patterns of the past. The range of potential subjects in this category is nearly limitless. What follows is only suggestive of activities that require students to step way back from our spinning planet, as it were, to take in broad vistas and long spans of time.

The Roman city of Timgad, East Central Algeria. Photo by Ross Dunn

Migrations of Africans to the Americas:
The Impact on Africans, Africa, and the New World*
by Patrick Manning

Manning writes of the involuntary migration of Africans to the Americas and the interaction of Africans with Native Americans and European settlers. The essay examines African, American, and global dimensions of this great migration, which spanned four centuries. The author draws on quantitative data to analyze the migration and its impact in the Americas.

Patrick Manning is Professor of History and African-American Studies at Northeastern University. He is author of *Slavery and African Life* and other books on African social and economic history. He is currently working on topics in modern world history.

The movement of Africans to the Americas from the seventeenth to the nineteenth centuries may be accounted as mankind's second-largest transoceanic migration. This migration, along with the concurrent African migration to the Middle East and North Africa, was distinct from other major modern migrations in its involuntary nature, and in the high rates of mortality and social dislocation caused by the methods of capture and transportation. A related migratory pattern, the capture and settling of millions of slaves within Africa, grew up in eighteenth- and nineteenth-century Africa as a consequence of the two patterns of overseas slave trade.

These three dimensions to the enslavement of Africans—which I have elsewhere labelled as the Occidental, Oriental, and African slave trades—were interrelated, so that there are advantages to treating them as an ensemble. At the same time, my purpose here is to focus on migration to the Americas. where Africans interacted with native American inhabitants and with European settlers. This paper is therefore divided into three sections, considering the migration of Africans to the Americas first in an American perspective, then in an African perspective, and finally in a global perspective including the Americas, Africa, and the Atlantic.

To simplify the presentation, I have restricted the quantitative data to the period from 1600 to 1800. The earlier slave trade, before 1600, was quantitatively small but socially significant. The later slave trade, after 1800, was large and significant, bringing nearly three million slaves (roughly one fourth of the total) to the Americas; African captives reached the shores of Cuba and Brazil into the late 1860s. Still, the pattern I describe below for the period 1600-1800 apply, in large measure, to the entire period of the Atlantic slave trade.

The American Perspective

David Eltis posed, in a 1983 article, a striking contrast in the population history of the Americas. By 1820, there had been about 8.4 million African immigrants to the Americas, and 2.4 million European immigrants. But by that date the Euro-American population of some 12 million exceeded the Afro-American population of about 11 million. The rates of survival and reproduction of African immigrants were, apparently, dramatically lower than those of European immigrants. Eltis's contrast drew attention to me range of demographic comparisons necessary to make sense of this puzzle: the rates of fertility and mortality, the timing and location of immigration, the sex ratios and the social identification of persons.

The table below shows estimated numbers of immigrants from Africa up to 1800, by the region to which they immigrated. These figures, despite their apparent precision, are very rough indeed: they involve a number of assumptions, extrapolations and interpolations,

*Reprinted from *The History Teacher*, Vol. 26 , No. 3 (May 1993), pp. 279-296.

including the inevitable confusion between numbers of slaves exported from Africa and imported to the Americas. As a result, all the figures, and particularly the smaller ones, must be seen as having margins of error of perhaps twenty percent. Nonetheless, they are worth presenting for the clear patterns they reveal. The table accounts for a total of about 7.6 million immigrant slaves up to 1800; nearly three million more slaves would arrive, principally to Brazil and Cuba, during the nineteenth century.

African Immigrants, by Period and Place of Arrival
(All figures in thousands of persons)

Region	to 1600	1600-1640	1640-1700	1700-1760	1760-1800
North America (Br, Fr, Sp)	–	1	20	171	177
Caribbean-non-Spanish	–	9	454	1623	1809
British Caribbean	–	8	255	900	1085
French Caribbean	–	1	155	474	573
Other Caribbean	–	–	44	249	151
Spanish America	75	269	186	271	235
Spanish Caribbean	7	20	14	27	140
Mexico & Cent America	23	70	48	13	5
Venezuela-Colombia-Peru	45	135	93	160	60
La Plata-Bolivia	–	44	30	71	30
Brazil	50	160	400	960	726
Total	125	439	1060	3025	2947
Annual average, in thousands	1	11	18	50	70

To display some of the immigration data in schematic form, I have prepared Figure 1, which gives estimates, for various regions of the Americas, of the numbers of African immigrants in the 1620s (before North European entry into the trade), in the 1700s (once the Caribbean sugar trade had become fully established and the prices of African slaves had risen sharply), and in the 1780s (at the height of the Atlantic slave trade).

The figure, while it indicates the wide geographical distribution of African slaves throughout the Americas, also emphasizes their concentration in the English and French Caribbean. There, on the sugar plantations of the eighteenth century, over three million slaves were consigned to oblivion. The African-descended population of the Caribbean is today about twenty-five million, or less than a fifth of the more than one hundred and fifty million people of African descent in the Americas.

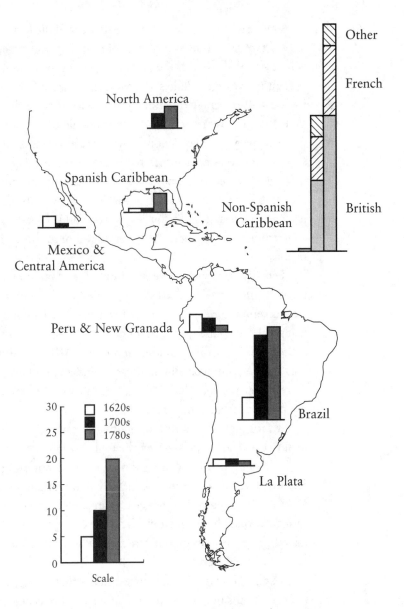

Figure 1. Immigrants from Africa

The migratory history of African slaves, once they landed in the Americas, sometimes continued for several further stages. The initial period of seasoning can be considered as migration through a change in status. Further, slaves were physically transshipped, often over considerable distances. Slaves brought by the Dutch to Curaçao and by the English to Jamaica were transshipped to Cartagena, Portobelo, and on to various Spanish colonies. From Cartagena, some slaves were settled down in Colombia. A larger number of slaves went to Portobelo in Panama, walked overland, and then went by sea to Lima. Most remained there, but some went into the highlands. Slaves landed in the Rio de La Plata went overland for 900 kilometers to Tucuman and then on for another 600 kilometers to the silver mines at Potosi. In Brazil, with the gold rush in Minas Gerais at the turn of the eighteenth century, slaves were sent overland to the mining areas, 300 kilometers from Rio and a much longer distance overland from Bahia. Slaves entering the Chesapeake and South Carolina came, in significant proportion, after stopping in Barbados. A final stage in the migration of some slaves was their liberation—either by emancipation, by self-purchase, or by escape.

One reason for emphasizing the number of distinct stages in the migration of Africans is to draw attention to the distinct rates of mortality and fertility at each stage. The mortality which is best known is that of the Atlantic crossing. (Crude mortality rates averaged about fifteen percent per voyage. While slave voyages averaged from two to three months in length, mortality is usually calculated on an annual basis. If slaves had encountered Middle Passage conditions for a full year, their mortality rate might have come to over five hundred per thousand per year. We will return below to Middle Passage mortality.) The point here is that slaves who survived the crossing had then to undergo various other types of elevated mortality: that of further travel within the Americas, that of seasoning in the locale where they were settled, and that of daily existence in slave status, where mortality was generally higher than for equivalent persons of free status. To this list must be added the fact that most slaves were settled in low-lying tropical areas where the general level of mortality was greater than in higher, temperate regions.

Fertility rates were generally lower for populations of slave status than for free populations. Fertility rates for slaves in the course of transportation, while not recorded in any detail, were certainly at an exceptionally low level. Most studies on fertility of African-American populations have focused, as is traditional and simplest, on the fertility of women. But because of the large excess of men among immigrant Africans, and because they did have children not only with African women but also with Indian and European women, there is an argument for more systematic consideration of the fertility of the male Africans and African-Americans than has been undertaken thus far.

A thorough accounting of the migration of Africans to the Americas would include the regional African origins—even the ethnic origins, age and sex distribution—of those disembarking in each American region. Such an accounting could now be estimated, based on recently developed evidence, though I will not attempt such an estimate here. In this regard, it is perhaps of interest that in recent years, and especially for the eighteenth and nineteenth centuries, scholars have given more attention to regional breakdowns and global synthesis in migratory movements on the African side of the Atlantic than to the equivalent details of immigration to the Americas.

To give but two of the many examples that could be given of the specificity and change in African origins of American populations: In Louisiana, the initial slave population settled by the French in the early eighteenth century drew heavily on Bambara men from the upper Niger valley. This male slave population maintained and passed on its traditions because the Bambara men married Native American women, also enslaved. After 1770, the larger number of slaves entering Louisiana under Spanish rule was dominated by slaves from the Bight of Benin, including a large minority of women; these slaves brought the religion of vodoun to Louisiana. Second, while slaves from Congo and Angola were numerous among those imported to all regions of the Americas, they were virtually the only slaves imported to Rio de Janeiro from the seventeenth into the nineteenth century. The black populations of Rio, and to a lesser extent of Minas Gerais, had a degree of cultural homogeneity unusual for slaves in the Americas.

The debates of the 1960s and 1970s focused on the total number of slaves crossing the Atlantic, and obscured questions of the distribution of African migrants over time, by age and by sex. The steady assemblage of slave trade data is permitting these issues to be addressed in increasing detail, and clear patterns have now come to light (Figure 2.) With the passage of time from the seventeenth to the nineteenth centuries, the proportion of adult male slaves shipped increased slightly, the proportion of adult female slaves shipped decreased significantly, and the proportion of children shipped, both male and female, increased over time.

For slave men, women, and children, the rate of labor force participation was generally high, as compared to free populations. Most of the work of slaves could be categorized into the occupations of mining, plantation work, artisanal work, transport, and domestic service. In Spanish America, slaves were concentrated most visibly in mining and artisanal work until the late eighteenth century, when sugar and tobacco plantation work began to dominate Cuba while slavery decline elsewhere. In Brazil, sugar plantation work dominated the sixteenth and seventeenth centuries, while mining work expanded greatly in the eighteenth century. The English and French Caribbean focused on sugar production, though coffee and livestock occupied significant numbers of slaves. Tobacco production occupied large numbers of slaves in Bahia and North America; cotton production expanded from the 1760s in Maranhao, and later in North America.

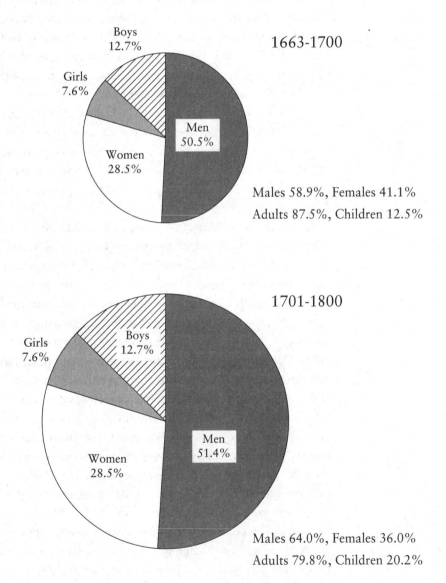

Figure 2. African immigrants by age and sex

The rise to profitability of this succession of industries seems to have provided the main "pull" factor driving the movement of slaves to the Americas from Africa. The demand for sugar workers in sixteenth-century Brazil, the seventeenth-century Caribbean and nineteenth-century Cuba brought a supply response from Africa. Similarly, the demand for mine workers in eighteenth-century Minas Gerais and New Granada brought an African response. Overall, the African and African-descended population of the Americas grew steadily through the seventeenth and eighteenth centuries, though it went into decline for as much as several decades whenever and wherever the import of additional slaves came to a halt.

The African Perspective

From the standpoint of the African continent, the slave trade to the Americas interacted with other migratory movements, including slave trading within Africa. Before the seventeenth century, sub-Saharan African societies lacked the powerful states and the lucrative trade routes necessary to support an extensive system of slavery, so that slavery in Africa was almost everywhere a marginal institution. The exceptions were the large states of the Saharan fringe, notably Songhai. The trade in slaves to Saharan oases, to North Africa and West Asia took an estimated ten thousand persons per year in the sixteenth century. The oceanic slave trade from Africa in the sixteenth century was dominated by the movement of slaves to Europe and to such Atlantic islands as the Canaries and Sao Thome.

By the mid-seventeenth century the migration of slaves to Europe and the Atlantic islands had declined sharply, and the trans-Atlantic trade had expanded to the point where it exceeded the volume of the Saharan trade. The expansion of the Occidental trade brought, as a by-product, the development of an Africa trade: growth in slave exports led to the creation of expanded networks of slave supply, and these permitted wealthy Africans to buy slaves in unprecedented numbers.

In the eighteenth century, the continued expansion of the Occidental trade brought a substantial growth in the African trade, particularly as female slaves were held within African societies. The effects of this slave trade were felt mostly in West Africa and West Central Africa. Then, late in the eighteenth century, the slave trade expanded to much of Eastern Africa. Occidental merchants began purchasing slaves from Mozambique. Growing Middle Eastern demand for slaves (occasioned by an apparent growth in Middle Eastern economies that is still not well explained) led to expansion of the slave trade in modern Sudan, the Horn, and the Indian Ocean coast of Africa. Expanded slave exports in turn stimulated the development of enslavement within Eastern Africa, a development which accelerated sharply during the nineteenth century. These general movements provide the context for the examples of African emigration to the Americas given in Figure 3.

The movement of so many slaves to the African coast for export entailed large-scale capture and migration. Distances for the movement of slaves to the coast could be small (an average of less than 100 kilometers for the large number of slaves from the Bight of Benin in the early eighteenth century), or they could be immense (some 600 kilometers for the Bambara slaves from West Africa who formed the nucleus of the Louisiana slave population; similar distances for slaves of the Lunda who passed through Angola on their way to Rio). These distances, travelled slowly and over long periods, brought elevated mortality with them.

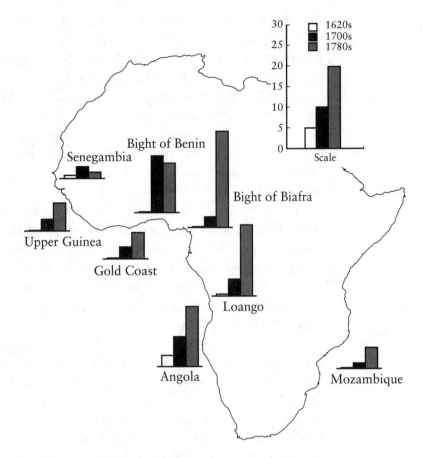

Figure 3. African emigrants to the Americas

Overall, then, the mortality of slaves within Africa was high, and their fertility was low. The considerations summarized above, with regard to the fertility and mortality of slaves in the Americas as they passed through transportation, seasoning, slave life and occasional liberation, apply in equivalent terms to the roughly equal numbers of persons in slave status at the same time in Africa. It must be emphasized that the high levels of mortality applied not only to the slaves delivered to the coast to be exported across the Atlantic, but to the nearly equal number of persons (most of them female) captured, transported to distant areas, and purchased as slaves within Africa.

This grim tale of slave mortality is not the whole of the story, of course, in that the purpose of the slave trade was to deliver live workers to the purchasers. We should therefore mention, at least, the economic network developed for supply of the trade in Africa. Considerable labor and investment were required to provide transport, finance, food, clothing, lodging, guards, and medicine for the slaves. These systems of slave delivery, though they differed from region to region, became a significant element in he African economic landscape.

The slaves held within Africa, numerous though they were, did not become readily visible to outside observers until the nineteenth century. This was because, along the western coast of Africa, most eighteenth-century slaves were women: they were held within families, and their productivity was mainly aimed at expanding the family economy. However, the Scottish explorer Mungo Park, travelling in the Senegal and Niger valleys at the end of the eighteenth century, found large proportions of the population to be held in slavery. He encountered a type of economic system that was to spread widely through the continent in the nineteenth century.

Adult males as well as females were held in slavery in large numbers, and slave men and women now tended to live apart from their masters as a slave class; their productivity was focused on marketable commodities. These included such African exports as palm oil, peanuts and coffee, but were more focused on yams, grains and cotton for the domestic market.

The evidence of transformation in African economic life through the expansion of slavery gives some hint of the accompanying social and ideological changes. Classes of merchants and monarchs rose with the export trade, and classes of landowners rose with the nineteenth-century growth of market-oriented slavery. Values emphasizing hierarchy arose in the societies holding and trading in slaves; egalitarian values were reaffirmed in societies resisting enslavement.

The most obvious "push" factors sending African slaves across the Atlantic were war and famine. The savanna areas of marginal rainfall—Angola and the grasslands extending from Senegambia east to Cameroon—underwent periodic drought and famine, and in these times desperate families sold both children and adults. The relation between warfare and enslavement is in one sense obvious, but on the other hand there have been two centuries of debate over whether the African wars broke out for purely domestic reasons, or whether the European demand for slaves stimulated additional wars.

Overall, the export of slaves from Africa halted and then reversed growth of the continent's population. During the seventeenth century, such population decline took place in restricted areas of coastal Senegambia, Upper Guinea and Angola. After about 1730, the decline became general for the coast from Senegal to Angola, and continued to about 1850. The decline was slow rather than precipitous. Even though the number of slaves exported averaged little more than three per thousand of the African regional population, and even though the trade took more males than females, the combination of the mortality of capture and transportation with the concentration of captures on young adults meant that Africa lost enough young women to reverse an intrinsic growth rate of five per thousand. The same processes transformed the structure of the population, causing the adult sex ratio to decline to an average of 80 men per 100 women.

A Global Perspective

Despite—indeed, because of—the immigration of Europeans and Africans, the total population of the Americas declined in the sixteenth and seventeenth centuries. While estimates of the pre-Columbian populations must remain speculative, the population of the Americas fell to perhaps as little as five million persons during the seventeenth century.

The threatened void of population in the Americas encouraged the transformation of African slavery from a marginal institution to a central element in a global system of population and labor. The global market for slaves encompassed the Americas, Africa, the Indian Ocean and Western Asia in the eighteenth and nineteenth centuries; it interacted more broadly with the regimes of population and labor in the Americas, Europe and Western Asia. When slave prices rose sharply (as they did at the turn of the eighteenth century) or fell significantly (as they did in the eastern hemisphere in the early nineteenth century), slave laborers were moved in new directions in response to economic incentives. Free workers on every continent moved, similarly, in response to these changes in the value of labor.

Before 1600, African migration to the Americas, while it may have exceeded European migration, was small in magnitude. During the time when the Indian population was declining but still large, Africans in the Americas, while usually in slave status, were nonetheless often persons of relatively high value, serving in the military and in artisanal tasks. In Brazil, large-scale enslavement of Indians for work on sugar plantations characterized the late sixteenth century. African laborers, concentrated at first in the skilled occupations on the plantations, gradually displaced the disappearing Indians at all levels of work.

In the seventeenth century, the scarcity of Indian laborers made Africans appear, by comparison, more plentiful. Still, for much if not all of the century, the addition of African and European immigrants and their progeny was insufficient to offset the decline in Indian population.

By the eighteenth century, all the major population groups—those of Indian, European, African, and mestizo or mulatto ancestry—were growing, though from a very sparse base. However, in this period the large-scale removal of Africans from their homes to serve as slaves in the Americas, with all its attendant carnage, brought population decline for region after region in Africa, and finally for the western African coast as a whole. Consequently, the African addition to the population of the Americas (both by immigration and by natural reproduction) was insufficient to make up for the loss of population in Africa.

The centrality of African labor was costly to the slaves, and was costly in the longer run to their societies of origin. In the eighteenth and nineteenth centuries the populations of Europe, the Americas and Asia grew at unprecedented rates, apparently as a result of improved immunities, certain social changes, and perhaps improved public health conditions. In the nineteenth century these rapidly growing populations spun off millions of migrants, who searched near and far for the means to make a better living. For Africa, in contrast, the population remained stagnant or in decline, and labor migration mostly took place, even within the continent, by the forcible means which interfered with population growth.

If we link the American pull and African push factors noted above, we find that they do not yet cohere into a full theory for the migration. Three main factors have been advanced, by different groups of scholars, to explain the migration more generally. The first factor is epidemiology: the relative immunity of Africans to the diseases of the tropics enabled them to survive at a greater rate than Americans or Europeans. Hence they were more valuable and more sought after as plantation laborers. Second is relative productivity. Given the technical limits of African hoe agriculture in comparison to the more productive plow agriculture of Europeans, even a highly productive laborer in Africa could not produce as much food as an ordinary laborer in Europe. In these terms, the value or price of a European laborer was greater than that of an African. European merchants, therefore, were able to buy slaves by paying Africans more than the value of an average laborer in Africa, yet bring laborers to the Americas that were far cheaper than European laborers. The third factor is transportation costs. When Africans sought to buy goods on the world market, they had to offer local goods in exchange. Such export goods needed a high ratio of value to weight, or the high costs of transportation would consume all profits. Africa did export gold, but lacked minerals in many regions; African textiles and art work were not recognized as luxury goods overseas. Slaves were the next most valuable commodity, and so they came to dominate Africa's export trade. (In the nineteenth century, as transportation became more inexpensive, Africans turned steadily from the slave trade to exporting peanuts, palm oil and other agricultural commodities.) The prices of slaves reflect the sum of these three factors, and perhaps others as well. Slave prices, however, have yet to be studied in a fully comparative and comprehensive fashion. We may hope that further studies will reveal more of the relative dominance and the interplay of these three factors—or, more simply, more of the reasons why the slave trade continued so long.

One way to signal the cost to Africa of this sort of participation in the world economy is to estimate the number of persons who died in the Middle Passage. Since the mortality schedule for the Middle Passage was somewhere between five and ten times higher than the normal mortality schedule, one is not far off by saying that all the deaths taking place on slave ships would not otherwise have taken place. Rough estimates of the cumulative total of deaths as sea come to a total of sixty thousand for the period before 1600, three hundred thousand for the seventeenth century, a million for the eighteenth century, and half a million for the nineteenth century. To get the total excess mortality brought about by the slave trade, aside from that of the condition of slavery itself, one would have to add the death in the course of African capture and transportation, and those in the course of resettlement and seasoning in the Americas.

On the other hand, we may choose to emphasize life rather than death. As of the mid-eighteenth century, when the population of the Americas had rebounded to perhaps as much as ten million, that total included roughly two million black slaves and another million free persons of color, with the latter concentrated in the Portuguese and Spanish territories. Two million free whites and five million Indians rounded out the total. The regional distribution included a million inhabitants in the Caribbean, the most densely populated area. North America and Brazil each had populations of roughly one and one-half million, and the Spanish mainland colonies had roughly five million inhabitants. The Americas grew rapidly in population during the eighteenth century, but trailed the Old World distantly. The population of sub-Saharan Africa totaled some fifty million persons, about twenty million of whom lived in the areas of the western coast of Africa from which slaves were dispatched across the Atlantic. Western Europe's population, far denser and in a smaller area, totaled roughly one hundred million.

The European and African migrations to the Americas shared a number of characteristics in the seventeenth and eighteenth centuries. The migrants were dominantly male, and they suffered elevated levels of mortality. But several distinctions between European and African migration stand out. Africans had no pattern of return migration eastward across the Atlantic parallel to that of the Europeans, and Africans were not able to repatriate earnings to their home societies. Thus, while emigration strengthened the external trade of Africa, it did so with a weaker multiplier than that for Europe. African migrants underwent an extra mortality cost in Africa and in the Middle Passage because of the violence of enslavement.

African rates of emigration were substantially higher than those of Europe. For the eighteenth century, the overall rate of emigration from the affected areas was three to four per thousand per year; this figure rose to as much as thirty per thousand per year for the Bight of Benin in the early eighteenth century. Since many more males than females left Africa, the sex ratio and marriage patterns on both sides of the Atlantic felt new pressures. In Africa, the relative surplus of adult women seems certain to have expanded the rate of polygynous marriage, and to have changed the sexual division of labor. In the Americas, very few men were able to have more than one wife, and many were unable to find a mate. This suggests a further contrast between African and European migrants: European males, because of their higher social status, had a wider range of choices of women among Europeans, African and Indian populations, and were thus more likely to have offspring than African men.

To return to the puzzle posed by David Eltis, we can now recapitulate though not yet in rank order, the factors responsible for the differential growth in American populations of European and African origin. Africans went in larger proportion to the high-mortality areas, the tropical lowlands. They arrived later than Europeans, on average, so that those populations which did become self-sustaining had less time to grow. In addition, the condition of slavery

282

increased the mortality and reduced the fertility of African immigrants. Finally, it may well be that the populations known as "white" and "mestizo" today include larger components of African and Indian ancestry than is now realized.

The transatlantic migration of slaves brought a rich African contribution to the culture of the Americas—in religion, cuisine, dress, language and philosophy. In language the African impact can be seen in two ways. First is in the development of the Creole languages, such as Haitian Creole, Jamaican Patois, Papiamento of the Dutch West Indies, and Gullah of South Carolina. In these languages the vocabulary is both European and African, and the grammar is mostly African. Haitian Kreyol is now a written official language of the country, and the similar Creole of the French Antilles is becoming the leading language of a new wave of multicultural music. Second is the impact of African speech on English, Spanish, French, and Portuguese as spoken in the Americas. The single biggest reason for the differences in these languages on the two sides of the Atlantic is the contribution of African expressions in the Americas.

These and other cultural patterns of the migration can be looked at in two ways. The first is in terms of survivals: that is, the continuity of West African religion in the vodoun of Haiti, or of West African cuisine in the gumbo or hot barbecue sauce of the American South. But we can also see African contributions to New World culture in patterns of change and innovation. Here the obvious example is in jazz music, which by definition is always in change, but where the rules for musical innovation can be traced back to Africa.

In addition to the heritage from Africa, the heritage of slavery created distinct patterns of community for Africans in the Americas. Other immigrants, arriving as free persons, had the opportunity to establish their own communities, in which people of similar linguistic and cultural background built up strong local units, usually maintaining some contact with the homeland—these ranged from Swiss farming towns in the American Midwest to Cantonese merchant communities to rural Japanese communities in Brazil. African communities in the Americas were largely prevented from recreating their home societies in this way because they were not free to move, and people of varying ethnic groups were often mixed purposely by their owners to reduce solidarity. As a result, inhabitants of African settlements in the Americas tended to refer back to Africa in general rather than to particular African regions, they thought of a romanticized African past rather than of the latest news because they were cut off from home, and they constructed a new, creolized culture out of the traditions available to them rather than maintain the traditions of a particular Old World region. Quite logically, therefore, the idea of the unity of Africa grew up in the Americas.

Most of the slaves died early and without progeny. In the Americas, much of their produce was exported, consumed and soon forgotten. Still, we can find ample remains of the investments of slaves in the construction of cities and the clearing of farms. I want to give particular emphasis to the value of the work done by African slaves—in the Americas, in Africa, and in the Orient—because the tradition of racist ideology in the last 150 years has done so much to deny their importance in constructing the world we live in, as well as to deny that the underdevelopment of Africa resulted in part from their forced migration. The very term, "Western Civilization," which we use to describe the continents of Europe, North and sometimes South America, reflects this denial of Africa's role in the modern world. The term carries with it the implication that the wealth and the achievement of these continents springs solely from the heritage of Europe. The migration I have discussed above is one of many ways to demonstrate that there is more to the modern world than the expansion of Europe.

Sample Student Activities

> ### Long-term changes and recurring patterns in world history.

Grades 5-6

▶ Using outline maps of the world, plot the major cities that existed in both the Eastern and Western Hemispheres in about 1000 BCE, 1 CE, 1000 CE, 1900 CE, and 1990 CE. *What new cities have appeared in recent times? What cities have vanished or fallen into ruins? What differing functions have cities had? What changing patterns of city-building around the world do you observe? How can these changes be explained?*

▶ Analyze definitions of the terms "slave" and "slavery." *Why throughout much of human history have some people held others in bondage? What are basic distinctions among domestic slavery, military slavery, and gang slavery in fields or mines?* Give examples of each from world history. *Should instances of forced or low-paid child labor today be regarded as a form of slavery? What have people done since the 18th century to abolish slavery?*

Grades 7-8

▶ Conduct a dialog between two citizens living in Athens in the 5th century BCE, Florence in the 15th century, Philadelphia in 1790, Paris in 1795, London in 1850, Moscow in 1950, New Delhi in 1980, or Los Angeles in 1990. *What does citizenship mean to you? What rights and obligations does your citizenship carry? How important to you is civic participation? How do you imagine your civic life as a citizen is different from that of a "subject" living under the rule of a monarch in a neighboring state?*

▶ After viewing the film "World Populations" produced by Zero Population Growth, analyze major shifts in world population since paleolithic times. *Why did world population remain low and relatively stable for hundreds of thousands of years? When did the first major spurt of population growth appear, and why? Why has world population exploded in the 20th century?*

▶ Research and write comparative definitions of the following terms: city-state, micro-state, empire, monarchy, constitutional monarchy, and nation-state. Give several examples of each from world history. *How have modern empires differed from ancient ones? What factors led to the rise of nation-states in modern times?*

Grades 9-12

▶ Role-play a Chinese merchant trading rice and wheat in the 11th century, an aristocratic land-owner in Britain in the 13th century, an Arabic-speaking merchant trading in the Indian Ocean in the 14th century, a banker in Italy in the 16th century, a textile factory owner in Manchester, England in the 19th century, a Nigerian oil broker in the 1970s, or the CEO of a multinational corporation in the 1990s. *Are your economic enterprises capitalist? Do your economic activities have some elements that are capitalist and some that are not? What distinguishes capitalism from other forms of economic organization? Why do you think historians differ on the issue of where and when capitalism emerged?*

▶ From a global perspective, analyze why a group of countries clustered at the western end of Eurasia came to achieve such military, political, and economic dominance in the world in the 19th and early 20th centuries. *Can this dominance be explained by cultural or other "traits" that Europe or Europeans possessed? What changing circumstances in the world after 1500 may have favored this development? In what ways did European dominance in the world come to an end in the half-century following World War I?*

▶ Define the terms "Western civilization" and "the West." Make a chart listing what you believe historically have been the major cultural characteristics of Western civilization. *Which of these characteristics may be historically associated in similar form with other civilizations, such as Chinese, Indian, or Islamic? Do civilizations have "inherent" traits? Are cultural institutions, customs, and ideas always subject to change, transformation, or dissolution? How does the concept of Western civilization differ from that of "the West" in connection with post-World War II geopolitics?*

▶ Analyze the periodization of world history as presented in this book. *What historical factors justify the "turning points" selected here?* Devise an alternative periodization of human history from early times to the present or from 1500 to the present. *Why is any historian's periodization design a creative construction reflecting that historian's particular aims, preferences, and cultural or social values?*

"Nairobi Rush Hour," painting by Ancent Soi, 1973

Students at Lakeview Junior High School, Santa Maria, CA

III

Teaching Resources

Introduction to Resources

While traditional printed sources are still invaluable, the revolution in information-processing technologies provide a new wealth of possibilities for studying the past. Today's teachers and students have a wide array of sophisticated resources and materials available for the improved study of history. The rapid advances in telecommunications and satellite technologies enable learners to engage in a variety of "distance learning experiences," including interactive field trips to historical sites and the use of modems and communications software to tap into distant data banks and sources. Making use of current technology, students have the opportunity to interview policy makers, conduct oral history projects, and explore different perspectives through links to individuals and students from throughout the world.

The evolution of CD-ROM and laserdisc technologies also provide access to an abundance of diverse printed, audio, and visual data. In addition, publishers increasingly incorporate such multimedia resources into their textbook packages. Finally, an extensive variety of public history resources and materials are available to enhance the study of history. Museums, art galleries, and folk art exhibits provide information and resources for studying history while local historical societies offer another avenue for exploring the impact of world events on local communities.

The following list is meant to be suggestive rather than inclusive and needs to be updated periodically.

Symbols

Media resources

CD-ROM and computer software

Text-based resources

Primary resources

Art

General Resources

"Africa: A Voyage of Discovery with Basil Davidson"
RM Arts, 1984, VHS, video cassettes

A comprehensive overview of African history and culture produced in England in association with Nigerian Television. The four programs in the series examine the civilizations of Africa, medieval trade, imperialism, and nationalism. Recommended for grades 7-12.

Africa and Africans (4th edition) by Paul Bohannan and Philip Curtin.
Prospect Heights, IL: Waveland Press, 1995.

This general survey explores the peoples, institutions, and history of the African continent. Recommended as a resource book for teachers and students, grades 9-12.

African Civilization Revisited, edited by Basil Davidson
Trenton, New Jersey: Africa World Press, 1991

The story of Africa from antiquity to modern times as told in chronicles and records. Recommended as a teacher reference and for grades 10-12.

African History from Earliest Times to Independence (2nd edition) by Philip Curtin, Steve Feierman, Leonard Thompson, and Jan Vansina.
London: Longman, 1995.

This standard survey of African history provides systematic coverage of the entire continent. Recommended as a resource book for teachers and students, grades 9-12.

African History in Maps by Michael Kwamena-Poh, John Tosh, Richard Waller, and Michael Tidy
London: Longman, 1982

A visual treatment of African history in maps. Recommended for grades 5-12.

The Africans: A Reader, edited by Ali A. Mazrui
New York: Praeger Special Studies, 1986

A series of diverse readings to accompany the video series "The Africans." Selections are historical, political, and literary sources to coordinate with basic themes and questions in African history. Recommended as a teacher reference and for grades 9-12.

The American Historical Association's Guide to Historical Literature (4th edition), edited by Mary Beth Norton
New York: Oxford University Press, 1995

Hundreds of historians have selected and provided commentary on the best and most useful works in their fields for this new edition the *AHA Guide to Historical Literature*. This two-volume work, the starting point for researching any topic in the field of history, provides unprecedented bibliographic guidance from prehistory to the 1990s. Each citation includes all essential data, along with a brief critical annotation written by a specialist in the field. Recommended for teachers.

Americas
A magazine published bimonthly in English and Spanish by the Organization of American States. Articles cover a variety of topics from art and music to travel with historical articles published in virtually every issue. Recommended for grades 9-12.

An Annotated Bibliography of Historical Fiction for the Social Studies, Grades 5 through 12, edited by Fran Silverblank
Dubuque, Iowa: Kendall/Hunt Publishing Co., 1992

A bibliography of historical fiction with grade level recommendations. Brief annotations of hundreds of children's trade books in world and United States history. Recommended for teachers.

"Arab World and Islamic Resources" (AWAIR)
Berkeley, California

A complete range of K-12 teaching materials about the Arab world, including a K-7 across-the-curriculum teaching manual, "The Arabs: Activities for the Elementary School Level," and a similar 7-12 manual, "The Arab World Notebook: For the Secondary School Level." Extensive materials and resources.

Aramco World Magazine
Excellent free monthly magazine on all aspects of the Islamic world.

Art Resources
Major art museums provide free or low cost rental of video cassettes and slide programs of historic themes such as The National Gallery of Art's "Treasures of Tutankhamen," "The Search for Alexander," "African Art," and "Ancient Moderns: Greek Island Art and Culture, 3000-2000 BC." Art prints are also available from galleries and publishing companies. Commercially produced series such as "Museum without Walls" and "The Grand Museums" offer detailed studies of artists and their works and tours of the world's most noted museums. Art resources may be used at different grade levels depending on student maturity.

"Art through the Ages"
Universal Color Slide Co.

A complete series of slides sets for world history through art. Recommended for grades 5-12.

"Art With a Message: Protest and Propaganda, Satire and Social Comment"
Center for the Humanities, 1971, VHS video cassette from still photographs

A probing view of the power of art to sway minds. The program examines issues such as political corruption, legal injustices, wars, and contemporary issues. Recommended for grades 9-12; however the program may be adapted for grades 7-8.

"Before Cortés: Sculpture of Middle America"
Sandak Color Slides

A set of 50 slides which illustrate 3000 years of sculpture from central Mexico to Panama and the Caribbean. Objects include works from the Olmec to the Aztec. Sandak offers a wide variety of slide collections including "Art Through the Centuries: The Americas," "Introductory Survey of Chinese Art," and "Global Art Slide Set." Recommended for grades 5-12.

British Heritage
A bimonthly magazine devoted to articles on British history and traditions. The magazine was formerly published as *British History Illustrated*. Recommended for grades 7-12.

"The Buried Mirror: Reflections on Spain and the New World"
Films Incorporated, 1993

A series of five video tapes hosted by Carlos Fuentes available in both English and Spanish. The series explores the Indian and Spanish heritage of the Americas from the pre-Columbian era to the present and examines the impact of history on contemporary Latin American society. Recommended for teachers and grades 9-12.

Calliope, World History for Young People

A magazine for students, grades 5-8, which focuses on a different in-depth topic or theme in world history in each issue. Usually includes plays, biographical articles, word games, archaeology, and history presented in practical and interesting ways. Published five times a year. Recommended for grades 5-8.

The Cambridge Encyclopedia of Japan, edited by Richard Bowring and Peter Kornicki
New York: Cambridge University Press, 1993

A one-volume reference providing a general survey of Japan's history, geography, politics, religion, and culture. Recommended for grades 8-12.

Cambridge Introduction to World History Series
Cambridge University Press

A series of 18 well-illustrated topical books on Western Civilization. Books in the series include *Life in the Stone Age, Pompeii, Iron and the Industrial Revolution, Life in a Medieval Monastery, The Rebellion in India, 1857,* and *Railways.* Recommended for grades 7-8.

Chinese Civilization: A Sourcebook (2nd edition), edited by Patricia Buckley Ebrey
New York: The Free Press, 1993

A collection of primary source selections reflecting the social history of China. Recommended as a teacher reference and for grades 10-12.

CITE Books
New York, 1988

A series of books entitled Through African Eyes, Through Chinese Eyes, Through Indian Eyes, and Through Japanese Eyes which provides an introduction to culture and history. The books include multiple primary source readings and visual documents on traditional and contemporary history. The documents focus on a few major themes and present materials that try to recreate the reality of life. Recommend for Grades 8-12.

"Civilization"
BBC, not dated, VHS video cassettes

These thirteen highly acclaimed 50-minute programs, narrated by Kenneth Clark, explore art, architecture, philosophy, music, and literature of Western Civilization from the Middle Ages. Recommended for grades 9-12.

Classroom Plays and Simulations
Numerous short classroom plays and simulation activities enhance the study of history. A number of companies have produced interactive activities in world history including classroom plays and readers' theater such as "Plays of Great Achievers" and "Children of the Holocaust." Simulations such as "Great Eras in History," "Civilization Game," and "World History Trials" are among many from which to select. A review of objectives for each of these activities is recommended. Grade level recommendations vary.

CLIO Project
University of California, Berkeley

The Clio Project publications contain overview essays and lesson plans covering a variety of topics from geography to changing gender roles in Asian cultures. Units include "Teaching and Learning About India" and "Teaching and Learning About Traditional China."

Cobblestone: A History Magazine for Young People
A monthly history magazine for young people that often contains information that is valuable for research and for classroom debates. Recommended for grades 5-8.

Cultural Atlas of the World Series
Stonehenge Publications

A multi-volume reference collection of the history and culture of different regions of the world and historical eras. Volumes in the series include: *Mesopotamia*, *The Jewish World*, *Medieval Europe*, *Islamic World*, *China*, *Japan*, and *Africa*. Recommended as a teacher reference and for grades 9-12.

Documentary Photographs
A number of companies produce documentary photographs and posters which may be used as an integral part of instruction. Among the many documentary visuals are: "Talkabout Posters," which present photographs, paintings, or posters along with explanatory text on the reverse side and "Then and Now: The Wonders of the Ancient World," which use current photographs and acetate overlays to re-create architectural wonders of the world. Poster art of the world wars and sets of dramatic photographs of the Nazi Holocaust are also available from several publishers. Documentary photographs may be used across all grade levels.

Documents in World History, Vols. I and II, edited by Peter N. Stearns
New York: Harper and Row, 1988

A complete collection of primary source readings for an entire world history course. Documents cover political, cultural, and social history and are amenable to cross-cultural comparison. Introductions to the documents are included along with questions to guide student reading. While designed for a college course, many readings can be adapted for high school use. Recommended for grades 10-12.

East Asian Curriculum Project
Columbia University, New York

Multiple resources and curriculum guides are available for teaching about Korea, Southeast Asia, South Asia, Japan, and China. These annotated guides for teachers present major recurring themes in areas under study. They include activities, lesson plans, art and cultural history resources in addition to teacher suggestions and pamphlets on developing central themes for each region. Recommended for grades 7-12.

Echoes of China
Boston Children's Museum

Seven separate curriculum units developed by the Greater Chinese Cultural Association and the Boston Children's Museum. Titles for world history include "Jia: The Chinese Family," "Chinese American Families," "China and Her Land," "Travels with Marco Polo: Life in 13th-Century China," "Fine and Folk Arts of China," and "Chinese Architecture." Recommended for grades 7-12.

Encyclopedia of World History, edited by William Langer
Boston: Houghton Mifflin, 1980

A one-volume reference encyclopedia. Recommended for teachers and students, grades 9-12.

"Eyes: Images from the Art Institute of Chicago"
Voyager Co., interactive laserdisc, Macintosh

Over 200 works from the Chicago Institute with music, poetry, sound effects, and narration about each work. The program provides an introduction to the world of art for younger students. Recommended for grades K-6.

Eyewitness to History, edited by John Carey
Cambridge: Harvard University Press, 1988

Short, readable eyewitness accounts of major events in world history. The selections include observations by both notable personalities and unfamiliar individuals of events such as the eruption of Vesuvius, Wat Tyler's revolt, Napoleon's entry into Moscow, the suppression of the Bulgarian revolt of 1876, the destruction of Guernica, and the fall of Philippine President Marcos. Recommended as a teacher reference and for grades 9-12.

FACES

A monthly magazine of world cultures. Published with the cooperation of the American Museum of Natural History, New York. Recommended for grades 5-8.

The Global Experience: Readings in World History, Volumes I and II, edited by
Philip F. Riley, et al.
New Jersey: Prentice Hall, 1992

A brief, balanced collection of primary materials organized chronologically and focused on global themes. Materials represent global change and exchange as well as the distinct achievements of major civilizations. Introductory comments and questions to consider appear for each reading. Recommended for grades 10-12.

Global Filmstrips and Videos
Upper Midwest Women's History Center, St. Louis Park, Missouri

Complete set of nine sound filmstrips and videos to introduce the subject of women's history in areas of world history including Africa, China, India, the Middle East, Japan, the USSR (CIS), Ancient Greece and Rome, Medieval/Renaissance Europe, and Latin America. Each comes complete with a full script guide, discussion questions and picture credits. Recommended for grades 9-12.

Greenhaven World History Program
Greenhaven Press, Inc. (originally published by George Harrap Publishers, London)

Sixty-four different pamphlets covering the complete range of world history issues: "History Makers," "Great Civilizations," "Great Revolutions," "Enduring Issues," and "Political and Social Movements." Recommended for grades 7-12.

"The Hermitage"
PBS, 1994

This three-part video uses art treasures from the Hermitage to present an overview of Russian history from Catherine the Great through World War II.

Historical Maps on File
Facts on File, 1983

Three hundred reproducible maps which cover historical topics from early civilizations to the 1980s. Although one-third of the maps pertain to U.S. history topics, others include the Crusades, world religions, revolutions, trading routes, and colonial empires. Recommended for grades 5-12.

A History of Africa by Kevin Shillington
New York: St. Martin's Press, 1995

This single volume, written in clear language, provides a good introduction to African history from earliest times to the present day. Recommended for grades 9-12.

"History of the World: A Complete and Authoritative World History Reference on CD-ROM"
Bureau Development, 1992

A storehouse of information on world history. The program includes short documents, complete books, and excerpts from seminal works. Students may compare legal codes of different civilizations, examine conflicting economic philosophies, or investigate leading historical figures. The IBM program requires 640K with VGA graphics and headphones or speakers; Macintosh requires a Mac Plus or greater and at least 1 MB with a color monitor recommended. Recommended for grades 7-12.

A History of Their Own: Women in Europe from Prehistory to the Present, edited by Bonnie Anderson and Judith Zinsser
New York: Harper Perennial, 1989

A two-volume study of women in European history. Information is drawn from diaries, letters, wills, poems, plays, and art works. Recommended as a teacher reference.

The History Teacher

The History Teacher is a quarterly publication by the Society for History Education. Articles include reports on promising new classroom techniques and methods, analyses of new interpretations by leading historians, and critical review essays on audio-visual materials and textbooks. The articles have wide appeal for history teachers at secondary schools, community colleges, and universities. Recommended for teachers.

"History through Art and Architecture"
Alarion Press

World history as seen through art and architecture. Multiple video offerings for many regions and periods. All videos are accompanied by teaching manuals and class posters. Recommended for grades 5-9.

History Today
An exceptional monthly magazine devoted primarily to British and European history with some articles dealing with topics in United States and world history. It is published in Britain. Recommended for grades 9-12.

The Human Record: Sources of Global History, edited by Alfred J. Andrea and James H. Overfield
Boston: Houghton Mifflin Company, 1990

A complete selection of primary sources for world history. This two volume work includes maps, charts, letters, diaries, and selections from literature. All sections have thorough introductions and leading questions to guide the reading. Many documents are used comparatively. Recommended for grades 10-12.

Illustrated History of the World
New York: Kingfisher Books, 1993

An illustrated dictionary of world history from ancient times to the present. The short descriptions of major events are enhanced by numerous illustrations and maps. Recommended for grades 5-8.

"Japan: The Changing Tradition"
Great Plains National Television Library

A series of sixteen 30-minute documentary-style programs that cover the history of modern Japan from the first contacts with the West in the 1500s to the 1970s. Produced in cooperation with the Japan Broadcasting Corporation and other Japanese institutions. Recommended for grades 9-12.

"Japanese Art and Architecture"
Alarion Press, 1992, VHS video cassettes

This series of five programs on three video cassettes examines the evolution of Japanese art and architecture from primitive bronze and clay objects to elaborate Buddhist shrines. Common themes such as inspiration drawn from nature, religious beliefs, and inspiration from other cultures are emphasized. Recommended for grades 9-12.

Journal of World History

The *Journal of World History*, published biannually, includes scholarly articles by prominent historians. The book review section is especially helpful in keeping abreast of current studies in world and comparative history. Recommended for teachers.

"Legacy"
Maryland Public Television, 1991, VHS video cassettes

Host Michael Wood explores the core values and cross-cultural influences of ancient civilizations, including Egypt, Mesopotamia, India, China, and Mesoamerica. Short segments recommended for grades 7-12.

Lost Civilizations Series
Time-Life Books

A series of well-illustrated books on ancient civilizations. The series includes *Sumer: Cities of Eden, Ramses II: Magnificence of the Nile, Africa's Glorious Legacy,* and *China's Buried Kingdoms.* Recommended for grades 5-8.

Mac TimeLiner and TimeLiner (IBM version)
Tom Snyder Productions, Inc., 1990, Macintosh, Apple, IBM

This timeline maker sorts the entered events into chronological order and arranges them proportionally. Recommended for grades 4-8.

Makers of World History, Volumes 1 and II, edited by J. Kelley Sowards
New York: St. Martin's Press, 1992

This is a collection of information and essays on 28 key individuals in world history including Akhenaton, Ashoka, Muhammad, Murasaki Shikibu, and Eleanor of Aquitaine. A series of review-and-study questions are included along with suggestions for further reading. Recommended for teachers; however, some documents may be used with students, grades 10-12.

"Medieval Studies for Secondary Schools"
NEH Seminar on Medieval Studies, 1986

A series of nineteen papers with classroom applications and bibliography produced by teachers who attended a NEH summer institute on Medieval Studies. Among the topics are: courtly love, medicine, architecture, medieval marriages, and Anglo-Saxon values. Recommended for grades 9-12.

Middle East Muslim Women Speak, edited by Elizabeth Warnock Fernea and
Bassima Qattan Bezirgan
Austin, TX: University of Texas Press, 1977

A collection of readings to unveil a dimension of Middle Eastern history which has been hidden by the notion that the Islamic world was created by men for men. The purpose of this anthology is to provide readers with a clearer view of the conditions, aspirations, struggles, and achievements of Muslim women. Recommended for teachers.

"The Mighty Continent: A View of Europe in the Twentieth Century"
Time-Life

A video series written and narrated by John Terraine with commentaries by Peter Ustinov. The program uses documentary films and contemporary footage to examine the political and cultural history of Europe in the 20th century. Recommended for grades 9-12.

Motion Picture and Made-for-Television Films
Numerous films are available for classroom use. "Gandhi," "Cromwell," "Shogun," "Lust for Life," "The Mission," "The Last Emperor," "Great Expectations," "Battle of Algiers," "Breaker Morant," and "Gallipoli" represent only a few of the available videos. Foreign films such as "Danton" with English sub-titles are also effective teaching tools. The length of major motion pictures may preclude using the entire work; however, selections are appropriate. Movies on laserdisc are especially useful as pre-selected sections are easily accessible. Various motion picture guides are available and should be consulted for additional titles. Each of the videos must be reviewed prior to showing to determine the appropriateness for grade levels and student maturity.

National Gallery of Art
Laserdisc (CAV) or Macintosh HyperCard stack

The program consists of two documentaries, "The History of the National Gallery of Art" and "A Tour of the National Gallery of Art," and offers visual access to over 1600 works of art from 8th-century Byzantine paintings to contemporary works of Pollock and Rothko. Recommended for grades 5-12.

"The Pacific Century"
Pacific Basin Institute, Annenberg/CPB Collection, 1992

Ten one-hour television programs that can be divided into half-hour segments for classroom use. The series features interviews, maps, charts, and archival footage on such topics as "Asia and the Challenge of the West" and "From the Barrel of a Gun: The Remaking of Asia." Text-book and study guides available along with a teaching guide. Recommended for grades 9-12.

Picture Atlas of the World
National Geographic Society, 1992, CD-ROM for IBM

Photographs, motion pictures, maps, statistical graphs, and audio clips of music and voices from every continent are incorporated in this National Geography program. Students access areas of the globe or focus on individual countries. Recommended for grades 5-8.

Political Graphics: Art as a Weapon by Robert Philippe
New York: Abbeville Press, 1980

The work examines broadsides and leaflets from the Renaissance and Reformation to the wall posters of the late 20th century. Recommended for grades 9-12.

Readings in World Civilization, Volumes I and II, edited by Kevin Reilly
New York: St. Martin's Press, 1992

Lengthy selections of both primary and secondary sources with brief introductions. Many interpretive pieces give teachers access to an analysis of a time period. Student questions are geared toward developing interpretive and critical thinking skills. Recommended for teachers.

Religions on File
Facts on File, 1990

A collection of religious texts, chronologies of historical events, charts, maps, diagrams, and other information on the world's major religions. Approximately 200 reproducible pages are included. Recommended for grades 5-8.

"Religions of the World"
Holt, Rinehart and Winston Video Series, 1989

A series introducing five of the world's main religions: Buddhism, Christianity, Hinduism, Islam, and Judaism. Tapes present the social, political, historical, and geographic impacts of each religion on the past and present. Recommended for grades 7-12.

Social Education
Published periodically by the National Council for the Social Studies with articles of interest to educators. The magazine regularly features annotations of children's trade books, reviews of newly developed computer programs, and lessons using primary source documents. Recommended for teachers.

Social Studies and the Young Learner
A quarterly magazine of the National Council for the Social Studies which includes articles of interest to K-6 teachers. Issues provide critiques of children's trade books. Recommended for teachers.

Sources of Indian Tradition (2nd edition), compiled by Ainslie T. Embree and Stephen Hay
New York: Columbia University Press, 1988

A standard reference collection of primary source selections on India from ancient times through modern history. Similar sourcebooks published by Columbia University Press include: *Sources of Chinese Tradition* compiled by William Theodore de Bary, Wing-tsit Chan, and Burton Watson (1864) and *Sources of Japanese Tradition* compiled by Ryusaku Tsunoda, William Theodore de Bary, and Donald Keene (1964).

Stanford Project on International and Cross-cultural Education (SPICE)
Stanford University

The Stanford Project offers over sixty titles which include curriculum units, resource guides, and research reports specifically designed for world history. Materials available include such units as "Two Visions of the Conquest," based on visual representations, primary and second documents, and maps for the period of Spanish conquest of Mexico; and "The Modernization of Japan: Continuity and Change," analyzing life in Japan at the end of the feudal period and during the Meiji period (1868-1912). Recommended for grades 5-12.

Teaching About Islam and Muslims in the Public School Classroom (3rd edition)
Fountain Valley, CA: Council on Islamic Education, 1995

Teaching About Islam is a basic handbook on Muslim religion, customs, society, and history designed to assist teachers.

TimeFrame
***Time-Life* Books**

A series of 25 well illustrated books that present the sweep of human history chronologically rather than civilization by civilization. Titles in the series include *Light in the East, The Domestic World, Winds of Revolution, The Pulse of Enterprise,* and *The Nuclear Age.* Recommended for grades 7-12.

"Time Table of History, Science and Innovation"
Software Toolworks, 1991.

A general historic survey of science from the origin of the universe to the present. Students scroll along a timeline which includes over 6,000 developments in all branches of science. Recommended for grades 5-8.

"Time Traveler: A Multimedia Chronicle of History"
New Media Schoolhouse, 1992, CD-ROM for Macintosh

A historical record from 4000 BC. Students may follow a topic through the centuries or investigate events around the globe for a given year. The program includes notes on the history and culture of a region and some entries include recorded speeches or period music. Recommended for grades 5-8.

"War: 100 Paintings"
Films for the Humanities

Five ten-minute segments which analyze in detail the style, significance, and history of Uccello's "The Rout of San Romano," Altdorfer's "The Battle of Issus," Velazquez's "The Surrender of Breda," Delacroix's "The Massacres at Chios," and Picasso's "Guernica." Recommended for grades 9-12.

Women in Islamic Biographical Collections by Ruth Roded
Boulder: Lynne Rienner Publishers, 1994

Roded makes a reassessment of the role of women in Muslim society by examining the large number of female scholars, philanthropists, and other prominent contributors who have figured in this Muslim historical genre from early Islam to the 20th century. Recommended for teachers and students grades 9-12.

Women in Muslim History by Charis Waddy
New York: Longman Group, Ltd., 1980

This book gives a comprehensive survey of Islamic views of women from a doctrinal and historical perspective, and presents fascinating portraits of women in Muslim history from the pre-Islamic period to the present. Recommended for teachers and students grades 10-12.

Women in the Muslim World, edited by Nikki Keddie and Lois Beck
Boston: Harvard University Press, 1978.

This collection of essays surveys an astonishing variety of topics from history, sociology, and anthropology, all anchored in studies of real women from various historical periods and regions. Recommended as a teacher reference.

Women in World Area Studies
Upper Midwest Women's History Center, St. Louis Park, Minnesota

Designed to integrate women's history into world history courses, this set of thirteen books and teacher's guides includes *Women in Africa, Ancient Greece and Rome, Medieval and Renaissance Europe, Traditional China, Modern China, and Latin America.* Each book covers the diversity of female experience both within a given period and over time. Materials include essays, activities, and primary sources, both visual and written, plus selected bibliographies. Recommended for grades 9-12.

Women in the World
Curriculum Resource Project, Berkeley, California

Selected units in women's history include "A Message for the Sultan: Suleyman the Magnificent's Ottoman Turkey" and a series of "Spindle Stories," six units including "The Bird of Destiny: Ancient Egypt," "The Garney-Eyed Brooch: Anglo-Saxon England," plus others. Recommended for grades 5-9.

World Eagle

Monthly publication of charts, maps, graphs, and general statistics for the social studies and world history. Excellent comparative maps (updates) and world data on many topics. Publications also include teaching units for world history. Recommended for grades 7-12.

"World Population: A Graphic Simulation of the History of Human Population Growth"
Zero Population Growth, 1990 (revised)

Illustrating population growth from 1 CE to the present and projecting future growth to the year 2020, this six-minute program uses dots of light appearing on a map to indicate the increase in world population. Historic references, at the corner of the screen, place population changes in context. Recommended for grades 5-12.

"The World: A Television History"
Network Television Production

This 26-part video series is an introduction to the triumphs and misfortunes of humankind from the emergence of humans on the African savanna through the post World War II era. Each program weaves together archaeological artifacts, computer-enhanced maps, artwork, location footage, and an informative narration to chart the rise and fall of empires, cultural advances, and scientific achievements in world history. Recommended for grades 7-12.

World History
TAP Instructional Materials, Center for Learning, 1986

A series of books with self-contained lessons on topics in world history. Each lesson lists objectives, prerequisites, teacher notes, and recommended procedures. Student handout masters incorporate art, graphs, maps, poems, and short documents. Recommended for grades 9-12; however, some lessons may be adapted for grades 7-8.

World History: An Annotated Bibliographic Index for Children and Young Adults
by Vandelia Van Meter.
Englewood, CO: Libraries Unlimited, 1992.

This is a handy bibliography of non-fiction and fiction trade books appropriate for students in grades K-12. The book is divided into the following categories: General works, World War I, World War II, Africa, Asia and Oceania, Europe, North America, and South America. Each entry includes grade level appropriateness. Recommended for teachers.

World History Videodisc
Instructional Resources Corp.

Complete world history videodisc providing instant access to 2400 images for use in world history, including more than 950 color images and 71 maps. Interactive capacity, IBM or MAC: Africa and the Middle East, Latin America, Japan, Korea, China, South Asia, Australia, New Zealand, and Canada; 320 images on art, 115 on architecture, 241 on religion. A complete master guide accompanies the videodisc and each frame is described in depth. The addition of bar code selected makes frame access almost instant and easy for students as well as teachers to use. Recommended for grades 6-12.

World Literature
Center for Learning

This two-volume teaching resource offers a variety of activities on world literature. Volume One examines works including *The Odyssey, Don Quixote, One Day in the Life of Ivan Denisovich,* and *The Madwoman of Chaillot.* Volume Two looks at the works of great writers from four continents. Recommended for grades 9-12.

Era Specific Resources

ERA 1

Archaeology: A Brief Introduction (5th edition) by Brian M. Fagan
New York: HarperCollins, 1994.

A lively introduction to the work of archaeologists. Recommended for grades 9-12.

The Atlas of Early Man
New York: St. Martin's Press, 1993 (revised edition)

A large format book of photographs, drawings, and charts which examines eight aspects of culture including art, architecture, technology, and religion between 35,000 BCE and 500 CE. Recommended for grades 5-12.

The Great Human Diasporas: The History of Diversity and Evolution by Luigi Luca Cavalli-Sforza and Francesco Cavalli-Sforza
Reading, MA: Addison-Wesley, 1995

This work by two prominent human geneticists incorporates the findings of archaeologists, linguists, anthropologists, and molecular biologists to track human migrations in colonizing the earth some 100,000 years ago. Recommended for teachers.

The Great Journey: The Peopling of Ancient America by Brian M. Fagan
New York: Thames and Hudson, 1987.

The Great Journey is an account of the long and demanding trek of peoples to ancient America. Recommended for teachers and as a research work for students, grades 9-12.

The Journey from Eden: The Peopling of Our World by Brian M. Fagan
New York: Thames and Hudson, 1990.

A global view of human evolution and early migration. Recommended for grades 9-12.

"The Making of Mankind"
BBC Video series

Narrated by Richard Leakey, this series approaches the study of early hominid development through seven video tapes. Each segment follows evolution chronologically, providing background on discoveries about the distant past and extending the discussion to basic questions about contemporary society. Recommended for grades 7-12.

The Neolithic Revolution: The First Farmers and Shepherds
National Center for History in the Schools Teaching Unit. Los Angeles: Regents, University of California, 1991

Children study archaeological illustrations to learn about the domestication of plants and animals between 8000 and 3500 BCE and the resultant cultural changes during the Neolithic Revolution. Recommended for grades 5-8.

"In Search Of Human Origins"
Nova, WGBH, Boston, 1994

A three-part video series in which anthropologist Donald Johanson examines fossils and other evidence to theorize about early hominids and investigate possible links between *Homo erectus*, Neanderthals, and modern humans. Recommended for grades 5-12.

ERA 2

The Beginning of Civilization in Sumer: The Advent of Written Communication
National Center for History in the Schools Teaching Unit. Los Angeles: Regents, University of California, 1991

In this unit students explore the beginnings of written language. Students read colorful contemporary documents and compare cuneiform notation to the Morse code. Recommended for grades 5-8.

The Code of Hammurabi: Law of Mesopotamia
National Center for History in the Schools Teaching Unit. Los Angeles: Regents, University of California, 1991

This unit examines various law codes of the sophisticated culture of Mesopotamia. Students read the precedent-setting case of "The Silent Wife" and examine how societies arrive at a system of justice by drawing on both divine and natural laws. Recommended for grades 9-12.

Myths from Mesopotamia: Creation, the Flood, Gilgamesh, and Others translated by Stephanie Dalley.
New York: Oxford University press, 1989

Myths from Mesopotamia is a collection of tales, written in readable English, that provides insights into the beliefs and ritual practices of ancient Mesopotamians. The translator makes links between the ancient folklore and more recent stories such as the "Tale of Babylon" in the *Arabian Nights*. Recommended for grades 9-12.

Nile: Passage to Egypt
CD-ROM for Mac or Windows, Discovery Channel, 1995

Students board a *felucca* and journey down the Nile from its headwaters to the delta at Alexandria. Narrated slide shows and video clips provide insights about the natural wonders, great monuments, and diverse peoples who live along the river. The program includes a 3-D tour of Abu Simbel and information about hieroglyphs. Recommended for grades 5-8.

The Origins of Greek Civilization: From the Bronze Age to the Polis, ca. 2500- 600 BCE
National Center for History in the Schools Teaching Unit. Los Angeles: Regents, University of California, 1991

This unit of study includes readings and activities for students at different grade levels. Older students learn how historians use archaeological evidence to reconstruct the history of Mycenae, Crete, and Troy. Younger students delve into Homer's Odyssey with a variety of projects including making puppets, drawing murals, and making maps. Recommended for grades 5-12.

"Pyramid"
PBS Home Video

David Macaulay guides students in a step by step tour of the Great Pyramid of Giza. The video combines live footage with Macaulay's pen-and-ink drawings. "Roman City," a companion video provides a glimpse of the monumental buildings and everyday life in a Roman city.

Pyramid: Challenge of the Pharaoh's Dream
CD for Windows 3.1 and Windows 95. McGraw-Hill, 1996

Assuming the role of a turn-of-the-century archeologist who has discovered an unexcavated Egyptian pyramid, students use the tools and technology of the time to solve challenges of pyramid building. This computer game is recommended for grades 5-8.

Tutankhamen and the Discovery of the Tomb
Golden Owl Publishing Co.

This Jackdaws kit traces the story of the excavation of Tutankhamen's tomb using primary source documents, wall paintings, and a working model of the outer shrine. The portfolio includes a study guide with reproducible masters. Recommended for grades 7-12; materials may be easily adapted for grades 5-6.

ERA 3

American Classical League
Miami University, Oxford, Ohio

Various books, pamphlets, posters, maps, slides, and teaching units on ancient Greece and Rome. Recommended for all grade levels.

Book of Greek Myths by Ingri D'Aulaire and Edgar Parin D'Aulaire
New York: Doubleday, 1980

A well-illustrated collection of 46 Greek myths written for young students. Recommended for grades 5-8.

Crossing to Salamis by Jill Paton Walsh
Portsmouth, NH: Heinemann, 1977

The story of an Athenian family fleeing Athens in 497 BCE in the wake of Xerxes's invasion of Attica. Recommended for grades 5-6.

Early Chinese History: The Hundred Schools Period
National Center for History in the Schools Teaching Unit. Los Angeles: Regents, University of California, 1995

In this unit students explore the Golden Age of Chinese philosophy when philosophers sought to account for the political fragmentation of the Zhou period and articulate solutions to restore order. Recommended for grades 9-12.

The First Emperor of China
Voyager, 1993, interactive laserdisc (CAV) or Macintosh HyperCard stack

Original film footage of the excavation of the tomb of Qin Shi Huang Di with a bilingual soundtrack with narrative in English or Mandarin Chinese. Recommended for grades 5-12.

The Golden Age of Greece: Imperial Democracy, 500-400 BCE
National Center for History in the Schools Teaching Unit. Los Angeles: Regents, University of California, 1991

This unit explores the achievements and tensions of Greece's most glorious century, the high point of Athenian culture. All lessons are based on a rich array of primary sources including architectural designs and numerous artifacts. Topics include: The Persian Wars, Athenian Democracy at Work, The Rebuilding of the Acropolis, Pericles' Funeral Oration, The Melian Dialogue, and The Last Days of Socrates. Recommended for grades 5-12.

The Hellenistic Period in World History by Stanley Burnstein
Essays on Global and Comparative History Series. Washington, DC: American Historical Association, 1995

The Hellenistic civilization produced by Alexander the Great's short-lived empire shaped the course of political, social, and cultural developments on three continents. Burnstein argues that the Hellenistic period represented one of the most intense and fruitful eras of global, inter-cultural exchange in the classical age. Recommended for teachers.

The Kingdom of Kush: The Napatan and Meroitic Empires by Derek A. Welsby
London: British Museum Press, 1996

A well-illustrated and authoritative study by a noted archaeologist who has been directing fieldwork in the Sudan for over ten years. Welsby uses ancient classical sources and modern data from archaeological excavations to illustrate aspects of Kushite life and show how the kingdom interacted with Pharaonic, Ptolemaic, and Roman Egypt. Recommended for teachers.

Locadio's Apprentice by Chelsea Quinn Yarbro
New York: Harper and Row, 1984

Against the background of Pompeii, Yarbro tells the story of a Roman boy's desire to become a doctor's apprentice. Recommended for grades 5-8.

Myths and Legends of Mount Olympus by Charles F. Baker and Rosalie Baker
Peterborough, NH: Cobblestone Publishing, Inc., 1992

This book highlights Greek myths and legends for young students. It includes a genealogy chart, a complete listing of the gods, a map of the Greco-Roman world, and a teacher's guide. Recommended for grades 5-6.

Rome Under the Emperors by Ellis Dillon
Nashville, TN: Thomas Nelson, 1974

This historical novel set in 110 CE gives a view of Roman life from the perspective of four boys. Recommended for grades 5-6.

In Search of the Indo-Europeans: Language, Archaeology and Myth by J. P. Mallory
New York: Thames and Hudson, 1989

The author traces the origins of each of the Indo-European peoples of Europe and Asia and draws conclusions about their common cultural heritage. Recommended for teachers.

Song for a Dark Queen by Rosemary Sutcliff
New York: Thomas Y. Crowell, 1978

The legend of Queen Boadicea and the attempt to stem the tide of Roman conquest in Britain in 62 C.E. Recommended for grades 5-8.

Spotlight on Ramayana: An Enduring Tradition edited by Hazel Sara Greenberg
American Forum for Global Education, 1995

This resource kit studies Indian civilization through the Ramayana's plot and characters. The kit includes 25 lesson plans, applicable at different grade levels, and a 57-minute video on the history and sociological significance of the *Ramayana*. Recommended for grades 5-12.

Wang Mang: Confucian Success or Failure?
National Center for History in the Schools Teaching Unit. Los Angeles: Regents, University of California, 1992.

This unit requires that students critically and creatively examine the reign and eventual demise of Wang Mang. Through the enactment of a mock trial, students determine whether Wang Mang was a victim of circumstances or a morally corrupt ruler. Ideas for good government and just rulers, as propounded by Confucius and Mencius, are interwoven throughout the text offering students a standard by which to measure Wang Mang. Recommended for grades 7-8.

Warriors, Gods, and Spirits from Central and South American Mythology by Douglas Gifford
New York: Schocken Books, 1983

A well-illustrated work which retells legends from Indian mythology. The book includes stories from Maya, Aztec, and Inca as well as oral traditions passed down from other societies in the Amazon basin. Recommended for grades 5-8.

The Weaving of a Dream by Marilee Heyer
New York: Penguin, 1986

Based on Chinese legend, this tale of the intense love and respect of a youngest son for his aging mother exemplifies Confucian values. Recommended for grades 5-6.

ERA 4

Ancient Ghana: Pre-Colonial Trading Empire
National Center for History in the Schools Teaching Unit. Los Angeles: Regents, University of California, 1992

This unit focuses on pre-colonial Ghana providing students with an introduction to the internal dynamics of an important West African kingdom before European colonization. Recommended for grades 5-8.

Exploring the Lost Maya
Sumeria, 1996

This CD-ROM combines text with original photography and videos taken at 40 archaeological sites to explore the history and cultural achievements of the Maya. Recommended for grades 7-12.

Gender and Islamic History by Judith Tucker
Essays on Global and Comparative History Series. Washington, DC: American Historical Association, 1994

This AHA essay explores the problems of scarce source material on ordinary people in the early history of the Middle East, the development in the ruling classes of the harem and seclusion of women, and the debate regarding the influence of gender in the study of Islam. Recommended for Teachers.

Islamic History as Global History by Richard Eaton
Essays on Global and Comparative History Series. Washington, DC: American Historical Association, 1990

This essay explores the rise of Islam and its continuing influential role in Asia, Africa, and Europe, making it the source of a truly global civilization. The author discusses such concepts as the nature of Islamic civilization and the sources of its cultural diffusion, Islamic institutions, and Islam as a world system. Recommended for teachers.

Jataka Tales by Nancy De Roin
Boston: Houghton Mifflin, 1975

These "birth stories" from sacred Buddhist works are re-told for young readers. Recommended for grades 5-6.

"The Lost Kingdom of the Maya"
National Geographic Society, 1993, VHS video cassette

A study of the collapse of the highly developed Maya civilization using recently deciphered hieroglyphics. The video also uses reenactments to dramatize ancient rituals. Recommended for grades 7-12.

Popul Vuh: The Definitive Edition of the Maya Book of the Dawn of Life and the Glories of the Gods and Kings translated by Dennis Tedlock
New York: Simon and Schuster, 1985

The *Popul Vuh* is the sacred book of the Quiché Maya, a powerful nation of Guatemala in pre-Columbian America. Written by an Indian after the European conquest, the *Popul Vuh* describes the mythology, traditions, and history of the Quiché Maya. Recommended for teachers and students, grades 9-12.

The Saga of the Volsungs: The Norse Epic of Sigurd the Dragon Slayer translated by Jesse L. Byock
Berkeley, CA: University of California Press, 1990

This thirteenth-century story, the work on an unknown Icelandic author, is based on legends kept alive in oral tradition. The saga recounts stories of princely jealousies, betrayals, schemes of Attila the Hun, and mythic deeds of Sigurd the dragon slayer. The saga has influenced the works of contemporary authors including the popular works of J. R. R. Tolkien. Recommended for grades 9-12.

Spain: The Moorish Influence
Encyclopedia Britannica Educational Corporation, 1989, laserdisc and video cassette

A complete history of Spain as the crossroads of two worlds. It shows the influence of Muslim scholars, translators, architects, and doctors on the development of Europe. Recommended for Grades 9-12.

ERA 5

The Adventures of Ibn Battuta: A Muslim Traveler of the Fourteenth Century by Ross E. Dunn
Berkeley, University of California Press, 1986

This study of Abu' Abdallah Ibn Battuta's account of his travels is a biography, an adventure story, and a study of human interchange in the 14th century. Recommended for teachers and students, grades 9-12.

Art of Courtly Love by Andreas Capellanus, translated by John Jay Parry
New York: Columbia University Press, 1941

This treatise gives a vivid picture of life in a Medieval court. Probably written to portray conditions in Queen Eleanor's Court at Poitiers (ca. 1170 CE), Andreas's work enjoyed popularity throughout late Medieval and Renaissance Europe. Recommended for grades 9-12.

The Black Death
Golden Owl Publishing Co.

This Jackdaw portfolio illustrates the misconceptions leaders during the Middle Ages had about the plague and the desperate, but ineffective, ways in which they tried to halt its spread. Recommended for grades 7-12.

"Castle"
Unicorn, VHS, video cassette

David Macaulay guides students on a tour of a fictional castle. Live footage is combined with animation to explore the building and defense of a medieval English castle and the surrounding town. A separate video, "Cathedral: The Story of Its Construction," by Macaulay examines the building of a medieval cathedral. Recommended for grades 5-8.

Cathay and the Way Thither edited by Henry Yule and Henri Cordier
London: Hakluyt Society, 1913-1916

This four-volume work is a collection of the writings of travelers to China from the Nestorian Christian missionaries through the journeys of Ibn Battuta and Marco Polo. Recommended as a research source for students, grades 9-12.

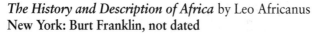

The Golden Trade of the Moors by E. W. Bolvill
New York: Oxford University Press, 1968

An extensive study of the great caravan routes linking the cities of North Africa with the markets south of the Sahara. Recommended for teachers.

The History and Description of Africa by Leo Africanus
New York: Burt Franklin, not dated

This publication by the Hakluyt Society is a reprint of an English translation in 1600 of Leo Africanus's account of his journeys in Africa during the 14th century. Recommended for teachers.

Ibn Battuta in Black Africa translated by Said Hamdun and Noel King
Princeton, NJ: Markus Wiener Publishers, 1994

Ibn Battuta's accounts of his travels in East and West Africa in the 14th century.

Leo Africanus by Amin Maalouf, translated by Peter Sluglett
New York: New Amsterdam Books, 1992

This novel of the travels of Leo Africanus provides a glimpse into the life of ordinary people in Muslim Granada, Arab North Africa, West Africa, Renaissance Rome, and the Ottoman Empire. Recommended for grades 9-12.

Magna Carta
Golden Owl Publishing Co.

This Jackdaw portfolio uses six short reproducible essays and nine historical documents to examine the quarrels between the barons and monarchy which culminated in the signing of the Magna Carta in 1215. Recommended for grades 7-12.

Mansa Musa: African King of Gold
National Center for History in the Schools Teaching Unit. Los Angeles: Regents, University of California, 1991

Students explore lessons in the history and geography of West Africa and read the fascinating descriptions of life in the court of Mansa Musa as recorded by 14th-century Arab scholars. Recommended for grades 6-8.

Medieval Universities
National Center for History in the Schools Teaching Unit. Los Angeles: Regents, University of California, 1992

The unit of study begins with a provocative description of the medieval student and uses primary sources to trace the development of the university system in late 12th-century Europe and its importance for curriculum advancement. Recommended for grades 9-12.

The Mongol Mission: Narrative and Letters of the Franciscan Missionaries in Mongolia and China in the Thirteenth and Fourteenth Centuries edited by Christopher Dawson
London: Sheed and Ward, 1955

This is a first-hand account of the journey of two Franciscan missionaries, John of Plano Carpini and William of Rubruck, to Mongolia. Recommended for grades 9-12.

The Peasants' Revolt
Golden Owl Publishing Co.

Rebels John Ball and Wat Tyler are the subject of this Jackdaw portfolio. The story of this popular revolution is told through contemporary chronicles and poetry. The kit includes short reproducible essays and a teacher's guide. Recommended for grades 7-12.

Picture the Middle Ages by Linda Honan
Amawalk, NY: Golden Owl Publishing Co., not dated

This resource book provides a self-contained lesson organized around the Medieval town, castle, monastery, and manor. Stories, poems, art, music, and dance help students gain a better understanding of life during the Middle Ages. Recommended for grades 5-6.

The Pit by Ann Cheetham
New York: Henry Holt & Co., 1987

Set in contemporary England, this novel tells the story of a boy who is hurled into the past to encounter life in plague-torn London. Recommended for grades 7-8.

The Role of Women in Medieval Europe
National Center for History in the Schools Teaching Unit. Los Angeles: Regents, University of California, 1992

Students examine women in the early Middle Ages with emphasis on the culture of the Germanic tribes that penetrated the Roman Empire; the property rights of women under feudalism; the participation of women in cultural life during the 11th through 13th centuries; and the occupational roles of women during the late Middle Ages. Recommended for grades 9-12.

The Ten Foot Square Hut and Tales of the Heike translated by A. L. Sadler
Westport, CT: Greenwood Press, 1970

These two classics in Japanese literature deal with society in thirteenth-century Japan from different points of view. *The Hojoki (Ten Foot Square Hut)* by Kamo no Chomei consists of reflections of a recluse who retired from a violent world. *The Tale of the Heike*, by an unknown author, is an epic story depicting the rise and fall of the Heike clan. Recommended for teachers, parts may be excerpted for students grades 7-12.

1066
Golden Owl Publishing Co.

Drawing evidence from the Bayeux Tapestry and other contemporary sources, this Jackdaw evaluates and recreates the background and the preparations for the Norman conquest. The portfolio includes reproducible masters and a teacher's guide. Recommended for grades 7-12.

The Travels by Marco Polo, translated by Ronald Latham
New York: Penguin Books, 1976

An account of Marco Polo's travels written while a prisoner of war in Genoa. The book gives vivid descriptions of a world remote from Europe in the 13th century. Recommended for teachers and students, grades 9-12.

The Travels of Ibn Battuta, A.D. 1325-1354 translated by H. A. R. Gibb
London: The Hakluyt Society, 1958-1994.

This four volume work, part of the Hakluyt Society's publication of the exploits of world travelers, is a translation of Ibn Battuta's narrative account of his journey from one end of the eastern hemisphere to the other. Ibn Battuta began his travels as a pilgrim but later rose to the position of a judge in the Sultanate of Delhi and envoy to the emperor of China. Recommended for teachers and students, grades 9-12.

The Treasure of the City of Ladies or The Book of the Three Virtues by Christine de Pisan, translated by Sarah Lawson
New York: Penguin Books, 1985.

Christine de Pisan, one of the most prominent literary figures in the courts of Medieval Europe, was a skilled poet and respected writer on moral questions, education, politics, and the conduct of war. Her works provide an exceptional view of political and social conditions in late Medieval Europe. Recommended for grades 9-12.

Voyages from Xanadu: Rabban Sauma and the First Journey from China to the West by Morris Rossabi
New York: Kodansha America, Inc., 1992

Rossabi gives an account of the little-known story of the life and travels of Rabban Sauma, a Christian monk, who left China for Europe about the time of Marco Polo's travels. Sauma's mission was to persuade the pope and kings of France and England to form an alliance against the Muslims. The author presents an analysis of the volatile international situation of the later thirteenth century. Recommended for grades 9-12.

The World System in the Thirteenth Century: Dead-End or Precursor? by Janet Lippman Abu-Lughud
Essays on Global and Comparative History Series. Washington, DC: American Historical Association, 1994

Most works on the rise of capitalism and European global hegemony begin around 1400 CE and focus on European development. This essay discusses the hundred years between 1250 and 1350 and reveals a complex system of world trade and cultural exchange that involved many advanced societies between northwestern Europe and China. Recommended for teachers.

The Way Home by Ann Turner
New York: Crown Publishers, Inc., 1982

This novel tells the story of a girl forced to flee her home in England at the time of the great plague. Recommended for grades 7-8.

ERA 6

Africa Remembered: Narratives by West Africans from the Era of the Slave Trade edited by
Philip D. Curtin
Madison, WI: University of Wisconsin Press, 1967

An African perspective of the slave trade drawn from primary source records. The book,
divided into three parts, concentrates on the works of African travelers from the eighteenth and
nineteenth centuries and accounts from the Gold Coast hinterland. Recommended for grades
9-12.

The African Slave Trade, A Census by Philip D. Curtin
Madison, WI: University of Wisconsin Press, 1969

Curtin examines both African and European participation in the slave trade and assesses the
number of slaves transported to the Americas by region and period. Recommended for grades
9-12.

The Age of Gunpowder Empires, 1450-1800 by William McNeill
**Essays on Global and Comparative History Series. Washington, DC: American Historical
Association, 1989**

This pamphlet in the AHA world history series explores the advent of gunpowder weapons
and how the use of these weapons changed the balance of power. The essay compares European, Russian, Islamic, Chinese, and Japanese uses of gunpowder weapons and how these
powers fit guns into their political, military, and cultural systems. Recommended for teachers.

The Agony and the Ecstasy by Irving Stone
Garden City, NY: Doubleday, 1963

This popular novel, set in Renaissance Italy, tells the story of Michelangelo. Recommended for
grades 9-12.

The Amethyst Ring by Scott O'Dell
Boston: Houghton Mifflin, 1983

A novel by a popular writer of historical fiction for young adults, *The Amethyst Ring* tells the
story of a young Spanish student who witnessed the conquests of Cortés and Pizarro. Recommended for grades 7-8.

The Armada
Golden Owl Publishing Co.

This Jackdaw kit of seven historical documents and reproducible essays illustrates the historical
significance of the events leading to the formation of the Spanish Armada and its deployment.
Recommended for grades 7-12.

The Captive by Scott O'Dell
Boston: Houghton Mifflin, 1979

The Captive tells the story of Julian Escobar, a Jesuit seminarian, who witnessed the enslavement and exploitation of the Indians. This novel is a sequel to O'Dell's *The Feathered Serpent*.
Recommended for grades 7-8.

Chushingura: Studies in Kabuki and the Puppet Theater edited by James Brandon
Honolulu: University of Hawaii Press, 1982

This work includes a Kabuki version of "The Forty-Seven Romin," a play which provides a
panorama of Japanese life in the early 1700s. Recommended for grades 7-12.

The Columbian Encounter
National Center for History in the Schools. Los Angeles: Regents, University of California, 1991

Drawing on a wide variety of sources, this complete teaching unit allows students to explore the Columbian Encounter from the perspective of Europeans, Native Americans, and Africans. The unit traces the background of the encounters, including motives for exploration and analyzes relations among the races as well as animal and plant exchanges. Recommended for grades 5-8.

The Columbian Voyages, The Columbian Exchange, and Their Historians by Alfred Crosby
Essays on Global and Comparative History Series Washington, DC: American Historical Association, 1987

This first essay in the AHA Global and Comparative History Series contrasts traditional interpretations of the Columbian voyages with analytic understanding made possible by quantitative study of population, economics, nutrition, and disease. Recommended for teachers.

The Crimson Oak by Edith M. Almedingen
New York: Coward-McCann, Inc., 1981

This novel, set in Russia in 1739, tells the story of a young peasant boy who chances to cross paths with the exiled Princess Elizabeth and comes to realize that his fate is linked to hers. Recommended for grades 7-8.

Cromwell's Boy by Erik Christian Haugaard
Boston: Houghton Mifflin, 1978

Set in the 1640s, this novel weaves the story of a young boy whose wit and horsemanship makes him invaluable to the Roundheads during the English Civil War. Recommended for grades 5-8.

Crowning the Cathedral of Florence: Brunelleschi Builds His Dome
National Center for History in the Schools Teaching Unit. Los Angeles: Regents, University of California, 1991

This unit recalls how the Renaissance architect Filippo Brunelleschi, with the backing of the government and guilds of Florence, designed the great dome of the cathedral of Santa Maria del Fiore, starting a new era in the history of architecture. Recommended for grades 7-12.

The Dream of the Red Chamber by Hsueh-chin Tsao, translated by Chi-chen Wang
New York: Twayne Publishers, 1958

The Dream of the Red Chamber also known as The Story of the Stone, is the tale of a large extended family and provides a good picture of the complexities of Chinese family structure. Recommended for grades 9-12.

Ecological Imperialism: The Biological Expansion of Europe, 900-1900 by Alfred Crosby
New York: Cambridge University Press, 1986

This work, by a renowned historian of human ecology and European migration, helps students understand the formation of settler colonies far from Europe. Recommended for grades 9-12.

Elizabeth I
Golden Owl Publishing Co.

A Jackdaw portfolio which details Elizabeth's life through short essays and historical documents and portraits. The kit includes a teacher's guide and reproducible material for classroom use. Recommended for grades 7-12.

The Feathered Serpent by Scott O'Dell
Boston: Houghton Mifflin, 1981

An adventure novel of a young Spaniard who witnessed the capture of Tenochtitlan. Recommended for grades 7-8.

The Fortunate Slave: An Illustration of African Slavery in the Early Eighteenth Century
by Douglas Grant
London: Oxford University Press, 1958

The account of the life of Job ben Solomon who was captured by enemies in Gambia in 1731 and sold to a slave trader. Job sent an letter to his father appealing for a ransom to buy his freedom. The letter fell into the hands of James Oglethorpe who, touched by Job's appeal, redeemed him from slavery and brought him to England. Grant's account traces Job's life from slavery to his return to Africa. Recommended for grades 9-12.

Four Major Plays of Chikamatsu translated by Donald Keene.
New York: Columbia University Press, 1961

This collection includes the "Love Suicides at Sonezaki," the story of a shopkeeper who refuses to marry the women chosen for him because of his love for another. Recommended for grades 9-12.

Equiano's Travels: The Interesting Narrative of the Life of Olaudah Equiano or Gustavus Vasa the African edited by Paul Edwards
New York: Frederick A. Praeger, 1966

Considered a best seller in the eighteenth century, Equiano's work went through a number of editions in both Britain and the United States. Captured at age 10, Equiano traveled widely in the service of an English sea-captain. Although treated considerably better than other slaves, Equiano describes the terrible treatment of captives in the West Indies. Recommended for grades 7-12.

The Japanese Family Storehouse by Ihara Saikaku, translated by G. W. Sargent
London: Cambridge University Press, 1959

Nippon Eitai-gura is a work by one of Japan's most distinguished writers of the Tokugawa period. The novel is a commentary on seventeenth-century Japan. Recommended for grades 9-12.

Kautilya's Arthashastra translated by R. Shamasastry
Mysore: Mysore Publishing House, 1960

This classic Indian play, written in the fifth century, relates the story of King Dusyanta and his love for Sakuntala. The reader can derive an understanding of Indian society through the dramatic narrative derived from the *Mahabharata*. Recommended for teachers.

The King's Fifth by Scott O'Dell
Boston: Houghton Mifflin, 1966

This is an adventure novel relating the story of Esteban de Sandoval, a young cartographer, who took part in the Coronado expedition. Recommended for grades 7-8.

Martin Luther
Golden Owl Publishing Co.

This Jackdaw portfolio outlines the life of Martin Luther and examines the development of his thoughts and ideas. Documents include a copy of the Ninety-five Theses, a Reformation woodcut satirizing the nature of the Church, Charles V's letter granting Luther safe conduct to attend the Diet of Worms, and a handbill attacking John Calvin. The kit includes a teacher guide and reproducible masters for classroom use. Recommended for grades 7-12.

Monkey by Wu Cheng-en, translated by Arthur Waley
London: Readers Union/Allen and Unwin, 1944

This sixteenth-century epic is a tale of a pilgrimage to India. The fictional Tripitaka (actually based on Hsuan Tsang's seventh-century journey to India) represents the ordinary man facing the difficulties of life while the monkey stands for the restless instability of genius. *Monkey* is a combination of folklore, allegory, religion, history, and anti-bureaucratic satire. Recommended for grades 7-12.

My Name is Not Angelica by Scott O'Dell
Boston: Houghton Mifflin, 1989

Using the fictitious story of Raisha, the daughter of an African chief, O'Dell tells the story of the West Indian slave revolt of 1733. Recommended for grades 5-8.

The New Hindu Tradition edited by Ainslie T. Embree
New York: Random House, 1966

This Modern Library edition of *The Hindu Tradition*, arranged chronologically, examines the complexity of Hindu tradition as it grew and developed over the centuries. It is a good exploration of the meaning of Hinduism.

Ramayana—King Rama's Way by William Buck
Berkeley: University of California Press, 1981

Valmiki's *Ramayana* is retold in English prose by William Buck. Buck's work began with a literal translation from which he extracted the story to make it more interesting for the modern reader. Recommended for grades 7-12.

The Samurai's Tale by Erik Haugaard
Boston: Houghton Mifflin, 1984

This young adult's novel of sixteenth-century Japanese warlords, poets, courtiers, spies, assassins, and monks is told through the perspective of a servant and later trusted aide of Lord Akiyama. Recommended for grades 7-8.

The Scientific Revolution
National Center for History in the Schools Teaching Unit. Los Angeles: Regents, University of California, 1992

Students explore the advances in scientific knowledge in Europe in the mid-16th century that radically changed humankind's basic notions of the very structure of the universe. The unit explores the contributions of key scientists and their basic discoveries and inventions through illustrations and short excerpts of their work. Recommended for grades 7-12.

Seeds of Change: A Quincentennial Commemoration by Herman J. Viola and Carol Margolis
Washington, DC: Smithsonian Press, 1991

An examination of the Colombian encounter prepared for a special exhibit at the National Museum of Natural History. Recommended for grades 7-12.

The Slave Dancer by Paula Fox
Scarsdale, NY: Bradbury Press, 1973

The novel, set on a slave ship wrecked in the Gulf of Mexico in 1840, relates the inhumanity of the slave trade.

The Spanish Inquisition
Golden Owl Publishing Co.

The Spanish Inquisition, first empowered in the 13th century, became an instrument for the expulsion, death, or forced conversion of non-Christians. This Jackdaw portfolio explores the attitudes and conditions of the Spanish Inquisition and other inquisitions in Europe. The kit includes reproducible masters and a teacher's guide. Recommended for grades 7-12.

"Suleyman the Magnificent"
Metropolitan Museum and National Gallery of Art, VHS, video cassette

A biography of Suleyman using treasures from the Topkapi Palace, scenes from illuminated manuscripts, mosaics, and cityscapes of Istanbul to examine his reign and the power and influence of the Ottoman Empire. Recommended for grades 7-12.

3000 Years of Urban Growth by Tertius Chandler
New York: Academic Press, 1974

A collection of maps and statistical information on urban growth and development. Recommended as a source for student research, grades 9-12.

The Tropical Atlantic in the Age of the Slave Trade by Philip D. Curtin
Essays on Global and Comparative History Series. Washington, DC: American Historical Association, 1991

The author traces the development of the "plantation complex" in tropical Africa and the Americas over a period of several centuries. The essay follows the patterns of the sugar and slave trades, their economic growth and decline, and their effects on Europe, Africa, and the Americas. Recommended for teachers.

The True History of the Conquest of Mexico Written in the Year 1568
by Bernal Diaz del Castillo
La Jolla, CA: Renaissance Press, 1979.

Written some years after the conquest of Mexico, Bernal Diaz felt compelled to write what he called "the true history" of the conquest. Upset with accounts that were inaccurate, he, as a participant in the conquest, wrote what has become the authoritative history of the period. Recommended for grades 9-12; however excerpts are appropriate for students, grades 7-8.

ERA 7

Annals of Labour: Autobiographies of British Working Class People, 1820-1920
edited by John Burnett
Bloomington, IN: Indiana University Press, 1974

A social history of nineteenth-century Britain drawn from workers autobiographies and diaries. Recommended for grades 9-12.

Aleppo and Devonshire Square: English Traders in the Levant in the Eighteenth Century
by Ralph Davis
London: Macmillan, 1967

Using primary records of individual merchants and business invoices, Davis examines the extent of English trade in the eastern Mediterranean during the eighteenth century.

As We Saw Them by Masao Miyoshi
Berkeley, CA: University of California Press, 1969

A historical essay on the first Japanese mission to the United States drawn from copious records of the travelers. Confronted by a strange society, the samurai recorded their impressions of American society and government. Recommended for grades 9-12.

Colonial Rule in Africa: Readings From Primary Sources edited by Bruce Fetter
Wisconsin: University of Wisconsin Press, 1979

Colonial rule in Africa through the eyes of the principal actors, administrators, missionaries, and the colonized peoples themselves. Recommended as a teacher reference and for grades 9-12.

Commodore Perry in the land of the Shogun by Rhoda Blumberg, 1985
New York: Lothrop, Lee and Shepard, 1985

Popular children's author, Rhoda Blumberg illuminates the human side of the negotiations between the Untied States and Japan with the arrival of Commodore Perry. Recommended for grades 5-6.

A Critical Edition of Mary Wollstonecraft's A Vindication of the Rights of Woman with Strictures on Political and Moral Subjects edited by Ulrich Hardt
Troy, NY: Whitston Publishing Co., 1982

Professor Hardt's edition of Mary Wollstonecraft's *Vindication of the Rights of Woman* analyzes the subtle and substantive changes that have appeared in editions over time. He reprints the 1792 edition in full and includes extensive notes on the work. Recommended for grades 9-12.

The Enlightenment
National Center for History in the Schools Teaching Unit. Los Angeles: Regents, University of California, 1992

Unit lessons on the "Age of Reason" are based on the English political thinkers Hobbes and Locke; the French *Philosophes* Condorcet, Rousseau and Montesquieu; Voltaire and his student, the "enlightened despot" Frederick II of Prussia; and Denis Diderot's *Encyclopedie*. The unit illustrates the social concerns of 18th-century philosophers on society, politics, and education and concludes by tracing the influence of the Enlightenment in America through excerpts from *Poor Richard's Almanack* and the United States Declaration of Independence. Recommended for grades 9-12.

Factory Girls: Women in the Thread Mills of Meiji Japan by E. Patricia Tsurumi
Princeton, NJ: Princeton University Press, 1990

The "Meiji miracle" produced the infrastructure of Japan's modern industrial establishment. This study examines the "factory girls" employed in the Japanese cotton spinning and silk reeling industries. It adds a new dimension to the study of Meiji Japan.

The French Revolution
Golden Owl Publishing Co.

This Jackdaws portfolio uses six historical documents to tell the story of the French Revolution from the events leading to the storming of the Bastille to the Reign of Terror. The kit contains a teacher's guide and reproducible masters. Recommended for grades 7-12.

Gender, Sex, and Empire by Margaret Strobel
Essays on Global and Comparative History Series Washington, DC: American Historical Association, 1994

The intersection of gender, sexuality, and race is a new area of exploration within the study of European imperialism. This essay focuses on British Africa and India although other areas are touched upon.

Germinal by Emile Zola, translated by Hanelock Ellis
Gloucester, MA: Peter Smith, 1968

Emile Zola, a French naturalist writer, describes working and living conditions during the Industrial Revolution. Excerpts recommended for students, grades 9-12.

"High" Imperialism and the "New" History by Michael Adas
Essays on Global and Comparative History Series Washington, DC: American Historical Association, 1994

This essay probes the many controversies surrounding the study of European conquest and colonization. The experiences of women, peasants, and urban working people of the colonial regions have recently been given voice through the use of oral accounts and other nontraditional sources. These studies have helped shift the focus from Eurocentric political, diplomatic, and economic interpretations to a more global perspective. Recommended for teachers.

The History of Cotton Manufactures in Great Britain by Edward Baines
New York: Augustus Kelley, 1966

This is a reprint of a 1831 publication that examines the cotton manufacturing industry, inventors, and the state of British manufacturing in the eighteenth and early nineteenth centuries.

Human Documents of the Industrial Revolution in Britain, edited by E. Royston Pike
London: George Allen & Unwin, 1978

All documents are originals, prepared and written during the Industrial Revolution. The work emphasizes social history. Recommended as a teacher reference and for grades 9-12.

Industrialization and Gender Inequality by Louise Tilly
Essays on Global and Comparative History Series. Washington, DC: American Historical Association, 1994

This essay compares early industrialization and urbanization in Britain, France, Germany, the United States, Japan, and China, and examines the impact of changing socioeconomic structures on gender inequality. Recommended for teachers.

Interpreting the Industrial Revolution by Peter N. Stearns
Essays on Global and Comparative History Series. Washington, DC: American Historical Association, 1991

An examination of the causes and changes—economic, social, political, and technological—of the Industrial Revolution that first influenced European and American societies and then were felt on a global basis. Industrial revolutions in Britain, Germany, France, the United States, Japan, Russia, and other nations are studied. Recommended for teachers.

James Watt and Steam Power
Golden Owl Publishing Co.

This Jackdaws kit follows the development of steam power from its earliest known application to its use as an economically satisfactory power source by James Watt. The portfolio includes nine historical documents, six short reproducible essays, and a teacher's guide. Recommended for grades 7-12.

The Last Years of the English Slave Trade, Liverpool 1750-1807 by Averil Mackenzie-Grieve
New York: Augustus M. Kelly, Co., 1968

The author captures the spirit of the abolitionist movement in Britain by drawing from contemporary documents. The political acumen of William Wilberforce is central to the story of British abolition of the slave trade. Recommended for grades 9-12.

Nectar in a Sieve by Kasmala Markandaya
New York: John Jay, 1954

This novel dramatizes the crushing impact of social and economic forces on rural Indian families. Recommended for grades 9-12.

Peasants, Rebels, and Outcasts: The Underside of Modern Japan by Mikiso Hane
New York: Pantheon Books, 1982

Starting with the Meiji Restoration of 1868, Hane weaves a tale of what it was like to be an ordinary person during the development of industrial Japan. The author draws evidence from a variety of sources including diaries, personal recollections, trial testimony, and popular Japanese fiction. Recommended for grades 9-12.

Ram Mohan Roy: Social, Political and Religious Reform in Nineteenth Century India
by S. Cromwell Crawford
New York: Paragon House, 1987

This account of Raja Ram Mohan Roy and his efforts to achieve social and political reform in India looks at different perspectives and concludes that he was a man ahead of his time. Recommended for grades 9-12.

Ta T'ung Shu': The One-World Philosophy of K'ang Yu-wei
London: George Allen and Unwin, Ltd, 1958

This utopian work, unique to Chinese writing, calls for a universal society in which decisions are made by the process of public discussion and voting. Autonomy rests in local areas and governments exists solely to ensure equality. Recommended for teachers and students, grades 9-12.

Things Fall Apart by Chinua Achebe
London: Heinemann, 1958

Achebe's work is an account of African experience in the era of the New Imperialism. The novel examines traditions and human conflicts in an Ibo village facing European imperial rule. Recommended for grades 9-12.

Tools of Empire by Daniel Headrick
New York: Oxford University Press, 1981

The progress and power of industrial technology and imperialism are two of the most important events of the 19th century. Headrick links the two adding a technological dimension to the factors usually explored as causes for the new imperialism.

Victorian Women: A Documentary Account of Women's Lives in Nineteenth-Century England, France, and the United States edited by Erna Hellerstein, Leslie Parker Hume, and Karen Offen
Stanford, CA: Stanford University Press, 1981

A collection of historical documents by and about women in three different, although related, Western societies. The editors present a picture of Victorian society drawn from a wide range of autobiographies, diaries, letters, medical and legal records, and case studies. Recommended for grades 9-12.

ERA 8

Children of the Resistance by Lore Cowan
New York: Pocket Books, 1969

A collection of true adventure stories, from eight different European countries, of young men and women in the underground who helped the escape of Nazi victims, harbored Allied pilots, and sabotaged factories. Recommended for grades 7-12.

Cigarette Sellers of Three Crosses Square by Joseph Ziemian, translated by Janina David
Minneapolis: Lerner Publications, 1975

The true story of Jewish children who managed to escape from the Warsaw ghetto in 1942. The children kept themselves alive by peddling cigarettes in Warsaw's Three Crosses Square. The book was written by a member of the Jewish underground in Poland who helped the children, many of whom survived the war.

The Coming of War
Golden Owl Publishing Co.

This Jackdaws kit uses 11 historical documents to trace the history of the years leading up to World War II. The portfolio includes a study guide with reproducible masters. Recommended for grades 7-12.

"The Diary of Anne Frank"
20th Century Fox, laserdiscs (CLV—"letterbox") or VHS video cassettes

The compelling story of Anne Frank and her family starring Shelly Winters and Millie Perkins. Recommended for grades 5-12.

An Encyclopedia of the Twentieth Century
New York: Oxford University Press, 1989-1992

A set of well illustrated resource books which chronicle the 20th century. Volume titles are: *The Family: A Social History*; *The Arts: A History of Expression*; *Passing Parade: A History of Popular Culture*; *Science: A History of Discovery*; *Wealth and Poverty: An Economic History*; *Power: A Political History*; *Nations: A Survey of the Twentieth Century*; and, *Events, A Chronicle of the Twentieth Century*. Along with two companion volumes, *The Experiences of World War I* and *The Experiences of World War II*, this series provides an ideal reference for the 20th century. Recommended for grades 9-12.

Ethnic Conflict: The Balkans
Golden Owl Publishing Co., 1996

This Jackdaw portfolio explains through short essays, historical documents, photographs, and illustrations the historical and political background of the Balkans. Although background information on the Ottoman Empire is included, much of the material presented in this study deals with the Balkan Wars of the early 20th century and the treaties ending World War I. Recommended for grades 7-12.

Hitler's Germany
Appian Way, 1991, IBM

This computer software program incorporates primary and secondary source material including excerpts from diaries, speeches, poems, and historical appraisals of the period. Each disc contains short documents on all aspects of life in Nazi Germany. Teachers and students may add documents to the program. Recommended for grades 9-12.

The Holocaust
Golden Owl Publishing Co.

This Jackdaws kit includes photographs, contemporary newspaper reports, portions of the Wannsee protocol, and Hitler's secret directive signed by Martin Bormann banning discussion of the "Jewish Question." A study guide and reproducible masters are included in the portfolio. Recommended for grades 7-12.

The Holocaust: An Annotated Bibliography and Resource Guide by David M. Szonyi
New York: KTAV Publishing House, Inc., 1985

An annotated bibliography of non-fiction, fiction, media, curricular materials, oral histories, and music resources on the Holocaust. Recommended for teachers.

Homage to Catalonia by George Orwell
Boston: Beacon Press, 1959

A classic study of the Spanish Civil War, told by one of the twentieth century's most noted writers. Orwell, a participant in the conflict, wrote of the ravages of the war and expressed his disillusionment with Communism. Recommended for grades 9-12.

I Never Saw Another Butterfly: Children's Drawings and Poems from Terezin Concentration Camp, 1942-1944
New York: Schochen Books, 1978

A collection of poems and drawings by children confined at Theresienstadt in Czechoslovakia. The camp funneled many of the children to Auschwitz. While held in confinement, the children of Theresienstadt secretly painted the reality they saw around them. Recommended for grades 5-12.

"Last of the Czars"
Discovery Channel, 1996

New material released from the Russian archives since the collapse of the Soviet Union sheds light on the private lives and struggles of the Romanovs as they faced social upheaval and revolution. The program includes rare footage, photographs, selections from letters and diaries, and cameo interviews with surviving witnesses to portray conditions in Russia at the turn of the century. Recommended for grades 7-12.

"Makers of the 20th Century"
News Multimedia, 1996

Based on a series from the Sunday magazine of the London *Times*, this CD-ROM digital archive provides accounts of the life stories of key individuals of the 20th century. Recommended for grades 7-12.

Night by Elie Wiesel
New York: Avon, 1960

This is a powerful personal record of the trauma of a young boy witnessing the atrocities of the Nazi genocide. Recommended for grades 9-12.

Propaganda, The Art of Persuasion: World War II by Anthony Rhodes
Secaucus, NJ: Wellfleet Press, 1987

A well-illustrated book which demonstrates the power of visual images through art, architecture, motion pictures, poster art, cartoons, and caricatures. Recommended for grades 7-12.

The Russian Revolution
Golden Owl Publishing Co.

Documents in this Jackdaws portfolio include a draft of Lenin's April Theses, excerpts from the *Manchester Guardian* and *Ivestia* on the October Revolution, and Civil War propaganda posters. A teacher's guide and reproducible masters are provided. Recommended for grades 7-12.

"Schindler's List"
MCA, 1993, laserdisc or VHS, video cassette

The story of a German industrialist, Oskar Schindler, who risked his life and fortune to save over 1000 Jewish workers from deportation and death. This award-winning film by Steven Spielberg contains graphic violence and should be previewed before showing. Recommended for mature students, grades 9-12.

Survivors: An Oral History of the Armenian Genocide by Donald E. Miller and Lorna Touryan Miller
Berkeley: University of California Press, 1993

A comprehensive study of the Armenian genocide based on oral histories, U.S. State Department files, missionary and ambassadorial accounts, and the Parliamentary Bryce-Toynbee Report. Recommended for grades 9-12.

20th-Century Art at the Metropolitan Museum
Metropolitan Museum, 1987, VHS video cassette

A tour of the American and European art in the Lila Acheson Wallace Wing of the Metropolitan Museum examines the works of leading 20th-century artists such as Picasso, Matisse, Pollock, and de Kooning. Recommended for grades 7-12.

And the Violins Stopped Playing: A Story of the Gypsy Holocaust by Alexander Ramati
London: Hodder and Stoughton, 1985

This novel based on historical events, traces the plight of Gypsies in Poland during World War II. The story focuses on a Gypsy clan which was given permission to live in the houses of former Jewish residents in Warsaw and then rounded up by Nazi soldiers and sent to death camps in Poland. Recommended for grades 9-12.

When Hitler Stole Pink Rabbit by Judith Kerr
New York: Coward, McCann and Geoghegan, 1972

The story of a Jewish refugee family who fled Nazi Germany in the 1930s. Recommended for grades 7-8; excerpts may be used with students in grades 5-6.

The Wild Children by Felice Holman
New York: Charles Scribner's Sons, 1983

This fictional account of life in Russia in the 1920s is based on historical records of the depravations following the Communist Revolution of 1917. The central character, Alex, finds that circumstances place him in the midst of a band of homeless, desperate children. Recommended for grades 7-8.

"Witness of the Holocaust"
Anti-Defamation League, VHS video cassettes

The program begins with an overview of the Holocaust followed by segments examining topics such as ghetto life, resistance, and liberation. Students must be prepared for the graphic scenes of atrocities. Recommended for mature students only after preview, grades 9-12.

ERA 9

Beyond Safe Boundaries by Margaret Sacks
New York: Lodestar Books, 1989

Set in South Africa, Sacks tells the story of encounters with Apartheid through the eyes of a white girl whose older sister joins an anti-government movement. Recommended for grades 7-8.

Communism and the Cold War
ABC News InterActive, 1991

This interative videodisc presents information on the major events of the cold war. With Macintosh HyperCard programs students can print documents and use video clips to compile individual or group reports. Lesson plans and curriculum integration charts are provided in the guidebook. Recommended for grades 7-12.

"Cry Freedom"
Universal Pictures

Based on the books *Biko* and *Asking for Trouble* by Donald Woods, the film tells the story of activist Stephen Biko who died under suspicious circumstances while in police custody in a South African jail. Recommended for grades 9-12.

Holding up the Sky: Young People in China by Margaret Rau
New York: Lodsestar Books, 1983

The author presents diverse portraits of young adults in a post-Cultural Revolution China. Recommended for grades 5-8.

In the Holy Land
ABC News InterActive, 1989

In the Holy Land is an interactive videodisc that presents information on the conflict in the Middle East. Topics include a survey of the history and geography of the region, political issues, and points of view of children affected by the conflict between Israelis and Palestinians. Recommended for grades 7-12.

Kaffir Boy: The True Story of a Black Youth's Coming of Age in Apartheid South Africa
by Mark Mathabane
New York: Macmillan, 1986

An account of the author's early life in a South African ghetto and his escape to the United States in 1978. Recommended for grades 9-12.

"Land of Demons"
ABC News, 1993, VHS video cassette

An examination of the crisis in Bosnia and the long-standing hatreds that fueled the dismemberment of Yugoslavia. The program is narrated by Peter Jennings. Recommended for grades 9-12

Live from the Past: The Rise and Fall of the Soviet Union"
New York Times Media, 1995.

Each teaching module in this kit includes 18 to 24 reproducible archival sheets of key *New York Times* articles and editorials, a poster, educator's guide, and video. The modules trace the rise and fall of communism in Russia and Eastern Europe from 1917 to 1991. Recommended for grades 9-12.

The 1993 Time Magazine Compact Almanac
Compact Publishing, 1993, CD-ROM for IBM, MPC compatibles, and Macintosh

A full text reference of every issue of *Time* for 1989 through January 4, 1993 with CNN videos of major stories. The disk also includes a "*Time* Capsules" section with some articles dating to the first issue of the magazine in 1923, a "Compact Almanac," maps, and the CIA World Factbook with State Department notes. Recommended for grades 9-12.

The People's Republic of China: Who Should Own the Land?
National Center for History in the Schools Teaching Unit. Los Angeles: Regents, University of California, 1991.

This highly participatory unit gives students the opportunity to analyze the issue of land distribution in China since the 1940s. Students read primary sources depicting disparities in land distribution and the impoverished state of Chinese peasants in 1947. Recommended for grades 7-8.

Shapes of World History in Twentieth-Century Scholarship by Jerry Bentley
Essays on Global and Comparative History Series. Washington, DC: American Historical Association, 1995

In this wide-ranging essay, the author reflects on the main approaches to the writing of world history from standard works, such as those by Toynbee and Spengler, to the innovative departures that dominate current works in the field. His survey leaves little doubt that studies with a global perspective will continue to influence research and teaching in history and related disciplines. Recommended for teachers.

Videoletters from Japan
The Asia Society

Units consist of a video cassette, teaching manual, and classroom poster. Six different video cassettes in all, including the "Living Arts," which introduces traditional dance, kabuki theater, the tea ceremony, and flower arrangement. Recommended for grades 5-7.